Presented to:

From:

Date:

David Jeremiah

Morning and Evening Devotions

Holy Moments in the Presence of God

Thomas Nelson
Since 1798

David Jeremiah Morning and Evening Devotions

Published in Nashville, Tennessee, by Thomas Nelson. Thomas Nelson is a registered trademark of HarperCollins Christian Publishing, Inc.

Thomas Nelson titles may be purchased in bulk for educational, business, fund-raising, or sales promotional use. For information, please e-mail SpecialMarkets@ThomasNelson.com.

ISBN: 978-0-7180-9261-0

Printed in China

17 18 19 20 DSC 6 5 4 3 2 1

Introduction

None of us would dispute that our world is complicated—even hectic at times. We long for shelter from the chaos, a place of refuge where we can rest and be refreshed. Frequently, we plan our vacations to accomplish that goal, but too often, soon after the vacation is over, we are back into the frantic cycle of life. How do we find moments, minutes, or even hours of peace and harmony? Turn to the Word of God.

The instruction of the Lord is perfect,
renewing one's life;
the testimony of the Lord is trustworthy,
making the inexperienced wise.
The precepts of the Lord are right,
making the heart glad;
the command of the Lord is radiant,
making the eyes light up.

(Psalm 19:7–8 HCSB)

True refreshment is found when we spend time studying God's Word. No matter the time of year, the season of life, or the time of day, when you go to the Scriptures for instruction and inspiration—you will find the peace and comfort you long for amidst the daily distractions of life today.

That time with Him makes the complicated issues of life seem small when seen in light of His truths for living. Your life journey will suddenly experience a turning point—the demanding job, or the need for a job, challenging family issues, medical or financial expenses—all of those important needs will be laid at the feet of the Master during those moments in His presence. Spending time with Him allows us to gain an eternal perspective, which draws our thoughts away from the daily events that often drain strength from our lives.

Of course, the most important decision for each of us is when we make Jesus Christ the Lord and Savior of our lives. Once He becomes Lord of our life, the path we formerly traveled is no longer our road of choice. Instead, we, like Christian in *The Pilgrim's Progress*, begin a journey toward the Celestial City. It won't be a journey without trials. There will be places along the path that may temporarily distract us, but our focus will no longer be on the diversions we encounter here, but on our eternal dwelling place there.

This book, *Morning and Evening Devotions: Holy Moments in the Presence of God*, is a collection of daily meditations from God's Word that will equip you to live with God's perspective. Whether you are an "early bird" or a "night owl," commit yourself to spending time each morning and evening with God. A moment in time may seem fleeting, but it is never futile when spent in the presence of the Lord—your days and nights will be richer for it.

JANUARY

Do you not know that your body is the temple of the Holy Spirit who is in you, whom you have from God?

—1 Corinthians 6:19

The Awesome Face of God

Give unto the Lord the glory due His name;
Worship the Lord in the beauty of holiness.

Psalm 29:2

As you meet with God in the light of morning, as your thoughts turn to Him in the adrenaline rush of the day, as you move into the silent sanctuary on the Lord's Day, know that He takes His place upon the throne whenever you give Him your praise. Your bowed head, your humbled heart, and your attentive spirit open the door to heaven. It's a door that swings both ways, for God comes to us no matter where we are.

The wonder of worship is the wonder of His very real presence. It's music from another world, wonder that floods out all the darkness and the dust of death this life contains. We rediscover the innocence of children again as we praise and exalt God's name, for He opens Himself to us. It's the most awesome moment of life—more awesome than holding your first child in the delivery room, more awesome than meeting the person you're destined to marry, more awesome than seeing the earth from the window of the space shuttle. You've seen something more beautiful: the face of God Himself.

Realistic Resolutions

Therefore, my beloved brethren, be steadfast, immovable, always abounding in the work of the Lord.

1 Corinthians 15:58

In December 2001, the American Society of Plastic Surgeons issued a report suggesting that many Americans are making plastic surgery one of their New Year's resolutions. If you haven't been able to keep all those other resolutions from years past—like lose weight, protect yourself with sunscreen, and exercise more—a nip here and a tuck there can take care of the damage. It's the American way—have your cake and lose it too.

New Year's resolutions are a traditional part of life, but it takes more than a "1" on the January calendar to bring about real change. Instead of trying to start something brand-new this year, consider taking something you're already doing to the next level: living with passion for God.

Christians have God-given passion already at some level; you couldn't have said yes to Christ without it. But how deep is it? Are you more passionate about God than about anything else in life? When your family and friends think of you, do they know that you love Jesus more than anything?

Make a realistic resolution this year—to go further on the road you're already traveling with Christ.

Long-Distance Father

The eyes of the Lord are on the righteous,
And His ears are open to their prayers.
1 Peter 3:12

When you became a son—when you were adopted into His family as a son or daughter of God—He opened up for you, through Christ's death on the cross, a way of fellowship and relationship that makes it possible for you to go right into His presence.

Do you relate to God like that? Are you in fellowship with Him? The way God "fathers" us will change the way we father our own children. Now that my children are grown and out of the house, I've had to apply God's principles of being available in new ways: I'm learning to be a "long-distance" father. I have entered into a deeper "relationship" with my Internet server so as to fulfill my fathering responsibilities. Fathering from a distance has added some new expenses, but it is what I need to do to remain a father to my children.

Now, if I am like that as an earthly father with limited resources, how available do you think your spiritual Father in heaven is? You don't need a long-distance calling card or an 800 number. He is waiting for you to come into His presence in prayer at any time.

A Clean Heart

Create in me a clean heart, O God.

Psalm 51:10

D. L. Moody did not want any sin to disrupt his intimacy with God. Because of this, Moody kept short accounts with God, immediately confessing any known sin. Each night he also allowed the Lord to shine an interrogating spotlight on all the events of the day. Before retiring for the evening, Moody would review his day with the Lord, asking God to reveal anything that displeased Him.

D. L. Moody exemplifies the kind of heart preparation needed before coming to God in worship. When we worship God, we must make sure we come with a clean heart, confessing any known sin in our lives. It is also good to prayerfully ask God to examine our actions, thoughts, motives, and words. Because God is perfectly holy, He cannot tolerate sin or commune with unrighteousness. Light has no fellowship with darkness (1 John 1:5–7).

In the Psalms, David offered up a prayer, very similar to D. L. Moody's. He, too, desired to come to God with a clean heart. Today, take a moment to make the following prayer your own: "Search me, O God, and know my heart . . . and see if there is any wicked way in me" (Psalm 139:23–24).

Trust the Character of God

You are my hope, O Lord GOD;
You are my trust from my youth.
Psalm 71:5

Sometimes during trials we focus so intently on our experience that we forget to focus on God. But the psalmist didn't. Over and over in this psalm he calls to mind the character and attributes of God: His glory, His power and strength, and His faithfulness.

And five times he mentions God's righteousness. The one thing that we must never lose sight of in the midst of our own suffering is the righteousness and goodness of God. It is because of God's inherent goodness that we are able to trust Him in all things.

When you are in the middle of trials, everyone will have an opinion or a suggestion or a remedy—and if they are from people you trust, you should consider them. But after all is said and done, there is only one thing that you can put all your trust in, and that is the character of God.

Praise the Lord

Let everything that has breath praise the Lord.

Psalm 150:6

Many Christians have sung Charles Wesley's famous hymn "O for a Thousand Tongues to Sing." But did you know there is an earlier German hymn entitled "O That I Had a Thousand Voices"? It was written by Pastor Johann Mentzer, who labored in the seventeenth century in the little village of Kemnitz in eastern Germany.

Pastor Mentzer was known for his attitude of praise and thanksgiving, and he encouraged his flock to praise the Lord whatever the circumstances. One night as he returned home from a nearby village, Mentzer saw flames shooting into the sky. Hastening to the scene, he found his home—the church parsonage—engulfed. Later, as he inspected the smoldering ruins, someone tapped him on the shoulder. "So, Pastor," said the man, "are you still in the mood for praise and thanksgiving?"

Pastor Mentzer was still in the mood for praise and thanksgiving, and out of that experience he wrote his hymn wishing for a thousand voices with which to praise the Lord.

We praise the Lord because it's a great therapy for the soul, but we praise Him most of all because He is worthy of praise. Let everything that has breath praise the Lord!

Filled with the Encourager

When [Barnabas] came and had seen the grace of God, he was glad, and encouraged them all that with purpose of heart they should continue with the Lord.

Acts 11:23

The Holy Spirit is the Encourager. Anyone who wants to be an encourager of others must be filled with the Encourager as Barnabas was. Because of the Spirit's presence in him, he could readily yield to the leading of God. Our own ego and drive for self-promotion is so strong that only the Spirit can bring about the transformation needed to accomplish God's purposes. When we build up and encourage others, we know that God is at work in and through us.

The fact that Barnabas was good, generous, gracious, and godly was not because of his upbringing or his education or his heritage. It was because he was filled with the Holy Spirit. The same Holy Spirit who indwelt Barnabas is the Spirit who is given to every believer in Jesus Christ. We receive the Holy Spirit when we are born again, and we remain filled with the Holy Spirit as we confess our sins and yield to His leading in our lives. God wants every Christian to be filled with the Encourager so that we might become encouragers as Barnabas was. The same glory brought to God through Barnabas's life can be brought to Him through our lives.

Chaos Under Control

He who is the blessed and only Potentate,
the King of kings and Lord of lords.
1 Timothy 6:15

In the 1960s, meteorologist Edward Lorenz proved that accurate long-range weather forecasting is impossible. This seemingly common-sense "discovery" was an outgrowth of what scientists call "chaos theory," which states that systems behave unpredictably due to the conditions in which they started. In other words, the slightest influences in the beginning can result in completely unpredictable results as systems develop. These are called "chaotic systems."

Many people, without understanding the science, subscribe to the "chaos theory." They believe the world is totally out of control and is careening through the universe on a collision course with some accidental destiny.

It is not wrong to think of this world as a "system." Indeed, the Greek word *kosmos* (translated "world") means an ordered arrangement. But it is completely wrong to view this world in terms of modern chaos theory. While the earth was at one time chaotic—"without form, and void" (Genesis 1:2)—it is now being carried in the hands of "Him who works all things according to the counsel of His will" (Ephesians 1:11).

Every headline that surprises us should be a reminder that there is no news in heaven.

Love's Power

[Love] bears all things, believes all things, hopes all things, endures all things.

1 Corinthians 13:7

Love hopes all things. Love that hopes has a confident expectation. It is a definite, persistent, absolute truth. There is no situation that divine love within us cannot face with full hope. That's what love is all about. Love hopes.

Hope is not refusing to face the truth. Hope is having a confidence in God to see you through each difficult trial. Jesus was always the epitome of truth, but He never failed to bring hope to others. When He met the woman taken in adultery, He inspired her to hope again. When He met the thief on the cross, Jesus made sure that man left this life with hope. He told the story about the lost coin that was found, and the lost son who came home, and the lost sheep that was found. Over and over again, what Jesus said in His messages was, "There's hope!" Though He was mocked, disbelieved, and crucified, He never doubted the glory that was yet to be, and He endured the cross for the joy that was set before Him. He had hope.

Love hangs on with tenacity when other hands let go in despair. To hope when faith has been disappointed is a greater thing than to have believed the sure thing. Love hopes all things.

Defined by Contentment

Not that I speak in regard to need, for I have learned in whatever state I am, to be content.

Philippians 4:11

Two teardrops were floating down the river of life. One teardrop asked the other, "Who are you?" The second teardrop replied, "I am a teardrop from a girl who loved a man and lost him. But who are you?" The first teardrop replied, "I am a teardrop from the girl who got him."

That's the way life goes, isn't it? We cry over what we don't have, not realizing we might have cried twice as hard had we gotten it. One of the reasons the apostle Paul lived a life characterized by such joy and gratitude was because he had learned the secret of being content. He was thankful for what he had and not sorry about what he didn't have (Philippians 4:12).

Paul passed on that secret to his new converts. While living in the end of the age, he told the Corinthians to be content where they were. He urged them not to be envious and try to gain what they didn't have, because "the time is short" (1 Corinthians 7:29). We live two thousand years later, so the time is shorter. Learn to be content where you are and with what—and who—you have.

People who are content live with a flexible cup; it expands or contracts to fit what God has supplied.

Let's Sing!

Oh come, let us sing to the Lord!
Let us shout joyfully to the Rock of our salvation.

Psalm 95:1

Isn't it wonderful that you could be on your hands and knees, scrubbing a filthy floor and singing the music of Zion?

Music helps you transport your spirit from mundane corners to majestic splendor. The body follows where the heart leads—and vice versa, as a matter of fact. Your prayers will be more focused and your mind more alert if you've aligned yourself on your knees. Some of your best worship might occur when you're jogging or driving a car, when your body is tensed to the task. Do you want to know how to incorporate worship into every moment of your day? Music is an excellent place to start.

Let's sing unto the Lord because it's one more way to give our bodies to His praises. Let's sing because music expresses levels of adoration we can't find in the spoken word. Let's sing because the people of the world will be attracted to our music. And let's sing because we absolutely can't help it! Our Lord reigns!

Chicken Soup

Faith without works is dead.

James 2:20

"I believe some chicken soup will help Johnny get over his cold," said Grandma as she put a chicken in the pot, peeled some vegetables, and prepared the tonic. Later that afternoon, she said, "I believe those flowers need some water." She filled her watering can and gave them a good dousing. "I believe I need a good night's sleep," she said that evening and headed toward bed.

Grandma's "I believes" were all followed by activities, illustrating a vital point: we behave according to our beliefs. As James put it, "I will show you my faith by my works" (2:18). Faith leads to action, and faith in God leads to obedience. He hasn't asked us to put our trust in warm, fuzzy feelings about Him. He tells us to put our trust in the revelation He has already given—His Word. When we obey, we are exercising faith. If you want an accurate measurement of your faith, see if you're obeying God's commands.

George MacDonald once said, "You can begin at once to be a disciple of the Living One—by obeying Him in the first thing you can think of in which you are not obeying Him. We must learn to obey Him in everything, and so must begin somewhere. Let it be at once, and in the very next thing that lies at the door of our conscience."

Temple on Wheels

I will dwell in [you]
And walk [with you].
I will be [your] God
And [you] shall be My people.
2 Corinthians 6:16

We, the saints, were never meant to be restricted to one roof. What if you began to see yourself as a saint in circulation, a temple on wheels, so that God could say, "I will dwell in [you] and walk [with you]. I will be [your] God, and [you] shall be My people" (2 Corinthians 6:16). What if you took your worship on the road so that you rejoiced, prayed, expressed your thanksgiving, and exalted Him everywhere you went? You could think of yourself as a beautiful temple, a place fit for encasing the law of God, a place where all people could come to experience Him—for that's one essential element of a temple, isn't it? It's a place for others to come together in God's name. You may not have a ceiling and large rooms, but through you people can experience the living God just as they did in the old temple of Jerusalem. That's the very idea of having the Holy Spirit come to live within us. It isn't for the purpose of our having some private experience, but in order that we can serve God.

The Twelve Spies

Caleb quieted the people before Moses, and said, "Let us go up at once and take possession, for we are well able to overcome it."

Numbers 13:30

During Operation Iraqi Freedom, U.S. Army Special Forces operated inside Iraq well in advance of the war, and American spy agencies had operatives in place long before the first missile was fired. In impending war, "human assets" are critical, and that's why Moses sent twelve men to spy out Canaan in advance of the anticipated invasion by the children of Israel.

In this case, however, the human assets became liabilities. Ten spies returned with daunting tales of giants, walled cities, and overwhelming foes. Only two—Joshua and Caleb—had a faith-based perspective. The ten compared themselves with the giants; the two compared the giants with God. Rather than aiding the victory, the ten spies discouraged the people.

Are you facing challenges today? Do you have some giant problems? Don't be discouraged. Don't compare yourself with the giants; compare the giants with God. He has promised victory in advance. Though the future appears daunting, you have a divine Commander in Chief who does all things well. Trust Him, for with Him you are well able to overcome.

Family of God

Behold what manner of love the Father has bestowed on us, that we should be called children of God!

1 John 3:1

Perhaps you've been exposed to the idea of the "Fatherhood of God and the brotherhood of man." This idea suggests that God is the Father of us all, and we are all brothers regardless of who or where we are in life. In reality, there are two families in this world. There is the family of God, and there is the family of the devil. Until you are spiritually born again, you are not part of God's personal family—you cannot call Him "Father." There are many people who have gone all their lives without knowing God personally. They have prayed the Lord's Prayer, but to no avail, because you cannot pray "My Father" if He isn't really your Father. The way He becomes your Father is by your putting your trust in the gift He provided of His Son, Jesus Christ. When you accept Christ as Lord and Savior of your life, you become a child of God—you are born into His family, and He becomes your Father.

Being Before Doing

As the branch cannot bear fruit of itself, unless it abides in the vine, neither can you, unless you abide in Me.

John 15:4

Harriet Beecher Stowe once wrote a wonderful book titled *How to Live on Christ*, in which she said, "How does the branch bear fruit? Not by incessant effort for sunshine and air; not by vain struggles. . . . It simply abides in the vine, in silent and undisturbed union, and blossoms and fruit appear as of spontaneous growth." We often forget that our walk with the Lord is more important than our work for the Lord. Abiding in Christ comes before abounding in labor.

Before the Bible records the mighty miracles of Moses, it describes the eighty years God spent preparing him for his mission. Before we read of Joseph's exploits in Egypt, we read chapter after chapter describing his preparation—before the palace came the pit and the prison. Even our Lord spent thirty years in Nazareth before devoting three years to public ministry.

If you feel that your life isn't making an impact, that your ministry is fruitless, give that over to God. Focus instead on abiding in Him. Spend much time in secret, in the Word and in prayer. We're often enamored by what a person does, but God is more concerned with who we are. Being always comes before doing in His eyes.

From Silence to Singing

You have turned for me my mourning into dancing;
You have put off my sackcloth and
clothed me with gladness,
To the end that my glory may sing
praise to You and not be silent.

Psalm 30:11–12

God is certainly with us when things are going well, but He is also with us when things aren't going so well. God is there when we achieve a major accomplishment or victory in life, but He is also there in the hospital room when we receive the bad news we were hoping not to hear. Whether in the ups or the downs, God is with us in every case.

The key thought is this: Whether you are going through weeping or joy, give thanks to God. Whether you are in an up time or a down time, give thanks to God. If you are experiencing prosperity or poverty, give thanks to God. If you are in times of dancing or of mourning, give thanks to God. Don't ever forget that the one constant in all of life is God's presence with you, and for that He deserves to be praised.

A Choice to Make

Choose for yourselves this day whom you will serve. . . .
But as for me and my house, we will serve the Lord.

Joshua 24:15

The American poet Robert Frost wrote simple yet powerful poems about life and nature. "The Road Not Taken" is about the different choices we make: "Two roads diverged in a wood, and I—I took the one less traveled by, and that has made all the difference."

Frost's road "less traveled by" reminds the reader of Jesus' "narrow" gate and "difficult" way (Matthew 7:14). Many are called to discover that less-traveled-by way, but few ultimately find it (Matthew 22:14).

Abraham was one who did find the way. We sometimes want to excuse those who don't find Christ or who make destructive choices in life. Given the times, we say, it's almost inevitable that we cannot escape corruption. But some do; and because some do, it means that all may. The difference is in choice: whom do we choose, this day, to serve? Abraham chose to serve the living God, while others chose to serve the gods of this life. If you are contemplating choices in your life today, make the ones that lead to life, now and forever.

A wise choice delayed is a wise choice not made. Choose life for you and yours today.

Take His Hand

I have come that they may have life, and that they may have it more abundantly.

John 10:10

Jesus Christ has proven that He has our absolute best interests at heart. What could He do that He has not done? He gave His life for us. Romans 5:8–10 says it this way:

"But God demonstrates His own love toward us, in that while we were still sinners, Christ died for us. Much more then, having now been justified by His blood, we shall be saved from wrath through Him. For when we were enemies we were reconciled to God through the death of His Son, much more, having been reconciled, we shall be saved by His life."

He is the one who said, "I have come that they may have life, and that they may have it more abundantly" (John 10:10). He gave His life for you, and if you will give Him your trust, not only will He give you today and forgive your sins, but He will give you the future. You can walk into that future with your hand in His, with a sense of confidence and with fear dispelled, knowing that He is your refuge and your strong tower.

How to Save a Marriage

Be kindly affectionate to one another with brotherly love, in honor giving preference to one another.

Romans 12:10

Randy and Victoria got engaged in February 1994. A short time later, Randy's doctor informed him that the diabetes he had suffered with since age twelve had ruined his kidneys. He would need a transplant to live. Victoria volunteered to be tested, and their immune systems matched perfectly. A month after their marriage, they underwent surgery to share equally Victoria's two healthy kidneys.

Randy had originally taken Victoria to the doctor's appointment so she could be sure she wanted to go through with being married to someone who might die. Little did he know that she was not only willing to marry him but to sacrifice part of herself to save his life. What a powerful example of everything that makes a marriage work: voluntary submission, willing sacrifice, generous sharing, and humble gratitude. While most biblical exhortations regarding love in marriage are given to the husband, love is a mutual responsibility. If your spouse has a need, do what you can to meet it. Sharing generously is a prescription for marital health.

Proof of possession is realized only in the giving away of possessions to benefit another.

He Is the Light

The city had no need of the sun or of the moon to shine in it, for the glory of God illuminated it. The Lamb is its light.

Revelation 21:23

Revelation 21:23 says plainly that there will be no sun or moon in heaven to provide illumination, because "the glory of God illuminated it. The Lamb is its light." We forget sometimes that there was light before God said, "Let there be light" (Genesis 1:3). God Himself is light "and in Him is no darkness at all" (1 John 1:5). Jesus said we are the light of the world (Matthew 5:14), but in reality we are only reflectors of His light. He is the only source of eternal light, for even our sun is slowly dying out. Light in heaven for eternity would have to come from the Light, which is God Himself.

No sun or moon means there will be no night. We will live constantly in the light in heaven. Think what that means for our lives: continual, uninterrupted fellowship and activity. The depression and discouragement that often accompany the darkness will be found nowhere in heaven.

Keep Reading

Your word is truth.

John 17:17

Do you find the Bible confusing? It's one book with two great sections—the Old and New Testaments. These are divided into sixty-six books, 1,189 chapters, and 31,102 verses, written by forty-plus authors. Even the newest parts of the Bible are nearly two millennia old. So is the Bible outdated? Incomprehensible? Untrustworthy? Irrelevant?

Not at all. The Bible is timeless. It reveals the mind of an eternal God who is the same yesterday, today, and forever. He was, is, and is to come. He is "I Am," the self-existent One who knows tomorrow's headlines before they're printed.

The Bible is timely, giving us daily encouragement and guidance. Missionary Amy Carmichael said, "Whatever need or trouble you are in, there is always something to help you in your Bible, if only you go on reading 'til you come to the word God specially has for you."

The Bible is knowable. It can be both taught and learned. It may seem puzzling to you now, but if you'll prayerfully keep on reading, hearing, and studying it, you'll increasingly understand its themes, discover its truths, claim its promises, echo its prayers—and share its message.

Don't get discouraged. Bible study is a lifelong habit. Keep reading!

Following God's Schedule

I have glorified You on the earth. I have finished the work which You have given Me to do.

John 17:4

Counselors often use a demonstration to help people see how they have compressed time with their frantic lifestyles. They will ask the client, on the "start" signal, to guess when they think a minute has passed. Most compulsive people and people suffering from addictions (even many normal people living in modern times) will say "stop" long before a minute has actually passed. For them, a minute is an eternity, and they drastically overestimate the speed of actual time. Why? Because their lives have become governed not by reality but by unreality. It is unreal what people now try to accomplish in their lives. And because no one can live indefinitely at such a frantic pace, they turn to other things to sustain them.

Our perception of time must be geared to God's eternal perspective, not the perspective of the twenty-four-hour day. The way Jesus lived His life is how we should live ours. Not in a hurry, not under insignificant deadlines, not burdened by unnecessary pressures. Rather, we should be moving in step with God's schedule. Following God's schedule, Jesus accomplished more in three years than anyone else could accomplish in a lifetime.

Struggles to Strength

Recall the former days in which . . . you endured a great struggle with sufferings.

Hebrews 10:32

The cocoon of the emperor moth is flask-like in shape. To develop into a perfect insect, the moth must force its way through the neck of its cocoon with hours of intense struggle. Entomologists explain that this pressure is nature's way of forcing a life-giving substance into its wings.

Wanting to lessen the seemingly needless trials and struggles of the moth, an observer said, "I'll lessen the pain and struggles of this helpless creature!" With small scissors, he snipped the restraining threads to make the moth's emergence painless and effortless. But the creature never developed wings. For a brief time before its death, it simply crawled, instead of flying through the air on rainbow-colored wings! If only the moth had been allowed to finish struggling, its life would have been transformed into beauty. Similarly, sorrow, suffering, trials, and tribulations are wisely designed to grow us into being like Christ.

Today's temptation can become tomorrow's strength; today's trial, tomorrow's triumph; today's crisis, tomorrow's crown. Christians suffer from spiritual atrophy when they are not strengthened through struggles. The refining and developing processes are oftentimes slow; but through grace, we emerge triumphant.

God's Providence

You gave me life and showed me kindness,
and in your providence watched over my Spirit.

Job 10:12 NIV

When Roger Williams arrived in the New World seeking religious liberty, he was opposed by some Puritans unfriendly to his views. Fleeing to Narragansett Bay, he purchased land and founded a settlement that later became the capital of Rhode Island. He named it Providence. It was a word, he felt, that aptly described God's ordering and overruling of his life.

We often find ourselves in difficult circumstances. But in both personal matters and global affairs, we can trust the overruling hand of our sovereign God, who turns negatives into positives, valleys into hills, and questions into exclamation marks. We can trust the providence of Him who has promised to work all things together for good.

Do you have a burden today? Worried about world events? Anxious about circumstances? A. W. Tozer wrote that the child of God travels in an appointed way. "Accidents may indeed appear to befall him," wrote Tozer, "but these evils will be so in appearance only and will seem evils only because we cannot read the secret script of God's providence."

Guess Who Moved?

For the perverse person is an
abomination to the Lord
But His secret counsel is with the upright.

Proverbs 3:32

A couple was driving home from their twenty-fifth wedding anniversary dinner, she in the passenger seat and he behind the wheel. Dreamily, the wife said, "Honey, remember when we used to sit right next to each other in the car?" The husband answered, "Well, sweetheart, I haven't moved. I've been right here all the time."

Sometimes Christians remember the early days of their walk with God. They have memories of a more intimate relationship with God. Over time, that relationship became formal and distant. But God never wanted it that way; He desires intimate relationships with all His children.

Abraham, the friend of God, found out just how close God wants to be. Before destroying Sodom, God said, "Shall I hide from Abraham what I am doing?" (Genesis 18:17). God shared His plans with His friend and gave Abraham the chance to respond—which he did! Christianity is a relationship, not a religion; and relationships demand time together if they are to grow. If God wanted to tell you a secret, would you be available?

If God doesn't seem as close as He used to, guess who moved?

Friendship and Comfort

If you then, being evil, know how to give good gifts to your children, how much more will your Father who is in heaven give good things to those who ask him!

Matthew 7:11

Many people remain lonely because they fear rejection. They think rejection hurts worse than loneliness and spend much of their time and money trying to avoid it. But that is a wrong attitude. Those who expect to be rejected usually will feel that they are. Those who expect to receive friendship and comfort usually will.

When you need friendship and comfort, offer friendship and comfort, and don't expect rejection. Accept yourself where you are, whatever your need, and remember that Christ will not reject you. When you reach out to Him, He will always respond with loving acceptance. He says in Matthew 7:11, "If you then, being evil, know how to give good gifts to your children [and your friends and all those around you], how much more will your Father who is in heaven give good gifts to those who ask Him!"

Your greatest source of comfort and hope is Christ Jesus.

Thanking God for Health

Beloved, I pray that you may prosper in all things and be in health, just as your soul prospers.

3 John v. 2

Following World War II, Field Marshall Montgomery was sitting in a session of the English House of Lords when he turned to the man next to him and said, "Excuse me, but I'm having a coronary thrombosis." He then quietly left the chamber to seek medical help.

Granted, heart attacks and other illnesses aren't always preceded by such clear warning signs. But if the signs were there, would we recognize them? To paraphrase old Timex watch commercials, it's amazing how much of a licking our bodies can take and still keep on ticking. Stress, too little sleep and exercise, too many empty calories—we take our good health for granted. The body's ability to stay healthy is truly a gift from God.

None of us enjoys now the perfect health we look forward to in heaven. But until then, we can express our gratitude to God for the health we have by being good stewards of these miraculous "earth suits" in which we work, serve, and play each day. Giving thanks for health (whether good or bad) is evidence that we understand this truth: our bodies are not our own (1 Corinthians 6:19).

Our Immortality in Christ

So when this . . . mortal has put on immortality, then shall be brought to pass the saying that is written: "Death is swallowed up in victory."

1 Corinthians 15:54

People addicted to the need for recognition want their name to live forever. A famous real estate developer in our day has built and acquired numerous properties and buildings in New York City and attached his name to all of them. Perhaps he thinks that if he can get his name on enough things he will be immortal and that, after his death, his name will live on. The problem is that moth and rust eventually corrupt, and thieves break in and steal (Matthew 6:19). To what will the name be attached then?

If you know the Word of God, you know that immortality does not come from our achievements but from a relationship with the Lord Jesus Christ. While it is true that every person will live forever, only those in Christ will truly live.

If you know the Lord, you don't have to worry about immortality. It's yours. God has given it to you as part of your gift of eternal life. You don't have to do all the things people do today to make sure they are remembered forever. If you live and die in Jesus Christ, you will be immortal.

What Keeps Us Going

Then Jonathan, Saul's son, arose and went to David in the woods and strengthened his hand in God.

1 Samuel 23:16

Army historian Brigadier General S. L. A. Marshall, after extensive interviews with soldiers returning from combat, concluded that the primary motivation for a soldier to fight is a sense of unity with his immediate combat unit. "I hold it to be one of the simplest truths of war," he said, "that the thing which enables an infantry soldier to keep going . . . is the near presence or presumed presence of a comrade."

Paul didn't go to the mission field alone; he always had partners. Jesus sent His evangelists two by two. The three Hebrews in Daniel 3 proved that "a threefold cord is not quickly broken" (Ecclesiastes 4:12). What would David have done without Jonathan's support in the wilderness? Even our Lord Jesus wanted His closest friends near Him in Gethsemane. Our faith is strengthened when godly peers stand with us in difficulty.

But the question isn't, "Do I have a close friend on whom I can lean?" It's, "How can I be such a friend?" Look around today for someone needing encouragement. Spend extra time praying for one in need. Be cheerful at work or school. Speak to the custodian. Share a verse with a neighbor. Brighten the corner where you are!

Crown of Creation

What is man that You are mindful of him,
And the son of man that You visit him?
For You have made him a little lower than the angels,
And You have crowned him with glory and honor.
Psalm 8:4–5

The night sky casts a divine, pensive spell over us, as people have found through the ages; God designed it to do so. David the psalmist, who gazed out upon those stars during so many nights of watching over his sheep, must have continually marveled. And he must have realized who was watching over him. As he considered his Lord, according to the psalm, he finally was brought to consider himself. "Who am I that I would be worthy of even a thin moment of Your attention?" he wondered. "I look upon the crown of Your creation, and I wonder: how is it that You could place a crown upon me?" For David, of course, a royal destiny did beckon. But true worship has this effect upon us: it simultaneously humbles and uplifts us. In other words, worship places us exactly where we should be, in the realization that we are small, yet a little lower than the angels; we are tiny creatures in the presence of God, but tiny creatures whom He adores.

The Best Medicine

Love never fails.

1 Corinthians 13:8

"Love, true love," wrote psychiatrist Karl Menninger, "is the medicine for our sick old world. If people can learn to give and receive love, they will usually recover from their physical and mental illnesses." He's right; but when the Bible talks about love, it isn't talking about the glossy, romantic, starry-eyed passion portrayed in songs or movies. It's talking about a reasoning, redeeming, choosing type of sacrificial love. It is the power that moves us to respond to someone's needs with no expectation of reward.

That kind of love is preeminent; it never fails.

An evangelist wrote about a wise physician who told a young doctor, "I've been practicing medicine for a long time. I've prescribed many things. But in the long run, I've learned that the best medicine is love."

"What if it doesn't work?" asked the young man.

"Double the dose," replied the doctor.

If things are tense at home, if you're having trouble with a loved one, if someone has insulted or hurt you, love that person anyway. And if that doesn't work, double the dose.

Call upon God

The Lord gives wisdom;
From His mouth come knowledge and understanding.
Proverbs 2:6

The prerequisite to obtaining help in dealing with our troubles is to realize that we lack sufficient wisdom to sort them out! The argument is this: "When facing trials, it is important to know how to cope with them. The only way we will be able to understand these trials and respond to them properly is by asking for the wisdom that only God can give." When our friends and loved ones are going through trials, we may think we see what God is doing through the ordeal. But when we are the sufferers, when we are the ones going through the fire, viewing the situation from God's perspective is a little more difficult. For this reason we are to ask God for wisdom.

As James motivates the troubled believer to seek wisdom (James 1:5), he describes God in such a way as to make us wonder why we have waited so long to reach out for His help.

We know from the Scriptures that God is the source of true wisdom. He is a good God who is not partial to any. He will always answer the prayer for wisdom, never turning away such a request. He may not always answer on our time schedule, but He always answers.

Isaac's Blessings

Bless me—me also, O my father!
Genesis 27:34

Every child needs his parents' blessing. Isaac longed for his father's blessing, love, and approval. Ross Campbell, in *How to Really Love Your Child*, suggests that most parents really do love their children, but they don't always convey that love to their children in a way that really makes the kids feel secure. A child doesn't just need to be loved; he needs to feel loved. He needs to experience his parents' blessings.

There are several excellent ways to bless our children with love. We can, of course, tell them we love them. But we can also convey our love through our eye contact, by the amount of time we spend with them, and by appropriate physical interaction with our youngsters—touching, holding, hugging, roughhousing, and kissing.

We also bless our children by pointing out their strengths. Motivational expert Zig Ziglar said, "Children who are raised in a spirit of praise and approval are going to be happier, more productive, and more obedient than the ones who are constantly criticized."

After all, our heavenly Father liberally dispenses His blessings on us. He expects us to do the same to others, especially to our children.

Received Into His Presence

He who did not spare His own Son, but delivered Him up for us all, how shall He not with Him freely give us all things?

Romans 8:32

If there was ever a person who had room to complain of injustice, it was Jesus. He was the only innocent man to be punished by God. If we stagger at the wrath of God, let us stagger at the cross. The cross was at once the most horrible and the most beautiful example of the wrath of God. God loves us with an everlasting love and wants to bring us to be with Him forever. But God is absolutely holy, and in order for us to be with Him, He had to deal with the issue of holiness. So He sent His holy Son and let Him suffer the penalty of sin for everyone. And then He gave those who trusted in His Son the full benefits of righteousness. He gave us the holiness of His Son.

When we stand before God in His holiness, He looks at us and sees the righteous clothing of His flawless Son. He is able to receive us into His presence. God is so holy that He would not even spare His own Son in order that we might have fellowship with Him.

Better Days Ahead

. . . a living hope through the resurrection of Jesus Christ.

1 Peter 1:3

"The best is yet to be," said poet Robert Browning. For the Christian, that isn't just a nice sentiment about growing older; it's a reality based on the resurrection of Christ. Our futures are just as bright as the flash of glory that burst from the tomb on the first Easter morning. Our tomorrows are just as promising as the first words of the risen Christ to the astonished disciples: "Peace be with you" (John 20:19).

You may have a heavy load to bear just now. Perhaps you've received bad news from the doctor. Maybe you've been rejected by the school to which you applied. Perhaps the bank turned down your loan request. Maybe you're worried about a child. Or maybe you've been struck by depression.

Jesus' friends were depressed the day before Easter. It was a Saturday filled with disappointment, discouragement, depression, and despair. They were whipped. But what a difference a day made!

Among other things, the resurrection of Christ validates all His other claims and promises. Because He rose again, He proved that He is who He said He was, and He can do what He promised to do. Because He lives, we can rest in His promises, knowing that the best is yet to come.

Putting It Into Words

I cry out to the Lord with my voice;
With my voice to the Lord I make my supplication.
Psalm 142:1

When we verbalize our feelings and concerns to God, it is like entering into a conversation with an intimate friend. It is, in fact, a healthy way for us to open up and reveal what is inside, to bring up from the depths of our heart those things we may have stuffed down inside. Fortunately, God is not shocked or surprised by anything, so there is nothing we cannot tell Him. It is an insult to the One who tells us to cast all our cares upon Him not to do so (1 Peter 5:7).

Why would He tell us to verbalize our problems to Him if He did not mean for us to? Even psychologists tell us that verbalizing our problems, whether in writing or out loud, is a good way to bring clarity and definition to what are often very confusing feelings. Suddenly, as we put our feelings into words, we actually begin to see things more clearly ourselves—all because God is willing to listen.

Our Glorious Hope

Our citizenship is in heaven, from which we also eagerly wait for the Savior . . . who will transform our lowly body that it may be conformed to His glorious body.

Philippians 3:20–21

Scottish Presbyterian Robert Baillie learned in 1684 that he would be hanged for his faith, then drawn and quartered with his head and hands nailed to a local bridge. Referring to Philippians 3:20–21, Baillie replied, "They may hack and hew my body as they please, but I know assuredly nothing will be lost, but that all these my members shall be wonderfully gathered and made like Christ's glorious body."

At the resurrection, the bodies of Christians will be raised and reconstituted to resemble the risen body of our Lord. When Jesus rose on Easter, He had a body that was the prototype of the ones we'll have throughout eternity.

Some things about Jesus' glorified body were similar to the one He had before He died. He resembled Himself; He could eat and drink; He could be touched. Yet He could pass through walls, and He appeared in various places without traveling by recognized means. His transformed body no longer aged, nor was it subject to sickness and death.

If you're battling aches and pains or if you're afflicted with illness or disease, take comfort. One day you'll have a body like His.

God's Family

When Jesus therefore saw his mother, and the disciple whom he loved standing by, He said to his mother, "Woman, behold your son!" And he said to the disciple, "Behold your mother!"

John 19:26–27

Our Lord emphasized the human family, but even more, He emphasized the spiritual family of God. The genuine and abiding relationship is not that of the flesh but of the Spirit. As wonderful as earthly relationships are, there is a more intimate relationship between the children of God. John, as a believer, was a better choice to care for Jesus' mother than His brothers and sisters who did not believe.

Jesus brought into being the brotherhood of believers. He created a new society that is not segregated by race or nationality, nor predicated upon social standing or economic power. It consists of those whose faith meets at the cross and whose experience of forgiveness flows from it. Jesus commended His own mother into the hands of a brother. At Golgotha that terrible day, Christ called upon a brother in the family of faith to minister to someone in need. That is still part of His call to those in God's family.

Trusting God for Work

And let the beauty of the Lord our God be upon us,
And establish the work of our hands for us;
Yes, establish the work of our hands.

Psalm 90:17

One story goes that a company's employees found this note on the office bulletin board: "It has come to management's attention that workers dying on the job are failing to fall down. This practice must stop, as it makes it impossible to distinguish the dead employees from those still working. Any employee found dead in an upright position will be immediately dropped from the payroll."

Many Christians have to be reminded that work is a sacred calling. The sacred or secular mentality infects many: anything related to "the spiritual life" is sacred, while work is secular. Nothing could be more unbiblical! Man was created for a lifetime of service to God, making all of life a sacred endeavor. While work became more difficult after sin entered the world, it did not change the fundamental value of work. It is meaningful and required of all who bear God's image. Whether you work for money or as a volunteer, in the home or the community, work is a gift and calling from God.

Do you know a person who is discouraged with his or her work? Your encouragement may help that person's toil become work that reflects the beauty of the Lord.

The Missing Piece Is Christ

In Him dwells all the fullness of the Godhead bodily; and you are complete in Him.

Colossians 2:9–10

Insight into who you are and why you are here is available only from the Creator, because you were created for Him. The missing piece in your life is not more education or better therapy. The missing piece in your life, if you don't know Christ, is to put Him at the center where He belongs. God created you uniquely for Himself. He put a vacuum within you that cannot be filled with anything else but Him. When you stuff in all the pleasure and all the madness of this age trying to find meaning in life, you will never discover it. But something happens when you say a simple prayer, giving in to God and receiving Him into your life.

Then Jesus comes to live within you. God loves you, He knows you, He has a plan for your life. He wants you to know who you are and why you are here, and if you will put your trust in Him, He will give you that perspective in your life. You were created in God's image, so you are really only yourself in relationship to God. When you let God take control of your life through His Son, life begins to have some meaning.

The Joy of Worship

Let the hearts of those rejoice who seek the Lord!

Psalm 105:3

Charles Spurgeon once said, "My happiest moments are when I am worshipping God, really adoring the Lord Jesus Christ, and having fellowship with the ever-blessed Spirit. In that worship I forget the cares of the church and everything else. To me it is the nearest approach to what it will be in heaven."

Worship has a way of refreshing our hearts and rejuvenating our spirits. As we reflect on God's attributes—His power and sovereignty—we view our circumstances through a different lens—God's lens. In the light of His power, giant-sized problems become mouse-like. Although we may enter into His presence with a heavy heart, we leave with a new sense of hope and joy. Through worship we are reminded of the following truth—God Almighty is in control of our lives, and He is fully capable of managing our concerns. The psalmist sums it up precisely with these words: "Why are you cast down, O my soul? . . . Hope in God" (Psalm 42:5).

Rejoice, believer! God has given you "the garment of praise for the spirit of heaviness" (Isaiah 61:3). When you worship Him, darkness and despair are dispelled.

God Is the Cure

He Himself has said, "I will never leave you nor forsake you."

Hebrews 13:5

What is loneliness? I don't know how to define it; all I can do is describe it. It's an underlying anxiety at having no one close, a sharp ache in a moment of grief, and an empty feeling in the pit of the stomach when we know we have no one to whom we can turn. There is no anguish like loneliness.

But God has a cure for loneliness. In our walk with Him, He offers friendship, a family, and a peace that passes all understanding. When we meet Him, we are not guaranteed never to feel lonely, but we are promised that we will never be alone. After all, He is the one who said, "I will never leave you nor forsake you" (Hebrews 13:5).

The Currency of Communicators

These are the things you shall do: Speak each man the truth to his neighbor.

Zechariah 8:16

On May 13, 2003, the United States Bureau of Engraving and Printing introduced a new twenty-dollar bill into circulation. The new bill incorporates advanced security features in an attempt to stay one step ahead of currency counterfeiters: a thin security thread imbedded in the bill, ink that changes color in changing light, watermarks that can be seen on both sides of the bill, and a redesigned portrait of Andrew Jackson.

Official Federal Reserve notes (dollar bills) are the currency of our country—they're how we do business. If someone uses a counterfeit bill, the transaction is invalidated because no real money changed hands.

There is a currency for communicators as well—especially marriage partners who want to communicate successfully. The currency of communicators is truth. The truth is what enables spouses to accomplish the "business" of marriage. If couples don't communicate honestly, then trust is destroyed. And as trust goes, so goes the marriage. Don't be a communication counterfeiter in your marriage. When you speak, speak the truth—in love.

False words create a foundation of fantasies on which no house can permanently stand.

Prepare for Tests

Of His own will He brought us forth by the word of truth, that we might be a kind of firstfruits of His creatures.

James 1:18

James reminds us that we experience temptation because we are God's special people. We are members of His family because we have been born again by the word of truth. When James uses the word *firstfruits* to describe believers, he is reminding us that we belong only to God. In the Old Testament, firstfruits were the firstborn of cattle and the early fruit of the ground, both of which belonged to God.

The enemy targets us because of our relationship with God. There would be no inner battle if we were truly lost.

The tests God allows to mature us can become temptations from Satan that malign us. We must be prepared for tests, realize that they can become temptations, and then overcome them through the strength of our relationship with God.

Home Before Dark

Teach me, O Lord, the way of your statutes,
And I shall keep it to the end.
Psalm 119:33

It'd be nice if the power of temptation lessened as we grew older, but there's no security in age. King David was fifty when he fell into sin with Bathsheba; and in that culture fifty was older than it is now, for life expectancy was much shorter. The hot blood of youth was no longer flowing through David's veins, but he fell into sin anyway.

Midlife and old age have their own sets of temptations, and we must never let down our guard. It's true that we should grow wiser and stronger as we grow older. We should grow in grace. But don't think you'll ever be immune from temptation in this life, whatever your age.

J. Oswald Sanders wrote, "Nothing is easier for the aging person who is growing increasingly infirm and experiencing some depression as a result than to turn inward and become self-occupied. That attitude of mind only exacerbates the problem. It is when with firm purpose we turn away from our own grief, aches, and ailments, and busy ourselves to relieve those of others, that we will obtain relief from our own."

Worship and Wonder

They were filled with wonder and amazement at what had happened to him.

Acts 3:10

Worship and wonder, which are so closely connected, are all about coming to the end of our measurements. In the presence of Almighty God, as the apostle John discovered, the sense of wonder comes naturally and leaves us changed. How could we respond any other way? But without the capability of awe, where we stand at the edge of ourselves and gaze beyond, we will never come into His presence.

Do you ever wonder? How long has it been since you've been a child again, gaping with wide eyes? How would it change your life if you could live like that every day? How would it change the people around you?

I hope you're already sensing it—your heart's very desire. This is what has been lacking in so many lives. We've wandered through the emptiness when we could have been wondering at the fullness of the love of God. Your heart's desire, even if you haven't come to realize it, is to live every moment in the wonder of worship.

Rewards for Holding On

For I consider that the sufferings of this present time are not worthy to be compared with the glory which shall be revealed in us.

Romans 8:18

In 1946, Akio Morita invented the world's first transistor radio in Tokyo. An American company offered to buy him out at a generous price, but Morita wanted his company's name on the product. He declined and struggled to stay in business. But his perseverance paid off as his company, Sony, became a world leader in electronics.

Far too often our focus is on today's suffering instead of tomorrow's reward. Morita could have sold out early and relieved his cash-strapped condition. But he was convinced that if he held on, greater rewards would come his way. And he was right!

The Christian life is like that. We frequently experience significant, unexplained, even undeserved suffering in this life. But the apostle Paul tells us to hold on—don't sell out! The suffering of this life—or the temporary relief we might enjoy by giving up our faith—cannot compare with the glory and rewards that await us in heaven.

Has the devil made you an offer you can't refuse? Don't sell out! What you'll lose in heaven is far more valuable than what you'll gain on earth.

Joy in the Morning

Weeping may endure for a night,
But joy comes in the morning.

Psalm 30:5

It's interesting that David follows a pattern of looking at the day that was begun in the creation account in Genesis. He says that weeping comes in the night, but joy comes in the morning. If you remember, when God created the heavens and the earth, He said, "The evening and the morning were the first day" (Genesis 1:5). We think just the opposite, don't we? We think of a day as the morning followed by the evening.

I think there are wonderful truths embedded in God's perspective on life. If you will look at your day as the evening and the morning instead of the morning and the evening, you will begin your day in the evening by meditating on what you need to accomplish the next day and asking God's blessing on it. Then He is free to work in your heart and mind as you sleep to prepare you for accomplishing those things. When Christ returns, there will be no more weeping. Weeping is ours during the night, but our eternal joy is coming in the morning of Christ's return.

A Lesson in Humility

When pride comes, then comes shame;
But with the humble is wisdom.

Proverbs 11:2

Booker T. Washington, the renowned black educator, was an outstanding example of this truth. One day he was walking in an exclusive section of town when a wealthy white woman stopped him. Not recognizing him, she asked if he would like to earn a few dollars by chopping wood for her. Professor Washington smiled, rolled up his sleeves, and proceeded to do the humble chore she had requested.

The next morning, the embarrassed woman went to see Mr. Washington and apologized profusely when she learned who he was. "It's perfectly all right, madam," he replied. "Occasionally I enjoy a little manual labor. Besides, it's always a delight to do something for a friend." Not long afterward, the woman showed her admiration by persuading some wealthy acquaintances to join her in donating thousands of dollars to the Tuskegee Institute.

Human nature desires attention and credit for good deeds, but God calls us to be humble and to offer the praise to Him. Just as Christ humbled Himself and gave His life for the world, we are called to let go of arrogance and to be servants.

Are you concerned with impressing people, or are you concerned with having a humble spirit? A truly humble man is hard to find, yet God delights to honor such selfless people.

A Resource of Power

I tell you the truth: It is expedient for you that I go away; for if I go not away, the Comforter will not come unto you; but if I depart, I will send Him unto you.

John 16:7 KJV

As a child of God, the Holy Spirit lives within my heart. Christ came into the world; He died; He was buried; He was resurrected; and He ascended into heaven. Before He ascended, He said, "Before I go, I want you to know I am going to send a Comforter who is not only going to be with you—He is going to be in you." The Holy Spirit is that Comforter whom Christ sent to live within us. By virtue of my sonship, I have a permanent spiritual resource—the Holy Spirit living within me. He helps me to walk, talk, and live like a son of God, something I couldn't do if He weren't within me. The standard for living life as a child of God is far beyond anything I could ever produce on my own. But when Christ came to live within my heart, He put His blessed Holy Spirit within me. Because I have the Spirit of the Father in me, I am identified as one of His children.

The Holy Spirit in me is far better than a calling card. With the Holy Spirit, I have access to my heavenly Father at any time. That is a resource of power that I cannot have any other way.

God's Heart, My Heart

I have found David the son of Jesse, a man after My own heart, who will do all My will.

Acts 13:22

Ruth Bell Graham wrote of an encounter she had with a young Indian student named Pashi. She spoke with Pashi about Christ, to which he replied, "I would like to believe in Christ, and many in India would like to believe, but we have never seen a Christian who was like Christ."

A friend of Mrs. Graham told her to tell Pashi, "I'm not offering you Christians. I am offering you Christ." Good point. No one will ever be excused for not believing in Christ on the basis of Christians' lack of faithfulness. On the other hand, we should ask ourselves the question, "What does a person look like who says he's a follower of Christ? Should Christians be like Jesus Christ?"

Perhaps the most well-known answer to that question is the description given of David: a man after God's own heart, committed to doing all of God's will. Perhaps, then, that's what a Christian should be—a person committed to doing all of God's will. If a government order were issued to arrest everyone who appears to be a Christian, would you be incarcerated?

The person after God's heart is the person whose own heart seeks first the kingdom of God.

The Deserving One

The hour is coming, and now is, when the true worshipers will worship the Father in spirit and truth; for the Father is seeking such to worship Him.

John 4:23

When Lawrence of Arabia was in Paris with some of his Arab friends after World War I, he took them to see the sights of the city. His friends showed little interest in the Louvre, the Arch of Triumph, or Napoleon's tomb. The thing that really interested them was the faucet in their bathtub. They spent much time turning it on and off; they thought it was wonderful. All they had to do was turn the handle and they could get all the water they wanted.

When they were leaving Paris, Lawrence found them in the bathroom with wrenches, trying to get the faucet off so they could take it with them. "You see," they said, "it is very dry in Arabia. What we need are faucets. If we have them, we will have all the water we want." Lawrence had to explain to them that the effectiveness of the faucet depended on the water system to which it was attached.

Our study of worship reminds us that the effectiveness of all that we do in the church is not to be found in outward activity or service, but in the One who stands behind it. The One we serve. The One deserving of our worship.

Grand People

When I call to remembrance the genuine faith that is in you, which dwelt first in your grandmother . . .

2 Timothy 1:5

Do you enjoy Fanny Crosby's great hymns, like "Blessed Assurance," "To God Be the Glory," "All the Way My Savior Leads Me," and "He Hideth My Soul"? They would not have been written but for a grandmother's love.

Fanny was blinded at six weeks of age by a spurious doctor, but her grandmother Eunice was determined that Fanny would never grow up feeling disabled or disadvantaged. Eunice spent years training Fanny in all sorts of things—teaching her the Bible, helping her explore nature, and enabling her to develop remarkable powers of memory. With her grandmother's encouragement, Fanny memorized large portions of the Bible. From that vast storehouse of memorized scripture, she later produced her hymns. "My grandmother was more to me than I can ever express by word or pen," Fanny wrote long afterward.

Don't underestimate the influence you can have as a grandparent. As you pour yourself into your grandchild, you will be molding a mighty servant of the Lord. Grandparents have the joyous responsibility of showing God's strength and power to the generations that follow.

Change Through Christ

Therefore, if anyone is in Christ, he is a new creation; old things have passed away; behold, all things have become new.

2 Corinthians 5:17

I believe that for marriage to become the treasure the Bible says it can be, Jesus Christ must be at the center. When Jesus Christ comes into a life, that person gains the basic equipment necessary to become "one" with another person, to be secure in identity, someone who doesn't have to prove personal worth because he or she recognizes that worth in Jesus Christ. The best thing that can happen to any marriage is for both partners to know Jesus Christ as their personal Savior and walk with Him by faith.

Would you like to know a priceless secret? Here it is: God is awesome, and He'll change your life, He'll change your marriage, He'll change your family, and He'll change your future for generations to come. That's what God, through Christ, will do!

He is waiting for you to give Him an invitation into your life. He does not barge in where He is not wanted. If you will take the initiative today, you can begin right now to live as you were meant to live. When you do, you will start to personally experience the awesomeness of God at work in your marriage and family. And when that happens, anything is possible.

Grocery Shopping

Fathers, do not exasperate your children; instead, bring them up in the training and instruction of the Lord.

Ephesians 6:4 NIV

A man in the supermarket was pushing a cart that contained, among other things, a screaming baby. As the man proceeded along the aisles, he kept repeating softly, "Keep calm, George. Don't get excited, George. Don't get upset, George. Don't yell, George."

A lady watching with admiration said to the man, "You are certainly to be commended for your patience in trying to quiet little George."

"Lady," he declared, "I'm George."

Every parent can relate to George. Doesn't it sometimes seem like Ephesians 6:4 should read, "Children, don't annoy your fathers while in the supermarket"? But it doesn't. Perhaps the reason is that parents are to be the example of God's love, and children learn the best from observation. Even shopping at the grocery store is an opportunity to show your children the proper way to behave.

There is no greater role model for children than a parent. Colossians 3:21 says, "Fathers, do not provoke your children, lest they become discouraged." Be an example of patience and love to your children. From potty-training to driver's education—parents are set in place by God to be a tool that transforms the precepts of the Bible into a living testimony to their children.

Jesus Is the Life

Jesus said to her, "I am the resurrection and the life. He who believes in Me, though he may die, he shall live. And whoever lives and believes in Me shall never die."

John 11:25–26

The King of kings came into the world humbly. He was born in a stable, His cradle a feed trough. In His thirty-three years of earthly life, He owned no possessions. He had to depend on others to provide for His needs, and He had to borrow everything He used. The stable where He was born was borrowed. He borrowed money to pay His taxes, a boat to stand in and preach, a cross on which to die. Even His tomb was not His own.

But He had a mission that He alone could accomplish: He, the Son of Man, came "to seek and to save that which was lost" (Luke 19:10). He bore our sins "in His own body on the tree" that in the age to come we might have eternal life (1 Peter 2:24; Mark 10:29–30; and John 3:13–17). Of Himself He says, "I am the resurrection and the life. He who believes in Me, though he may die, he shall live. And whoever lives and believes in Me shall never die" (John 11:25–26). He "put away sin by the sacrifice of Himself . . . so Christ was offered once to bear the sins of many. . . . We have been sanctified through the offering of the body of Jesus Christ once for all" (Hebrews 9:26–10:10).

Redeemed or Religious?

For there is one God and one Mediator between God and men, the Man Christ Jesus, who gave Himself a ransom for all.

1 Timothy 2:5–6

Don't think of Christianity as a religion, a ritual, a routine, or a set of rules. It may have elements of all those things, but it is primarily and essentially a relationship with the living God through Christ our Redeemer.

As quarterback for the Oakland Raiders, Rich Gannon enjoyed his share of fame and fortune. But the high point of his life came while playing backup quarterback with the Minnesota Vikings. "I went to chapel, and I heard a speaker give his testimony. I felt so guilty inside," he said. "I was a young, strapping athlete who had basically everything. But I felt I wanted something he had. I knew what he had was that inner joy and peace that a relationship with Jesus brings."

It's a relationship with Jesus that brings joy to our lives. Someone said that religion is man seeking God; Christianity is God seeking man. Becoming a Christian isn't primarily a matter of doing good works, but of coming to Christ in simple faith and asking forgiveness for sin. When you receive His forgiveness, gained through His shed blood, your sin is washed away and His righteousness takes its place.

If you've never done that, why not today? Why not now?

God Always Knew You

For you formed my inward parts;
You covered me in my mother's womb.

Psalm 139:13

God knew you before you were born. He knows the moment when you were conceived. In every phase of development, from that moment on, He is there. The human embryo is not the result of a biological accident. God is aware of the union of the sperm and the egg and the attachment of the embryo to the uterine lining and the development of human life. God formed the inward parts and arranged the genetic structure. God knows about that human life and loves that human life from the very moment of its union.

In every cell of your body there is enough information to re-create your adult person as if no other cell were necessary. And every time that cell divides in the process of your growth, all the information contained in each cell is part of the division. Someone has reasoned that if all of the instructions in the DNA of one cell were written out, it would take a thousand six-hundred-page books to put all that information down. And God put it in a cell that no one can see without magnification. And it's in every cell of your body. God did it so you would have your identity. You are unique. You are individually precious to God.

RSVPing to God

Come to Me, all you who labor . . . and I will give you rest.

Matthew 11:28

Many of the practices of Western etiquette came from the French court of King Louis XIV in the late seventeenth and early eighteenth centuries. At his palace, Versailles, Louis XIV had the rules for court behavior written on "tickets," or etiquette. It's also why our familiar RSVP means "*Répondez, s'il vous plait*"—Respond, if you please.

Jesus told a parable about how the Jewish nation politely RSVPed to God—but with the wrong reply. When God sent Jesus to the Jews as their Messiah, they should have interpreted His invitation to "come to Me" (Matthew 11:28–30) as an invitation to enter God's eternal kingdom. But they made up excuses to reject God's invitation. In the parable, the recipients of the invitation to a great banquet replied that, sorry, they were too busy. So the host reissued the invitation to the forgotten of society, the inhabitants of the highways and byways, and brought them in. Those to whom the invitation was originally sent missed out on that chance to enter the kingdom.

If you've RSVPed to God with a "Sorry, too busy," you might want to reconsider—and accept! When an invitation comes from God, failing to respond is the same as saying no.

Maybe Not!

Lift up your eyes and look at the fields, for they are already white for harvest!

John 4:35

Tennessee pastor Robert Shockey doesn't believe in chance encounters. To him, every contact is an opportunity to evangelize. When he answers the phone, for example, and hears the person on the other end saying, "Sorry, I must have the wrong number," Bob responds, "Maybe not!"

Usually there is a pause on the line, followed by something like, "What do you mean?" That gives Shockey an opening to initiate a conversation about the Gospel. He has led more than one person to faith in Christ that way.

Evangelist Billy Graham once answered the phone in his hotel room. The person on the other end asked for so-and-so, and Mr. Graham told him he had the wrong number. There was a pause, and the person said, "You sure sound a lot like Billy Graham."

"This is Billy Graham," replied the evangelist. During the ensuing conversation, the caller gave his life to Christ. There are opportunities all around us to witness for Christ, some in unexpected places. We are ambassadors for Christ—harvesters, witnesses. Perhaps the Holy Spirit will lead you to someone today who needs a word from the Lord.

Little Foxes

The little foxes that spoil the vines . . .

Song of Solomon 2:15

According to *Psychology Today*, 70 percent of high school students and nearly half of college students confess to cheating. *USA Today* reported that 91 percent of Americans lie routinely.

Our culture says, "If you want to get ahead, you have to break a few rules." But the Bible warns that "little sins" can be just as damaging as the big ones—or more so. Commentator Matthew Henry wrote, "Adam's eating forbidden fruit seemed but a little sin, but it opened the door to the greatest."

Are you being tempted to compromise your integrity? Tempted to cheat at school? Pressured to be dishonest at work? Drawn into an "innocent little relationship"? We must live by biblical principles, faithful to the standards of a holy God. As evangelist Charles Finney put it, "A person who is dishonest in little things isn't really honest in anything." On the other hand, Jesus rewards those who are "faithful over a little" (Matthew 25:21 ESV).

Make sure the little, hidden areas of your life are governed by your convictions, not corrupted by your compromises.

FEBRUARY

In the world you will have tribulation, but be of good cheer; I have overcome the world.

—John 16:33

Rest in Jesus

In the world you will have tribulation, but be of good cheer; I have overcome the world.

John 16:33

When we don't know how this is all going to work out, we have to hold tightly to the Lord Jesus Christ Himself and rest in Him. That's the message we often find in the New Testament.

In John 16:33, Jesus said to His disciples, "These things I have spoken to you, that in Me you may have peace. In the world you will have tribulation; but be of good cheer, I have overcome the world." Jesus had been talking about His future death, but then He said, "Don't get caught up in that. Make sure in the midst of these tumultuous times your trust is in Me."

When we go through a tough time, if we've spent any time at all in the Word of God, that tough time is like a magnet that draws us to the Lord Jesus. Nothing will happen in the future that will catch Jesus Christ by surprise. And there's nothing that will happen that He can't help His children work through.

So rather than spending our time trying to figure out the nuances of what will happen, we should spend at least as much time getting to know Him better.

Self-Judging

If we would judge ourselves, we would not be judged.

1 Corinthians 11:31

Jonathan knew he shouldn't use the company computer to access personal websites, but he did it anyway. As a result, his boss appeared in his office one day, asked for Jonathan's keys and files, and summarily marched him outside the building, firing him. Jonathan was humiliated, but he had no one to blame but himself. If he had evaluated and corrected his behavior, others would not have done so. If he had judged himself, he would not have been judged.

To judge our sins means to see them as God sees them. It means to hate those sins and to know that God wants to put them out of our lives. It means to honestly acknowledge moral failures in our lives and to deal with them through genuine, lasting confession and repentance.

King David did this in Psalm 32:3–5: "When I kept silent, my bones grew old through my groaning all the day long. For day and night Your hand was heavy upon me; my vitality was turned into the drought of summer. I acknowledged my sin to You, and my iniquity I have not hidden. I said, 'I will confess my transgressions to the Lord,' and You forgave the iniquity of my sin."

Does anything in your life need to be evaluated and corrected today?

The Poor Rich Man

For where your treasure is, there your heart will be also.

Matthew 6:21

A certain Muslim lived in a cottage on a hill. Every week he rode his camel to a little stream. And every week as the camel stopped to drink, it nosed up the pebbles in order to make a deeper place for drinking. Again and again, the Muslim picked up the bright stones the animal uncovered and took them home with him.

One day a traveler told the Muslim of the easy comfort and riches that certain men in the city enjoyed; the traveler filled the Muslim's eyes and heart with discontent. So he sold his cottage and wandered the earth looking for money. Finally he died in rags and poverty, and was buried. The man who bought the cottage found the stones and preserved them.

One day a merchant came to his home and discovered that these well-preserved stones were diamonds. The owner of the diamonds immediately became a millionaire. The first man had great wealth but, being ignorant of it, sold it and traveled the world looking for it. The second man simply made use of what he had. All people have eternal life at their disposal. Some respond to this treasure like the first man, some like the second.

Lots of Lots

. . . for you are still carnal.

1 Corinthians 3:3

Not long ago, a man in Louisville, Kentucky, stole a credit card from a woman at church who, noticing her purse open, called the police. Authorities soon caught the man. He was using the card at a Christian bookstore to buy ten copies of a Bible study called *Moving Beyond Your Past*.

We don't know the thief's spiritual condition, but we do know that many Christians never move far beyond their past. They come to Christ, but the evidence of maturity and spiritual growth is sparse. Paul called such people "carnal."

The carnal man is saved and Spirit indwelled, but he is controlled and dominated by his own life. The Holy Spirit is a resident, but He is not president. Lot is a good biblical example. He was enamored with the world, pitching his tent toward Sodom. Soon he was in Sodom, sitting at the gate, all wrapped up in materialism and with the world.

You have to read all the way through the Bible until you come to 2 Peter 2:7 before you find out that Lot was a believer. There are lots of Lots today. If you had to indict them for Christianity, you couldn't get enough evidence for a conviction.

Are you a "carnal" Christian? Renew your wholehearted commitment to Christ, and let Him be President, Lord, Boss, and King of your life.

Count It All Joy

My brethren, count it all joy when you fall into various trials.

James 1:2

Persecution was the most common trial among Jewish believers in James's time. Today, a trial can be a number of things: the loss of a job, a divorce, trouble with our children, severe financial strain, illness or death in the family, or relational problems over which we seem to have little control. Though our trials may not seem as severe as the persecution of James's day, note that James does not say "if" we encounter trials, but "when" we encounter trials. And when these trials come, our first strategy, according to James, is to "count it all joy."

To count, or consider, it all joy in the midst of our trials is to respond with a deliberate, intelligent appraisal of our situation. We must learn to look at our situation from God's perspective and recognize that, though the trial is not a happy experience in itself, it is God's way of producing something of great value. The word *count* means "to think in terms of the future." James is not saying we are to rejoice over pain, but we are to rejoice because God's purposes are being accomplished in our lives.

Fervent Prayers

When you have shut your door, pray to
your Father who is in the secret place.
Matthew 6:6

Bishop Joseph Hall, an ardent seventeenth-century Anglican once imprisoned in the Tower of London for his faith, spent his final years on a farm in the countryside writing devotional classics. Here's what he said about prayer:

> An arrow, if it be drawn up but a little way, goes not far; but if it be pulled up to the head, flies swiftly and pierces deep. Prayer, if it be only dribbled forth from careless lips, falls at our feet. It is the strength of [discharge] and strong desire that sends it to heaven, and makes it pierce the clouds. It is not the arithmetic of our prayers, how many they are; not the rhetoric of our prayers, how eloquent they be; nor the geometry of our prayers, how long they be; nor the music of our prayers, how sweet our voice may be; nor the logic of our prayers, how argumentative they may be; nor the method of our prayers, how orderly they may be; nor even the divinity of our prayers, how good the doctrine may be—which God cares for. Fervency of spirit is that which availeth much.

The Lord uses men and women who pray earnestly. Were you going to rush through your prayers today? Why not pause and talk to your Father awhile?

Stand Amazed

God saw everything that He had made,
and indeed it was very good.

Genesis 1:31

Genesis begins, as everyone knows, with the creation of the world. None of us was there to witness it, but we're given the account of how God fashioned the heavens and the earth with His powerful hand. Through writing inspired by the Spirit of God, we can stand and behold the moment when God said, "Let there be light," when He divided the waters from the dry land, when He caused the earth to bring forth grass, and when He placed the sun, the moon, and the stars in the sky. On each occasion we know that God said, "It is good."

Yes, it is good! That's our most basic response, too, when we look into the star-filled sky or see the sun rise in glory over a mountain, bathing the skies in orange and deep blue. But when we see that which is perfect, that which God has proclaimed good, we respond also with our emotions. We stand amazed; we wonder. And that's a point we must stop and consider, for the ability to marvel lies at the very center of our identities as human beings created in the divine image.

Stand before that sunset. Not only will your eyes be filled, but also your very soul and imagination.

Lost and Found

Have mercy upon me, O God,
According to Your lovingkindness;
According to the multitude of Your tender mercies,
Blot out my transgressions.

Psalm 51:1

John Vassar was an agent for the American Tract Society in the 1850s. He left a Bible in the home of a Christian woman whose husband was an infidel. When the husband discovered the Bible, he chopped it in two. Later, in an hour of despair, he began reading Luke 15, the story of the prodigal son, in his half of the Bible. Desperate to read the conclusion, he begged his wife for her half, read the story over and over, and was saved.

It's easy to tell when the grace of God has opened the spiritual eyes of a sinner—he comes to a clear conclusion that he is a sinner! And it's also easy to tell when personal sin is not clear to an individual—he sees sin in everyone but himself. The parable Jesus told of the two brothers (Luke 15:11–32) has an example of each. The younger, prodigal brother recognized his sin and repented before his father. The older brother, however, was indignant that his younger sibling had been forgiven. He couldn't extend grace to others, probably because he may not have experienced it himself.

Which "brother" would you have been in Jesus' parable? Being forgiven by God only makes sense to those who know they've sinned.

From Weeping to Joy

I will turn their mourning to joy, will comfort them, and make them rejoice rather than sorrow.

Jeremiah 31:13

Sadness is an everyday truth in this life, and one we have to reckon with. But just as a day can bring sadness with it, it is also true that the day of sadness passes. We can be accused of being trite or trivial when we say it, but it is true that "things are going to get better; just hang on; you'll get through this." That's the truth. Sadness does turn to joy.

I don't know how many times I have faced a group of family and friends who have lost a loved one unexpectedly—a funeral can be the saddest day of our lives. Looking at people's faces, we wonder if they will ever smile again. And yet, I will see those same people in a matter of weeks or months and the joy has returned. It's just the process of life. We weep and then we rejoice. God gives us the grace to move from one phase to the next, from one day to the next.

The Sympathizing Jesus

He gently leads those that have young.

Isaiah 40:11 NIV

Though brilliant and well liked, young Aurelius Augustine (354–430) lived in utter immorality. For more than three decades, his mother, Monica, prayed for him, following him to Carthage, to Rome, and on to Milan, weeping, pleading, and assaulting heaven with perpetual missiles of prayer. The Lord finally answered in wondrous ways, for Monica's wild and wayward son became one of the most influential figures in the history of Christianity.

There was never a distraught parent in the Gospels who came to Jesus on behalf of a troubled child and found Him unresponsive. Notice how sympathetically He dealt with the distressed father in John 4:46–54.

But God's miracles come in many packages, and He deals with us all differently. As we see in the Gospels, for example, Jesus did not always heal in the same way. Sometimes He touched, sometimes He spoke, sometimes He healed in stages, and sometimes He made mud from spittle, smeared it on a blind person's eyes, and told him to wash it off.

He custom designs His aid to fit our circumstances, to develop our souls, and to meet our needs. If you're troubled about a loved one today, trust Jesus and await His special miracle for you.

Your Will Be Done

Your kingdom come, Your will be done
on earth as it is in heaven.

Matthew 6:10

It is a helpless, hopeless feeling to be caught in a whirlpool in which other people and their priorities are sucking you under. I know that my priorities are God first, my wife next, my children next, and my vocation and ministry last. What a joy it is to go to God in prayer each day and pray what I have learned from the Lord's Prayer: "Lord, Your kingdom come, Your will be done. By the grace of God, with all that I have within me, Lord, help me this day to make Your will manifest in my life."

I have to keep praying that every day. I pray those priorities back to God, not only because I want God to hear them, but because I want me to hear them, so I don't ever forget. God changes us through prayer—when we pray, we get on the same wavelength with God. And as we pray, if we pray according to the will of God, little by little He takes all the things that are out of sync in our lives and puts them into sync so that we can take this big deep breath and say, "Oh, yes, that's the way it's supposed to be!"

Worshiping God Alone

And when He had sent the multitudes away, He went up on the mountain by Himself to pray.

Matthew 14:23

Jesus Christ was unique in that He was both human and divine. Because we tend to think of Him as the Son of God more than the Son of Man, we often overlook what we can learn from His human experience.

When Jesus miraculously fed five thousand people near the Sea of Galilee, His divine power and prerogatives were clear (Matthew 14:13–21). Yet after this event, we see the humanity of Jesus in ways we should be able to easily identify with. After dismissing the crowd and sending His disciples away, Jesus withdrew to a solitary spot on the mountainside to be alone with God.

How is it that the Son of God needed to be alone with God? While that mystery may remain, one thing is clear: the stark contrast between the crush of a huge crowd and the solitude of being completely alone. Most Christians today only experience the former. Note that Jesus created His solitude by sending the others away. When was the last time you created time for the express purpose of worshiping God by yourself?

People are necessary for many things, but worshiping God alone is not one of them.

Parenting by Faith

Children, obey your parents in the Lord, for this is right. . . . And you, fathers, do not provoke your children to wrath, but bring them up in the training and admonition of the Lord.

Ephesians 6:1, 4

There is no such thing as painless parenting. Pain—even excruciating pain—is a natural part of the family process in our broken world. Women know better than anyone that pain is how the family got started. And the aches and pains, the hurts and hassles, will continue to intrude into the parenting pathway through the years, whether we like it or not.

That's why a vital faith in Jesus Christ is so crucial to a happy family. God equips us through faith to meet all the challenges of parenting, even in a toxic environment. Consider Ephesians 6:1, for example: "Children, obey your parents." How? "In the Lord." Or read Ephesians 5:25: "Husbands, love your wives." How? "As Christ loved the church." Or Ephesians 5:22: "Wives, submit to your own husbands." How? "As to the Lord." All these instructions to the family wrap around a core of faith in God and Jesus Christ.

Don't try to build your family without faith in God. Throw yourself on His grace and mercy and say to Him, "Lord, I know that apart from You, I can't do anything but mess this thing up. So I'm going to hang on to You with both hands. Together, we'll make this family work."

John, the Loyal Disciple

Now there was leaning on Jesus' bosom one of His disciples, whom Jesus loved.

John 13:23

The Greek word *agape* is one of the most important words in the New Testament. It means "unconditional love"—the no-strings-attached love with which God loves us. *Agape*'s Hebrew parallel in the Old Testament, *hesed*, is less familiar but no less important. It means "loyal love" and describes God's everlasting love for His people, Israel (and Israel's spiritual descendants, the church).

Loyalty is almost a lost value in today's world. Everything seems to be for sale, including friendship, affection, and devotion—the things that make up loyalty. Even Jesus' disciples found themselves lacking in loyalty on the day Jesus was crucified—all the disciples except one, that is. The disciple named John seems to have had a devotion to Jesus that the others lacked prior to His resurrection. John was the only one of the original band of disciples who stood at the foot of the cross in Jesus' final hours. John was loyal to the very end. Every Christian should ask himself, "Would I have been there with John? Will I be loyal to Jesus regardless of the price?"

The deeper our understanding of God's *agape*, the deeper the manifestation of our hesed.

God Is Gracious

If any of you lacks wisdom, let him ask of God, who gives to all liberally and without reproach, and it will be given to him.

James 1:5

James says that God gives to all men "liberally," which means two things. First, the word means "to stretch out," and it pictures God stretching or spreading out His table of wisdom. God dispenses His wisdom to those of us who ask by lavishly pouring out to us the full supply of that which we need. The second meaning reflects the word *singly.* God is the opposite of the "double-minded" man mentioned in James 1:8. God gives His wisdom simply, plainly, and individually to all who will ask of Him.

God also gives His wisdom without reproach (that is, without insult). When we pray for wisdom, God does not scold us for coming. He is a God who is generous and gracious, so seekers should approach Him in faith. If we approach God without faith, we have decided to live life our own way, to make our own decisions, to separate ourselves from Him.

James says the person who prays while doubting is like a wave of the sea, blown and tossed about by the wind. However, the faithful man is stable, looking in only one direction for the wisdom he needs. And he knows that the God to whom he prays is able and willing to respond to his need.

Warning: God at Work!

For it is God who works in you both to will
and to do for His good pleasure.
Philippians 2:13

Before the apostle Paul encountered Christ on the Damascus road, his entire life had been dedicated to the study of the Old Testament. When he became a follower of Christ, it is likely he first thought all his years of meticulous study as a Pharisee were wasted. Yet God had providentially prepared Paul to show how Christ was the fulfillment of the Old Testament scriptures he knew so well.

It's easy to fall into the trap of thinking that God doesn't begin working in our lives until the day we come to know Christ. But Scripture says He "foreknew" us, meaning He chose us and prepared us long before we ever met Him (Romans 8:29–30). David said that God wrote out all the days of his life before they ever came to pass (Psalm 139:16), and we can assume He has done the same for us.

God is at work in our lives in ways we know nothing about. When the road gets bumpy and the fog rolls in, don't project your confusion onto God. Even when you can't see His hand at work, He is always active in you to bring about His good pleasure.

Faith changes the question "Is God at work?" into a declarative statement of faith: "God is at work!"

Christ Cures

[Christ] Himself bore our sins in His own body on the tree, that we, having died to sins, might live for righteousness—by whose stripes you were healed.

1 Peter 2:24

For true comfort we must turn to the Master Healer. The apostle Peter gives us the promise of healing when we turn to Christ, "Who Himself bore our sins in His own body on the tree, that we, having died to sins, might live for righteousness—by whose stripes you were healed. For you were like sheep going astray, but have now returned to the Shepherd and Overseer of your souls" (1 Peter 2:24–25).

We are comforted by the knowledge that because of our Savior's lonely suffering and death and His glorious resurrection, we also will rise again to have eternal life in heaven. Even when our loved ones die and leave us behind, we can become true survivors in Christ and not be overwhelmed by the pain of separation and aloneness, for we are not forever separated from them, nor are we ever truly alone. Our Savior is always with us, and through His power we know that the death of an earthly body is not the end of life, but the beginning of eternal happiness. Knowing this gives us comfort.

A Good and Faithful Servant

Well done . . . you were faithful over a few things,
I will make you ruler over many things.

Matthew 25:21

Several years before slaves were legally set free by Lincoln's "Emancipation Proclamation," a Virginia slave agreed to purchase his freedom from his master. He was released to find work where he could. When Lincoln freed all slaves, this man still owed his master three hundred dollars. In spite of his legal freedom, the slave walked from his home in Ohio to his master's home in Virginia to pay his final debt. His reason? He had given his word, and he would not be able to enjoy his freedom without fulfilling his promise.

Daniel the prophet had been made a slave of the Babylonian and, later, Persian Empires in Mesopotamia. Separated from Jerusalem and his own spiritual culture, he nonetheless continued to worship God faithfully. At the time of the evening offering in Jerusalem (3:00 p.m.), Daniel was found to be faithfully in prayer in Persia—and this after being separated from Jewish practices for nearly seventy years (Daniel 9:21). Without the support structure of your friends and local church, would you remain faithful to God as Daniel did?

Faithful servants are those who live obediently even when they don't have to—and they are rewarded by God accordingly.

Walk by Faith

For we walk by faith, not by sight.

2 Corinthians 5:7

Faith is seeking and finding God in Christ—desiring Him and being fulfilled by Him. To say it another way, faith is wholly leaning on Christ for everything in your life. It is trusting Him for eternity. Faith is the acceptance of a gift at the hand of Almighty God. That's what faith is, and anything that doesn't meet that standard, while it may be a spiritual term, is not faith. The Bible tells us that not only do we walk by faith and live by faith every day, but faith also plays a part in our life as we continue to seek a deeper relationship with God through Jesus Christ.

We have a problem in that we have isolated faith to the act of becoming a Christian instead of living the ongoing Christian life. Certainly, faith is at the center of our entrance into salvation. But if we leave it there and do not continue to exercise faith daily, we will fail to live an obedient spiritual life. We literally must walk by faith as believers or we will not walk at all.

Shadrach, Meshach, and Abed-Nego

Our God whom we serve is able to deliver us . . . and He will deliver us. . . . But if not . . . we [will not] worship the gold image which you have set up.

Daniel 3:17–18

In 1555, in Oxford, England, Hugh Latimer and Nicholas Ridley were burned at the stake for their biblical views that failed to conform to the ruling (Catholic) church. As the flames consumed them, Latimer called out, "Be of good comfort, Master Ridley, and play the man. We shall this day light such a candle by God's grace in England as I trust shall never be put out!"

God didn't deliver Latimer and Ridley from the flames on earth, but He did deliver them from the flames of eternal judgment by their faith in Christ. These two martyrs were imitating the faith of three who came before them in the Old Testament—Shadrach, Meshach, and Abed-Nego. They were thrown into a fiery furnace for refusing to worship a golden image; but God delivered them, though they didn't know that was His plan. Their faith had prepared them to die or be delivered—the choice was God's, and they were fine with that. Has your faith prepared you to be fine with the choices God is making in your life today?

Faith sees no difference between kinds of deliverance, as long as the deliverance is from God.

No Quality Without Quantity

You shall teach [God's commands] diligently to your children, and shall talk of them when you sit in your house, when you walk by the way, when you lie down, and when you rise up.

Deuteronomy 6:7

It's not the quantity but the quality of time that really counts. Simply defined, that statement means that one can make up for having minimal moments with his family by making certain that the time he does have is quality time.

On the surface, this concept seems to make a lot of sense. It is possible to spend much time with one's family that is seemingly meaningless. All of us experience times when we are at home physically but our minds are wandering miles away. I can remember days with the family that could have been "scratched" in terms of quality.

So what is the "quality time" myth? It's as phony as the fake diamond in a one-dollar ring. The fact is, there is no quality without quantity. Too many parents live with the regrets of abandoned moments. It takes time to be silly, to share a secret, to heal a hurt, to kiss away a tear. Moments of uninhibited communication between child and parent cannot be planned; they just happen. The only ingredient we bring to that dynamic of family life is our availability . . . and that is spelled T-I-M-E.

Abiding

Abide in Me, and I in you.

John 15:4

When the great missionary J. Hudson Taylor was badly overworked and worried, he read a letter from a friend who had discovered the secret of abiding in Christ. The letter deeply moved Taylor, and he realized that his oneness with Christ should produce joy and fulfillment, not worry and stress.

Soon thereafter, Taylor wrote his sister, saying, "As to work, mine was never so plentiful or so difficult; but the weight and strain are now gone. The last month has been perhaps the happiest in my life; and I long to tell you a little of what the Lord has done for my soul. . . . I looked to Jesus and saw that He had said, 'I will never leave you.' Ah, there is rest. For has He not promised to abide with me? As I thought of the Vine and the branches, what light the blessed Spirit poured into my soul!"

Are you abiding in Christ? You are if you have come to Him in simple faith, taking Him at His word, trusting in His promises of forgiveness and blessing, and seeking to live a life of daily obedience. "Abide in Me," said Jesus, "and I in you. As the branch cannot bear fruit of itself . . . neither can you, unless you abide in Me" (John 15:4).

Finding Real Love

But the fruit of the Spirit is love.

Galatians 5:22

I'm convinced that what we need most in our world today—in our churches, in our homes, and in our personal lives—is a great outpouring of agape love. It is not an accident that God has put love at the top of the list of the fruit of the Spirit, because when that is right, everything else has the greatest potential to fall into place.

How can we get this love in our lives? By finding out how much God really loves us. We love Him because He first loved us.

If your heart is filled with bitterness, resentment, and hard feelings, God loves you just as you are in spite of that. But when you go to His Word and contemplate His love for you, when you see the price He paid that you might have Him and His love, when you drink deeply of His love and thank Him for loving you, the wonder of it all begins to break in on your consciousness.

Then real love, agape love, God's love, can begin to develop in your life. Get caught up in how God loves you, and watch your life respond. The more we know about God and His love for us, the more that love begins to fill our being until we become like Him.

The Freedom of Slavery

Likewise he who is called while free is Christ's slave.

1 Corinthians 7:22

In a speech to a regiment of Union soldiers during the Civil War, Abraham Lincoln said, "Whenever I hear anyone arguing for slavery, I feel a strong impulse to see it tried on him personally." He was referring, of course, to the coercive form of slavery. But many people have personally, and permanently, made themselves slaves of a different kind.

Some of the most unusual language of the New Testament comes from the pens of the apostles Paul, Peter, James, and Jude. Each of these church leaders, along with other coworkers, referred to themselves as slaves. Modern Bible translations soften the Greek word *doulos* to "servant" instead of "slave." But in the first century, a *doulos* was a person who voluntarily submitted himself to a master to be a permanent slave. A *doulos* willingly laid everything he had at the feet of his master, then picked it up again to accomplish his master's will.

The apostles were free to live or free to die because of their obedience to their Master. Have you considered living your life as a voluntary *doulos* of the Lord Jesus Christ?

If perfect freedom is found in perfect obedience, how would you measure your own freedom?

The Best Love

Let each of you look out not only for his own interests, but also for the interests of others.

Philippians 2:4

There is an inscription on a small tombstone in an English village that reads, "Here lies a miser who lived for himself. He cared for nothing but gathering wealth. Now, where he is or how he fares, nobody knows and nobody cares."

The root of all evil in human nature is the desire to have one's own say. Self-centeredness is the exact opposite of agape love. Agape love is love that seeks the best interest of the one loved. Selfishness seeks the best interest for one's own self, so the two are exactly opposite. It is not possible to have agape love and to have self-seeking or self-interest. R. C. H. Lenski, the well-known commentator, has said, "If you can cure selfishness, you have just replanted the Garden of Eden." It was selfishness that caused Adam and Eve to reject God's way in favor of their own desires. Self replaced God in their hearts, and they determined to go their own way. Love, on the other hand, is not interested in its own way but is preoccupied with the interests of others.

Love does not seek its own. Love considers the other person and gets excited about seeing that their needs get met.

Too Thankful to Be Anything Else

My brethren, count it all joy when you fall into various trials.

James 1:2

When Mike McAdams's wife, Cheryl, was in the intensive care unit in a Nashville hospital, she was barely able to respond. When a friend asked how she was doing, Mike replied, "It's touch and go. We held hands, prayed, and remembered James 1:2: 'Count it all joy.' You know, it's impossible to be thankful and anxious at the same time."

It's hard to be thankful and negative at the same time. When was the last time you felt thankful and resentful? Thankful and lonely? Thankful and angry? Thankfulness seems to take the edge off our negative or self-centered thoughts and actions. Why? It's because our focus is taken off ourselves and turned toward God. Fifteen times in the Old Testament we find the phrase, "Give thanks to the Lord." It's a little hard to imagine saying, "Thank You, Lord" and "Lord, I'm so lonely (or mad, or depressed)" at the same time. After all, if God provided the circumstances that we find to our liking, isn't He also in control of the circumstances that don't suit us? Yes—and genuine thankfulness will acknowledge Him in both cases.

A thankful life is not an escape from reality but an evidence of true spirituality.

Only Love

If God so loved us, we also ought to love one another.

1 John 4:11

A famous psychiatrist once said, "Love, true love, is the medicine for our sick old world. If people can learn to give and receive love, they will usually recover from their physical and mental illnesses."

Before Christ, the concept of love was a love for the best. If something was deemed worthy of love, it was loved. Christ dying on the cross changed all that, for He offered a love for which we are completely unworthy. Christ revealed God's love. He lavished that holy love on people with no thought about whether they were worthy or not. Now when a Christian wants to know what real love is, he looks to the cross. Having experienced God's love while yet a sinner, and having been transformed by that great love, the Christian recognizes the people around him as the objects of God's love. They are love-starved, in need of the transforming power that only Christ's love can bring.

Jesus set an example by giving Himself totally in love, with no thought of receiving anything in return. We, as Christians, are called by God to reflect that love to our spouses, our families, and our world. And the more we reflect it, the more we give it away to others, the more we experience it in our own lives.

The Locket of Your Heart

Teach me your way, O Lord;
and I will walk in your truth;
give me an undivided heart,
that I may fear your name.
Psalm 86:11 NIV

A young woman in England always wore a golden locket that she would not allow anyone to open or look into. Everyone thought there must be some romance connected with the locket, and within the locket must be a picture of the one she loved. After the woman died, someone opened the locket and found a little slip of paper with these words written upon it: "Whom having not seen, I love." Her Lord Jesus was the only lover she knew and the only lover she longed for.

This woman was wholeheartedly devoted to Christ. She exemplifies the kind of devotion God desires from each of us in worship. He wants us to worship Him with our whole heart, with our minds focused solely on Him. In a world that aggressively competes for our affections, we must make a deliberate effort to keep God first.

If someone were to open the locket of your heart, what or who would they find there? Has your devotion to God been replaced by other affections? By money? Sports? Success? A relationship? Today, take time to pray and ask God to give you an undivided heart.

LISTEN TO JESUS

I am the First and the Last. I am He who lives, and was dead, and behold, I am alive forevermore.

REVELATION 1:17–18

Who is Jesus? He's the Son of God and the Son of man. He is the God-man and the man-God. He is Jesus Christ, the Son of the Living God. He is God walking around in a body. He is God forever enthroned in heaven, now at the right hand of the Father. Jesus Christ is God.

One of the greatest illustrations of who Christ is and why we should listen to His words is found in the prologue of the book of Revelation. John was in exile on the isle of Patmos, and he saw this One to whom we are appealing and said, "When I saw Him, I fell at His feet as dead. But He laid His right hand on me, saying to me, 'Do not be afraid; I am the First and the Last. I am He who lives, and was dead, and behold, I am alive forevermore. Amen'" (1:17–18).

There is no one like Jesus Christ. He is the only one who has ever lived or ever will live who has a true grasp of the future. Because the Lord Jesus Christ as God lives in the time about which He speaks, He views all of time as if it were the present. He is the Eternal One, the Alpha and the Omega, the Beginning and the End, the First and the Last.

Faithful Is He

If we are faithless, He remains faithful;
He cannot deny Himself.
2 Timothy 2:13

In 1947, Dr. Chandrasekhar, professor of astrophysics at the University of Chicago, was scheduled to teach an advanced seminar. He lived in Wisconsin at the time, but he planned to drive in the dead of winter twice a week to the class. When only two students signed up for the class, everyone expected him to cancel. But all winter, twice a week, he made the 100-mile trip—for two students, each of whom later won the Nobel Prize.

Dr. Chandrasekhar, a Nobel Prize winner himself, displayed one of God's characteristics: faithfulness. The response or commitment of the students did not dictate his actions. He had promised to teach the class, and that is what he did—and that is how God relates to us. God is faithful regardless of our attitudes or actions. Even when we are faithless—when we have no faith—He is faithful. God's faithfulness is based in His character and revealed in His promises. For instance, when we sin, "He is faithful and just to forgive us" (1 John 1:9).

Faithfulness is acting like God regardless of how others act toward us.

The Peril of Religion

The Pharisee stood and prayed thus with himself, "God, I thank you that I am not like other men—extorters, unjust, adulterers, or even as this tax collector."

Luke 18:11

One of the terrible possibilities suggested by the Pharisee's attitude in prayer is this: a person can be religious and not be right. This man's religion became the cause of his ruin. He did everything right from a religious perspective—in fact, more than right! His problem was that he had totally excluded God from the picture of his life. His religion was all about him.

Every Sunday, people attend houses of worship with other worshipers. They sing hymns, recite liturgies, pray prayers, listen to sermons. And they will leave feeling better about themselves than when they went in. Unfortunately, they will still be deeply rooted in their sins. If our religion does nothing more than make us feel better about our sin, then that religion has doomed us, not saved us.

The Pharisee was a religious man who was lost in his religion. Along with everything else we learn in this story, we learn about the dangers of religious pride. And that doesn't mean we are to go to a church where we leave feeling bad. It means we are to leave feeling good about the Savior whose mercy has saved us from our sins. We leave feeling good about God's justification, not our own.

Better Safe Than Sorry

Therefore, whether you eat or drink, or whatever you do, do all to the glory of God.

1 Corinthians 10:31

In the early years of his Christian faith, General Thomas "Stonewall" Jackson, the great battlefield leader of the Civil War, purposed to glorify God in all things. He tithed his income and gave up all activities that might distract his thoughts from holy things. If he was asked about the good or evil of a particular activity, he would smile and reply, "Well, I know it is not wrong not to do it, so I'm going to be on the safe side."

Many Christians today flirt with sin, hoping to stop themselves just before they cross the line. Technically, they don't sin. But General Jackson's attitude is the biblical one: move toward God in all things, and sin will lose its strength. In other words, better to be safe than sorry.

How about you? How much of your life is given to the pursuit of the glory of God? Even in times of sickness, of testing, of suffering, of doubt—are you still committed to staying close to God and allowing Him to be glorified by being your strength? Paul said even his difficulties could "cause thanksgiving to abound to the glory of God" (2 Corinthians 4:15).

Bringing glory to God in all things is the only way to stay safe and avoid sorrow.

Alone with God

In the morning my prayer comes before you.
Psalm 88:13

I believe the best time to get alone with God is early morning—it sets the tone for your entire day. He'll show you things and tell you things that will make the difference at crisis points during the next twelve hours or so. After you talk with the Lord and walk with Him through the schedule that lies ahead of you, He'll strengthen and encourage you to make every point of your day an act of worship.

Another advantage to a morning time with God is that He'll plant His Word in your heart. You'll be amazed at how often the very verse you studied over your morning coffee will have key significance a few hours later. Ask the Spirit to illuminate your study, and then go over your Scripture passage reflectively. Try to take that verse with you the rest of the day so that it's never far from your mind. The Word of God is essential to the worship of God, and there's simply nothing so encouraging as His timeless and powerful Word. One little verse is enough to give you a divine perspective throughout the day.

The Church's One Foundation

For no other foundation can anyone lay than that which is laid, which is Jesus Christ.

1 Corinthians 3:11

In 1972, Dean Kelley wrote a book that has become a classic in the study of church growth: *Why Conservative Churches Are Growing.* He chronicled the decline of mainstream, liberal churches and the growth of conservative, Bible-teaching churches. There was a direct correlation between churches' acknowledgement of the authority of the Bible and whether or not they grew.

While we can be thankful for Kelley's historical analysis, we might have looked no further than the book of Acts for an earlier example of his thesis. The greatest numerical growth in the history of the church took place when Jesus was preached in the power of the Spirit by the apostles in Jerusalem. No gimmicks—just the message about Jesus. And people responded by the thousands (Acts 2:41, 47). Just as no building can be erected without a firm foundation, so the church cannot be raised except on the foundation of Jesus Christ her Lord.

Whatever your role is in your church, are you making sure nothing replaces Jesus Christ and His Word as the foundation?

God's Always There

When my spirit was overwhelmed within me,
Then You knew my path.

Psalm 142:3

A friend of mine likes to tell about the time his granddaughter told him what she learned in Sunday school: that God never says, "Oops!"

There is profound theological truth in that little girl's remembrance of her lesson. God didn't look down from heaven surprised to find David in a cave in a fit of discouragement—and David knows it. He says to God, "When my spirit was overwhelmed within me, then You knew my path." God knew right where David was the whole time—all the time David was discouraged, deserted, depressed, and defeated. God was there the whole way.

For some reason, we are greatly tempted to think that because no one else is around, God isn't either; because no one else knows how we feel, God doesn't either; because no one else is willing to listen, God isn't either. God is always there, and to recognize that is the first step toward meeting His solutions to our dilemma.

Work on That Relationship

Work hard and cheerfully at whatever you do.

Colossians 3:23 NLT

For hundreds of years, inventors have been working on various versions of perpetual motion machines, trying to invent a device that will keep going without any input of energy. No one has yet succeeded.

Many people think love, marriage, and friendship are perpetual motion machines that will keep going without our energy and effort. They aren't. We have to work at spending time together, being patient with each other, and listening to what the other is saying. We have to work at serving the other person without complaint.

Whether with our spouse, kids, or friends, a good partnership takes work; otherwise, at some point, the relationship will lose steam.

Contrary to popular opinion, love is not having a trouble-free relationship. It's caring deeply about the needs of the other person even if and when there is stress in the relationship. Love means putting up with the faults, flaws, and failures of the other. This kind of love isn't of the earth, but from above. It flows into imperfect hearts and heals imperfect circumstances, for it comes from an infinite and infallible God who loves us.

Do you need to work a little harder on that troubled relationship? Why not start today?

One Day at a Time

Give us this day our daily bread.

Matthew 6:11

Every day I try to pray, "God, I want Your will to be done on earth as it is in heaven. Please meet my needs today." To trust Him daily presupposes that you talk to Him daily. Praying week to week is not in the Lord's Prayer. The challenges of life come daily, not weekly. For us to remain free of worry, we have to pray and trust Him daily.

It's not wrong to think about tomorrow, to plan for tomorrow, or to make provision for tomorrow. It's just wrong to worry about tomorrow. I believe God expects me to plan as if it all depends on me but pray as if it all depends on Him.

The only way we get through crises with our kids is one day at a time. The only way we get through sickness is one day at a time. The only way we get through times of financial stress is one day at a time. Why? Because God has ordained that life moves at the pace of one day at a time. All He wants us to do is be in step with Him—to trust Him for today.

Connecting the Dots

I am the Alpha and the Omega, the Beginning and the End . . . who is and who was and who is to come, the Almighty.

Revelation 1:8

One of the most popular documentary series ever shown on public television was titled *Connections*. It was based on the work of the British scientific historian and author James Burke. In each segment of the series, Burke explored the development of scientific advancements and showed how seemingly unconnected discoveries were in fact related—like fast food and black holes in space, and corn flakes and Einstein's theory of relativity.

It takes a scientist or historian to tediously follow the chain of events that lead from one discovery to another, to connect history's seemingly random dots. What about God's plan of redemption? Who would have thought that God's calling of a Mesopotamian pagan worshiper named Abram would result in spiritual blessing for the whole world (Genesis 12:1–3)? Every seemingly mundane event in world history has taken place as part of God's plan. And He knows everything about your life as well—the beginning, the middle, and the end. His plan is perfect and will be fulfilled.

When the parts of your life seem disjointed, remember: God has all the dots connected.

The Energy to Wait

He did not waver at the promise of God through unbelief . . . being fully convinced that what He had promised He was also able to perform.

Romans 4:20–21

One of the hardest things for us to do is wait on God. Sometimes God's promises don't materialize as soon as we would like, and we wonder if God has forgotten us.

What God has promised He is able to perform. Think of the many wonderful promises He has made. How do we know He is able to do what He has promised? Because He is the Almighty God. As we wait for the fruition of God's promises, we can find confidence in knowing that God is not only in charge of the event, but He is in charge of the timing. What energizes us as we wait for Him is this thought: God has never promised anything to any of us that He is not able to do, and He is faithful to do what He has promised.

God will not prostitute His power to give us desires that will in the end be destructive to our walk with Him. But if we are consumed with a passion to find God's will through His Word and His Holy Spirit, we can always be in the place where God can shower down His power upon us.

Refiner's Fire

Every branch in Me that does not bear fruit He takes away; and every branch that bears fruit He prunes, that it may bear more fruit.

John 15:2

As evidenced by the devastation in California in 2003, wildfires have an out-of-control nature. Each year, more than one hundred thousand wildfires occur in the United States. Did you know that these fires are a natural way of clearing old growth in order to make room for new growth? In fact, some trees cannot survive without periodic blazes—and most animals escape and even benefit from wildfires. They simply find a new place to live. Thus the forest's cycle of life starts over—lasting decades or centuries, until the forest grows back and the departed animals return.

Sometimes there is no way to stop the out-of-control flames but to pray and wait for the flames to fall silent.

How do we handle the fires that rage through our lives—divorce, unemployment, or disappointments? Remember that God is with you in the midst of those trials. He has plans for new growth in your heart. His reasons are not always known, but the benefits of trusting God through hard times are eternal.

Meditate on these lyrics from Brian Doerksen's worship song "Refiner's Fire": "Refiner's fire, my heart's one desire is to be holy, set apart for You, Lord. I choose to be holy, set apart for You, my master, ready to do Your will."

Pray for Your Children

The effective, fervent prayer of a righteous man avails much.

James 5:16

If I had to reduce it to just one thing, I would pray for my child's personal relationship with the Lord Jesus, because if that's solid, most of the other stuff will settle in.

Some days I have felt so burdened for my family that I have spent my whole prayer time praying for my children, either out loud or in writing, making sure I said everything I wanted to say. And God has answered my prayers in a way that would take ten books to describe.

Perhaps your children are (or will be) scattered around the country or the world. Remember this: though you are separated by hundreds of miles, you can feel a sense of oneness in the presence of God, a sense of security that God will do what He has promised. Or your children may still live with or near you, but through prayer you can draw even closer to them than physical proximity allows.

Through prayer, righteous parents can change the course and direction of their family. The prayer of a righteous parent can put a child's heart into the hand of the Lord, who then directs it like a watercourse wherever He pleases.

Enjoy What You Have

Better is the sight of the eyes than
the wandering of desire.
This also is vanity and grasping for the wind.
Ecclesiastes 6:9

In his book *Racing to Win*, NFL coach and racecar owner Joe Gibbs recounts some of his financial failures. As a young coach seeking to make more money, he invested in three different ventures, all of which failed—the last taking nearly five years of frugal living to pay off. It was only after he started seeking God instead of wealth that he became successful.

When Benjamin Franklin wrote that "a bird in the hand is worth two in the bush," he might have been paraphrasing King Solomon, who wrote that "a living dog is better than a dead lion" (Ecclesiastes 9:4). In other words, God's provision is far more secure than something that exists only in our dreams and fantasies. Solomon also said that "the hand of the diligent makes rich" (Proverbs 10:4). Get-rich-quick schemes are a dime a dozen, and they usually confirm the old saying, "If it sounds too good to be true, it usually is." Focus today on your work and enjoying the fruits of your labor. Both are gifts from God.

Truth is better than time, talent, and treasure. The truth of abundant life is about enjoying what we have been given, not lusting after what we have not.

Live for Jesus

Go out into the highways and hedges, and compel them to come in, that my house may be filled.

Luke 14:23

Purely as an illustration, suppose the Lord Jesus told you you've got one year left on earth. Do you think He would then tell you to spend your time stockpiling food? Hardly! I think He would say, "Friend, you've got one year left to go up and down the highways and the byways and the corridors of this land with the Gospel of Jesus Christ, sharing about Me as you never have before. Sell everything you've got to buy literature, and get it to those who don't know. Give everything you have so that by the time I come back at the end of this year, you will have touched every human being you could possibly touch with the message of Jesus Christ, the Lord of glory."

It's not my task or purpose to make people feel guilty. Every one of us knows we could be doing a better job of telling other people about our Lord. I'm not talking about buttonholing people and being obnoxious. That's not what we're supposed to do. I'm just talking about starting every day by praying, "Lord, today I'm going to live for You. If You bring someone across my path who needs You, help me to sense it, and help me to do the right thing."

Streams in the Desert

. . . and that Rock was Christ.

1 Corinthians 10:4

Have you experienced deserts in your life? Ever felt you were wandering in a wilderness, surrounded by problems, hemmed in by distress? Charles Weigle was an itinerant evangelist who enjoyed traveling and preaching, despite the rigors of the road. His wife, however, grew disillusioned with her frequently absent husband. One day Charles returned home to find this note: "Charlie, I've been a fool. I've done without a lot of things. . . . From here on out, I'm getting all I can of what the world owes me. I know you'll continue to be a fool for Jesus, but for me it's good-bye!"

Charles was stunned, and depression swept over him like a tidal wave. One day, sitting on the porch of a cottage in Florida, he contemplated suicide. *Your work is finished*, said an inner voice. *No one cares . . .* But another voice pierced his gloom: *Charlie, I haven't forgotten you . . . I care for you.* Instantly, Charles was on his knees, rededicating himself to Christ.

Sometime later, he wrote the words to the well-known gospel song: "No one ever cared for me like Jesus; there's no other friend so kind as He. No one else could take the sin and darkness from me; O how much He cared for me."

He cares for you too—even in the desert.

THE INWARD MAN

Even though our outward man is perishing, yet the inward man is being renewed day by day.

2 CORINTHIANS 4:16

It is easy in our world to lose touch with the value of the inward man. Because we are an accomplishment-oriented society, it is hard to "rank" the inward man on those scales that our culture deems important. Therefore, in order to feel significant, we focus on developing the outward things that give us credibility in the eyes of others.

Paul said that the "outward man is perishing." No amount of working on it is going to change that. How sad it is to see people wanting to look youthful in their obituary picture in the paper when they are as dead as everyone else! But Paul had a different philosophy. He accepted the fact that the outward man is perishing and the inward man is going to live forever.

But how exactly do we demonstrate that we value the inward man? How do we invest in that part of us we know is most important? We have to go into the spiritual gymnasium and work out with the inward man just as we would work out with the outward man to build up muscles or lose weight.

Just as the outward body needs food, so the inward man needs food, and the Bible tells us that food is God's Word.

Trusting God for Family

Train up a child in the way he should go,
And when he is old he will not depart from it.

Proverbs 22:6

The line of kings of Judah from Rehoboam to Jehoram represented five generations of fathers and sons: Rehoboam (bad), Abijah (bad), Asa (good), Jehoshaphat (good), and Joram (bad). Bad fathers produced both bad and good sons, and good fathers produced both good and bad sons. Where is the predictability?

There are no guarantees when it comes to family. True, Proverbs 22:6 says to invest in our children so they become wise adults. But the book of Proverbs contains guidelines, not promises. Sometimes, good parents (like King David) produce bad sons (like Absalom) who bring shame to their fathers. David might have wondered if the line of promise was going to fizzle out with his sons, given their character. But the grace of God was at work in David's son, Solomon; and the Messiah appeared right on schedule (Matthew 1:1–16; Luke 3:23–38). Salvation came to the earth through human families just like yours. Even our familial flaws can't keep God's purposes from being accomplished!

Take a moment to thank God that His purposes don't depend on your perfection as a parent or child, but on His faithfulness.

Talk to the Lord About Troubles

The righteous cry out, and the Lord hears,
And delivers them out of all their troubles.

Psalm 34:17

David testified, "This poor man cried out, and the Lord heard him, and saved him out of all his troubles" (Psalm 35:6).

C. S. Lewis once wrote, "Down through the ages whenever men had a need of courage they would cry out, 'Billy Budd, help me' and nothing happened. But for 1900 years, whenever men have needed courage and have cried out, 'Lord Jesus, help me' something always happened."

I love the Hebrew definition of the word *trouble*. The word literally translates "hang-ups." It means to be inhibited, tied up, and restricted. When we lay hold of Christ, we are freed from our hang-ups.

Sound too simple? It is! Yet when I've counseled with so many Christians in deep trouble, I've asked them, "Have you talked to the Lord about this?" They looked at me with a blank stare. "You mean tell Him?" Yes. When you acknowledge the reliability of the One who is in charge of your life and then admit your fear, you have to appropriate the power He has promised to give you. You have to tell it to Jesus.

Redeeming the Time

Teach us to number our days,
That we may gain a heart of wisdom.
Psalm 90:12

Alarm to the Unconverted is a little book written by Joseph Alleine (1634–1668). Though not as recognized as it once was, it has left its mark in Christian history as a Puritan classic.

Alleine was a serious young man who felt that his commitment to Christ required the wise use of his time. He wanted to use every moment, in one way or another, for the Lord. As a student, he often neglected his friends for his studies. "It's better they should wonder at my rudeness," he explained, "than that I should lose time; for only a few will notice the rudeness, but many will feel my loss of time."

As a minister, Joseph habitually rose at four in the morning, praying and studying his Bible until eight. His afternoons were spent calling on the unconverted. At the beginning of the week, he would remark, "Another week is now before us; let us spend this week for God." Each morning, he would say, "Now let us live this one day well!"

Though he died at age thirty-four, Joseph Alleine did more for Christ than many twice his age. Are you being a good steward of your time? Are you using your moments wisely for Christ?

February 25

In His Steps

To this you were called, because Christ also suffered for us, leaving us an example, that you should follow His steps.

1 Peter 2:21

After supper one evening, we decided to stroll along the beach to the boardwalk, about twenty blocks away. I remember pointing out to the children that they ought to be careful where they walked. We were barefoot and could easily step on broken shells or those horrid jellyfish.

Since my gait is usually about twice as fast as anyone else's, I was walking out in front of the rest of the family. Suddenly I sensed that someone was immediately behind me. The crunch of feet, not my own, was audible, and I looked over my shoulder to see one small son stretching to put his feet in the very footprints I was leaving in the sand. I guess he felt that the only way he could be sure that he avoided broken shells, jellyfish, and crabs was to step exactly where his father was stepping.

What a lesson I learned that day! Sometimes as I walk through the debris of this world, I shudder to think of all the spiritual jellyfish, broken shells, and crabs that lie in the path. There is no certain way to avoid these pitfalls apart from the steps of our heavenly Leader.

Just Try It

And try Me now in this.

Malachi 3:10

Before his death, Pastor Harvey Hill of Winter Haven, Florida, wrote out his life's story. He said that when he and his wife, Sylvia, were married, they didn't have a penny. It was during the Depression, and not many people had a car. They walked to church, to work, and to visit with friends; and they lived hand to mouth. One day the pastor of their church asked them if they tithed—that is, if they were in the habit of giving at least 10 percent of their income to the Lord.

"No," said Harvey. "We can't afford it."

"Just try it," the pastor replied, "and see if God doesn't bless you."

Struck by the challenge, Harvey and Sylvia agreed to try. From that day until their deaths within a few weeks of each other seventy years later, they never failed to bring God their tithes and offerings. And He never failed to meet their needs.

Malachi 3:10 says, "'Bring all the tithes into the storehouse, that there may be food in My house, and try Me now in this,' says the Lord of hosts, 'if I will not open for you the windows of heaven and pour out for you such blessing that there will not be room enough to receive it.'"

Are you tithing? You should just try it, and see if God doesn't bless you.

Little Pictures

God is able to make all grace abound toward you,
that you, always having all sufficiency in all things,
may have an abundance for every good work.

2 Corinthians 9:8

An old widow was living in poverty and want. A young man, hearing she was in need, went to visit her to see if he could be of any help. The old lady complained bitterly of her condition and remarked that her son in Australia was doing very well. Her friend inquired, "Doesn't he do anything to help you?" She replied, "No, nothing. He writes to me regularly once a month, but he sends me only some little pictures with his letters." The young man asked to see the pictures she had received. To his surprise, he found each of them to be twenty-pound notes. The poor old lady did not realize the value of this foreign currency, but had imagined them to be mere pretty pictures.

She had lived in poverty and want, whereas she could have had all the bodily comforts she desired and needed so badly. We smile at the foolishness of the old woman, but how many of us are like her, living as though we were paupers instead of sons and daughters of the King?

Problem Children

Please go and see if it is well with your brothers.

Genesis 37:14

Jacob was worried about his boys. They were strong-willed, immature "problem kids." Even when they were absent, he was concerned. Sometimes they acted like a band of thugs. Their shenanigans caused Jacob endless heartache. In Genesis 37, they were shepherding their flocks in Shechem, and Jacob, perhaps sensing trouble, sent Joseph to find out if all was well. The brothers saw Joseph coming, seized him, stripped him, threw him into a pit, and sold him to a passing caravan as a slave.

The situation seemed hopeless. But fast-forward to the end of Genesis: Joseph is prime minister of Egypt, he and his brothers are reconciled, Jacob is happy and honored, and his twelve sons become the patriarchs of the Jewish nation.

Don't give up on your children, even when they worry you, even when circumstances seem impossible. God can devise implausible solutions and do impossible things. Luke 18:27 says, "The things which are impossible with men are possible with God."

Maybe it's not your child—maybe it's your spouse, your sibling, your neighbor, or your best friend. We can't change another's heart, but God can. Do your best and then let Him do the rest.

Wisdom Multiplied

The wisdom that is from above is first pure, then peaceable, gentle, willing to yield, full of mercy and good fruits, without partiality and without hypocrisy.

James 3:17

Heavenly wisdom is continually coming from above, as evidenced in James's use of the present tense in 3:17. God's supply of wisdom never runs dry, but keeps coming to us to meet the demands of each hour (James 1:5). This wisdom is manifested through God's Son, made available through God's Holy Spirit, and written down in God's holy book, the Bible. The wise man is the man who has given himself to Jesus Christ and who, with the Spirit's help, keeps his intellect in submission to the will of God.

The comparison of heavenly and earthly wisdom is instructive. The world's wisdom results in "confusion" (v. 16), but God's wisdom always brings "peace" (v. 18). The result of the world's wisdom is "every evil thing" (v. 16), but God's wisdom produces fruit. In the fruit of God's wisdom are the seeds of more fruit; the fruit of righteousness is sown in peace (v. 18). God's wisdom automatically multiplies.

For Want of a Wall

Whoever has no rule over his own spirit
Is like a city broken down, without walls.
Proverbs 25:28

The Great Wall of China was erected in the third century BC as a defense against raids by nomadic peoples from the north. Throughout succeeding centuries, especially during the Ming dynasty (1368–1644), the Great Wall was repaired and extended in length, finally stretching for 13 thousand miles.

Centuries before the Great Wall was begun, biblical cultures used walls to protect themselves from marauders as well as to draw boundaries around themselves for purposes of identity. To be effective, walls had to be maintained. The slightest foothold in a fortress wall could give the enemy a fateful advantage (Ephesians 4:27 NIV).

Modern armaments have made walls obsolete as defensive structures. But there is one wall that is the Christian's primary defense against personal destruction: the wall of self-control. Failure to maintain self-control is like opening the city gates to the enemy, like issuing an invitation to the devil and his legions. Make a defensive assessment today, and fix what has fallen into disrepair.

Kingdoms have been lost for want of a strong wall. Don't let a lack of self-control be the ruin of yours.

Give Me Souls!

My heart's desire and prayer to God . . .
is that they may be saved.

Romans 10:1

A recent survey by Christian pollster George Barna found that only half (53 percent) of born-again Christians feel a sense of responsibility to tell others about their faith. Compare that with these quotes from earlier generations of believers:

"I cared not where or how I lived, or what hardships I went through, so that I could but gain souls for Christ."

—David Brainerd

"Lord, give me souls or take my soul."

—George Whitefield

"Here let me burn out for God."

—Henry Martyn, on the shores of India

"I am very tired, but must go on. . . . A fire is in my bones. . . . Oh God, what can I say? Souls! Souls! Souls! My heart hungers for souls!"

—General William Booth

"I would rather win souls than be the greatest king or emperor on earth. My one ambition in life is to win as many as possible."

—R. A. Torrey

Great Expectations

And they were greatly amazed in themselves beyond measure, and marveled.

Mark 6:51

Canada has suffered its share of natural disasters in recent years, prompting the Canadian Red Cross to begin a preparedness program to help schoolchildren deal with sudden crises. The slogan is "Expect the Unexpected."

In the Gospels, the disciples were often left slack-jawed and wide-eyed at Jesus' behavior, His words, and His miracles. When He healed the paralytic in Mark 2, for example, "all were amazed and glorified God, saying, 'We never saw anything like this!'" (v. 12). They learned to expect the unexpected when they were with Him.

If you're a disciple, you're learning to expect the unexpected, for we never know what Christ is going to do next for us, in us, around us, or through us. It's an exciting, adventuresome way to live. Discipleship is an experience that dispels boredom and keeps the Christian looking up in amazement.

Expect Him to answer your prayers and to overrule the problems of your life and cause all things to work together for good. Expect Him to open doors, create opportunities, meet your needs, and bless your efforts. Say with the psalmist, "My soul, wait silently for God alone, for my expectation is from Him" (Psalm 62:5).

MARCH

I cried out to You, O Lord:
I said, "You are my refuge;
My portion in the land of the living."

—Psalm 142:5

Living on the Living God

I cried out to You, O Lord:
I said, "You are my refuge,
My portion in the land of the living."
Psalm 142:5

David would have agreed with the old preacher who said, "There's no living in the land of the living like living on the living God." That preacher was right. The land of the living is not a reference to eternity or heaven. It is a reference to living right now. The Bible is written for people who are living in the land of the living, not for people who dream of "pie in the sky by and by."

The land of the living is where you and I live every day. We rise and face the challenges that the living face, and God is our portion in that land. He does not remove us from the land where we live in order to help us. Rather, He joins us where we are—our private world, our family, our job, our church—to meet our needs. The God of David is our God, and He is still our refuge and our portion.

Remember to Forget

For I will forgive their iniquity, and their sin I will remember no more.

Jeremiah 31:34

Diane Sollee of the Coalition for Marriage and Family reports a powerful fact concerning conflict in marriage: couples who are happy and stay married have the same number of disagreements and conflicts as couples who are unhappy and get divorced. So it is not the absence of conflict that preserves marriages, but the ability to manage conflict when it happens.

What does it mean to "manage conflict"? It certainly means practicing the kind of self-control that keeps conflicts from mushrooming into hurtful and divisive standoffs. But it also means knowing what to do with hurt feelings, anger, disappointment, and dashed expectations. It means, in other words, knowing how to forgive and forget. But what does that mean?

Emotional hurt and tension is almost impossible to forget; the harder we try, the more we remember. Therefore, couples have to remember to forget. They have to act like God, who chooses not to hold against us what He knows about us. If you are holding something against your spouse, why not choose to forget it?

You may never forget how you've been hurt, but you can choose to forget about it.

Never Fail to Forgive

Forgive us our debts, as we forgive our debtors.

Matthew 6:12

When I was a teenager, I disobediently took my father's car out for a joyride when he wasn't home. Unfortunately, I ended up running the car off a country road and into a ditch. I went to him and said, "Dad, I've got to tell you, I feel terrible about what I did. I was wrong, deceitful, dishonest. I knew better than to do that. I'm sorry, and I want to ask you to forgive me." He said, "You are forgiven—but you will pay for the car."

When I damaged my father's car, did I cease to be my father's son? No. But my relational forgiveness was in deep trouble. If you want to know oneness with the Lord in your daily relationship with Him, if you want to feel the reality of your forgiveness when you pray to God, don't hold grudges against others and fail to forgive them. You can't come to God and expect to enjoy His forgiveness of your sins when you have not confessed your own sin of unforgiveness and forgiven your brother. If you want to know the daily sense of your forgiveness in your walk with the Lord, then you must forgive those who have wronged you.

Tighten Your Resolve

Resolve this, not to put a stumbling block
or a cause to fall in our brother's way.

Romans 14:13

J. Wilbur Chapman, a powerful evangelist of an earlier era, formulated what he called "my rule for Christian living." He said, "The rule that governs my life is this: Anything that dims my vision of Christ, or takes away my taste for Bible study, or cramps my prayer life, or makes Christian work difficult, is wrong for me, and I must, as a Christian, turn away from it."

We can also add: "Anything that hurts my testimony or stunts the growth of another Christian is likewise wrong."

There are many issues, habits, and convictions that differ among Christians. The apostle Paul deals with these "gray areas" in Romans 14 and 1 Corinthians 10, and he warns us against allowing our Christian liberty to become a stumbling block to ourselves or to others. If we practice our Christian liberty in such a way as to tempt others to violate their consciences or to engage in activities that may for them be doubtful, we are not exercising our freedom in a wise or loving way.

Is there an area in your life that needs to be tightened? Is there an activity that needs changing?

How to Fear God

Only fear the Lord, and serve Him in truth with all your heart; for consider what great things He has done for you.

1 Samuel 12:24

In July 1861, in an act declaring September 26 as a National Day of Prayer and Fasting, Abraham Lincoln wrote, "It is fit and becoming in all people, at all times, to acknowledge and revere the Supreme Government of God; to bow in humble submission to his chastisement; to confess and deplore their sins and transgressions in the full conviction that the fear of the Lord is the beginning of wisdom. . . ."

That may be one of the best summaries ever penned of what it means to "fear the Lord." Note the action words: "to acknowledge . . . revere . . . bow . . . confess and deplore." To fear the Lord means more than just one thing. Indeed, it is a phrase that gathers together a number of attitudes and actions. In short, when we fear the Lord, we recognize God's proper place as Creator over us, His creation. If someone followed us around for a week, what evidence would they see that we fear the Lord? Which would they hear most—grumbles or gratitude, complaints or compassion?

A nation that fears the Lord is one whose citizens fear the Lord. Plan a "Personal Day of Prayer and Fasting" soon—a day to reaffirm your own fear of the Lord.

Dad, I'm Sorry

Blessed is he whose transgression is forgiven.

Psalm 32:1

"Dad, I'm really sorry." Jeremy could barely get the words out. Having borrowed his dad's credit card for groceries, he had used it to purchase beer for his buddies. His dad might never have known about it, but for that little device inside the human heart called a conscience. "I shouldn't have bought the beer, I shouldn't have lied about my age, and I shouldn't have used your credit card to do it. You trusted me, and I let you down. I'm sorry. I will never do it again."

That's confession. That's what we must do in our prayers.

In the New Testament, the Greek word translated "confession" means to agree with God concerning His opinion about a matter. It means to admit our guilt. When we confess our sins, we are agreeing with God concerning the sin in our lives as revealed through His Word and by the Holy Spirit. When we confess, we verbalize our spiritual shortcomings and admit our sin.

Confession is painful, but it keeps our relationship with our heavenly Father clear, open, and close. Hiding our sin builds a barrier between us and God.

Do you have a sin to confess? "If we confess our sins, He is faithful and just to forgive us our sins and to cleanse us from all unrighteousness" (1 John 1:9).

As Your Soul Prospers

Beloved, I pray that you may prosper in all things and be in health, just as your soul prospers.

3 John v. 2

Verse 2 contains a revealing concept: prospering in all things as your soul prospers. As I was studying this verse, I began to wonder what it would be like if one Sunday everyone arrived at church in the same physical condition their souls were in. That is, our outward manifestation of "prosperity" would be in direct correlation to the prosperity of our souls. It might be a very interesting sight!

How would you arrive if that happened? In a wheelchair? On crutches? Would you need assistance getting in the door? Or would you arrive in fine shape, physically fit because your soul was in such fine condition? John knew that Gaius was a godly man, so he did not hesitate to pray that he prospered in all things in the same way his soul prospered.

If the church is going to accomplish all it is supposed to, we need many more vigorous workers than we have now. We need people who are willing, like Gaius, to play a supporting role, empowering others in their spiritual walk. The Bible promises spiritual blessings for those willing to work in such a way.

When Jealousy Is a Good Thing

For you shall worship no other god, for the Lord, whose name is Jealous, is a jealous God.

Exodus 34:14

In the late sixth century, Pope Gregory the Great codified various lists of major sins circulating in the church, settling on seven deadly ones (listed by him in the decreasing order of their offense against love): pride, envy, anger, sadness, avarice (greed), gluttony, and lust. In the seventeenth century, sadness was replaced by sloth. Interestingly, jealousy isn't one of the seven deadly sins.

Jealousy probably doesn't appear because it has both a positive and a negative dimension (see if you can find a positive aspect of any of the seven above). Jealousy can be focused on self ("I am jealous of someone or something because of what I can't have"), or on others ("I am jealous for you because of what I want you to have"). The former is self-centered; the latter is others-centered.

God's jealousy for His children is others-centered, for our benefit. He is jealous for us that we might remain pure and holy. God moves aggressively against idolatry not because He is threatened (jealous), but because He cares for (is jealous for) us.

The proper response to God's jealousy is to have no other gods before Him.

Blessed Are Those Who Trust in the Lord

Let us not grow weary while doing good, for in due season we shall reap if we do not lose heart.

Galatians 6:9

"Blessed is the man who trusts in the Lord, and whose hope is the Lord. For he shall be like a tree planted by the waters, which spreads out its roots by the river, and will not fear when heat comes; but its leaf will be green, and will not be anxious in the year of drought, nor will cease from yielding fruit" (Jeremiah 17:7–8).

The person who loves God is like a tree with deep roots. During a drought, when all the other trees are perishing, that tree will remain healthy and strong. There is no anxiety, for the commitment of that tree reaches beyond the circumstances of the storm.

If we are to succeed in the midst of trouble, and if we are not to quit when the going gets tough, we need to get our roots down deep into the Lord, establishing a commitment in Christ that goes beyond our circumstances. As the apostle Paul put it, "And let us not grow weary while doing good, for in due season we shall reap if we do not lose heart" (Galatians 6:9).

Following Your Way to Fellowship

If we say that we have fellowship with Him, and walk in darkness, we lie and do not practice the truth.

1 John 1:6

Think of the last time you experienced tension in a relationship—perhaps with a family member or someone at work. Conversation is superficial, and you're more comfortable apart than together. When something happens between people who are normally close, the first thing to vanish is the evidence of fellowship.

It's the same way with the Lord. We think we can stop following Him without damaging our relationship. The conversation is surface ("Lord, please bless this food"), and we avoid spending time with Him ("I just don't have time for my devotions").

The main prerequisite for experiencing fellowship with Jesus is following Him and obeying His commands. It's like when Peter and the disciples were fishing, and the Lord told them to cast their nets on the right side of the boat. When Peter obeyed, something greater than catching a boatload of fish happened—he saw Jesus. What followed was an intimate meal, a sweet time of fellowship with the Lord. Fellowship follows obedience.

If you're feeling out of fellowship with Jesus, chances are good that you've either stopped following or started disobeying.

When in Doubt, Don't!

Shall not the Judge of all the earth do right?

Genesis 18:25

Everyone has doubted God's justice at times. We may not think of it that way; we may just wonder, *Why did God allow an event to happen that way?* I know I have wondered the same thing on many occasions.

I have learned to take many things in my Christian walk purely by faith. I have learned enough about God through Scripture and His faithfulness in my life that when I come to a place where I am tempted to doubt—I don't. I take by faith the fact that God is good, that the Judge of all the earth shall do right (Genesis 18:25). Not to have that core conviction governing one's thoughts daily is to live in a world of vacillation and shifting shadows.

If we do not live our lives based on the fact that God is righteous, we have no basis for righteousness in our own lives.

Journaling

Remember His marvelous works which He has done,
His wonders, and the judgments of His mouth.

1 Chronicles 16:12

Jim Elliot was an intensely committed missionary who was killed in 1956 by the Ecuadorian Indians he was trying to reach. Indians were not his only challenge: "My devotional reading pattern was broken. I have never restored it. . . . Prayer as a single man was difficult. . . . Now it's too hard to get out of bed in the morning. . . . I've made resolutions on this score before now but not followed them up."

Jim Elliot was a godly young missionary who struggled with spiritual disciplines like every believer. But unlike most, he kept a written record of spiritual defeats as well as victories in his journal. Keeping a journal can help us remember God's works, retain our honesty, reflect on our hearts, register our progress, regain lost momentum, reject bad habits, reinforce good habits, and reach our spiritual goals. What other discipline offers such benefits? Consider making a journal your personal place to be honest with God and yourself. You, and perhaps others, will benefit from your faithfulness.

A journal is a record of a journey, a written account of your travels on the road to heaven.

Loved!

God is love.

1 John 4:8

When Scottish teenager George Matheson learned he was losing his eyesight, he determined to finish his studies at the University of Glasgow as quickly as possible. Blindness overtook him while he pursued graduate studies for Christian ministry, but his family rallied to his side. His sisters even learned Greek and Hebrew to help him in his assignments.

The real blow came later, when his fiancée determined she just couldn't marry a blind man. George was devastated. Years later, when he was a beloved pastor in Scotland, his sister became engaged, and the news opened old wounds in his heart. More mature now, he turned to God and out of the experience wrote a prayer that later became a much-loved hymn:

O love that wilt not let me go,
I rest my weary soul in thee;
I give thee back the life I owe,
That in thing ocean depths its flow
May richer, fuller be.

Have you been disappointed recently? God's love will never let you go, and in its continuous, compassionate, costly flow, your life will richer, fuller be.

Giving to the Giver

For all things come from You, and of
Your own we have given You.

1 Chronicles 29:14

Sixteen of Jesus' thirty-eight parables were concerned with how to handle money and possessions. In the four Gospels, one out of every ten verses deals directly with the subject of money. The Bible has five hundred verses on prayer, less than five hundred verses on faith, but more than two thousand verses on money and possessions.

Do you think God is trying to tell us something? It seems to be a truism in life that generous people are comfortable talking about money and even more comfortable giving it away. Stingy people, on the other hand, obsess over keeping what they have and how to get more. Maybe that's why Jesus, the most generous person in history, spoke so much about money—He understood its source, its use, and who owns it all.

Jesus' ancestor David understood those same things. King David gave generously to build the temple and left us the basis for understanding money and material possessions: all things come from God, and from His gifts to us we give back to Him. When we get comfortable with that truth, we will be comfortable in giving generously as He directs.

If you are uncomfortable with giving, you may be opening your Bible less often than your checkbook!

What Will We Do in Heaven?

They sing . . . the song of the Lamb, saying: "Great and marvelous are your works, Lord God Almighty! Just and true are your ways, O king of the saints!"

Revelation 15:3

We will never get bored! We will sing. Those who could never carry a tune on earth will be able to sing in heaven and never grow weary of exalting the name of the King of kings. We'll serve perfectly, enabled by the power that is able to conform all things to the pleasure of His sovereign will. We'll share unbroken fellowship with angels, members of the church, God the Father, Jesus, and the spirits of just men made perfect. Never again will we have to say good-bye to a loved one or give a farewell party. Through our resurrected bodies, we will have instant access to each other at all times.

God has different things for different people to do. God made each of us unique, with a special ministry and a responsibility. Each of us in our own right is peerless in what God has called us to do. There are many distinct groups in heaven, all unique in their responsibility before God.

When we get to heaven, we are going to praise God perfectly. All of heaven will be filled with music. Throughout eternity, worship will be our privileged occupation.

Careless Talk

Let your speech always be with grace, seasoned with salt, that you may know how you ought to answer each one.

Colossians 4:6

Have you noticed the similarities between the New Testament letters of Ephesians and Colossians? Many verses in Colossians have a parallel in Ephesians. For example, notice how Colossians 4:6 corresponds with Ephesians 4:29, which says: "Let no corrupt word proceed out of your mouth, but what is good for necessary edification, that it might impart grace to the hearers."

Our words shouldn't be "salty," but seasoned with salt—tasteful and appropriate, useful for helping others and building them up.

The Chinese Christian leader Watchman Nee devoted a chapter in his book *The Normal Christian Worker* to this subject. He wrote, "Because of unrestrained speech, the usefulness of many Christian workers is seriously curtailed. Instead of being powerful instruments in the Lord's service, their ministry makes little impact on account of the constant leakage of power through their careless talk."

If you're in need of wiser, more gracious, salt-seasoned speech, here's a prayer for you: "Set a guard, O Lord, over my mouth; keep watch over the door of my lips" (Psalm 141:3).

The Power of One

What man of you, having a hundred sheep, if he loses one of them, does not leave the ninety-nine in the wilderness, and go after the one which is lost until he finds it?

Luke 15:4

Jesus said that His purpose for coming into the world was to seek and to save that which was lost (Luke 19:10). It is at this point that Christianity is separate from all other religions of the world. Christianity is God searching for man. Christianity is the Shepherd looking for the sheep. How different it is! And how blessed we are to be part of it!

And how glad we are that Jesus didn't work on the basis of percentages. The shepherd had 99 percent of his flock safely at home. A modern businessman might have figured that the cost of finding the one wasn't worth the value of the sheep. *Take your losses and move on*, he might have thought. Yet the shepherd left the ninety-nine and went to find the one. The woman who lost the coin had 90 percent of her wealth. But the man with the lost son had only 50 percent of his. With God, the percentages don't matter, for every single one is important and worth finding.

Every Single Law

Submit yourselves to every ordinance
of man for the Lord's sake.

1 Peter 2:13

Georgi Vins, a pastor in Russia before the fall of Soviet communism, was severely persecuted for his faith. But no matter how severe the repression and mistreatment became, he and his fellow Christians determined they were going to obey every single law on the Russian books, just or unjust. With the exception of laws that would force them to cease worship or disobey God's Word, these brave pastors bent over backward to be good citizens. Even in concentration camps, they obeyed the rules unless these rules conflicted with their worship or directly countermanded a truth in the Word of God.

Their example made them heroes not only among the Christians but among the citizens of Russia. In the eyes of the world, the cause of Christ was advanced.

Both Peter and Paul told their readers (who were living under the tyranny of the Roman government) to obey the laws of the land, respect civil authority, and pay their taxes (Romans 13:1; 1 Peter 2:13). God ordained human government for our good, and He desires us to obey even those laws that we dislike. He will bless us as we do so.

The Spirit and the Word

Let the word of Christ dwell in you richly in all wisdom, teaching and admonishing one another in psalms and hymns and spiritual songs, singing with grace in your hearts to the Lord.

Colossians 3:16

Ephesians points to our being filled with the Spirit. Colossians points to our being filled with the Word of God, which dwells within us richly. Then, by psalms and hymns and spiritual songs, we partake in wisdom and teaching together. Combine the two passages and we see a melody and countermelody of being filled with God's Word and God's Spirit, responding with beautiful music in both cases.

We need both of these, the Spirit and the Word, to be Christians. Subtract either and it's simply not possible. One reshapes the heart and the other the mind, and together they make us whole persons molded to the image of Christ. The Word of God provides the content; the Spirit of God applies it. He impresses the teachings of the Scriptures upon us, applies them to us, and reminds us of them at need. Throughout time, many believers have been inspired to create hymns as they've read God's Word. Very often, they've said they were convinced that God gave them the melody as well. How could powerful songs like "Amazing Grace" and "Joy to the World" have any other source but God?

Why Worship?

Because He is your Lord, worship Him.

Psalm 45:11

An old gospel song goes like this:

Jesus, I'll never forget what You've done for me,
Jesus, I'll never forget how You set me free,
Jesus, I'll never forget how You brought me out,
Jesus, I'll never forget, no never!

The song goes on to proclaim, "He's done so much for me, I cannot tell it all, He's taken all my sins away!"

Whether we worship God for His attributes (who He is) or His actions (what He has done), worship is our response to Him. Worship is a measure of our perception, appreciation, or understanding of who God is and what He has done.

When a child erupts with squeals of delight and hugs of affection upon receiving a surprise, we are seeing the response of joy. In a similar way, because God's mercies are new every morning to us (Lamentations 3:22–23), we have good reason never to stop worshiping Him. A good exercise for the Christian is to spend some time remembering the things God has done, which flow from who He is. If we consider carefully, we will agree with the songwriter: "He's done so much for me, I cannot tell it all."

To remember God's greatness and goodness is to respond with a heart of gratitude.

Peace in the Storm

He calms the storm, so that its waves are still.

Psalm 107:29

Remember the story in the Gospels about Jesus and the disciples in a boat on the Sea of Galilee (Matthew 8:23–27)? A fierce storm arose, and the disciples were certain they were about to perish. The disciples learned a great lesson that day, one that could only be taught in a storm—not in a classroom. Jesus had gone to the back of the boat to take a nap, and a huge storm blew up. Their fear is most evident in Luke's account: "Master, Master, we are perishing!" (8:24). It would appear they didn't make the connection immediately that riding in the boat with them was the One who created the wind and the waves. Perhaps it did click with them, and that's why they woke Jesus up and were chastised by Him for their "little faith" (Matthew 8:26).

But we can understand how they felt because it's how we feel when the storms of our lives come up. We forget that we know the very One who allowed the storm in the first place and that He can cause it to stop or see us through it.

The Value of Uniqueness

But one and the same Spirit works all these things, distributing to each one individually as He wills.

1 Corinthians 12:11

Author Stu Weber's two oldest sons did well in high school athletics. To encourage his youngest son, Ryan, to find his niche, Stu spent lots of time camping and hiking in the outdoors with him. Ryan's identity developed around a favorite pocketknife he always carried on their trips. But the real value of the knife was revealed the day Ryan gave it to his dad as a birthday gift.

What Ryan Weber did for his dad is a reflection of what Jesus Christ has done for us. Jesus, by His Holy Spirit, has given every believer a personal spiritual gift especially suited for who we are. Jesus gave up His physical ministry on this earth when He returned to heaven, then He distributed His ministry to us to help carry out for Him.

That's what spiritual gifts are—individual portions of the ministry of Jesus with which each individual Christian has been gifted. Others may have the same gift as you, but no one else will be led to use that gift in the same unique way. Excitement and joy in ministry come from recognizing how special the gift of God to us really is.

The combination of you and your spiritual gift occurs nowhere else in the world.

Develop a Spiritual Immune System

How can a young man cleanse his way?
By taking heed according to Your word.

Psalm 119:9

One of the things I've learned a lot about in the last few years is the immune system. Our God-given immune systems help us fight off the forces that would destroy our bodies. If our immune systems are functioning at 100 percent, we don't have to take medicines because they will just fight off the disease seeking to take over our bodies. But if our immune systems aren't healthy, then we become susceptible to lots of things. If we get to the condition of an AIDS patient, our bodies lose their ability to fight off almost anything. To fight off sickness, we have to strengthen the body's immune system. That may mean stopping some things we enjoy doing and starting some things we haven't been doing. It's a matter of critical importance.

The same is true spiritually. In order to increase our immunity to sin, we must strengthen ourselves through prayer, the Word, and fellowship with other strong Christians.

The Essence of Aging

You shall come to the grave at a full age, as a sheaf of grain ripens in its season.

Job 5:26

Ben Patterson says old age has a way of whittling a person down to his or her bare essence—what is left of us is what we were all along. He cites his wife's grandmother, who, in her eighties, couldn't remember family names, but her prayers were heaven on earth. A distant uncle, on the other hand, spent his life making money and was obsessed with it at the end of his life.

When mind and muscle leave us, what remains is who we really are. Some of us, like Moses, will minister right up to the end (Deuteronomy 34:7). But for most of us, aging will take its toll. If Patterson is right . . . what will stand out in your life?

Abraham and Sarah were just getting started when they hit the century mark. They had their first child together and set out to build a nation that would cover the earth like the sand on the seashore. That's called walking by faith, and the older we get, the more it ought to characterize our life.

If today was your last day on earth and the essence of your life was revealed, what would it be? Start building a life of faith so that when all else passes away, your legacy of faith will remain.

For the Christian, growing old gracefully means growing old, full of grace.

THE TRUTH ABOUT MERCY

Through the LORD's mercies we are not consumed,
Because His compassions fail not.
They are new every morning;
Great is Your faithfulness.
LAMENTATIONS 3:22–23

When Thomas Chisholm wrote the words to the song "Great Is Thy Faithfulness," he made a tiny error. The song is based on this scripture. He wrote, "Morning by morning, new mercies I see." But the point of this passage is that the prophet Jeremiah did not see any new mercies. He didn't see a thing. He had no visible evidence of God's mercies at all. Morning by morning brought horror and pain and dread—not new mercies. Jeremiah was not saying, "I trust You because I understand everything that is going on in my life." He was saying, "I trust You because You are God and You cannot fail. And I know You cannot lie."

There are times when life is not easy, when it is hard to believe in the faithfulness of God. We try to hold on and find out what God is up to, and sometimes He seems to have disappeared. And we listen to the words of the enemy, who tries to pull us away from what we know and cause us to operate on how we feel.

God is faithful whether you feel like He is or not, whether you think He is or not, whether you observe His faithfulness or not. God, who cannot lie, is faithful.

Delayed Dreams

God meant it for good.

Genesis 50:20

Are you wrestling with disappointment, a broken dream, or a setback in life? Think of Joseph. His brothers called him a "dreamer" (Genesis 37:19), but all his dreams died—or seemed to—in an act of brotherly betrayal that led to Egyptian imprisonment.

God's heroes have always been dreamers, men and women who sensed what God wanted them to do and who were willing to trust Him to perform it. But sometimes those dreams have died. Perhaps yours have too.

We must remember that when God seems to say no, there is still a lot left, a lot to be thankful for, and a lot to do for Him. We should learn to say, "I don't understand why my dream hasn't come true, but thank God for all He's done for me anyway."

And we must go on dreaming and persevering. When Joseph's dreams seemed to have died, he remained faithful anyway. He decided to bloom where he was planted, even if it was in a filthy jail, falsely accused as a rapist. Later, in God's own mysterious way, He took Joseph from the prison to the palace, and all Joseph's God-given dreams were fulfilled.

If your dream has been set aside by God, don't quit. Seek out what God has for you in the days ahead. Trust Him, and keep dreaming.

Depending on God

Our God . . . will deliver us from your hand, O king. But if not, let it be known to you, O king, that we do not serve your gods.

Daniel 3:17–18

I don't care how strong a Christian you are; peer pressure today is so intense that you cannot cope with it apart from the Lord. If you don't depend on God with all of your heart, if you don't ask God to give you the strength you need to stand up and be counted, and if you don't realize that He is your ally and goes with you every day, you cannot possibly make it through these years without the risk of ruining your life.

Three young men from the book of Daniel (chapter 3)—Shadrach, Meshach, and Abed-Nego—are models for depending upon God when the heat is on. When everyone in Babylon was bowing down to the king's idol (including, apparently, the rest of the Jewish captives), these three refused. One way to get noticed in a crowd is to remain standing when everyone else is bowing on their knees!

Their dependence was on God alone, and He delivered them. Every person who walks with God must be prepared to depend on Him when the pressure comes to conform.

Don't Be Surprised

We are hard-pressed on every side.

2 Corinthians 4:8

"I don't know why this is happening," Jill cried. "Just a month ago I turned my life over to Christ. Now my car has died, my child has mononucleosis, and my promotion at work fell through."

While it seems logical that God would shield us from all pain, that isn't the way He worked in the Bible. Study the great biblical heroes—Abraham, Joseph, Moses, David, Peter, Paul—and trace their trials and tribulations. Despite what certain false teachers say, the Christian life is not unbridled health and wealth. Jesus put it bluntly when He said, "In the world you will have tribulation; but be of good cheer, I have overcome the world" (John 16:33).

In other words, we shouldn't be surprised when, in seeking to do God's will, we find ourselves in painful, frightening, difficult, or impossible situations. God hasn't promised us exemption from the trial but grace in the trial. He has promised never to leave us nor forsake us, and to work all things together for our good. Peter said, "Beloved, do not think it strange concerning the fiery trial . . . as though some strange thing happened to you; but rejoice . . . be glad with exceeding joy" (1 Peter 4:12–13).

The Lord will see you through.

Trials Versus Temptations

No temptation has overtaken you except such is common to man; but God is faithful, who will not allow you to be tempted beyond what you are able.

1 Corinthians 10:13

A consumer protection group will test a car to find its flaws, while the car manufacturer tests a car to find its strengths. In the same way, Satan tempts us to bring out the bad (James 1:13–18), while God tests us to bring out the good (vv. 1:1–12). Nothing tests the integrity of our faith like our response to temptation.

When we hear of people falling prey to temptation, we are not surprised. But when we face temptation ourselves, we are often shocked. We shouldn't be surprised, for temptation is inevitable. The more we grow toward the Lord, the more we are tempted.

Unless we acknowledge the reality of temptation, we have set ourselves up to fail. Paul agrees with James that temptation should not be considered unusual in the life of a Christian but common to every believer.

Stop the World!

Finally, my brethren, be strong in the Lord.

Ephesians 6:10

Ever wonder if you can press on? Life is difficult, and we often feel like saying, in the words of the old musical, "Stop the world—I want to get off!" It's hard to bear up under chronic pain, to keep going against constant opposition, and to remain joyful in cheerless surroundings. Within ourselves, we haven't sufficient courage or morale.

But we can be strong in the Lord. When our strength is gone, His is ready to be tapped. We can give Him our burdens, trust Him with our hurts, tell Him our cares, and claim the promises of His Word. As J. B. Phillips put it in his paraphrase of Ephesians 6:10: "Be strong—not in yourselves but in the Lord, in the power of his boundless resource."

Commentator Matthew Henry said about this verse: "We have no sufficient strength of our own. Our natural courage is as perfect cowardice, and our natural strength as perfect weakness; but all our sufficiency is of God. In His strength we must go forth and go on."

Focus your mind today on the strength of our Lord Jesus Christ. Tell Him you feel weak, but don't dwell on that. Don't dwell on your problems either. Dwell on Christ. Let Him be your strength and solution today.

Opportunities

May the God of all grace, who called us to His eternal glory by Christ Jesus, after you have suffered a while, perfect, establish, strengthen, and settle you.

1 Peter 5:10

Problems are often given to us by God to provide us greater opportunities. As God's children, we need to learn how to look for the possibilities in our problems. God's people have always worked this way. An entire section of Scripture, the "prison epistles," was written while Paul was incarcerated in a Roman jail cell. The book of Revelation was written by John while he was exiled on the isle of Patmos. It was in prison that John Bunyan saw the great allegory that would later become the immortal *Pilgrim's Progress*. Sometimes good things come from bad times.

Joseph learned from his prison experience that he was not forgotten by God. As a matter of fact, God used a relationship formed while Joseph was in prison to accomplish His plan.

I remember hearing Charles Colson say that his lowest times as a believer have been far more fulfilling that all his glory days in the White House when he was an unbeliever. During the lonely days of prison, he learned to know God. Sometimes loneliness and difficulties are necessary in our lives, because the problems are the means God uses to provide opportunities for us.

Christian Books

Bring the cloak that I left with Carpus at Troas when you come—and the books, especially the parchments.

2 Timothy 4:13

The Left Behind series of Christian novels has sold tens of millions of copies, and *The Prayer of Jabez* was the best-selling nonfiction book in America in 2001. So strong is the Christian publishing market that some major evangelical publishers have been sought by secular media companies.

If there is a danger in the rise of Christian publishing in recent years, it is the temptation to read more books about the Bible than the Bible itself. But keeping all things in balance, the wealth of good resources for Christians is a modern blessing that believers ought to take advantage of. For instance, try a good biography of a famous saint to find a stimulating role model or a devotional classic to keep you in the Word daily. Or perhaps you'd enjoy a missionary tale or exciting novel with biblical themes to read aloud as a family. Reading good Christian books can reinforce and illustrate the themes we read in Scripture. What are you reading this week?

Looking for dependable guidelines for choosing books to read along with the Bible? Check out Philippians 4:8.

Confidence in God's Presence

The Lord, He is the One who goes before you. He will be with you, He will not leave you nor forsake you; do not fear nor be dismayed.

Deuteronomy 31:8

When Susanna Wesley was on her deathbed, she gathered her children around her. As she was about to be called home to heaven, she admonished them not to weep but rather to "sing a hymn of praise." Then with her last breath, she reminded them that the greatest comfort we have in any circumstance is the fact that "God is with us."

We often need that reminder! It is especially reassuring to hear these words when God has given us a difficult assignment, one that seems impossible and for which we feel totally unqualified. We are not the first to have experienced fear and hesitation in accepting God's assignment.

Moses certainly didn't do any cartwheels when God asked him to lead the Israelites out of Egypt. He was not excited about the task because he felt ill equipped to accomplish it. That's when God spoke these courage-infusing words: "I will certainly be with you" (Exodus 3:12).

Those few precious words remind us that with God's presence and help, we can accomplish any assignment. His presence instills confidence in our hearts.

God With Us

. . . Christ in you, the hope of glory.

Colossians 1:27

Patrick was born in what is now called Scotland. He was kidnapped by pirates as a lad and enslaved in Ireland, but after a dramatic escape, he returned home to Ireland as an evangelist. During his ministry, he planted about two hundred churches and baptized one hundred thousand converts.

Patrick once said this about the Lord Jesus: "Christ with me, Christ before me, Christ behind me, Christ in me, Christ beneath me, Christ above me, Christ on my right, Christ on my left, Christ when I lie down, Christ when I sit down, Christ when I arise, Christ in the heart of every man who thinks of me, Christ in the mouth of everyone who speaks of me, Christ in every eye that sees me, Christ in every ear that hears me."

All the promises of our almighty Father can be encapsulated in the name prescribed for the Lord Jesus at His birth—Emmanuel, God with us. Jesus Christ is the embodiment of all His grace, the fulfillment of all His promises, the satisfaction of all our needs.

The reliability of God's promises to us is found in the presence of Christ among us. When He is near, we have all we need.

The Best Violins

We also glory in tribulations, knowing that tribulation produces perseverance; and perseverance, character; and character, hope.

Romans 5:3–4

An old violin maker was much envied by fellow artisans because of the superior quality of the instruments he produced. He finally disclosed the secret of his success. He said that while the others went into the protected valleys to cut wood to make their violins, he climbed the rugged crags of a nearby mountain in order to secure trees that had become severely twisted and gnarled by storms. From these weather-beaten monarchs of the forest he then fabricated his violins—famous for their tone and beauty.

He knew that the fierce trials of the mountain gales caused such trees to strengthen and toughen their fibers. It was this—their storm-tortured heart and grain—that produced the deep, colorful sound when the instrument was played. Likewise, the Lord allows sore difficulties to come into our lives that we may more fully bring forth the music of His grace when our soul-trying experiences have done their sanctifying work.

Peculiar People

The Lord hath chosen thee to be a peculiar people.

Deuteronomy 14:2 KJV

When the older translations talk about us being "peculiar" people, they mean we're to be different from everyone else on earth, caring little for the things of the world and living instead for Jesus alone. That sometimes makes us seem peculiar—and some Christians really are.

The nineteenth-century backwoods evangelist Bob Sheffey is a good example. He was known for the unique nature of his prayers, which were often answered in astonishing ways. On one occasion, encountering moonshiners in the mountains, "Uncle Bob" dismounted, knelt, and offered a long prayer for God to "smash the still into smithereens." He rose, smoothed his trousers, and continued his journey. A heavy tree fell on the still, wrecking it. The owner rebuilt it, and Sheffey prayed again. This time a flash flood did the job. Sheffey's unorthodox prayers and sermons made him seem peculiar, but they ushered many mountaineers into the kingdom of God.

While we don't want to be peculiar in a negative sense, we are to be separate from the world, different, living for Christ alone. Is your Christianity enough to make you peculiar?

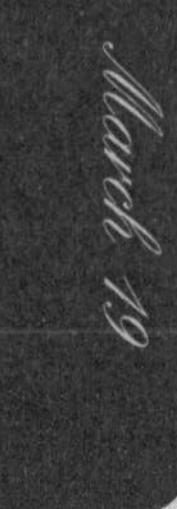

Not by Sight

Trust in the Lord with all your heart,
And lean not on your own understanding;
In all your ways acknowledge Him,
And He shall direct your paths.
Proverbs 3:5–6

At the beginning of flight training, a student flies with an instructor by his side, over familiar terrain, and in perfect weather. All his decisions are based on sight. But at the end, when a student pilot receives his "instrument rating," he has learned to fly by himself, over unfamiliar terrain, and in total darkness. He has learned to trust not his sight but his instruments—compass, altimeter, air speed, and radar. He has learned to "fly blind."

Just as a flight instructor's ultimate goal is to see a student get his instrument rating, so the father in Proverbs had the same goal for his son. What is the spiritual equivalent of an instrument rating? It is trusting in the Lord, not in one's own understanding. Every parent, teacher, and leader knows his protégés will one day encounter darkness, storms, and unfamiliar terrain in life. The key to their graduation and promotion is learning to live by faith, not by sight (2 Corinthians 5:7).

"Flying blind" in life doesn't mean closing your eyes; it means keeping them on the Lord.

Make the Connection

For since the creation of the world His invisible attributes are clearly seen . . . even His eternal power and Godhead.

Romans 1:20

In a seminary missions class, Herbert Jackson told about a car he was given as a new missionary. Because the car would not start without a push, for two years he made a habit of always parking on a hill—or just leaving the car running. When he left that mission assignment, he passed the car on to his replacement. Curious about the starting problem, the new missionary raised the hood, twisted a wire, turned the key, and the car roared to life!

Failing to take advantage of a car's power for two years is bad enough, but not nearly as bad as living a lifetime without God's power. Look at the evidences of God's power all around us. From the countless galaxies in the universe to the tiniest atoms of which they are made, from the marvelous complexity of the human body to the stunning simplicity of a one-cell bacterium, from the grandeur of the Himalayas to the mysteries of the ocean floor—God's power is clearly seen wherever we look. Are you connected to God as your power source, or do you need a push just to get started every day?

Don't let a loose connection with God leave you powerless in this life.

The Pursuit of Happiness

[Jesus] opened His mouth and taught them, saying, "Blessed are the poor in spirit, for theirs is the kingdom of heaven."

Matthew 5:2–3

Malcolm Muggeridge once called the pursuit of happiness the most disastrous purpose set before mankind, something slipped into the Declaration after "life and liberty" at the last moment, almost by accident. In his *Screwtape Letters*, C. S. Lewis had the archdevil, Screwtape, advise his apprentice demons on the lure of happiness. He called it "an ever-increasing craving for an ever-diminishing pleasure." That's exactly how the pursuit of happiness works in this world.

Pleasure is an anesthesia for deadening the pain of empty lives. There seem to be few happy people around today. That's why I appreciate the words of Jesus in the Sermon on the Mount. Nine different times Jesus uses the word *blessed*, which roughly translates to "happy." The core values Jesus offers in the Beatitudes describe life that is really worth living.

Saving Versus Spending

Wealth gained by dishonesty will be diminished,
But he who gathers by labor will increase.

Proverbs 13:11

Albert Einstein believed the rule of seventy-two (the compounding of interest) was a more important discovery than his theory of relativity. Here's the rule: divide seventy-two by the interest rate of your savings to discover the number of years in which your savings will double. For instance, one thousand dollars saved at 6 percent interest becomes two thousand dollars in twelve years. No wonder compound interest is called the eighth wonder of the world!

But credit card issuers also know the rule of seventy-two. If you make a one-thousand-dollar purchase on a credit card at 18 percent interest and don't pay it off, that balance becomes two thousand in four years ($72 \div 18 = 4$). Instead of earning you money, your one thousand dollars is earning big bucks for the credit card company.

Saving versus spending is a daily battle in a wealthy and materialistic economy. But God's economy is designed to repay savings. Save and sow a single tomato seed, and you'll get thousands in return—it's only a matter of time. And it's the same with money. Take time today to evaluate your savings practices. Remember, a penny saved is (another) penny earned!

The very day we think we can't afford to save is the day we can't afford not to!

Break Out in Praise

Praise the Lord, for the Lord is good;
Sing praises to His name, for it is pleasant.
Psalm 135:3

Praise and worship are refining processes. We can't be in God's presence without a deep awareness of our sin and without confessing and allowing the purification that only He can provide. Worship cleanses our hands and hearts, and then we can see how to fight. Then we can clear the sinful mists from our eyes and do things God's way.

Some have said that Satan has an allergic reaction whenever there is true worship. That's an interesting way of visualizing it; perhaps when we break out in praise, the devil breaks out in hives. I don't know whether he itches, sneezes, or coughs, but I do know he becomes very uncomfortable on those occasions when we take our eyes off ourselves and place them squarely and worshipfully on the Lord of grace. That's when God's mighty works finally come to pass. That's when we take powerful weapons in hand, crying, "Onward, Christian soldiers!" and advancing on the enemy's holdings. The forces of hell cannot prevail against the uplifted name of Christ.

Defending the Children

And give my son Solomon a loyal heart to keep Your commandments and Your testimonies and Your statutes.

1 Chronicles 29:19

Irene Park is a committed Christian with a tragic background: she was a high witch in the state of Florida, seducing boys and girls into abusive occult activities. She has stated that the only children she could never reach were those who had Christian parents who protected their children by pleading the blood of Christ over them in prayer.

Today, occultism has made its way directly into the public school systems of our land under the guise of the New Age movement. Well-meaning parents provide children every kind of protection possible—cell phones, pagers, nannies, cars—but too often fail to provide the most powerful defense of all: prayer in the name and through the blood of Jesus. Technology will never overcome Satan like the blood of Jesus can (Revelation 12:11). As you pray for your own children, pray for their teachers, schools, and classmates as well. The devil will take a foothold wherever he can.

What a tragedy to think of a single child walking through today's world without the protection of praying parents.

The Secret to Storms

They are glad because [the storms] are quiet;
So He guides them to their desired haven.

Psalm 107:30

God's purposes in the storms you encounter are always to guide you to a haven. Think about it: we don't just go out on the sea to sit there; we go for a purpose. If a storm interrupts that purpose, God will direct you through it, or He may change the purpose of your trip altogether.

I have learned this about storms: the place you thought you wanted to go heading into the storm is not always the place you think you want to go coming out of the storm. Sometimes storms can change your mind about things you thought you wanted.

The secret to experiencing these changes is starting the journey with a receptive heart. If you head into a storm saying, "Thy will be done," then your will and God's will become one.

Home Run

One's life does not consist in the abundance of the things he possesses.

Luke 12:15

In a *Sports Illustrated* interview, baseball hero Mickey Mantle once described his long battle with alcohol and his heartbreaking problems with his family. The interviewer then asked, "So how are things going with you today, Mickey?"

"Better," was the reply. "I haven't had a drink in eight months. I'm starting to get my life back together, but I just feel like there's something missing."

Here was a living legend who had played 2,401 games for the New York Yankees from 1951 to 1968, hit a record eighteen homers in twelve World Series, and had entered baseball's Hall of Fame in 1974. But he felt empty inside, for the accumulation of wealth, fame, and accomplishment didn't satisfy.

Is something missing in your life?

Near the end of his life, Mickey Mantle found what he had always been looking for—Jesus Christ. Another former baseball player, Bobby Richardson, led him to Christ. At Mantle's funeral, Richardson told of helping Mantle receive the Lord Jesus as his personal Savior. "I am trusting Christ's death for me to take me to heaven," Mickey Mantle said on his deathbed.

Only in Jesus Christ can we find our true identity. He alone gives us a fulfilled, abundant life.

Deliverance from Poverty

Behold, the eye of the Lord is on those who fear Him,
On those who hope in His mercy,
To deliver their soul from death,
And to keep them alive in famine.

Psalm 33:18–19

David gives us permission to pray for deliverance from poverty and need. This psalm talks about being kept alive in times of deprivation. God loves to deliver His people from that condition. We are always aware of those who are struggling materially and wonder how they are going to make it. God can deliver them from it.

I talk with Christian people all the time who are in the midst of great need. I always ask them, "Have you asked God pointedly, naming the details of this situation, to help you and deliver you from it?" They have often prayed in generalities, but not in specifics.

My friend, when you are in the lions' den, you need to pray about the lion—by name!

Investor or Trader?

On the first day of the week let each one of you lay something aside, storing up as he may prosper.

1 Corinthians 16:2

In the volatile world of commodity futures trading, investors rely on a critical document called the "Commitment of Traders Report." This document reveals what large commercial corporations are buying (for example, how much wheat General Mills is securing for its cereal production), which gives smaller investors an indication of a particular market's direction.

Once a huge corporation makes a commitment to buy a commodity like wheat, cotton, or lumber, its action sets a course for the rest of the market. An investment is a long-term proposition that requires careful consideration. And with millions of dollars at stake, companies make such decisions for the long-term only.

If a "Commitment of Christians Report" were issued on your life, what long-term investment decisions would it reveal? Would it show investments of time, talent, and treasure for the kingdom of God? Can others look at your life and get direction for their own?

The church needs long-term investors with commitment, not day-traders who are in the market and then out. God rewards patient commitment in every realm of life.

Unchangeable Personality

For I am the Lord, I do not change.
Malachi 3:6

If you have kids, have you ever noticed how they work you? Another word for this is *manipulation*. They live in the same house with you, so they study you. They know when you're in a certain kind of mood and when they should move in. If they see you're troubled or upset over something, they know it's not the time to make a request. If you've had a great day, they make their move.

You don't have to work God. He's always in a good mood. He's always the same. You don't have to sneak up on God when you think it is appropriate to ask Him for what you need. And that affects your fellowship with Him and your attitude toward Him. He loves you, and He wants to do as much for you as He can at any given time. It doesn't matter when you call. He's always there.

Imperfect Saints

Lord, I believe; help my unbelief!

Mark 9:24

None of the "heroes of the faith" described in Hebrews 11 was perfect. They all had lapses in their faith. Take Abraham. When a famine struck Canaan, he rushed to Egypt, where he became so fearful he lied about his wife (Genesis 12:10–20). How did Abraham recover? In Genesis 13:1–4, he returned to his altar at Bethel, "and there Abram called on the name of the Lord."

When we realize our faith is faltering, we need to go back to our place of commitment, and call on the name of our Lord. The Christian statesman George Müller was a spiritual giant, but this is what he once said about his faith:

> My faith is the same faith which is found in every believer. It has been increased little by little for the last 26 years. Many times when I could have gone insane from worry, I was at peace because my soul believed the truth of God's promises. God's Word, together with the whole character of God . . . settles all questions. His unchangeable love and His infinite wisdom calmed me. I knew, "God is able and willing to deliver me." It is written, "He who did not spare His own Son, but delivered Him up for us all, how shall He not with Him also freely give us all things?" (Romans 8:32)

Words of Life

Pleasant words are like a honeycomb,
Sweetness to the soul and health to the bones.
Proverbs 16:24

Karl Marx devoted his entire life to writing about the demise of capitalism and the coming of communism. He, along with Friedrich Engels, wrote one of the most well-known political treatises in all of history, the *Communist Manifesto*. As evidence of his keen understanding of the great power of words, Marx is credited with saying, "Give me twenty-six lead soldiers and I will conquer the world!" Who are the twenty-six lead soldiers Marx referred to? They are the twenty-six letters of the alphabet on a printing press.

All words have power and meaning (Isaiah 55:11). Jesus said we would be held accountable for even our idle words (Matthew 12:36–37), and Proverbs says that words have the power of life and death (18:21). So the question is not whether words have power. The question is, "What power am I releasing with my words?" If you have sent forth words that hurt, take them back with an apology and replace them with words that heal. The greatest untapped source of healing in life is "pleasant words." You may not consider yourself a physician, but you should—as long as you are dispensing words of life.

The Biggest Lie

Get behind Me, Satan!

Luke 4:8

A store manager heard his clerk tell a customer, "No, ma'am, we haven't had any for a while, and it doesn't look as if we'll be getting any soon." Horrified, the manager came running over to the customer and said, "Of course we'll have some soon. We placed an order last week." Then the manager drew the clerk aside. "Never," he snarled, "never say we're out of anything—say we've got it on order and it's coming. Now what was it she wanted?" The clerk replied, "Rain."

As absurd as it is to order rain for a customer, it is equally absurd to believe Satan's lies compared to God's truth. Satan wants us to believe that there is a sin that can separate us from God. But in John 8:44, Jesus reminds us, "He [Satan] is a liar and the father of lies" (NIV).

Satan used lies to trick Eve and to tempt Jesus, and today he tests our wills with his lies. But we can trust God. When Christ was being tempted, He fought back by quoting Scripture. Today, we have the power to ignore Satan's ploys by focusing on God's Word and prayer.

Don't forget that Jesus is the only way, the truth, and the life.

Change Your Thinking

Every good gift and every perfect gift is from above, and comes down from the Father of lights, with whom there is no variation or shadow of turning.

James 1:17

In contrast to the evil enticements that come from within us, every good gift comes from God, who is over us. The text literally says that such benefits come down to us in a steady stream from the Father of lights.

God's nature is unchanging. He will forever be both good and trustworthy. Jesus (Matthew 6:30; 7:11) and Paul (Romans 13:14) shared the same perspective. James might add to Paul's words that the believer should not only refrain from thinking about gratifying his desires but also avoid thinking about not gratifying his desires.

We are not to grit our teeth and make up our mind that we will not do a certain thing. The key to dealing with temptation is to fill our minds with other things. Since temptation begins with our thoughts, changing what we think about is the key to victory.

A Time for Celebrating

. . . absent from the body . . . present with the Lord.

2 Corinthians 5:8

When Christian author and speaker Dr. Bob Hill was seventy-one, his mother passed away. She was nearly ninety-four. Family and friends gathered in St. Louis for the memorial service, and Bob rose to open the funeral. "Friends," he said with a smile, "this is not a time for grieving but a time for celebration." At that moment, Bob suffered a massive brain hemorrhage and slumped to the floor. As his wife and children rushed to the platform and gathered around him, he slipped into glory.

Bob had written sixty books and had preached hundreds of times, but his last words were perhaps his most memorable. He had intended for them to be about his mother, but they became instead a comfort to those he himself left behind.

While it's necessary and normal for us to grieve, we also sense a celebration going on in heaven when a loved one falls asleep in Jesus, and we sorrow not as those who have no hope (1 Thessalonians 4:13). But such an occasion also causes us to revisit our own lives and reexamine our walk with the Lord.

Are we really living a life worth living? Are we doing those things that when we stand before the Lord, we'll wish we had been doing?

Love Authentically

Husbands, love your wives, just as Christ also loved the church and gave Himself for her.

Ephesians 5:25

Christ loved the church with an authentic love. By that, I mean it was real. It wasn't fantasy; it was the church as the church is. It was you and me as we were and as we are. Christ was under no illusion when He sought us in love. And of course, that is the way husbands are to love their wives—with realistic, authentic love.

We must recognize that our love will embrace all of our wife's faults and failures and all of her unlovable and disagreeable elements. When a young couple enters into marriage with unrealistic expectations, it doesn't take long before those expectations are brought back down to earth. Marriage is a mixture of ideals and reality. It's a wonderful thing to know that Christ loves us as we were and continues to love us as we are. He loves us in spite of our sins.

Christ's love for us is not idealized, romanticized, or stylized. It is simply authentic, meeting sinners like us exactly where we are.

Harmony

Finally, all of you, live in harmony with one another; be sympathetic, love as brothers, be compassionate and humble.

1 Peter 3:8 NIV

A fifth-grade music teacher asked her class to sing "Do Re Mi," a song about the musical scale that was made popular in the movie *The Sound of Music*. The children did so in unison, all singing the same notes as they worked their way up the scale. Then the teacher asked half the class to sing the song again while she led the remaining students in singing up the C-major scale, holding each note until it was time to go on to the next. In that way, she taught the class two-part harmony.

A lot of us need to learn the difference between unison and harmony. The Bible doesn't tell us to live our lives in unison. Your friends, family, and fellow believers all have different personalities, backgrounds, and opinions. We have different levels of spiritual maturity, different strengths and weaknesses, and different gifts. We aren't all going to agree about everything.

Instead of being argumentative, learn the secret of harmony. Respect the opinions and personalities of those the Lord has placed in your life, and don't always expect to have your own way or have the last word. Live in harmony with one another.

Stand, No Matter What

Stand fast in one spirit, with one mind striving together for faith of the gospel.

Philippians 1:27

Someone has said that a man who refuses to stand for something will sooner or later fall for anything. Because of his stand for the faith, Paul was facing the possibility of death, and he was willing to pay the supreme price if called upon to do so.

In writing to the Philippian believers, he shared his concern about their willingness to stand against the pressure of persecution. He hoped that he might be with them in person to encourage them if such a thing occurred, but he had no guarantee. So he sent them a strategy that would serve them well, even if he was not available to personally cheer them on.

Paul's game plan for the Philippians is needed in our day too. We are in the minority, surrounded by the enemy, and constantly being undermined by members of our own army. Many among God's people have adopted a philosophy that gives to survival the attributes of victory. But in our day, as in Paul's, anything short of victory is just the postponement of defeat!

True Spirituality

God is Spirit, and those who worship Him
must worship in spirit and truth.

John 4:24

Former Congressman J. C. Watts, Jr. (Republican, Oklahoma) made the statement famous in his speech at the 1996 Republican Convention, while one of the earliest references to it comes from the nineteenth-century evangelist D. L. Moody. Since Moody's day, and Congressman Watts's day, and up to the present day, this statement continues to ring true: "Character is what you are when no one is looking."

The issue, of course, is double-mindedness. Are we really who we say we are? If so, what is the essence of a Christian—that is, the true nature and character of a follower of Jesus Christ? One of the surest ways to discover the essence of true spirituality is to pull back the curtain on heaven and see what occupies its residents. Since we leave everything else behind when we enter heaven, perhaps whatever we take with us is close to the definition of true spirituality.

The book of Revelation suggests that one thing dominates heaven: worship (Revelation 4:8, 11; 5:9–10, 13–14; 7:11–12; 11:15–18; 15:3–4; 19:1–8). When we are stripped of all we pretend to be, worship is what will endure for eternity.

For the Christian, worship is what we should do even when no one sees us except God.

March 29

Preaching Christ Crucified

Then Philip went down to the city of Samaria and preached Christ to them.

Acts 8:5

Notice what Philip preached when he arrived in Samaria: Christ! What did that mean in the first century? Remember, they didn't have the New Testament to use. All they had was the Old Testament. So when Philip "preached Christ to them" (Acts 8:5), he was simply explaining how Jesus Christ fulfilled the Old Testament expectation of the coming Jewish Messiah. The only message the early church had was the birth, life, death, and resurrection of Jesus of Nazareth. "Christ and Him crucified" was the message (1 Corinthians 2:2).

The church today has so muddied the gospel water that we can preach forever and never get around to Christ crucified. We've added cultural issues and social issues and theological issues to the Gospel that probably would have just confused the first-century Christians. They only had an eyewitness story to tell of a Messiah who died and rose again. That was what Christ did, and that is what the church preached.

And look what happened when Philip preached that simple message. Multitudes of people responded to his preaching and the miracles he performed, "and there was great joy in that city" (Acts 8:6–8).

Bearing and Sharing Fruit

Therefore by their fruits you will know them.

Matthew 7:20

You drive up to a local roadside produce market with your heart set on buying a load of fresh summer vegetables. You see homegrown tomatoes, squash, cucumbers, and several varieties of peppers—everything you need and more. Just as you start to select your items, the farmer who owns the stand says, "Sorry, ma'am; this produce isn't for sale. I just like to grow it and enjoy looking at it until it rots. Then I throw it away."

Huh? You likely haven't encountered such an absurd situation, and probably never will. Farmers and consumers know that produce is for consuming. Sure, it's beautiful to look at, but its God-ordained purpose is to bring nutrition and health to people. Fruit that isn't consumed is no better than fruit that was never grown.

Similarly, if Christians aren't manifesting fruit in their lives that benefit other people, something's wrong. The fruit of the Spirit, as well as the good works we were made to walk in (Ephesians 2:10), are not for analyzing, discussing, and admiring. They're for sharing with others! Not to bear and share fruit in the Christian life is to keep others from being blessed as God intended.

Bearing fruit and sharing fruit are two sides of the same spiritual coin.

Use It or Lose It

Therefore take the talent from him, and give it to him who has ten talents.

Matthew 25:28

Each believer has talents given by God that we are to use for His glory. We can't claim that we have no gifts or that we have been given no opportunity. The fact is, what we do with what we have will be the basis of our judgment. I won't be judged on my inability to sing or play the piano, but I will have to give an account of the gifts that I have.

If we don't use our talent for God, we will lose it. It doesn't remain dormant. It won't remain hidden. We will end up not having the opportunity we had at the beginning. On the other hand, if we are faithful in the use of our abilities, God will multiply our opportunities for service. The way to grow in influence and service is to use what we already have—then the Lord will reward us with more opportunity.

Remember, someday we will have to give an account at the Judgment Seat of Christ. As Christians, we won't be judged for our sins—they have already been forgiven. But we will be judged for the stewardship of those things God has given us. We'll be judged on quality, not quantity. We have been given incredible potential for serving God. How are we putting ours to use?

Change Your World

These who have turned the world upside down have come here too.

Acts 17:6

Quick—name five Christians who literally changed the world by their presence (or, as young people might say, five Christians who "rocked their world"). Think about Martin Luther and the Reformation, John Wesley and holiness, William Wilberforce and slavery, C. S. Lewis and apologetics, and Billy Graham and evangelism. None of these men set out to change the world; they set out to obey God one step at a time.

That could also be said of the man who, besides Jesus Christ, was the greatest world-changer in history—the apostle Paul. Ironically, Paul set out to keep his world from being changed. He was content with being a Pharisee—keeping the Law and making sure others did too. He didn't like the changes the itinerant preacher Jesus of Nazareth was proposing. But when confronted by Jesus in all His glory, Paul's world was changed—and the whole world was changed as well.

What does it take to impact your part of the world, or the whole world, for Christ? If we use Paul as an example, we would have to say unreserved obedience. Jesus told Paul to take the Gospel to the Gentile world, and that's exactly what he did.

What has God directed you to do? Remember, your world has to change before you can change the world.

True Happiness

Blessed are the pure in heart, for they shall see God.

Matthew 5:8

Blessed means "happy, blissful, joyous, ecstatic." Those characteristics the Lord lists are like an explosion on His lips, a description of the inner joy we can experience. This expression was commonly seen in the book of Psalms. "Blessed is the man who walks not in the counsel of the ungodly," says Psalm 1:1. Anyone who has ever been burned by ungodly counsel will attest to the fact that a man who doesn't get mixed up with ungodly counsel is happy. "Blessed is he whose transgression is forgiven," we read in Psalm 32:1. We are to be blissful and ecstatic over the fact that the Lord has taken away our sins. That's the same expression Christ used when He began talking about the Christian life. Blissful, happy, joyous—these are the words that describe the Christian walk.

Matthew 5:1–12 describes nine characteristics of the happy Christian life. If you want to know what happiness is all about, search through this "happiness manifesto" from the Lord Jesus. He'll explain to you what true happiness is all about.

Ye of Much Faith

But Peter and the other apostles answered and said: "We ought to obey God rather than men."

Acts 5:29

The seventeenth-century Scottish pastor and theologian Samuel Rutherford wrote an important book in Christian history: *Lex, Rex, or The Law and the Prince: A Dispute for the Just Prerogative of King and People.* In this book, he argued that the laws of man can never supersede the laws of God; any just human law will be consistent with God's law.

It took faith for Rutherford to write that book, since he had already spent two years in a Scottish prison for his nonconformist views. He would have found a cellmate in the apostle Peter, who also spent time in a Jewish jail in Jerusalem for advocating Rutherford-like views. Peter, remember, had been "O ye of little faith" (Matthew 6:30 KJV) just before Jesus' crucifixion, unwilling to even be named as a follower of Jesus. But the coming of the Holy Spirit changed him completely. He was full of faith, and the rest of the fruit of the Spirit as well. When told to stop preaching, Peter said, "Not so fast—we have a higher command than yours to obey."

When was the last time your faith brought you into conflict with society's values, norms, or laws? Were you "of little faith" or "of much faith"?

It takes faith to obey—and faith to trust God with the outcome.

APRIL

I am not alone, but I am with the Father who sent me.

—John 8:16

Beware Foolish Friends

He who walks with wise men will be wise,
But the companion of fools will be destroyed.

Proverbs 13:20

It is important not to choose fools for friends because you will become just like them: "He who walks with wise men will be wise, but the companion of fools will be destroyed." This is important for young people to know, especially during the years when peer pressure is so great. Christians are not supposed to live like isolationists, walling ourselves off from those who need Christ. It is fine to have casual friendships with those who are not wise, but not committed friendships. It is when we begin to open ourselves up to others on a committed level that we are likely to be influenced to become like them.

Sometimes Christians forge friendships with unwise people thinking they can change them. But you will both be changed. Many Christian young people marry non-Christians thinking they can win them over after the marriage. It rarely happens. Everyone is on their best behavior during courtship, and after marriage, the mountain of unbelief looms larger than it did before. You shouldn't make committed friendships with fools, but you should look for faithful friends.

FATHER KNOWS BEST

For this child I prayed. . . . I also have lent him to the LORD; as long as he lives he shall be lent to the LORD.

1 SAMUEL 1:27–28

Carman, the well-known Christian performer, credits his parents with dedicating him to Christ as a child. "My parents held me up in a Bible study and dedicated my life to the Lord so that, whatever happened, my life would be used for the service of God," he wrote. "I guess that commitment really stuck because the presence of Jesus haunted me until I finally succumbed [to Christ] when I was twenty years old."

When we dedicate our children to God, we're saying, "Lord, this is the child You have loaned me, and I understand he belongs to You. I'll do everything I can as a mother (or father) to see that he grows up to know, love, and serve You." When you do that, you're giving your child back to the Lord.

What if God wants him to be a missionary in a faraway land? What if He wants your child to do something difficult? God's plan is always best—best for your child and best for you. You can trust your child to Him, for the Father knows best.

A NOTE OF VICTORY

Oh, sing to the LORD a new song!
For He has done marvelous things;
His right hand and His holy arm
have gained Him the victory.

PSALM 98:1

Did you know there is someone who really gets bent out of shape whenever you go to church? No, not that fellow in the next pew who objects to your singing. It truly torments the devil and every one of his "assistants" when you worship God, in the public sanctuary or the private one. It throws a wrench into the detailed agenda of demonic works. In all the other things we do, from watching television to grocery shopping to taking business trips, there are countless windows of opportunity for the devil to steal in and do his thing. But when you worship God devotedly, Satan is out of his league. He is completely stripped of power, and that's always been the one thing the devil can't abide.

Worship has always been our weapon. Consider that midnight in a Philippian jail, when two prisoners named Paul and Silas lifted their voices and sang praises to God. Think of all the psalms in which David begins in deep depression, lamenting the injustice of his enemies' success. In so many of these, he turns his attention and poetry to the praises of God, and his psalm finishes on a note of victory. Praise can become the pattern in your life.

Faith Over Reason

But without faith it is impossible to please Him, for he who comes to God must believe that He is, and that He is a rewarder of those who diligently seek Him.

Hebrews 11:6

Author Marshall Shelley suffered the deaths of two of his children—and grew in faith. As a child reading novels, he learned not to be confused by the introduction of many different characters, events, and subplots in early chapters. He learned that, if the author was skilled, all the disparate parts would come together by the end of the book. Thus, he said about his life, "I choose to trust that before the book closes, the Author will make things clear."

Who can understand the death of one child, much less two? How far can human reasoning go in explaining the facts, much less in healing the hurting heart? Because we possess strong minds, as those created in the image of God, our natural tendency is to seek solutions first in reason. But reason is not all the mind is good for. The spiritually minded have "the mind of Christ," which is first and foremost a mind of faith (1 Corinthians 2:16). Our challenge in the spiritual life is to be faithful first and reasonable second.

The Author of the story of your life has a plot in progress that will leave no question unanswered.

Take Hope in the Risen Christ

Blessed be the God and Father of our Lord Jesus Christ, who according to His abundant mercy has begotten us again to a living hope through the resurrection of Jesus Christ.

1 Peter 1:3

The resurrection of our Lord is the single greatest event in history. Had the Lord merely died, He would have been considered a great teacher and a moral leader, but He would not have proven Himself God. By coming out of the grave, He triumphed over death and hell, showed His sacrifice on the cross as being acceptable to God, and gave hope of eternal life to everyone who puts their trust in Him.

Every other religious leader lies buried in the earth. Mohammed lies dead and buried. Buddha, Confucius, Zoroaster, and all the others who have attempted to lead men and women into a religious experience apart from Almighty God could not defeat death. But Jesus Christ, in what is one of the best documented facts in history, rose victorious from the grave. In this troubled world today, we can take hope in the risen Christ.

Casting Out Fear

God has not given us a spirit of fear,
but of . . . a sound mind.
2 Timothy 1:7

Missionary Isobel Kuhn found herself imperiled when the Communists overran China. Taking her young son, she escaped on foot across the snow-covered Pienma Pass, arriving in Burma. There she was stranded at world's end with no money and no way to get home. "I cannot tell you the dismay and alarm that filled me," she later wrote.

But she made two decisions. "The first thing is to cast out fear," she said. "The only fear a Christian should entertain is the fear of sin. All other fears are from Satan sent to confuse and weaken us. How often the Lord reiterated to His disciples, 'Be not afraid!'" So Isobel prayerfully trusted God and rejected panic. Second, she sought light for the next step, and she eventually arrived home safely.

Anxiety disorders are at an all-time high in America. How prone we are to panic in a crisis! Fear comes so powerfully and naturally.

Yet the Bible tells us, as God's children, to fret not (Psalm 37:1), faint not (Deuteronomy 20:3), and fear not (Isaiah 41:10). With God's strength, we can learn to handle crises with sound counsel and calm faith.

Perhaps you're in a difficult spot today. By His grace, cast out fear and seek light for the next step.

He Is Sovereign

Yours is the kingdom and the power and the glory forever.
Matthew 6:13

A critic might suggest that, given the state of the world, Christ the King is not doing a very good job running His kingdom. But please understand that one day Christ will institute His kingdom over the kingdom of this world, and He will rule and reign and bring order out of the earth's present chaos. You may think that your personal life is a mirror of the world—out of control, headed for calamity. Just when I think things are rolling along smoothly and in control, something will happen that I never could have dreamed of. Out of order comes chaos! But what a wonderful thing it is to go to God in prayer, knowing that He is sovereign over my life. And not only my life, but all creation.

Sometimes God allows us to sense in a practical way that everything is on track and under control. That's just one of His blessings—icing on the cake, so to speak. Those are special times. But it's when we don't have that sense, when we don't have evidence our eyes can see, that we need to remember this prayer: "Yours is the kingdom!"

Equipped for Success

You have made known to me the ways of life; You will make me full of joy in Your presence.

Acts 2:28

Former U.S. senator Mark Hatfield told of touring Calcutta with Mother Teresa and visiting the so-called House of Dying, where sick children are cared for in their last days, and the dispensary, where the poor line up by the hundreds to receive medical attention. Watching Mother Teresa minister to these people, feeding and nursing those left by others to die, Hatfield was overwhelmed by the sheer magnitude of the suffering she and her coworkers faced daily. "How can you bear the load without being crushed by it?" he asked. Mother Teresa replied, "My dear Senator, I am not called to be successful, I am called to be faithful."

God has given us the tools to succeed. First Samuel 18:14 says, "In everything he did he had great success, because the Lord was with him" (NIV). When we are faced with overwhelming or seemingly impossible situations, it is our duty to remain faithful and to leave the definition of success to God.

How do you define success? Does it line up with the will of God? Meditate on these questions as you go through your day.

A Risen King!

But the angel answered and said to the women, "Do not be afraid, for I know that you seek Jesus who was crucified. He is not here; for He is risen, as He said."

Matthew 28:5–6

Every year people climb a mountain in the Italian Alps and stand at an outdoor crucifix. There they remember that the Lord Jesus died. A tourist noticed that a little trail led off from the shrine of the cross. He made his way down the trail, and to his surprise, he found another shrine overgrown with brush. This shrine symbolized the empty tomb. Unfortunately, it had been neglected. Reflecting on the experience, the tourist said it reminded him of many Christians who stop at the cross and never proceed to the empty tomb.

If we make our final stop at the cross, we miss the core of Christianity. Without the resurrection, our faith is dead. Because Christ rose from the dead, our past is forgiven and our future is secure. The empty tomb represents victory for every Christian.

Especially at Easter, we need to take time to reflect on the meaning of the resurrection. For the Christian, the resurrection is a cause for great celebration!

Are You a Learner?

The disciples were first called Christians in Antioch.

Acts 11:26

We're prone to think of disciples as turbocharged Christians, but originally the terms *disciple* and *Christian* were synonymous. Differentiating between the two has had the effect of watering down the original demands of following Christ.

Dallas Willard puts it this way: "The word *disciple* occurs 269 times in the New Testament. *Christian* is found three times, and was first introduced to refer precisely to the disciples. The disciple of Jesus is not the deluxe or heavy-duty model of the Christian—especially padded, textured, streamlined, and empowered for the fast lane of the straight and narrow way. He stands on the pages of the New Testament as the first level of basic transportation in the Kingdom of God."

Modern Christians don't often think of using the term *disciple* to describe themselves, but Jesus never put the terms of discipleship in small print. He's not content for us to be distant followers, and He will not rest until we learn to take His yoke upon us and learn from Him (Matthew 11:29).

The word *disciple* means learner, and it refers to someone who is committed to learning to live the Christ-life in conscious, daily obedience. Is that you?

To Help Us Grow

The testing of your faith produces patience. But let patience have its perfect work, that you may be perfect and complete, lacking nothing.

James 1:3–4

In order to use us, God sets in motion a plan for shaping us into the kind of people He wants us to be. Sometimes that means we experience awful pain, giving up what we want to keep and going forward into areas we'd rather leave unexplored. But if we are going to be used by the Lord for His purposes, that process has to take place. That's exactly what happened to Joseph. As a favored young man, beloved and chosen by his father as his heir, Joseph was unexpectedly dropped into a pit. Before he knew what was happening, he was a family slave in a foreign country, serving under a hard man. If ever a man had reason to be bitter, it was Joseph.

But the wonderful thing is that Joseph did not become bitter. He was able to dream, to recognize the fact that God was shaping him for ministry—using the tough times of his life to prepare him for something great. All of us go through trying times, and they don't happen by accident. God arranges those times to help us grow.

The Knowledge of Love

Knowledge puffs up, but love edifies.

1 Corinthians 8:1

Dr. Albert Schweitzer earned doctorates in philosophy and medicine and received a half-dozen additional honorary doctorates in medicine, theology, and music. He was an authority on Bach and won the Nobel Peace Prize in 1952. Yet despite his brilliance and acclaim, he is best known as a humble doctor who labored for decades in the equatorial jungles of Africa, bringing health and hope to the spiritually and physically needy.

When Albert Schweitzer dispensed medicine or performed surgery on a hurting African man or woman, they did not know how many languages Dr. Schweitzer could read and speak or how many academic degrees he possessed. They only knew him as the kind and gentle doctor who seemed to have a reverence for all of God's creation, whose words to them were comforting and encouraging.

In many ways, Albert Schweitzer was like the apostle Paul, who said we amount to nothing if our great knowledge is not couched in love (1 Corinthians 13:2). We can become more like Paul, who himself was like Jesus, when people discover first how much we care. Only then will they care how much we know.

People will always have a greater appreciation for your head once they appreciate your heart.

I Just Know

If a man dies, shall he live again?

Job 14:14

Four hundred years before Christ's birth, the Greek philosopher Socrates lay dying from poison. He was considered the wisest teacher in the world, but when his friends asked, "Shall we live again?" he could only answer, "I hope so, but no man can know."

In Job 14:14, another man asked the same question: "If a man dies, shall he live again?" It's an age-old question. It haunts many people and tests every religious persuasion—the most crucial question of the ages. In Hebrews 2:15, we find that some men live all their lives in bondage to the fear of death. Many are afraid that death will catch up with them. Without some assurance of life after death, death becomes a terrifying proposition. But that is exactly why we can celebrate Easter: the resurrection of Jesus Christ answers that age-old question once and for all. The resurrection takes Christianity out of the realm of philosophy and turns it into a fact of history. It proves that there is life beyond this life.

Student of the Scriptures

All Scripture is God-breathed and is useful for teaching, rebuking, correcting and training in righteousness, so that the man of God may be thoroughly equipped for every good work.

2 Timothy 3:16–17 NIV

When their son left for his freshman year at Duke University, his parents gave him a Bible, assuring him it would be a great help. Later, as he began sending them letters asking for money, they would write back telling him to read his Bible, citing chapter and verse. He would reply that he was reading the Bible, but he still needed money. When he came home for a semester break, his parents told him they knew he had not been reading his Bible. How? They had tucked ten and twenty dollar bills by the verses they had cited in their letters.

The rewards of Bible study are life-changing—even if there is no money between the pages. It is vital to spend time in God's Word because it is the guide to help you prosper in everything you do. Create new ways to revitalize your walk with the Lord—invest in new study materials, find an accountability partner, or rearrange your schedule to include a different environment in which to meet with God.

When you commit to reaching out to God, He has already committed to meeting you where you are.

A Gracious Offer

Be blameless and harmless . . . in the midst of a crooked and perverse nation, among whom ye shine as lights in the world, holding forth the word of life.

Philippians 2:15–16 KJV

When we "shine as lights" in the world, the testimony of our personal holiness makes an impact on those around us. But the testimony of a righteous lifestyle is incomplete if there is no explanation to accompany it. I never have believed too much in the power of the "silent" witness. But when a godly life is accompanied by the presentation of the Word of Life, the effect can be dramatic.

The Word of Life is the total message of God's Word. It not only brings life to those who are dead in their sins, but it also sustains life each day for the disciple who is nurtured by it. When we are told to "hold it forth," the word that is used is one that was often chosen to describe a host offering wine to a guest at a banquet. It is the picture of a gracious offer of the Gospel of Jesus Christ to those who do not know Him.

The Velvet Ant

Satan . . . transforms himself into an angel of light.

2 Corinthians 11:14

There's a strange little insect called the velvet ant—attractive, as ants go—garbed in a thick coat of tiny hairs that feel smooth and velvety. But it's all a disguise. This tiny creature isn't an ant at all, but a wingless wasp with a nasty sting. After injecting its victims with venom, it lays its eggs in their incapacitated bodies.

How like Satan! He's a venomous impostor who wants to implant his warped ideas into the dulled hearts of his victims. One of his cleverest strategies is to make evil seem desirable. Just consider today's movies. Sexual sin of every type is glamorized and glorified. Profanity appears as righteous indignation. Fame captivates. Fortune beguiles. Violence titillates.

Or take modern faith fads. Satan doesn't mind if we become religious, just so long as it remains politically incorrect to proclaim Jesus Christ as the only name under heaven whereby we must be saved.

Paul told the Corinthians, "I fear, lest somehow, as the serpent deceived Eve by his craftiness, so your minds may be corrupted from the simplicity that is in Christ" (2 Corinthians 11:3).

Be on guard! Don't fall for Satan's frauds.

Comfort in His Father

I am not alone, but I am with the Father who sent Me.

John 8:16

Although Jesus walked alone in His mission, suffered alone, was rejected by the world, and was denied by His friends, our lonely Savior had consolation. His heavenly Father was with Him: "And yet if I do judge, My judgment is true; for I am not alone, but I am with the Father who sent Me" (John 8:16).

Even though Jesus might have felt alone at times like we do, He knew He had a Father in heaven who would be with Him: "And He who sent Me is with Me. The Father has not left Me alone, for I always do those things that please Him" (v. 29).

Christ promises that people can find peace in Him: "Come to Me, all you who labor and are heavy laden, and I will give you rest" (Matthew 11:28).

Our Savior promises that He can relieve people's burdens, even the burden of loneliness. He has conquered loneliness for us by His death on the cross.

Spouses Who Never Give In

Therefore, what God has joined together, let no one separate.

Mark 10:9

On October 29, 1941, when England was being mercilessly attacked by German rockets and planes, Winston Churchill visited his alma mater. A verse honoring him had been added to one of the school songs; it spoke of "darker days." Churchill asked that it be changed to "sterner days." The days of the war were stern but not dark, he said. Churchill was committed to seeing the light of England's glory shine yet again.

Many marriages today are under attack by enemies such as discouragement, infidelity, unforgiveness, and bitterness. Spouses find themselves wandering through dark days, ready to declare defeat. What they need is a Churchill-like, biblical kind of commitment and perseverance. Marriages can go through stern days without entering dark nights if the partners enter their marriage committed to defeating any enemy that comes against them. When your marriage encounters a stern enemy, recommit yourself to your spouse—and never give up.

Don't be committed to commitment. Be committed to the one you told "'til death do us part."

Live above Deception

I am the way, the truth, and the life. No one comes to the Father except through Me.

John 14:6

In John 14:6, Jesus said, "I am the way, the truth and the life. No one comes to the Father except through Me." Jesus is the truth. God accomplishes His will on earth through truth, and Satan accomplishes his purposes on earth through lies. When the child of God believes the truth, then the Spirit of God can work in him, God's Word can work in him, and he can be set free from deception.

But when we play with the deceptive words of Satan and allow that deception into our hearts, we open the door for him to wreak havoc in our lives and in the lives of our families. Every time there is destruction among God's people, it's because the deceiver has been allowed to have just a little bit of a foothold in someone's life.

Today, the spirit of deception is rampant. But let's not forget that in the midst of this problem, there is Jesus. In the midst of the deception, there is the Truth. In the midst of all of the seduction of our society, there is the absolute, rock-solid person of the Lord Jesus Christ—the Way, the Truth, and the Life. When we put our trust in Him, we can live above deception and on the level of truth.

The Right to Sacrifice

All things are lawful for me, but not all things are helpful.

1 Corinthians 10:23

One of the biggest issues facing lawmakers today is whether there should be limits on damages awarded in lawsuits where injury has occurred. Opponents of tort reform say it's impossible to place a limitation of value on personal injury. Proponents say the lack of limits is driving doctors out of business, since they can't afford the premiums on malpractice insurance.

Whose rights are more important? A citizen's right not to be permanently injured? A doctor's right not to be driven out of business? A lawyer's right to profit? Or a jury's right to decide what's "right"? The pursuit of rights has made America the most litigious society in the world. What ever happened to people giving up their rights for a greater good?

The apostle Paul said everything is "lawful," but not everything is helpful. For instance, Paul had the right to be paid by those he served. But he gave up that right, and others, for the sake of spreading the gospel without criticism from others. Look at your rights and see if limiting them would give you a greater voice with those you seek to serve.

A right is only a right until we discover it makes us wrong.

TRUE JOY

Let them shout for joy and be glad,
who favor my righteous cause.

PSALM 35:27

I read a quote once from a man who said, "I think I must be the happiest man in the world! I have never met anyone who has had as much fun as I have had." The words were not spoken by a playboy or a globetrotter or an adventurer. They were spoken by a Christian missionary by the name of Frank Laubach, whose life was dedicated to the cultivation of literacy among the backward people of the world. He never went searching for happiness—he just found it as a by-product of his search for something more important.

Dr. Laubach described delighted men and women weeping for joy when they discovered how to read. "No other work in the world could possibly have brought me so much happiness," he said. He didn't live with prosperity or worldly success, but he found happiness. True joy is a by-product, not a goal.

Impact

Follow Me.

Mark 1:17

John Wesley once said, "If I had three hundred men who feared nothing but God, hated nothing but sin, and determined to know nothing among men but Christ and Him crucified, I would set the world on fire."

Missionary Jim Elliot said, "He is no fool who gives what he cannot keep to gain what he cannot lose."

Jonathan Edwards, whose ministry sparked the Great Awakening, made this his life's motto: "Resolved: To follow God with all my heart. Resolved also: Whether others do or not, I will."

John Eliot, early missionary to the American Indians, said, "I can do little; yet I am resolved through the grace of Christ, I will never give over the work, so long as I have legs to go."

C. T. Studd, one of England's greatest athletes, shocked the world when he gave up fame and fortune to be a missionary to China. "If Jesus Christ be God and died for me, then no sacrifice can be too great for me to make for Him," he explained.

What would be the impact of your life if you were totally yielded to God?

Take the Power of the Lord

Thou art holy, O thou that inhabitest
the praises of Israel.
Psalm 22:3 KJV

When we go forth into the battle—whether we battle through a family crisis or a career problem—we have two strategies. We can go in our own weakness and face defeat, or we can go in the power of the Lord. How do we do the latter? We simply love, adore, worship, and praise His name. We know that God makes His home in our praises, and He will march with us even to the farthest corners of the earth and the end of the age. As we worship, our life strategies come together in ways we never could have formulated on our own. Then, as we face the challenges head-on, we keep right on praising, right on singing to the Lord, who is greater and stronger than any challenge that might stand in our path. The wonder of worship, guiding our everyday experiences, will totally change the way we see everything that confronts us.

What is that challenge for you today? I would urge you to focus not on the misery of the crisis but on the mastery of Christ. Then follow Him into battle. See if the demons themselves don't turn and flee from the gateway, terrified by the sounds of godly praise and adoration.

Short-Term Missions Trips

So Jesus said to them again, "Peace to you! As the Father has sent Me, I also send you."

John 20:21

William Carey is often called the father of modern missions. The number of his accomplishments in India was almost equaled by the number of obstacles he overcame to get there. He was told by a group of English ministers, "If God wants to save the heathen, young man, He will do it without your help or ours."

When he developed a burden for the lost in India, William Carey was not a career missionary. He was a young Englishman in poor health with a pregnant wife and small children underfoot. That is, he was a lot like the average Christian today—just trying to make ends meet and keep life together. But he also had something else, a burning question he could not escape: "Who will reach the lost if I don't go?" He ultimately became a career missionary, but he started by saying yes to God.

From high schoolers to retirees, Christians today are discovering the blessing of sharing the Gospel and doing good works in other lands. Take a short-term missions trip, and see how God can change your life.

A career missionary is nothing more than a short-term missionary who keeps saying yes to God.

Come Out of the Grave

It was necessary for the Christ to suffer and to rise from the dead the third day, and that repentance and remission of sins should be preached in His name.

Luke 24:46–47

History is replete with those who have had delusions of grandeur about themselves. Some have even been willing to die for their cause. But, like all men, they were defeated by death. If we dug up their graves, we'd find their dead bodies. But that's what makes Jesus unique. He predicted His death, predicted His burial, and prophesied that one day He would come out of the grave victorious over death. Three days after His death, He did just that.

The Scriptures recorded it. All who have tried to disprove it have been defeated. Scientists, determined to destroy the Christian faith, have been unable, and many skeptics and atheists have been brought to faith after studying the death and resurrection of Jesus Christ. It is one of the most thoroughly documented events in the world's history.

Through His death we are redeemed, and through His blood our sin atoned, but all of that is meaningless if He did not come out of the grave. Christ's resurrection validated what He did on the cross.

The Heart of Worship

My heart greatly rejoices,
And with my song I will praise Him.

Psalm 28:7

In *Meditations from a Prison Cell*, F. Olin Stockwell, one of the last missionaries to leave Communist China, wrote about his imprisonment at a center where the Communist leaders were indoctrinating young people in Marxist ideology. Every afternoon and evening, the leaders would teach the young people and then set the teachings to music. China was singing herself into the Communist worldview, Stockwell wrote.

Everyone has had the experience of hearing a song on the radio or a hymn from childhood and being able to sing along "by heart." While it's our mind that remembers, we say "by heart" because of the emotional "hooks" these songs set in us. And it is from an emotional level—the level of the heart—that God wants us to worship Him as well as from the mind.

Some of the most heartfelt and theologically oriented worship in the Bible is found in the Psalms, the hymnbook of Israel. With the abundance of edifying Christian music available today in varying audio formats, there is no reason for the home and heart of every Christian not to be filled with worshipful songs.

Since God knows you "by heart," make sure yours is a heart of rejoicing.

Faithful over Few, Ruler over Many

Well done, good and faithful servant; you were faithful over a few things, I will make you ruler over many things.

Matthew 25:21

God owns everything and has decided to put some of it into our hands to manage. When the Lord looks down and sees an individual doing a good job administering a few things, He decides to put that individual in charge of a few more things. God evaluates our stewardship on the basis of how well we administer it, keeping His priorities in mind rather than our own. When He sees someone serving faithfully, He expands the responsibility, giving something else to be managed. But when He sees someone who manages God's resources based on a personal agenda, or who forgets to reflect the Spirit of God in his management, the Lord can choose to withhold any further responsibility.

That's why Jesus, in explaining the parable of the talents in Matthew 25:21, said, "Well done, good and faithful servant; you were faithful over a few things, I will make you ruler over many things."

Why?

Peace I leave with you, My peace I give to you; not as the world gives do I give to you. Let not your heart be troubled, neither let it be afraid.

John 14:27

There are six interrogative words commonly used in discourse between people: *who, what, when, where, why,* and *how.* Of these six, one is used more frequently than the others in times of personal anguish: why. It is human nature to want to know why things happen the way they do. And for Christians, why means, "Why did God allow it?"

The disciples of Jesus surely asked "Why?" questions more than once in their relationship with Jesus. But at no time did they wonder why more seriously than when their lives were in peril on the Sea of Galilee. A huge storm had come up while they and Jesus were crossing the water. While they feared for their lives, Jesus napped calmly in the back of the boat. They wondered, *Why doesn't Jesus do something?* When Jesus finally calmed the storm, He had a "Why?" question for them: why did they let their faith be overcome by fear (Mark 4:40)?

If you've been asking God "Why?" questions lately and receiving no answers, stay focused by faith on Jesus. He will still the storm at the right time.

It's okay to ask God why. It's even better to wait for the answer in faith instead of fear.

April 15

No Grumbling

Righteous lips are the delight of kings,
And they love him who speaks what is right.
Proverbs 16:13

Lest you think you will never be called to speak before the ruler of the land, remember that you do so at least once every year—on April 15. You communicate in writing, validated by your signature, certain things about your financial status over the previous year. It is your responsibility to communicate that information honestly and righteously and without grumbling.

A pastor friend of mine paid no taxes for many years because his salary was so low, and he told me how resentful he was the first year he had to pay income taxes. The first few years he even addressed his envelope on April 15 to the "Infernal Revenue Service" or the "Eternal Revenue Service." But he soon realized that he was not speaking righteously before the king and changed his attitude. It is our privilege as citizens to try to change the system through proper channels, but until it is changed we are to have "righteous lips" before the king.

Trusting in God for Friends

There is a friend who sticks closer than a brother.

Proverbs 18:24

Two young men, best friends since childhood, enlisted together in World War I. Their outfit came under a withering attack, and one of the men was mortally wounded. His friend crawled out amid the fire to rescue him and was mortally wounded himself. When he made it back to the trenches with the body of his friend, the rescuer was told he had wasted his life to reach a dead man. "It was worth it," he said. "The last thing my friend said before he died was, 'I knew you'd come, Jim.'"

These two men had the kind of friendship that Proverbs speaks about and that Jesus made reference to: "Greater love has no one than this, than to lay down one's life for his friends" (John 15:13). Those closest to God, like Abraham and the disciples of Jesus, were referred to as "friends" (James 2:23; John 15:15). In both cases, friendship meant being told the very plans and purposes of God. And in both cases, these friends repaid God's friendship with the highest human value: loving loyalty. Gaining loyal friends takes time, but you can start today by being a loyal friend yourself.

How good a friend are you? Think of a way this week to confirm your loyalty to those you value most.

What's Missing?

Faith is the substance of things hoped for,
the evidence of things not seen.

Hebrews 11:1

In a day of material prosperity, when it seems that we have no lack of anything, there is one thing we are missing: heroes. Too often, those we traditionally look to as heroes end up being tarnished in some way—leaving us to search again.

Some people are designated as heroes during their lifetimes for achieving great things. But those enshrined in Hebrews 11 are remembered for their faith—faith by which they changed the world of their day. The most compelling thing about the people listed in Hebrews 11 is that they were ordinary people—people like you and me. The only thing they had going for them is the same thing available to us: faith.

The Surprise Gift

[They] were astonished . . . because the gift of the Holy Spirit had been poured out on the Gentiles also.

Acts 10:45

C. S. Lewis's personal story in *Surprised by Joy* chronicles his journey to faith in Christ. The title reflects what he discovered: he was surprised by the joy he experienced once he received the free gift of salvation. He hadn't realized that joy would come as a result of faith.

The Bible is filled with examples of how God surprised people. The apostle Peter was certainly surprised when he learned it was God's intention to offer salvation through the gift of the Holy Spirit to Gentiles as well as Jews (Acts 10). And every Christian who truly understands the mercy and grace of God must stand amazed at the forgiveness God offers in Christ.

That we are accepted into, instead of banished from, God's presence is perhaps His biggest surprise ever. Knowing how good surprises feel, have you surprised anyone lately with a gift of grace, appreciation, encouragement, forgiveness? Give someone today the pleasure of being surprised by your unexpected gift of love.

The better people know our faults, the more meaningful are the surprise gifts we receive from them.

Investing in Our Children

Only take heed to yourself, and diligently keep yourself, lest you forget the things your eyes have seen. . . . And teach them to your children and your grandchildren.

Deuteronomy 4:9

The values that we instill in our children are the values by which they will raise their families. And so the life of our investment is not just one generation, it is generation after generation. The key issue is not only what our children are now, but what they will become after internalizing the values we have passed on to them. And the clearest evidence of what they have internalized is what they pass on to their own children. A parent's influence on his child will have a long-term, lasting impact. Just as a seed takes time to germinate in the ground and bring forth fruit, so our teaching and influence on our children takes time to bear fruit as well. But it will bear fruit, for better or for worse.

The parent who wonders if the stress and strain of raising children—going against the flow of the culture, teaching them biblical values, spending the necessary time and money to give them the best opportunities—is really worth it need only remember the law of deposit and return. That which is sown today will bear fruit in the years to come.

The Persistent Mercy of God

Through the Lord's mercies we are not consumed,
Because His compassions fail not.
They are new every morning.
Lamentations 3:22–23

Francis Thompson was a nineteenth-century English poet who failed at early ventures and ended up destitute until taken in by a benefactor who was impressed with his poetry. "The Hound of Heaven" is his most famous work, telling of God's persistent pursuit of him until finally Thompson surrendered to His love.

"Ah, fondest, blindest, weakest, I am He Whom thou seekest," says the Hound of Heaven to the object of His pursuit. The persistent mercy of God is what captured the poet's heart.

God's relentless grace is also what saved Lot in the wicked city of Sodom. Before God judged the city, He gave Lot repeated opportunities to escape. Lot, his wife, and two daughters were finally dragged—kicking and screaming, as it were—from the city of sin. God's mercy was greater than Lot's own spiritual reasonableness, as is often the case with us as well.

Only heaven will tell how many times God has saved us from ourselves by working harder at our salvation and deliverance than we did. Have you thanked God recently for His persistent mercy?

Fortunately, our resistance is not as great as God's persistence.

Spiritual Aspirin

The joy of the Lord is your strength.

Nehemiah 8:10

Doctors speak of the "threshold of pain," the level of awareness at which a person feels pain. Some people have a high threshold; others have a very low threshold. When you take an aspirin, it has no effect on your physical problem. All it does is raise your pain threshold so that you must experience more pain before you are aware of it. The aspirin makes you *feel* better because you don't know how bad you *feel.*

Joy is like that. Happiness and joy are spiritual aspirin. When you are filled with the joy of the Lord, the hurts around you don't touch you so quickly.

I have found that music raises my threshold of psychological pain. On days when I am discouraged, I'll go home, turn on the stereo, and begin to listen to music. God uses that to assuage my soul and bring me out of pain. Is it any wonder that Saul required David to come and play for him on the harp to bring him out of his depression? That's what music can do in our hearts.

Every Day

Every day of my life was recorded in your book.
Every moment was laid out
before a single day had passed.

Psalm 139:16 NLT

While Elvis Presley was filming *Roustabout*, he met Larry Geller, a hairdresser with whom he developed a close friendship. The two discussed spiritual issues and Eastern religions. "What you're talking about," Elvis told Geller, "is what I secretly think about all the time." While discussing Elvis's purpose in life, the singer admitted he felt "chosen" but didn't know why. "Why was I plucked out of all of the millions of millions of lives to be Elvis?" he asked. We don't know if he ever found the answer.

The Bible teaches that God has a life purpose for us, and we discover it only through our relationship with Christ. He has something for us to do, something special for us to do today. If God were finished with us, He'd take us immediately to heaven. But He saved us, not just to take us to heaven, but to use us on earth. Every day we should be looking into His face, saying, "Lord, what do You want me to do? How can I advance Your work today? How can I serve You now?"

Give this day to the Lord, and ask for His will to be done in your life. Use every moment to fulfill His great purpose for you.

Christian, Never Give Up!

I press toward the goal for the prize of the upward call of God in Christ Jesus.

Philippians 3:14

In one of many attempts to scale Mount Everest before the successful climb in 1953, a team of mountain climbers made a final dash for the summit. Their courageous attempt failed and today they lie buried somewhere in the eternal snow. One of the party, who had stayed below when the final ascent was attempted, returned to London. One day as he was giving a lecture on mountain climbing, he stood before a magnificent picture of Mount Everest. As he concluded his address, he turned around and, addressing the mountain, he said, "We have tried to conquer you and failed; we tried again and you beat us; but we shall beat you, for you cannot grow bigger, but we can."

Just as a true mountain climber can never give up as long as there is still an unconquered peak, so Paul could not let the Philippian believers give up until they had reached maturity. His challenge to them was to keep on walking, keep on growing, keep on climbing until they reached their potential in Christ.

Only One Missionary

I thank Christ Jesus our Lord who has enabled me.

1 Timothy 1:12

Because of her father's drinking problem, eleven-year-old Mary Slessor was putting in twelve-hour shifts in the mills, helping her family pay their bills. She found she could prop books on her loom while working. As she read about the land of Calabar (modern Nigeria), Mary grew convinced she should go there as a missionary. In 1876, she sailed for West Africa aboard the SS *Ethiopia*, which, ironically, was loaded with hundreds of barrels of whiskey. Remembering how alcohol had hurt her family, she said, "Scores of barrels of whiskey, and only one missionary."

But what a missionary! Mary was a combination circuit preacher, village teacher, nurse, nanny, and negotiator who single-handedly transformed three pagan areas by preaching the Gospel. She diverted tribal wars and rescued women and children by the hundreds. For forty years, she labored as God enabled her.

If you feel like you're the only Christian at your school, office, or factory, rejoice! Don't underestimate how God can use you. One plus God is a majority in any setting.

Gifts of Life

It is more blessed to give than to receive.

Acts 20:35

Too often we forget that it is a blessing to be able to give. If we were as eager to do things for others as we are to receive favors, we would better understand the words of Jesus, "It is more blessed to give than to receive." A spring of water continually gives, while a pool continually receives. That is why the spring is always fresh, while the pool becomes stagnant and filled with refuse. If we knew the blessing of giving, there would be no need for drives, schemes, rummage sales, car washes, entertainments, and circuses to support church work. The poor preacher would not need to plead and urge and beg to keep things going. A giving church cannot die, but when a people stop giving, the church dies—spiritually as well as materially.

After a minister had earnestly pleaded for the cause of missions, a stingy old deacon complained, "All this giving will kill the church." The pastor replied, "Take me to one church which died from giving and I will leap upon its grave and shout to high heaven, 'Blessed are the dead which die in the Lord!'"

It Takes an Expert to Tell

[The Bereans] . . . searched the Scriptures daily to find out whether these things were so.

Acts 17:11

Lots of people who want to adorn themselves with diamonds use the classic counterfeit—cubic zirconium. While it's pretty easy to tell the imitations from real diamonds, scientists have devised a way to actually create real diamonds in the laboratory. These lab creations are so good that gemologists have a hard time distinguishing manufactured diamonds from mined ones.

To tell the difference, an expert's checklist is applied: color, intensity, weight, brilliance, and hardness. Without it, an imposter could pass off a two-day-old diamond for one that took thousands of years to develop. The same is true with spiritual truth. If Christians don't know their Bibles, spiritual imposters can pass off all manner of lies as truth. It's not enough for someone to do miracles in Jesus' name. Even Satan can disguise himself as an angel of light. We have to own, use, and study our Bibles so that we can know the truth. We have to have the desire of an expert—a desire not to be deceived.

If study and care are taken in determining the quality of a precious stone, how much more should the same effort be applied to the precious Word of God?

Experience Peace

You have heard Me say to you, "I am going away and coming back to you." If you loved Me, you would rejoice because I said, "I am going to the Father."

John 14:28

In order for Jesus to give us what He promised, it was necessary for Him to go back to heaven. He says in verse 28, "You have heard Me say to you, 'I am going away and coming back to you.' If you loved Me, you would rejoice because I said, 'I am going to the Father.'" Jesus is reminding His disciples (and us) that before His peace could flood their hearts, it was necessary for Him to ascend back to heaven and be with the Father.

You may wonder why that was true. I believe it was because the peace of the Lord Jesus is resident in the Person of the Holy Spirit, and the Holy Spirit could not be poured out upon humankind as He was at Pentecost until Jesus Christ ascended back to the Father. Jesus had just told the disciples (vv. 25–26) that the Holy Spirit would be sent by the Father after Jesus was no longer present with them. Because the Holy Spirit is resident in the life of every believer, it becomes possible for every believer to experience peace (Galatians 5:22).

It's All His

He who is faithful in what is least is faithful also in much.

Luke 16:10–15

A few years ago, the *Wall Street Journal* changed its format, adding a section devoted to personal money and life management, entitled "Personal Journal." The paper realized that many of the leaders of America's top companies are skillfully handling their companies, but their personal lives are in turmoil.

The word *manage* comes from the Latin word *manus*, meaning "hand." It has to do with handling things. For the Christian, that means handling God's things. The concept of stewardship has to do with wise management of our lives—recognizing we don't own anything. God owns it all; we simply manage it on His behalf.

Tithing, for example, is my acknowledgment that all my money is His and that I'm managing it well enough to return at least 10 percent into the work of His kingdom. As someone has said, the real question is not, "Should I give God 10 percent of my money?" but "Should I keep 90 percent of His money for myself?"

The earth is the Lord's and the fullness thereof. We are not our own; we are bought with a price (Psalm 24:1; 1 Corinthians 6:19–20). Let's manage wisely what He has entrusted to us, that His work and Word might advance.

Happy Is He Who Obeys

Where there is no revelation, the
people cast off restraint;
But happy is he who keeps the law.
Proverbs 29:18

Roger Staubach, who led the Dallas Cowboys to the World Championship in 1971, admitted that it was difficult for him to be a quarterback who didn't call his own signals. Coach Tom Landry told Staubach when to pass, when to run, and only in emergency situations could he change the play. Even though Staubach considered Coach Landry to have a "genius mind" when it came to football strategy, pride told him he should have been able to run his own defense.

Staubach later said, "I faced up to the issue of obedience. Once I learned to obey, there was harmony, fulfillment, and victory."

Every Christian needs to come to terms with the issue of obedience as well. True happiness and fulfillment come in obeying God's commands. Many have turned down the wrong corridor in search of happiness. They have chased after possessions, pleasures, and positions, only to find themselves at a dead end. Disillusioned by a world that promised happiness, they stand before a chasm of emptiness and trouble.

Have you been searching for happiness in all the wrong places? True happiness awaits those who obey Christ.

The Refreshment of Grace

The words of a wise man's mouth are gracious,
But the lips of a fool shall swallow him up.

Ecclesiastes 10:12

The most unsettling TV commercial in 1999 showed close-ups of three individuals bearing noticeable physical injuries and scars. There was no explanation—only a familiar logo at the end and the words, "Just do it." What made the commercial moving was the Joe Cocker song playing throughout in the background: "You are so beautiful . . . to me."

Granted, the commercial was for shoes. But there was another message as well: true beauty and grace is not a matter of physical perfection. Some of the most refreshing people to be around are those who have overcome serious limitations in their lives. Their gracious attitude seems to say, "I may not have everything that's possible, but I'm doing everything possible with what I have been given."

There should be no bounds to the graciousness of those who know Christ since God has made all grace abound to us to make us sufficient in all things (2 Corinthians 9:8). Wherever we go as Christians, we should take with us the refreshment of the gospel of grace.

Instead of "Just do it," Christians should "Just dispense it"—the grace of God, that is.

The Man with a Plan

He who has begun a good work in you will complete it until the day of Jesus Christ.

Philippians 1:6

When a young teenage girl named Joni Eareckson broke her neck in a diving accident, she thought it was the last step on her road to life. In reality, her mishap was actually the first step on a path of fruitfulness that she could not have imagined at the time. From her wheelchair, the quadriplegic Joni Eareckson Tada has touched millions of lives through her books, art, music, and advocacy for the disabled.

Joni's story is more dramatic than anything most of us will ever experience. But the depth of her suffering serves all the more effectively to illustrate the point: the day we think life has come to an end is the day God's plans and purposes are brought into even sharper focus. What we call "accidents" in life are nothing of the sort if we mean that accidents are random occurrences outside of everyone's control—unpredictable events with no more meaning than a ricocheting steel ball in a pinball machine. The same God who has every hair on your head numbered has the days of your life numbered as well.

The child of God should rest in the knowledge that our Father in heaven has a plan—and He is never late.

Meeting God Anywhere

Then the king said to me, "What do you request?" So I prayed to the God of heaven.

Nehemiah 2:4

A woman was in the habit of praying while ironing. One day she was thinking about the different kinds of lines—bus lines, clotheslines, fishing lines, telephone lines. "Why not a prayer line?" she asked herself. So she strung a short rope with names of people she knew needed prayer.

Now as she irons, she prays for each person by name. Not surprisingly, she gets regular requests to "hang me on your prayer line."

Prayer is a conversation with God. It doesn't matter where you are or what you are doing; you can meet with Him and pour out your heart in prayer. Most dictionaries define *prayer* as a reverent petition made to God, a god, or another object of worship. So how do you define *prayer* in your daily routine? Do you come to God with your petitions, thanksgiving, and praise each morning and evening? While you are driving your car or taking a break at work?

Creating habits with prayer helps you meet with God no matter where you are or how hectic your schedule is.

Timeless Refuge

Therefore we will not fear
Even though the earth be removed,
And though the mountains be carried
into the midst of the sea.
Psalm 46:2

We, as humans, are tied to time and space—they are all we know. We do not have a sense of the eternal. This earthly planet where we make our home is our point of reference in the universe. If it is stable, we feel secure. If it trembles and quakes, then we do as well. But God our refuge is not tied to this earth. In fact, He is not tied to anything. The entire earth could be removed, and the mountains could be carried into the midst of the sea; the waters could roar and be troubled, and the mountains could swell and shake—and God, our God, would still be a refuge.

The comfort for us in this is that nothing can happen to us in the time-and-space existence we live in that can impact God. He is, and will always be, a refuge for us. When things change around us, God doesn't change. When things are in an uproar around us, He is not. When things of the earth are in a calamitous state, He is at peace. Therefore He is always a timeless refuge where we can seek shelter and safety.

Ecology of the Heart

Keep your heart with all diligence,
For out of it spring the issues of life.
Proverbs 4:23

Increasing importance is being placed every year in America on cleaning up our environment—and rightly so. As stewards of God's creation, we have not always done the best job of preserving and protecting His handiwork. But Jesus talked about a different kind of ecosystem that deserves an even higher priority—cultivating the soil of the heart.

Jesus told a parable of a sower, seed, and soil. But as any good gardener will tell you, the effectiveness of the sower and his seed is totally dependent on the condition of the soil. In fact, Jesus said this was a key to understanding all His other parables (Mark 4:13). The parable of the soils says this: when God's Word is sown into heart-soil that is prepared, and that seed springs up and the new life is nurtured, salvation is the result. But if kingdom truth is sown into hard heart-soil, or if the soil dries up or is rocky, it stands little chance of saving the soul.

The parable of the sower and soils is not just about being saved; it's also about living as saved. Because seeds of God's truth come continually to our hearts, our hearts must be continually kept soft and fertile.

The first order of Christian ecology is the purity of the heart.

We Can Do It!

The Lord is with us. Do not fear them.

Numbers 14:9

I love the story of the Israelites when they were in Kadesh Barnea (Numbers 13). Moses sent spies into the land to check it out. The majority came back and reported, "We can't do it. We checked it out, and we are like grasshoppers in front of the giants of the land." But Joshua and Caleb went to the same land, saw the same giants, and probably experienced the same initial fear, but they said, "We're no match for them, but they are no match for God. We can do it!" Joshua and Caleb were honored for their faith. That's why they got to go into the promised land while the other spies didn't.

When you worship God, when you praise Him, when you honor Him, when you hallow His name, your vision will be expanded. You will become a more visionary business-person, a more visionary spouse, a more visionary parent. You will see life not in the little restricted areas that are yours, but you will begin to see that part of your life expand into that which God wants to do through you.

Reading God's Word

As newborn babes, desire the pure milk of the word, that you may grow thereby.

1 Peter 2:2

Bible scholar Wilber Smith once wrote, "One single, normal issue of *The Saturday Evening Post* contains as much reading matter as the entire New Testament. Thousands of people read *The Saturday Evening Post* through every week. The number of Christians who read the New Testament through every week, or even one whole book . . . are so few that we need not talk about it."

When Josiah became king in Jerusalem, he assigned workers to repair the temple. There they discovered a copy of the Law in the ruins. No one had seen it in years! Josiah quickly reasoned that Judah's idolatry was directly tied to the absence of the reading of God's Word. So he gathered all the people of Judah together, personally read to them the Law of God, and led them in a rededication to live according to God's Word (2 Chronicles 34).

What connections can you make between your spiritual life and your consistency in studying God's Word? If you are not consistently in the Bible, it will be impossible for the Bible to be consistently in you.

See God as He Really Is

When He is revealed, we shall be like Him, for we shall see Him as He is.

1 John 3:2

When you see God as He really is, you will worship Him as He desires to be worshiped. When Moses saw God and worshiped Him, he ended up giving us the Law. When Job saw God and worshiped Him, his whole family was restored to him and he got his second start. When Isaiah saw the Lord high and lifted up, he was inducted into the role of a prophet. When Saul was struck by the holiness of God, he became Paul, the greatest missionary evangelist who ever lived. And when John saw God and fell down before him as dead, he got up and wrote the book of Revelation, the great apocalyptic story of the New Testament. *Worship* is not a noun; it's a verb. Worship is your whole life dedicated back to God.

Finally, when you see God as He really is, you will look forward to the day when you will be like Him. In the New Testament we are told that someday we shall be like Him because we will see Him as He is. On that day we will be holy in perfection. We will be changed and the sin of our lives will be taken away. We're going to be beautiful because God is beautiful in His holiness.

A Barnyard of Pigs

Always be ready to give a defense to everyone who asks you a reason for the hope that is in you.

1 Peter 3:15

Without Christ, we're left with nothing but despair. William Lane Craig, the brilliant professor, said that a worldview that omits God is tragic. "Mankind is a doomed race in a dying universe," he wrote, "because the human race will eventually cease to exist, it makes no ultimate difference whether it ever did exist. Mankind is thus no more significant than a swarm of mosquitoes or a barnyard of pigs, for their end is all the same. The same blind cosmic process that coughed them up in the first place will eventually swallow them all again."

We're living in a world in which several generations have been taught a philosophy of despair. If evolution is true, we're nothing more than random accidents that emerged from primordial slime. There is no basis for hope. We have no future, no everlasting life.

Look closely and you'll see despair in the eyes of those around you at school or work. But we know that there is no hope apart from God, no joy apart from Christ, and no eternal salvation apart from the Gospel.

Today, let hope shine through you that others, seeing it, will ask about it. And then tell them about Christ, the King of the ages.

April 27

Strengthen One Another

All things are lawful for me, but not all things are helpful; all things are lawful for me, but not all things edify. Let no one seek his own, but each one the other's well-being.

1 Corinthians 10:23–24

You and I are called to build up and strengthen one another. I am called to build you up. You are called to build me up. I must be very careful not to tear you down by my actions, inaction, or words.

Tearing down is the polar opposite of our calling in Scripture. Edifying one another doesn't happen accidentally. Be on your knees before God, asking Him to fill you with His Spirit and show you opportunities. Be filled with the Word of God and begin to see people as individuals who need to be built up. Fight off the inevitable distractions and interruptions.

Paul is saying, "There are many things I might do and many things I might say. But my first concern ought to be, 'Will this build up or tear down my brother or sister in the body?'"

Pray Everywhere

And [Joseph] was there in the prison. . . . But the Lord was with Joseph and showed him mercy, and He gave him favor in the sight of the keeper of the prison.

Genesis 39:20–21

A famous preacher tells how, when he was a child, his mother paid a neighbor girl to walk the eight blocks to school with him and back each day. He finally convinced his mother to let him walk to school and back alone.

Years later, at a family party, he bragged about his independence as a child, how he had walked to school alone. "Did you think you were alone?" his mother asked. "Those first few years, I walked behind you to and from school. You never saw me, but I was there every day just in case you needed me."

That preacher's mother might have taken a lesson from the experience of Joseph in Egypt. When Joseph was thrown into prison, being falsely accused by Potiphar's wife, the Bible says that God was with him during his two-year imprisonment.

When we find ourselves imprisoned spiritually or emotionally by our circumstances, we need to remember that God is with us. Though it is dark in prison, pray anyway, every day, for God is near you and listening to your prayers. You cannot be in a place where God isn't.

The day you stop believing God is with you is the day you stop believing God.

Look to the Past

I remember the days of old,
I meditate on all Your works;
I muse on the work of Your hands.

Psalm 143:5

One thing we can do as we stand at the threshold of transition is to remember how God has helped us in the past. Has He not been good to you? I know there has been some heartache, hurt, and tragedy in the last year. That's true for all of us, more true for some. As we survey all of what God has done, especially in perspective, God has been good to us. He has met our needs. As God has helped us in the past, He will help us in the future. I have witnessed how God has time and again helped our church. Sometimes we, too, have been at the Red Sea, the enemy has been right on our heels, the wall has been right in front of us, and at the last moment God has opened the way. That's the God we serve. God will lead us into the future. We have no need to fear since the God of the past is the God of the present.

Rewards for Being Faithful

And your Father who sees in secret
will reward you openly.
Matthew 6:4, 6, 18

An eleventh-century German king, Henry III, grew tired of ruling. He applied to a monastery to spend the rest of his life in quiet contemplation. The prior asked if he, a king, could live out a vow of complete obedience. "I will," said the king. "Then you are accepted," replied the monk. "Your first duty is to return to your throne and serve faithfully where God has placed you."

It is easy to grow weary of being a spouse, a parent, an employee, or an employer. Some days we just want to quit! One woman who resisted that temptation was Abigail, the wife of Nabal (1 Samuel 25). Abigail was understanding and beautiful; Nabal was harsh and evil. Abigail even saved Nabal from the sword of David because she chose to honor her husband instead of humiliate him. She drew joy and strength from God, not her surroundings. And God rewarded her when Nabal died. David was so impressed with Abigail that he took her for his wife.

Are you tempted to leave it all behind—to throw in the towel? Don't do it. Make God your joy, and wait for His reward.

We aren't faithful to get a reward, but we are rewarded for being faithful.

The Greater Works

He who believes in Me, the works that I do he will do also; and greater works than these he will do, because I go to My Father.

John 14:12

It is exciting to me to understand what begins to happen as we pray. It's not that we pray in order that we might do the work. Take another look at the verse: "And whatever you ask in My name, that will I do" (John 14:13). If you ask anything in His name, He will do it.

That is no small distinction! Sometimes Christians get weary because we forget. We think God wants us to do His work for Him. That will make you tired very, very quickly. You can't do it! I can't do it! Our legs are too short to run with God! What Jesus is saying is this: when we pray, God is going to do His work through us, and we will be channels for His work.

I remember hearing about a preacher who said he could build a great church even if there was no God. I'm not sure that's a compliment. Sometimes we do commendable, praiseworthy things in the energy of our flesh. But when God begins to do the work through us, it is an entirely different proposition altogether. Incredible things begin to happen.

An Equal-Opportunity Sin

[Pilate] knew that the chief priests had
handed Him over because of envy.

Mark 15:10

One of the largest and most active federal government agencies is the EEOC—the Equal Employment Opportunity Commission. They are responsible for the statement seen nearly everywhere today: "... does not discriminate on the basis of race, color, religion, sex, or national origin." The EEOC's goal is to make sure everyone gets treated fairly in the workplace and other public and private venues.

Many people are surprised to find that jealousy is an equal-opportunity sin. People think only the poor, the ungifted, the lower classes, the uneducated, or the common man ever get jealous. After all, of whom or what would "the rich and famous" have to be jealous?

Yet anyone can be jealous of someone who has something he or she wants but doesn't have. In Jesus' day, the Pharisees were jealous of Jesus because He was loved and appreciated by the people. Mark 15:10 says that the Pharisees handed Jesus over to Pilate "because of envy." Anyone who is dissatisfied and discontent is a prime candidate for jealousy and envy.

The strongest defense against the attacks of jealousy is a heart that is grateful for what God has done in your life and for what He is doing in the lives of others.

April 30

Our Hope for New Bodies

The Lord Jesus Christ . . . will transform our lowly body that it may be conformed to His glorious body.

Philippians 3:20–21

While we don't know exactly how our bodies are going to be changed in that glorious day, we do know that the limitations and pain and suffering and death will be forever gone! To the Corinthians, Paul said that our bodies will be buried in decay and raised without decay; they will be sown in humiliation and raised in splendor; they will be sown in weakness and raised in strength; they will be sown a physical body and raised a spiritual body (1 Corinthians 15).

Our new bodies will be like the glorious body of our Lord Jesus Christ. Apart from the resurrection of Jesus Himself, there are only three resurrections recorded in the Gospels: the son of the widow of Nain, the daughter of Jairus, and Lazarus. All of these situations began in mourning until Jesus came; then that sorrow was turned into joy and gladness. Jesus said of Himself, "I am the resurrection and the life" (John 11:25). Whenever the life of Jesus meets death, death is always defeated. When He comes again, death will be dealt its final blow. As Paul said to the Corinthians, "Death is swallowed up in victory" (15:54).

ROWING UPSTREAM

Put away the foreign gods which are among you, and incline your heart to the LORD.

JOSHUA 24:23

As John and Debbie canoed down the Arkansas River, they decided to turn around and try rowing upstream for a while. It took about ten minutes for exhaustion to set in, and they gladly reversed course and let themselves be carried.

The current of our culture is downward, and many people just drift along with the moral flow. Living for Christ is like rowing upstream. The entertainment industry churns out nonstop programs and movies designed to convert us to secular thinking.

Take romance and marriage, for example. If a visitor from space watched an evening of television, he'd think premarital sex was the greatest discovery in history. He would see divorce, cohabitation, same-sex marriage, and immodesty portrayed as glamorous and glorious.

Yet the Bible says, "Among you there must not be even a hint of sexual immorality, or of any kind of impurity, or of greed, because these are improper for God's holy people" (Ephesians 5:3 NIV). We can't escape our culture, but we don't have to be shaped by it. We have to paddle against the current.

How long can we stay at the oars? The Lord strengthens those who obey Him. Trust Him to row against the flow.

MAY

I will never leave you nor forsake you.

—Hebrews 13:5

Every Day with God

Every day I will bless you,
And I will praise Your name forever and ever.

Psalm 145:2

A good way to think of eternity in the future is to think of it in terms of today. Has God provided for you and cared for you today? Not yesterday or tomorrow, but today? Wherever you are today, as you are reading this, has the Lord sustained you today?

Things aren't perfect, I realize. They never will be on earth. But regardless of today's imperfections, we can still confess that God has blessed us and is watching over us.

Well, with God, every day is today. He is eternal. Do you think God is sitting up in heaven wringing His hands over what might happen to you tomorrow or the next day? God sees the end from the beginning. God lives in the eternal now. And if I am okay with God in the now, I have nothing to fear from the future, for every day with God is today, and He can be trusted.

Cherishing God's Word

How sweet are Your words to my taste,
Sweeter than honey to my mouth!
Psalm 119:103

In his famous volume *How to Read a Book*, Mortimer Adler notes the one time when everyone reads as they should: when reading a love letter. They read it over and over, between the lines and in the margins, taking into account context, insinuation, and implication. Words, phrases, punctuation, and style—all are important to the person in love. A love letter is the most cherished writing in the world.

Isn't it ironic that the world's greatest love letter has not been more cherished by those to whom it was written? The Bible can be rightly viewed as God's love letter to mankind—a disclosure of His love, a record of His sacrifice for His beloved bride, a promise of His faithfulness and fidelity.

How many of us still have shoeboxes filled with letters and cards from the days of our courtship, still savored after so many years? Our hearts and passions are stirred afresh when we read them, just as they would be if we pored over God's letter to us with equal fervor.

Next time you open your Bible, read it as a love letter from God to you and see what a difference it makes. To give God's words the honor they are due is to cherish them above all others.

God Never Sleeps

Behold, He who keeps Israel
Shall neither slumber nor sleep.
Psalm 121:4

It is one of the most amazing facts about our God that He never slumbers or sleeps. What good is a God who is not there when you need Him? Elijah caught the idolatrous prophets of Baal on this very point in 1 Kings 18.

Elijah arranged a contest on the top of Mount Carmel to demonstrate to the prophets of Baal that the God of Israel was the only real and true God. They set up an altar with sacrifices on it, and whichever "god"—either Baal or Yahweh—could consume the sacrifices with fire from heaven would be the true God.

Just when the prophets needed Baal to prove his existence, he was taking a nap. Elijah seized the moment and called out to the true God, who sent down fire from heaven that licked up the sacrifices on the altar in a mighty display of His existence and His power. Think of yourself in your time of need on your journey through this life. Which "god" would you rather call upon to help you? The God of Israel neither slumbers nor sleeps. He is there at all hours of the day for you.

Succeeding at Failing

Get Mark and bring him with you, for he is useful to me for ministry.
2 Timothy 4:11

One of the most unusual sets of circumstances in the New Testament is that surrounding Mark, the cousin of Barnabas. Paul and Barnabas took young Mark with them on a missionary trip, but he returned home before the end of the trip for reasons not revealed in Scripture. Whatever Mark's reasons, Paul apparently thought they were unjustified since he refused to take Mark along on a subsequent trip (Acts 15:38).

Did Mark fail at being a missionary? Judging from Paul's response, it would appear he did. While the New King James Version says Mark "departed" from Paul and Barnabas, the word probably is closer to "deserted"—a more negative connotation. It's probably reasonable to conclude that Mark did fail at being a missionary.

But did that make him a permanent failure? Apparently not, for the same apostle Paul who was so disappointed in Mark counted him a valuable coworker in ministry later in his life. This is a perfect example of how to succeed at failing: fall, get up, and continue on. The next time you fail, make sure it is a temporary experience, not a permanent label.

Don't get "failing" and "failure" confused. Failing is nothing more than the back door to success.

Whatever He Chooses

For who in the heavens can be compared to the Lord?
Who among the sons of the mighty
can be likened to the Lord?

Psalm 89:6

A young boy was waiting after church for his family, and the pastor struck up a conversation with him. Since the boy had just come from Sunday school, the clergyman decided to ask a little question to see how much he was learning. He said, "Young man, if you can tell me something God can do, I'll give you this apple." The boy thoughtfully replied, "Sir, if you can tell me something God can't do, I'll give you a whole box of apples."

There really isn't anything God can't do. The Bible speaks of God's almighty power by using the word *omnipotent*. To be almighty is to have all the power. Only God has all the power. A theologian has defined the omnipotence of God like this: it is the power of God, or His ability and strength, whereby He can bring to pass whatsoever He pleases, whatsoever His infinite wisdom may direct, and whatsoever His purity of will may resolve. In other words, God is able to do whatever He chooses to do.

Law of the Harvest

Do not be deceived, God is not mocked; for whatever a man sows, that he will also reap.

Galatians 6:7

In 1687, Sir Isaac Newton set forth a theory we call the law of gravity. While revised by Einstein and others along the way, the law has remained an immutable principle of nature that governs the universe. Another immutable law, found in both the physical and spiritual realms, was cited by biblical writers centuries ago: the law of the harvest.

The law of the harvest has three parts: no reaping without sowing; reaping is in proportion to sowing; and time separates sowing and reaping. We can understand how the law of the harvest works with money by observing the law of the harvest at work in nature. No farmer expects to reap a harvest without having first sowed his seed, nor does he expect to sow sparingly and reap bountifully. And no farmer expects to reap the day after sowing.

God applies those principles to our money as well: giving precedes receiving; we receive in proportion to our giving; and God chooses when to repay our giving. Unlike farmers, we can apply the law of the harvest anytime, anywhere—even today!

We bring pain on ourselves by violating the law of gravity. Are we doing the same thing spiritually by violating God's law of the harvest?

Angels Rejoice at Our Salvation

Likewise, I say to you, there is joy in the presence of the angels of God over one sinner who repents.

Luke 15:10

The Bible tells us that angels are aware of the moment each person repents of his sin and becomes a Christian. According to Luke 15:10, they rejoice. One writer says that "they set the bells of heaven to ringing with their rejoicing before the Lamb of God." Although the angels rejoice when people are saved and glorify God who has saved them, they cannot do one thing: they cannot testify personally to something they have not experienced. Angels have not been redeemed. They can only point to the experiences of the redeemed and rejoice that God has saved them. This means that throughout eternity, we humans alone will give our personal witness to the salvation that God achieved by grace and that we received through faith in Jesus Christ. As great as they are, angels cannot testify to salvation the same way as those who have experienced it.

It Takes Two

As a prisoner for the Lord, then, I urge you to live a life worthy of the calling you have received.

Ephesians 4:1 NIV

One story in circulation claims that a mother and son were eager to attend a concert by renowned Polish pianist Ignacy Paderewski. When the house lights dimmed, the mother discovered that the child was missing. As the curtain rose, the mother noticed in horror that her little boy was sitting at the keyboard, innocently picking out "Twinkle, Twinkle Little Star." At that moment, the great piano master made his entrance, quickly moved to the piano, and whispered in the boy's ear, "Don't quit. Keep playing." Leaning over, Paderewski reached down with his left hand and began filling in a bass part. Together, the old master and the young novice transformed a tense situation into a wonderfully creative experience.

Whether this story is true or not, it is a perfect example of the relationship we have with our heavenly Father. What we can accomplish on our own is hardly noteworthy. But with the hand of the Master, our life's work can be beautiful. Next time you set out to accomplish great feats, listen for the voice of the Master whispering in your ear, "Don't quit. Keep playing." Feel His loving arms around you. Know that His strong hands are there, turning your feeble attempts into true masterpieces.

Remember, God doesn't call the equipped; He equips the called.

Victory and Fruitful Labor

Therefore, my beloved brethren, be steadfast, immovable, always abounding in the work of the Lord, knowing that your labor is not in vain in the Lord.

1 Corinthians 15:58

The greatest encouragement man will ever know is the giving of Jesus Christ to our world. Through His death, burial, and resurrection, Jesus has written the word *hope* in every heart. Because He lives, we, too, shall live. Because He was victorious over death, our future is bright.

As we consider the encouragement of Christ's resurrection, we should respond in two definite acts of love. Both of these responses are illustrated for each of us by the great apostle Paul. They are recorded in the last two verses of 1 Corinthians 15, the Bible's great resurrection chapter.

First, we should express our gratitude to our Father in heaven: "But thanks be to God, who gives us the victory through our Lord Jesus Christ" (1 Corinthians 15:57).

And second, we should do as Paul did—use the truth of Christ's resurrection to encourage others: "Therefore, my beloved brethren, be steadfast, immovable, always abounding in the work of the Lord, knowing that your labor is not in vain in the Lord" (1 Corinthians 15:58).

A Second, Deeper Look

It is good for me that I have been afflicted,
That I may learn Your statutes.

Psalm 119:71

Many of Fred Astaire's movies rank as classics of the silver screen. But in 1932, when Astaire was just starting out in Hollywood, he went to a screen test to try out for a part. After the audition, the evaluator wrote, "Can't act. Can't sing. Can dance a little." That memo hung over the actor's fireplace in his Beverly Hills home throughout his successful career as an actor, singer, and dancer.

There is no end to the stories of people who succeeded wildly after failing miserably—often for years. The lessons are usually similar in every case: don't give up, try harder, dig deeper, don't settle for no, and winners never quit.

There's nothing wrong with such advice, but it only addresses one level of our lives. For the Christian, failure can represent an entirely different set of realities: God is at work in me for His own good pleasure (Philippians 2:13); God can take every event and cause it to work for good (Romans 8:28); God is shaping my character to be like Christ (Romans 8:29). If you have failed recently, take a second, deeper look. God is at work to accomplish what only He can.

Every time we fail, we eliminate one more option that is proven not to work.

The Adulterous Woman

Neither do I condemn you; go and sin no more.

John 8:11

Men have no right to judge others. No story better illustrates this than Jesus' encounter with the adulterous woman:

As [Jesus] was speaking, the Jewish leaders and Pharisees brought a woman caught in adultery and placed her out in front of the staring crowd. "Teacher," they said to Jesus, "this woman was caught in the very act of adultery. Moses' law says to kill her. What about it?" They were trying to trap him into saying something they could use against him, but Jesus stooped down and wrote in the dust with his finger.

They kept demanding an answer, so he stood up and said, "All right, hurl the stones at her until she dies. But only he who never sinned may throw the first!" Then he stooped down again and wrote some more in the dust. And the Jewish leaders slipped away one by one, beginning with the eldest, until only Jesus was left in front of the crowd with the woman. Then Jesus stood up again and said to her, "Where are your accusers? Didn't even one of them condemn you?" "No sir," she said. And Jesus said, "Neither do I. Go and sin no more." (John 8:3–11)

A Mother's Love

I will give him to the Lord all the days of his life.

1 Samuel 1:11

Nothing prepared Mary Lee Bright for the pain of losing a stillborn child and of nearly dying herself. When she learned she was expecting again, friends feared and were afraid. This pregnancy, too, appeared troubled. But Mary determined to carry the child to term, and she withdrew to her devotions. "I just searched the Scriptures and prayed without ceasing," she said. "As I did this, the strong feeling came over me that I would be all right and so would the child. It was at this time, before he was born, that I dedicated him to the Lord. And do you know, he turned out wonderfully well!" He did indeed, for that baby became a great evangelist—Bill Bright, founder of Campus Crusade for Christ.

It must have been difficult for Hannah to give her child to the Lord before he was even born. But dedicating something to the Lord is the surest way of keeping it, and entrusting our loved ones to the Lord is the safest path for them to follow.

Be Humble, Be Wise

When pride comes, then comes shame;
But with the humble is wisdom.

Proverbs 11:2

On December 6, 2001, American evangelist Billy Graham received a singular honor from the British Empire. He was given an honorary knighthood in recognition of his Christian service benefiting England and the world. When given his award by the British ambassador to the United States, the evangelist's remarks were characteristic: "I accept it with humility and unworthiness." He went on to say that he looked forward to laying his honorary knighthood, along with any other recognition he has ever received, at the feet of Jesus Christ, who deserves all the honor and praise.

One has to wonder if the impact of Billy Graham and his ministry around the world is in any way connected with his personal spirit of "humility and unworthiness." In light of biblical testimony concerning humility, the answer has to be yes. God gives skill and advancement to the humble and actively resists (stands in the way of) the proud. If you have a destination in view, you can remove at least one serious roadblock by being humble on the way.

Skills for living are not acquired as much as they are received in the form of grace—given by God as wisdom to the humble.

Faithful Provider

The Lord has heard my cry for mercy;
the Lord accepts my prayer.

Psalm 6:9 NIV

A little girl approached her father and asked for a nickel. The father drew out his wallet and offered her a five-dollar bill. But the little girl, not knowing what it was, would not take it. "I don't want that," she said. "I want a nickel."

Are there times when we deal with our heavenly Father as this little girl dealt with her earthly father? Do we sometimes ask for some small favor and refuse His offer of a blessing a hundred times more valuable?

When we come to God with petitions, He promises to answer. But it is not always the answer we want to hear. However, it is the answer that God knows is best for us.

We must believe that God will be a faithful provider, no matter what our circumstances. Psalm 111:5 says, "He provides food for those who fear him; he remembers his covenant forever" (NIV). What an amazing promise: He will never forget about our needs, and He will sometimes bless us beyond our wildest imagination. He will accept our prayers and our cries for mercy. What an awesome God we serve!

The Spirit's Translation

The Spirit helps us in our weakness. We do not know what we ought to pray for, but the Spirit himself intercedes for us with groans that words cannot express.

Romans 8:26 NIV

I heard a story about a pastor who frequently visited a woman who was dying from cancer. One day she told him, "I'm so often racked with pain that it's hard for me to gather my thoughts to pray. Even when I rally a little from the influence of the medication, my mind is still so dull I can't concentrate for any length of time."

He looked at her a moment and said, "Well, you can groan, can't you?"

"Oh yes," she replied. "My days are spent doing that."

"Well, never mind that you can't formulate prayers," the pastor told her. "The Holy Spirit translates your groans into eloquent petitions and presents them to the Father!"

Can you remember moments in your life when your heart was so heavy that you couldn't find words to speak to God? Sometimes, even though we're on our knees in an attitude of prayer, we can only manage to sigh or groan or whisper the Lord's name. And in those moments, according to Paul, the indwelling Holy Spirit takes our sighs and our groans and brings those prayers to God. He understands the inward turmoil in our life. He is the searcher of our hearts, and He knows us better than we know ourselves.

Joseph the Generous

And Joseph took the body and wrapped it in a clean linen cloth, and laid it in his own new tomb, which he had hewn out in the rock.

Matthew 27:59–60 NASB

Christian novelist Bodie Thoene once worked for Hollywood film star John Wayne as a scriptwriter. Wayne read an article she had written and liked it; a relationship developed, and she began writing for Wayne's production company. Later, when Thoene asked the famous actor why he had been so generous toward her, he answered, "Because somebody did it for me."

Receiving seems to stimulate giving. That was true for a man in the four Gospels, Joseph of Arimathea. He was a prominent member of the Jewish Council in Jerusalem, meaning he was wealthy and well-respected. But like another member of the Council, Nicodemus, Joseph had become a disciple of Jesus, albeit a secret one for fear of retaliation from the Jews.

But when Joseph watched Jesus suffer and die for him, he could remain a secret follower no longer. He went to Pilate and got permission to bury the body of Jesus in his own new tomb. Joseph was transformed by Jesus' generosity toward him. That ought to be true of everyone who claims to be His follower.

Generosity in giving is often a response to gratitude in receiving.

When God Delays

Can a woman forget her nursing child, and not have compassion on the son of her womb? Surely they may forget, yet I will never forget you.

Isaiah 49:15

Let's be honest. Sometimes when God delays, we feel forgotten. Someone has said that it is the length of the trial, not the severity of it, that is most threatening to us. When a painful trial begins, we rally our resolve, we call our comrades, and we determine to defeat our "enemy." But as the days wear on and nothing changes, we lose heart and begin to grow weary. We never imagined God would let us suffer so long!

God says it is as likely that He would forget us as it is that a mother would forget her nursing child (Isaiah 49:15–16)—though it doesn't seem like it in the midst of our trials. Not only can we feel forgotten—we can feel forsaken as well.

So when you pray to God in your hour of seeming abandonment, just remember: God has heard that prayer before, even from His own Son. He knows what you are going through. In fact, He deliberately turned His back on His own Son so that He would never have to turn His back on us. He tells us, "I will never leave you nor forsake you."

Trust in Him

None of them that trust in Him shall be desolate.
Psalm 34:22 (KJV)

Like most women, missionary Amy Carmichael wanted to be married. But her work would have been impossible for a married woman, and God gave her Psalm 34:22 as a special promise. Amy's struggle was deeply personal, one she didn't divulge for years. Finally she told the story. "I went away alone to a cave in the mountain. . . . I had feelings of fear about the future. . . . The devil kept whispering, 'It's all right now, but what about afterwards? You are going to be very lonely.' And he painted pictures of loneliness. . . . And I turned to my God in a kind of desperation and said, 'Lord, what can I do? How can I go on to the end?' And He said, 'None of them that trust in Me shall be desolate.' That word has been with me ever since."

In heaven, we'll have no loneliness, no loss, no privation, and no painful sacrifices. But it's our joy now to yield ourselves fully to God, for no one who trusts in Him will ever be desolate.

How to Value Anything

He who tills his land will be satisfied with bread,
But he who follows frivolity is
devoid of understanding.
Proverbs 12:11

Many men of the world have understood the necessity of commitment when trying to accomplish great things. Spanish explorer Cortez landed at Vera Cruz in 1519 to begin his conquest of Mexico with a small force of seven hundred men. It is said that when his entire crew came ashore, he purposely set fire to his fleet of eleven ships. Presumably, his men on the shore watched their only means of retreat sink to the bottom of the Gulf of Mexico. There was now only one direction to move—forward into the Mexican interior to meet whatever might come their way.

This illustration of diligence is a stark rebuke to those who believe that all of life's fruits can be had instantly and with little or no sacrifice. But in God's economy, the germination-cultivation-harvest cycle remains. And it is based on the application of diligence and commitment. Are you facing the temptation to give up on something important? What does your level of commitment say about the importance of the cause you have committed to?

The value we place on a relationship or project or opportunity can be measured directly by the degree of diligence we apply in working at it.

A Body of Praise

Now may the God of peace Himself sanctify you completely . . . spirit, soul, and body.

1 THESSALONIANS 5:23

One of the strangest individuals in early church history was Simon the Stylite. At age thirty-three, he began living atop a pillar in the desert. For thirty-six years, he lived on a platform that gradually reached a height of sixty feet. From there he preached to curiosity seekers who came by the thousands. After his death in AD 459, a monastery and sanctuary were built on the site of the pillar.

Simon the Stylite was an ascetic, a person who pursues spirituality by disavowing the material things of this world. Ascetics especially deny themselves any bodily pleasures—tasty foods, marriage, hygiene—believing that they are temptations to worldliness.

But ascetics miss an important point: the human body shares the same creation blessing as do the soul and spirit. Therefore, your body should be a medium for praise and a channel for worship just as your spirit is. In fact, "your body is the temple of the Holy Spirit," Paul said (1 Corinthians 6:19). Your body is that which the Spirit animates to bring glory to God.

An offering of your body to God brings glory to its Creator and Sustainer.

The God of All Grace

The God of all grace . . . called you to
His eternal glory in Christ.
1 Peter 5:10

God took Jacob through one experience after another to teach him to submit. Jacob even wrestled with God once, but his vow afterward rang hollow. Jacob didn't deserve any more chances, but God's grace stayed in effect. The Lord loved Jacob and disciplined him until he surrendered his life to God.

God is more forgiving than we can imagine. His continuing grace can take the sorry elements of a human life and use them for His blessed purposes. There is nothing more marvelous in the entire world than the power of God's grace. He forgives, He lifts up, and He transforms.

The great love of God's grace can heal broken hearts and mend broken lives. The Gospel comes to hearts that are broken by sin and despairing of redemption, and it offers peace, pardon, and purity. Only a God of grace could take a rebellious man like Judah and a wicked woman like Tamar and somehow use them in the line of our Blessed Redeemer. But that's what God does—redeem people. He came to reclaim the broken lives of His children. He is the God of all grace, and His grace abounds to you and me.

Survey Says . . .

He hears the prayer of the righteous.

Proverbs 15:29

The following statistics come from the Barna Research Group:

- Four out of five Americans believe that "prayer can change what happens in a person's life" (1994).
- Nine out of ten adults agree "there is a God who watches over you and answers your prayers" (1991).
- One out of five adults has a time of extended prayer with members of their household during the course of a typical week.

If someone were to take an inventory of your prayer life, how would you score? Although prayer isn't a competition between believers, it is a sign of constant communication in our relationship with God. When we don't take time to get on our knees, it is often evidence that we have strayed from our walk with Him.

So how do we approach God after being out of fellowship? Micah 6:6 says, "With what shall I come before the Lord, and bow myself before the High God?" We are to come back with praise and thanksgiving—and He will hear our prayers.

Psalm 3:4 reminds us, "To the Lord I cry aloud, and he answers me from his holy hill" (niv). Rewrite your survey, and be faithful in prayer.

One-on-One Care

Are not two sparrows sold for a copper coin? And not one of them falls to the ground apart from Your Father's will. . . . Do not fear, therefore; you are of more value than many sparrows.

Matthew 10:29, 31

God is the God of the individual. He is the God who would spare Sodom if someone there could demonstrate faith. When the destruction came, He got His people out because of His love for the individual. He was the one who saw Nathanael, sitting under a fig tree, and later talked to him one-on-one. He's the one who cared about Cornelius, who was praying by the sea. He's the one who sent two messengers to Rahab so that she could know what to do before the judgment came.

God knows who you are. He sees you in the massive crowd on this overpopulated globe! He knows you, He loves you, and He cares. The same God who is the God of patience is a God of passion for the individual.

He is the only one who can take us as we are and not only keep us from the judgment but also lift us up out of the mire and put our feet upon the Rock. He'll give us all we need to become all He ever wanted us to be.

Everybody Submits to Somebody

Let every soul be subject to the governing authorities. For there is no authority except from God, and the authorities that exist are appointed by God.

Romans 13:1

As mentioned earlier, the Scottish reformer Samuel Rutherford published *Lex, Rex, or The Law and the Prince* in 1644. In this book, he challenged the prevailing notion of the divine right of kings—that whatever the king says is the law. Rutherford reminded rulers that they are not authorities unto themselves, but they are all under God's authority. God is the ultimate source of all authority in this world.

No matter how much authority we think we have in any setting, we quickly discover there is someone with more. But no one's authority is ultimate, for all authorities are ultimately subject to God. From parents to potentates, the apostle Paul reminds us that God establishes all authorities on earth. Unless an authority requires us to break a law of God, we should make submission and honor a part of our lives (Acts 5:29).

Who are the authorities in your life? If there are some you find it difficult to submit to, make it a practice to pray diligently for them. It's hard to resist someone you're praying for.

Submission to authorities shows we understand the nature of authority.

Rooted in the Word of God

His delight is in the law of the Lord. . . .
He shall be like a tree
Planted by the rivers of water.
Psalm 1:2–3

Your strength comes from God's Word. The psalmist says the righteous person is like a tree planted by streams of water. Just like a tree is nourished by the constant supply of water—without which, under the blistering sun, the tree would surely die—so the life that is rooted in the Word of God will also be established and will be strong.

Your stability comes from God's Word. A fruit tree that is planted by the banks of the river suggests stability. The tree is firmly rooted in the soil so that it can resist the storm. There are trees standing today that were here when this country was discovered. If you go to the right place, you can see trees that are just as magnificent and beautiful as they were in their prime. Why? Because they've got a tremendous root structure and they are strong. If you've ever seen a redwood, a tree so big that you can drive your car through the middle of it, then you know what invincible means. That's the kind of stability God wants His people to have. And when you put your roots deep down into His Word, you will become a person of great stability.

The Riches of Grace

In Him we have redemption through His blood, the forgiveness of sins, according to the riches of His grace.

Ephesians 1:7

In 1997, the *New York Times* reported on a conference where Bill Gates, founder and CEO of Microsoft, gave an address. In the question-and-answer session that followed his talk, a medical doctor asked Gates whether, if he were to lose his sight, he would exchange all of his wealth to have his sight restored. Gates, who in 1997 was worth $35 billion, said he would indeed.

Microsoft's stock's highest-ever selling price was $119.75. If Gates had never sold any of his original Microsoft stock, on the day of that highest share price he would have been worth $384.3 billion. We can assume he would have traded all that to regain his sight as well.

But did you know those numbers pale in comparison to another set of riches that were exchanged that we might have sight? The riches of Christ's glory in heaven were exchanged that our spiritual eyes might be opened and we may recognize the love and forgiveness of God (Philippians 2:5–8). We may never have many of this world's riches, but we have been given riches of grace beyond comparison.

The riches of grace are not affected by the stock market or economic conditions. They represent wealth we cannot lose.

Joy That Stays

I will see you again and your heart will rejoice,
and your joy no one will take from you.

John 16:22

The joy of Christ doesn't go away. Have you noticed how easily earthly joy can leave? Have you discovered how simple it is for your gladness of today to become your sadness of tomorrow, for your sweetness of the morning to turn into the bitterness of the night? Have you discovered how the people you thought were your friends today can become your enemies tomorrow, the wisdom you thought was so great yesterday is foolishness today?

Nothing seems to be too stable in the world. You can't really count on much anymore. But the joy of Christ is a continual, never-ending, absolutely constant joy when we follow the principles of the Word of God. This joy survives all the difficult times in life. This joy is not hinged on happenings but on a Person.

In John 16:22, Jesus says, "Therefore you now have sorrow; but I will see you again and your heart will rejoice, and your joy no one will take from you." Isn't that something? Jesus says the joy He wants to give every one of His children is the kind of joy you don't have to lose. Nobody can take it away from you!

A Sacrificial Mother

When Jesus therefore saw His mother . . . He said to His mother, "Woman, behold your son!"

John 19:26

She was the twenty-fifth child in the English family of a religious dissenter; she had little education and lived in a male-dominated age; she married an older man and bore him nineteen children, nine of whom died. Her house burned down, her barn fell down, her health failed, and her pastor husband was either poor, jailed, or sick much of the time. But Susanna Wesley raised two sons, named John and Charles, who changed the world. Fortunately, Susanna Wesley wasn't a woman who thought the task of mothering to be beneath her.

And fortunately, a young Jewish woman named Mary didn't consider anything more meaningful than being the mother of the Son of God. From the beginning, she knew she was irreplaceable in the life of her child, and her sacrificial love remained strong to the end as she watched Him die for her and the world's sins. Jesus' efforts to care for Mary indicate just how much she meant to Him (John 19:27).

It is the heart of mothers to sacrifice and the need of mothers to be remembered. Surprise your mother this week with an unexpected token of love.

Motherhood is best defended by children who appreciate their mother's love.

When God Seems Unfair

You say, "The way of the Lord is not fair."
Hear now . . . is it not My way which is fair,
and your ways which are not fair?"
Ezekiel 18:25

That's not fair! Did you ever say that to your parents? Most of us have, and in some cases we have spoken the truth. But usually children feel that way because they're unable to see things from a more mature perspective.

In Isaiah 55:8–9, our heavenly Father says: "My thoughts are not your thoughts, nor are your ways My ways. . . . For as the heavens are higher than the earth, so are My ways higher than your ways, and My thoughts than your thoughts."

Abraham might have wondered if God was being too harsh with the population of Sodom, but he contented himself with this assurance: "Shall not the Judge of all the earth do right?" (Genesis 18:25).

He shall! God is righteous—that is, He is morally right, and He is right in His decisions and in all His ways. But God tempers His justice with mercy. If you sometimes feel God has treated you unfairly, tell Him so. Then ask Him to give you a higher understanding of His ways and a deeper dependence on His grace. You can trust the Judge of all the earth to do right.

Eventually Like Jesus

For whom He foreknew, He also predestined to be conformed to the image of His Son, that He might be the firstborn among many brethren.

Romans 8:29

Jesus Christ was both God and man. While it is difficult for us to comprehend such a union, the Bible makes it clear that Christ was a man of two natures. Though He was sinless, Jesus was like us in other ways. When we fail, we can draw encouragement from Hebrews 5:8: "Though He was a Son, yet He learned obedience by the things which He suffered."

Jesus had to "learn" obedience? Who does that sound like (besides your children)? It sounds like every Christian who has ever tried, and often failed, to put off the old man and put on the new (Colossians 3:9–10). Though we don't understand how or why the Son of God learned obedience, He did. And He suffered in the process. The way we know that He learned it is because when He faced the greatest test in His earthly life, He said to God, "Nevertheless not My will, but Yours, be done" (Luke 22:42).

Learning obedience is not easy. If you have recently chosen your will instead of God's, don't despair. You have been predestined to be conformed to the image of Jesus Christ. Let what you know you will become tomorrow keep you moving beyond what you are today.

The Indestructible Word

The grass withers, the flower fades,
But the Word of our God stands forever.
Isaiah 40:8

Down through the centuries, the Bible has always been hated and scorned by God's enemies. Men have gone out of their way to abolish it.

There have been some "heroes" of God's Word. William Tyndale devoted his life to spreading God's good news. He translated it, printed it, and distributed it. In the midst of the great distribution under Tyndale, the bishop got angry and wanted to get the Bibles out of circulation. He sent a friend to buy all the Bibles Tyndale had printed. "Whatever it takes, buy them and destroy them." The friend talked Tyndale out of the Bibles in spite of Tyndale's exorbitant price. The bishop's friend paid it, took the Bibles, and destroyed them. With the money from the Bibles, Tyndale bought materials to print thirty times as many Bibles and distributed them all over the country. When the bishop discovered more Bibles, he asked where Tyndale had gotten the funds to do this. His friend said, "You paid for it—you bought the Bibles and he distributed them."

Isn't that great! The Bible, defiantly, victoriously, convincingly, still stands. It remains the only inerrant, infallible, complete revelation man has ever received from his living God.

Today Is the Day

For this cause everyone who is godly shall pray to You
In a time when You may be found.

Psalm 32:6

A German farmer settled in Guatemala and became prosperous. While sailing back to Germany to visit family, he discovered that a tropical flea had taken up residence under a toenail and laid its eggs. Instead of dealing with the painful problem then and there, he let the toe fester so his family could see the foreign insect. By the time he got to Germany, blood poisoning had set in and the farmer died.

The farmer made a faulty assumption: that he had plenty of tomorrows in which to make a life-or-death decision. We are not guaranteed any set number of days on this earth, as the apostle James wrote: "[Life is] a vapor that appears for a little time and then vanishes away" (4:14).

Every person faces a life-or-death decision, spiritually speaking, and many put it off indefinitely. They think there will be plenty of time to consider God's place in their life: "I want to be saved, just not right now." Do you see the faulty assumption in that statement? None of us is guaranteed tomorrow. If you have been putting off a spiritual decision, make it today.

Today is the day of salvation for all who don't know what tomorrow holds.

Doing the Steps

The fear of the Lord is the beginning of wisdom,
And the knowledge of the Holy One is understanding.
Proverbs 9:10

A little boy comes to his father: "Daddy, I can't get this piece of my model car to fit. I know it goes right there, but there's just not room." After walking his son back through the directions, they discover together that the problem part should have been glued in on step four—but the little guy is nearly finished. "See what happens? They tell you to put this piece in early because they know there won't be room once the others are assembled."

Sometimes when life's pieces don't fit together, it may be because we skipped the first step. And the first step to gaining wisdom and God's knowledge is to fear the Lord. The word *beginning* can mean either "the first part" or "the main part." In both cases, the practical message is the same. The first step, and the continual priority, in fitting all the part of life together is to honor, revere, and worship God. Why? Because all knowledge and wisdom come from God, and we must seek answers through Him if we are to find them at all.

If you're stumped with a part of life that won't fit, humble yourself before the Lord. That's the first step in living life skillfully.

Strength

. . . strengthened with might through
His Spirit in the inner man.
Ephesians 3:16

In 1998, after speaking at a Christian rally in New Delhi, India, Dr. P. P. Job received threats against his family. At the time, his son Michael was training at the university to be a medical missionary. One evening, a white Fiat with Delhi plates, traveling at a high speed, changed lanes, rammed into Michael, and sped away without stopping. Michael died from the injuries.

Dr. Job was inconsolable. "It happened because I am a preacher of the Word of God," he said. "I was shattered. There are no words to describe the pain I went through." But as he read his Bible, he found Philippians 1:12: "The things which happened to me have actually turned out for the furtherance of the gospel."

That verse strengthened Dr. Job's faith, imparting courage to advance the Gospel. Today there is a Michael Job Orphanage, a Michael Job High School, a Michael Job Residential Art and Training College, and a Michael Job Memorial Chapel. Multitudes have been inspired by this story, and God is gaining glory for Himself throughout India because a father was inwardly strengthened by the Holy Spirit.

Ask God for His inner strength to meet the challenges of your life too.

Problems Prepare Us for Ministry

[God] comforts us in all our tribulation, that we may be able to comfort those who are in any trouble, with the comfort with which we ourselves are comforted by God.

2 Corinthians 1:4

Problems in our lives make us sensitive to the problems of others. How could the men and women of God reach out to a hurting world if they had never experienced that same pain in their own lives? How can we put our arms around a brother facing disappointment if we have never experienced disappointment ourselves? Sometimes God allows problems in our lives so that we can better minister to someone else. That's exactly what happened to Joseph. From his humbling slave and prison experiences, he was able to fairly administer grain to a starving populace.

You see, problems have advantages. They provide us with opportunities if we will but look for them. They promote spiritual maturity if we let them make us better instead of bitter. They prove our integrity, produce a sense of dependency, and prepare our hearts for ministry. God allows problems so that we can learn and grow. We don't like them, but they are necessary if we are to grow and change. Don't run from the pressures God wants to use to make you His perfect example of Christlikeness.

The Real Meaning of Sharing

Rejoice with those who rejoice, and
weep with those who weep.
Romans 12:15

Just before speed skater Dan Jansen was to race at the 1988 Winter Olympics, he received word his sister had succumbed to her yearlong battle with leukemia. He fell in that race and again in his second race four days later. Returning home, one of many letters of consolation he received was from a thirty-year-old medal winner in the Special Olympics, who wrote, "I want to share one of my gold medals with you because I don't like to see you not get one. Try again in four more years."

For Dan Jansen, receiving that medal from a fellow athlete must have come close to winning one of his own. That's an example of the *koinonia*—the oneness, the unity—that athletes share.

Christians are to share that same kind of oneness, which is the true meaning of *koinonia*, or what we call "fellowship." If a fellow Christian is suffering, then the rest of the church suffers. If we are rejoicing, then we're blessed when other believers rejoice with us. Because we are all part of one body, the experiences of one member of the body—whether joy or sorrow—are experienced by all.

God never intended for any of His children to laugh or cry alone.

Feeding Sheep

Jesus said to [Peter], "Feed My sheep."

John 21:17

The final chapter of John's Gospel records one of the last conversations between the resurrected Lord Jesus and Peter. Just days earlier, Peter had denied his Lord beside a fire. Now, beside another fire, he will be restored. Just as Peter had denied Christ three times, he would be given three opportunities to confess his love for Jesus.

That's the portion of the story most people remember. Jesus uses one word for love—a strong, intense word for committed love—and Peter, his confidence shattered, comes back with a weaker word in reply. That happens two times, until finally Jesus looks Peter in the eyes and uses Peter's own, weaker word, as if to say, "Peter, do you even care for Me as a friend?"

The question breaks the big fisherman's heart, but Jesus neither rejects nor casts the sorrowing man aside. On the contrary, He sends Peter into the kingdom. In no uncertain terms, He gives him a job to do.

That is the portion of the story so often overlooked. Every time Peter answered the Lord, the Lord gave him a strong, specific command: "Feed My lambs, Peter"; "Tend My sheep, Peter"; "Feed My sheep, Peter."

Peter got the message. Do you?

Strong Enough to Be Gentle

Blessed are the meek, for they shall inherit the earth.

Matthew 5:5

George Washington Carver, the scientist who developed hundreds of useful products from the peanut, said, "When I was young, I said to God, 'God, tell me the mystery of the universe.' But God answered, 'That knowledge is reserved for Me alone.' So I said, 'God, tell me the mystery of the peanut.' Then God said, 'Well, George, that's more nearly your size.' And He told me."

Meekness is having a patient and humble outlook on life. Meekness is being mild of temper, not easily provoked or irritated; patient under injuries, not vain, haughty, or resentful; forbearing; submissive.

This character trait seems like a tall order and hardly applicable to daily life. Meekness is truly hard work; it's being strong enough to be gentle in whatever situation you are placed. When you understand the importance and power of meekness, God can use you to glorify Him as well as be useful to others.

James 3:13 says, "Who is wise and understanding among you? Let him show by good conduct that his works are done in the meekness of wisdom." It doesn't matter so much what your position in life is—it matters how you respond to your position. And when you have the attitude of meekness, you are sure to succeed in the eyes of the Lord.

Unwilling Hope

This hope we have as an anchor of the soul, both sure and steadfast.

Hebrews 6:19

Scripture teaches us that hope is necessary because the will is often uncooperative. We all know we should possess hope. We know that as Christians, we should be filled with hope. But how many of us have found ourselves praying the prayer of Paul in Romans 7:19: "Lord, I know what I should do, but I don't do it. I know what I shouldn't do, and here I am doing it again" (my paraphrase).

Hebrews 6:18 is very interesting. It says, "That by two immutable things, in which it is impossible for God to lie, we might have strong consolation, who have fled for refuge to lay hold of the hope set before us."

Many of us have experienced difficult times and we know our hope ought to be in the Lord. But sometimes our will is uncooperative and we just have to forget everything, hang on to God, and flee to Him for our refuge.

Home Security System

Go, show your love to your wife.

Hosea 3:1 NIV

The United States now has a Department of Homeland Security to help ensure the safety of our American homes. It's an important safeguard against terrorism, but a lesson might be learned from the Great Wall of China, one of the wonders of history. Upon its completion, the Chinese emperors expected never again to worry about security. No enemy could ever get past the forty-five-hundred-mile defensive wall, or so they thought. But the enemy did invade—by bribing the guardians of the gates and walking in.

Our government is doing its best to protect our nation's homeland, but the real enemy—Satan—is effectively slipping into our homes. Almost everyone has been touched by divorce in one way or another, and America now has the highest divorce rate in the world.

Many divorces could be prevented if husbands and wives committed their homes to Christ and took time to build a spiritual friendship, one that included daily Bible study and prayer together. The hectic demands of our society make it important to spend time together having fun, going out to eat, taking in a ball game, chatting over tea, or enjoying a weekend getaway. Go, show your love to your husband or wife.

The enemy has a hard time bribing the guards in a marriage like that.

The Spirit's Gifts

To each one of us grace was given according to the measure of Christ's gift.

Ephesians 4:7

The Bible says that when you're saved you not only get the Giver, you get the gift! You receive the Spirit of God, but you also receive the gift of the Spirit. Every Christian is immediately endowed with a special gift of ministry. You will find those gifts listed in Romans 12, in Ephesians 4, and in 1 Corinthians 12.

In other words, every believer has a gift of the Spirit. We are to exercise that gift so that everyone else profits. I exercise my gift, and it helps you. You exercise your gift, and it helps me. And all of us using our giftedness help the whole body to grow. But you can't do that without the Spirit of God. The whole concept of service is based on the spiritual filling of the believer. No wonder so many of God's people are trying to figure out how to survive! Do you know what we're trying to do? We're trying to accomplish a supernatural task in the energy of our own weak flesh.

We run like crazy trying to keep up with everything, and we fall into bed at night totally exhausted. There is no human way for us to do the work of God in the energy of the flesh. If the Spirit of God doesn't fill us with His power, we're attempting the impossible.

Knockoffs

Take heed to yourself and to the doctrine.

1 Timothy 4:16

They're called "knockoffs"—counterfeit watches, sunglasses, pens, and ties, all sporting a designer label. "Counterfeiting is a booming international business," reported the *New York Times*, "accounting for an estimated 5 to 7 percent of global trade." Some people buy phony goods for fun because they enjoy sporting a "Rolex" watch or "Louis Vuitton" purse, but others are fleeced of their hard-earned money.

There are a lot of counterfeit religions being peddled today too. Visit any large bookstore, and peruse the titles in the religion/spirituality section. Surf through the channels on your television. Scan the religion section of your newspaper.

How can you tell the truth from the knockoffs? The best way is to carefully study the genuine article. It's easy to spot fakes if you know the authentic. That's why it's important to read the Scriptures and divide them rightly. It's important to listen to the sermons and study the writings of trustworthy pastors and teachers.

The apostle Paul warned Timothy to reject the claims of false teachers, "rightly dividing" the Word of God for himself (2 Timothy 2:15). Don't fall for the phony. Take heed to yourself and to the doctrine.

Ninety-Two Bananas

God shall supply all your need according to His riches in glory by Christ Jesus.

Philippians 4:19

The prophet Jeremiah and the apostle Paul discovered the same thing about prayer: when our hearts are right, God delights to give us more than we asked for. In Jeremiah 33:3, the Lord said, "Call to Me, and I will answer you, and show you great and mighty things, which you do not know." In Ephesians 3:20, Paul said that God "is able to do exceedingly abundantly above all that we ask or think."

In her autobiography *Evidence Not Seen*, missionary Darlene Diebler tells of being near starvation in a Japanese POW camp. Through her window she saw in the distance a banana. "Lord," she prayed, "just one banana." But she couldn't see how God could get her a banana through prison walls.

The next day she heard footsteps coming down the hall and the key turning in the door of her cell. In walked a guard with a bunch of bananas. "They're yours," he said. She sat down in stunned silence and counted them. There were ninety-two bananas!

As Darlene wept and thanked the Lord, she seemed to hear Him say in her heart, "That's what I delight to do, exceeding abundantly above everything you ask or think."

Sunday and Beyond

I beseech you . . . that you present your bodies
a living sacrifice, holy, acceptable to God.

Romans 12:1

Since the Reformation, Protestant churches have included two sacraments in their worship: baptism and the Lord's Supper. In both of these observances, the Christian worships with his body, physically participating in the ordinances of the Lord.

In the Old Testament, believers worshiped with their bodies by bringing offerings to the Lord as sacrifices and by participating in the various festivals throughout the Jewish year. Participation in appointed worship is important, but the New Testament gives a brand-new mandate to Christians: take your worship beyond the meeting of the church. Instead of only participating in sacraments, become a sacrament. Instead of bringing a sacrifice to God, be the sacrifice.

Offer your whole life to God in daily service. Like Jesus, there shouldn't be a time when we aren't serving the Lord (John 5:19; 8:28). Make a conscious effort this week to view every day as "the Lord's day." Instead of looking for a sacrifice to bring, look for ways to live sacrificially for Christ.

Think of the impact on the world if every Christian began worshiping God every day of the week.

May 23

A Reflection of Holiness

I will make all My goodness pass before you, and I will proclaim the name of the Lord before you.

Exodus 33:19

What happened to Moses when he experienced the Holy? Moses had seen some pretty amazing miracles in his life, but he still wanted to see God's glory. God decided to show Moses a little bit of His glory. God put Moses in the cleft of a rock and covered him with His hand as He passed by. Moses saw only a reflection of the holiness of God from a distant rear view, but it affected him so much that the people of Israel were afraid of him when they saw him. His face shone so brilliantly that the people were terrified. Moses had to wear a veil in order to talk to the people.

If we could see God as He really is, not only would we know Him as a God of compassionate love, but we would see Him as a God of holiness, quite apart from anything we have ever known.

Why is it important to see God as He really is in His holiness? Because only then will you see yourself as you really are.

Treasure in Heaven

By faith Moses . . . [esteemed] the reproach of Christ greater riches than the treasures in Egypt; for he looked to the reward.

Hebrews 11:24, 26

Scott Adams, creator of the popular Dilbert comic strip, creates his cartoons from his own experience as a corporate cubicle dweller: "I don't think I'll ever forget what it feels like to sit in a cubicle and realize . . . everything you did today will become unimportant in the next [corporate] reorganization."

That's not to say, of course, that working at a corporate job is not without eternal significance. However, it does highlight the fact that every aspect of our lives has both a temporal and an eternal aspect. And it's learning to invest our lives—our time, talent, and treasure—for eternity that is the goal of life.

At work, seeing a coworker come to Christ through your witness adds an eternal dimension to what may be a mundane job. And investing the earnings from your job in the lives of a missionary family engaged in cross-cultural evangelism adds an eternal perspective to temporal work. In how many ways is eternity benefiting from your investments of time, talent, and treasure?

The reason you never see a hearse pulling a trailer is because investing in heaven must be done now, not later.

A Family Focused on God

And Joseph situated his father and his brothers, and gave them possession in the land of Egypt, in the best of the land, in the land of Ramses, as Pharaoh had commanded.

Genesis 47:11

There are at least three lessons we can learn from the story of Joseph and his family. First, God provided for the entire family due to the faithfulness of one member. God provided good land, met their every need, and watched Jacob's family come back to Him, and none of it would have happened had it not been for Joseph. Christians, if we are the only godly people in our families, we can't quit. We have the potential of redeeming our entire family.

A second lesson we learn from this story is that we are to care for the elderly. Joseph sets an example for us to follow by offering tender, loving care to his father.

Finally, we learn that God puts a priority on the family. The family is part of God's perfect plan for the world. There are only two institutions that God ordained: the church and the family. In this day, when families are being torn apart, the story of Joseph is a clear indication of what the family can accomplish when it is intact and focused on the Lord.

Jesus With Skin On

I have been crucified with Christ; it is no longer I who live, but Christ lives in me.

Galatians 2:20

The story is told of a small boy who was terrified of thunderstorms at night. Whenever the lightning and thunder would begin, he would invariably end up at his parents' bedside saying, "I'm scared." On one particular night, his father told him, "You don't need to be afraid of the storm; Jesus is there with you." "I know He is," the boy replied, "but I need a Jesus with skin on."

Out of the mouths of babes, right? The phrase "Jesus with skin on" is not found in the New Testament, but it definitely expresses a biblical reality: Christ living His life through the heart and hands of the Christian. A Christian, to put it in a child's terms, is the Holy Spirit with skin on. Isn't that what Paul said in Galatians 2:20: "It is no longer I who live, but Christ lives in me"? We ought to ask ourselves, "Who do people see when they look at me?" If they see love, joy, peace, longsuffering, kindness, goodness, faithfulness, gentleness, and self-control, then they're seeing Jesus through the Holy Spirit in us (Galatians 5:22–23).

Just as a dirty window conceals what's on the inside, so an unclean life keeps Jesus from being seen in us.

No Cookie-Cutter Children

The father of the righteous will greatly rejoice,
And he who begets a wise child will delight in him.

Proverbs 23:24

Sometimes we have the parenting cookie-cutter mentality. We not only want our children to believe what we believe, but we want them to live out their beliefs exactly like we do. We lose sight of the fact that as children grow, they are going to develop some of their own ways of expressing the same commitments to truth that we have. But when we lose sight of the commitment to truth and we demand outward conformity in every single way, we foster rebellion, because rebellion is the only way they can get enough energy and power to be what they need to be.

You may have heard the story about the housewife who always cut off the end of a ham before baking it in her oven. When the reason was discovered, it was because her grandmother's small oven necessitated it—a practice that was blindly followed by succeeding generations without question. Values and beliefs should not change from generation to generation, but the expression of them likely will. When we force our children to express their beliefs as we do, we foster rebellion. They need freedom to become their own people.

Memorizing God's Word

Your word I have hidden in my heart,
That I might not sin against You.

Psalm 119:11

Seneca, the ancient Greek teacher of rhetoric, would impress his class of two hundred by asking each student to recite a favorite line of poetry. He would then recite all two hundred lines from memory in reverse order. Augustine had a friend who could recite all the poet Virgil's works—backward!

Okay, maybe those guys were gifted—but there are lots of things each of us can recite from memory too. Family members' names, birthdays, and other important dates; numerous phone numbers and addresses; and our Social Security, checking account, credit card, and driver's license numbers. And what about popular songs from high school, songs from summer camp, and favorite hymns?

These items have two characteristics in common: frequent use and indispensability. We've memorized them because we use them so often and because we can't get along without them. What would happen to our efforts at scripture memory if we viewed the Bible the same way?

Try this: pick a passage of Scripture that addresses a need you face (indispensability), and read it once a day (frequency). Before long, you'll know it by heart!

Meekness, Not Weakness

Blessed are the meek, for they shall inherit the earth.

Matthew 5:5

When you hear the word *meekness*, you may think of the word in its modern setting—someone who is spineless, spiritless, lacking in strength and virility. The meek person in today's world is not how we'd like to be known.

But the Bible says, "Blessed are the meek." The Bible says the meek are blessed of God and someday they will rule the earth.

Meekness is not weakness. It is not laziness. It is not compromise at any price, not just being born nicer than other people.

The word came to mean in classical Greek "to soothe, to calm, to tranquilize." Someone has described meekness as gentleness by those who have the power to be otherwise—power under control. Meekness is the grace that brings strength and gentleness together.

When Jesus invited us to Him, He did not appeal to us on the basis of His kingship, majesty, or authority. The Lord reaches out His arms and says, "Come to Me and I'll give you rest, for I am meek—you can be comfortable coming to Me" (see Matthew 11:28).

The Value of Persecution

Our God whom we serve is able to deliver us.

Daniel 3:17

On July 15, 2002, a seventeen-year-old Christian Pakistani girl resisted the sexual advances of a Muslim man in her workplace. Angry at her refusal, the man returned and doused her with acid. She was burned severely on her face and chest and lost sight in her right eye. The International Christian Concern lists sixty-eight countries around the world where there is severe persecution or discrimination against Christians.

When we read stories in the Bible of believers being thrown to the lions, put into a fiery furnace, stoned, beaten, or made to suffer other forms of torture (Hebrews 11:35–38), we tend to think in historical terms only. But the truth is, millions of saints around the world today live in daily fear of persecution, simply for identifying themselves as Christians. And it is even happening in America, though in much more subtle ways.

The irony associated with persecution is striking: historically, there has been a direct correlation between the growth of the church and the degree of persecution it suffers. God is never so present in our lives as when we suffer in His name.

The Spirit's Presence

Do you not know that your body is the temple of the Holy Spirit who is in you, whom you have from God?

1 Corinthians 6:19

Paul said to the Corinthians, "Do you not know that your body is the temple of the Holy Spirit?" Why was he telling them that? Because the Corinthians were doing things with their bodies that were an embarrassment to the Holy Spirit. They were living lives divorced from the awareness of His holy presence within them.

Perhaps you've found yourselves at certain crossroads recently where you didn't know whether you should go to a certain place or participate in a certain activity because you are a Christian. The fact is, where you go, the Holy Spirit goes with you. So before you go, you'd better ask Him if He wants to go. And whatever He tells you, do it.

Many Christians don't even think about that. They just drag the Holy Spirit everywhere, into all kinds of things that are dishonoring to His first name, which is Holy.

The Holy Spirit permanently indwells you. If you grasp that concept, it could have a life-changing impact on you. He is there. He is in you. He will never leave you.

It's Never Too Late to Begin!

For we must all appear before the judgment seat of Christ.

2 Corinthians 5:10

In 1980, a young woman named Rosie Ruiz was declared the winner of the women's division of the Boston Marathon—but not for long. It was discovered this was only her second marathon, she never practiced, and none of the other runners had seen her during the race. She had ridden a subway sixteen miles, entered the race near the end, and crossed the finish line first.

Perhaps as the marathon approached, Ms. Ruiz realized she had waited too late to begin training. Instead of cheating, she should have run the best race she could and gained the prize of satisfaction and a clear conscience.

Like the Boston Marathon, the Christian life is a long-distance race (2 Timothy 4:7; Hebrews 12:1). Every participant will stand before the final Judge, Jesus Christ, and be evaluated on how he or she has run. But unlike the Boston Marathon, the Christian life is a "grace race." We will be judged not on being first but on being faithful. Did we use time, talent, and treasure for His glory? Did we run the best race we could with the gifts we have?

Regardless of how you've run in the past, today is the day to get in the race! Don't worry about where you place. Just be there at the end!

Abundantly Good

Great is the Lord, and greatly to be praised;
And His greatness is unsearchable.
Psalm 145:3

When the Bible writers call God good, they are thinking of all those things about His character we admire: His perfection, His compassion, His mercy, His grace, and perhaps most of all, His generosity.

Whatever God is, He is abundantly! God is good in a generous way. That means God loves to lavish upon His children that which blesses them. God is blessed in His life when He brings joy and blessing to those who depend upon Him for sustaining grace. Just as we have a real sense of joy in our hearts when we are able to do something good for another person, God has an intense joy in His heart as He expresses His goodness to all of us.

Have you ever heard a sermon about the prodigal son where the father is described as prodigal? *Prodigal* means "lavish, unrestrained, and unlimited." If you want to see the prodigal in that story, examine the heart of the father who never stopped loving his wayward son. Who waited every day to see him come home. And who, when his wayward son walked back into the family home, put on a feast to welcome him back. There was nothing that father would not do for his son. That's the way God is. He lavishes Himself upon His people.

Willing to Be Wounded

Faithful are the wounds of a friend.

Proverbs 27:6

When George Whitefield, the eighteenth-century British evangelist, first sailed to America, he wrote in his journal that the ship's cook had a drinking problem. When he was reproved about his sins, the cook boasted that he planned to reform his life two years before he died, but not before. Whitefield noted that the cook died six hours later.

No one likes to be reproved about sin, but a wise person listens and repents. Indeed, Solomon said, "Open rebuke is better than love carefully concealed" (Proverbs 27:5). Not surprisingly, most of us love to give reproof more than we like to receive it. But Solomon also said that the person who receives correction is considered wise (Proverbs 15:5).

As a Christian, humility is perhaps the top priority in being open to reproof. God says He gives grace to the humble but resists the proud (James 4:6). That doesn't mean we have to be a doormat, but it means we are willing to receive godly reproof without becoming defensive and resentful. If you were lost on a journey, wouldn't you appreciate the person who pointed you in the right direction?

Receiving reproof could be the first step in reaching the goals you've set for your life.

The Sovereignty of God

God sent me before you to preserve a posterity for you in the earth, and to save your lives by a great deliverance. So now it was not you who sent me here, but God.

Genesis 45:7–8

I've noticed, as I've studied the life of Joseph, that God is just as intimate to him as breath. God is so much a part of Joseph's life that he sees the Lord in every circumstance, and he trusts the Lord through every difficulty. "God meant it for good," he tells his brothers, "in order to bring it about as it is this day, to save many people alive" (Genesis 50:20). Everything that happened to him, both bad and good, was viewed through the lens of God's will.

When Joseph interpreted Pharaoh's dream, he said that it was God who gave him the meaning. When Joseph presented his sons to Jacob, he introduced them by saying, "These are my sons whom God has given me" (48:9). Even when Joseph was dying, he was able to encourage those around him that "God will surely visit you" (50:24).

At the center of Joseph's life was the sovereignty of God. Everything that happened was for His purposes and part of His program. Even the darkest threads in the weave help to provide the overall beauty of the tapestry.

The Great Multiplier

Who has despised the day of small things?
Zechariah 4:10

In 1912, Dr. Russell Conwell, pastor of Grace Baptist Church in Philadelphia, had a young student in Sunday school named Hattie May Wiatt. The church was crowded, and one day Dr. Conwell told Hattie May that he would love to have buildings large enough for everyone to attend.

When Hattie May became ill and died, Rev. Conwell was asked to preach the funeral. The girl's mother told him Hattie May had been saving her money to help build a bigger church. Hattie's purse contained coins amounting to fifty-seven cents. Taking the coins to the bank, Conwell exchanged them for fifty-seven pennies, which he put on display and "sold." With the proceeds, a nearby house was purchased for a children's wing for the church. Inspired by Hattie's story, more money came in, and out of her fifty-seven cents eventually came the buildings of Temple Baptist Church, Temple University, and Good Samaritan Hospital.

Perhaps you feel your gifts, your time, your talents, and your efforts are too small to make a difference. But have you ever given them to God completely and asked Him to bless them richly? He's the Great Mathematician, and He can take our words of witness, our undertakings, and our gifts and multiply them beyond anything we can ask or imagine.

Single Peace

He who is unmarried cares for the things of the Lord—how he may please the Lord.

1 Corinthians 7:32

People are single for four kinds of reasons: physical, medical, spiritual, or they just want to be single (not everybody wants to be married and apparently that is a part of God's plan). Some of the greatest people who ever served God were single. Rejoice in all the gifts God has given you, including your singleness.

Seeking marriage is not wrong, but don't let that search dominate your life. We must not make finding a marriage partner the supreme goal of our lives by putting all our energies into searching for a mate. We must learn to be in God's will. A very wise person said, "There is something far worse than single loneliness, and that is marital misery." Learn contentment, for it is great gain.

If God has a mate for you, He knows how to bring the two of you together. Don't take things into your own hands.

Wherever you are, whatever your situation, use the time to grow both mentally and spiritually.

The Soil of Your Soul

Examine me, O Lord, and prove me;
Try my mind and my heart.
Psalm 26:2

Topsoil—that luxurious layer of soil in which plant life thrives—is disappearing in America. As modern agricultural and commercial development has spread, wind and water have removed more than a foot of this precious resource. Yet when soil leaves one grain at a time, it's hard to see it happening.

The erosion of one's spiritual life happens like the erosion of topsoil—one sin at a time. Erosion and sin are deceptive. A grain of soil breaks free, weakening others that soon follow. A sin is willingly committed and unconfessed, and others are likely to follow.

That's what happened to Saul, the king of Israel. He grew impatient for the prophet Samuel to come to Gilgal to offer a sacrifice before battle, and so he offered the sacrifice himself—a sin in God's sight (1 Samuel 13). He gave himself permission to sin once, and it became ever easier to sin again.

If you have sinned, repent quickly. The same clay that makes bricks to build a cathedral can create a gully by its absence. Don't let sin wash away the soil of your soul.

Don't Ask, Do

According to all that God commanded [Noah], so he did.

Genesis 6:22

Noah did "according to all that God commanded" (Genesis 6:22). Therein lies the key and secret to Noah's faith. When God told him to do something, he did it. He was a man who took God at His word. We have no record of Noah disagreeing with God or debating His instructions. He believed that his salvation depended on God's wisdom and good plan, and he chose to receive it and implement it just as God explained it.

For us to be saved and move ahead as men and women of faith, we have to do the same thing. God needs to know that we are not going to debate or disagree with Him. His Word to us becomes our command. You and I will likely never be in Noah's position—the only person on earth who will obey God. But we need to live like it anyway. If we do, God will remember us the same way He remembered His friend Noah (Genesis 8:1).

Flee Immorality

But immorality or any impurity or greed must not even be named among you, as is proper among saints.

Ephesians 5:3 NASB

L. M. Clymer was president of the Holiday Inn hotel chain when the corporate board made a decision to invest $25 million in a gambling casino in Atlantic City. As a committed Christian, he had protested the decision to invest in the gambling industry but was overruled. As a result of the decision, Clymer resigned his position as president of the company, being unwilling to compromise his moral and spiritual convictions.

Godly men and women cannot be content in the presence of wickedness. Some would say to Mr. Clymer, "You can't help what the board decides. Besides, you're not gambling; you're not doing anything wrong." But the apostle Paul told the Roman Christians that God's judgment is upon those who not only sin themselves but give approval to others who sin (Romans 1:32).

If our failure to speak out against wickedness can in any way be interpreted as approval of the practice, then we are guilty as well. Look around—is there sin surrounding you to which you have grown accustomed? Are you willing to take a stand regardless of the cost?

A voice of dissent unheard speaks as loud as any shout of approval.

JUNE

God is my strength and power, and
He makes my way perfect.

—2 Samuel 22:33

Come to Know Him

I know whom I have believed and am persuaded that He is able to keep what I have committed to Him until that Day.

2 Timothy 1:12

We worship whom we trust, and we trust whom we know. We come to this level of faith because we build trust, and we build trust because we spend time with God. Do you remember the experience of getting to know your best friend—perhaps the person you married? You didn't fully unburden your deepest thoughts because you didn't know whether you could trust your new friend. Alas, there are lesser relationships with people who fall by the wayside because they betray our trust in some way. But your best friend was that person who redeemed your trust, and you confirmed it only through the time and tears of relationship.

The same principle holds true with God. You must come to know Him before you can really, truly, deeply trust Him. Then and only then will you be able to worship in spirit and in trust. Then and only then will you be able to say, in a twenty-first-century paraphrase of Habakkuk, "I may lose my work, my loved ones, and all that I own. Still I will love God all the more. Still I will praise Him with the loudest voice I can muster. And He will lift me up, for I know whom I have believed and am persuaded that He is able."

Fire and Fence

Daniel purposed in his heart that he would not defile himself.
Daniel 1:8

F. Scott Fitzgerald wrote, "At 18 our convictions are hills from which we look; at 45 they are caves in which we hide." Another analogy would be: convictions are the fires that propel us and the fences that protect us.

Our inner convictions propel us to action. If I have a deep conviction the world is lost without Christ, I'm going to be a witness. If I have a deep conviction God answers prayer, I'm going to pray. If I deeply believe I should help the helpless, I'm going to get involved.

At the same time, convictions erect boundaries around our lives that protect us from sudden temptation. The backseat of a car is no place to decide what we believe about morality and purity. We'd better know about that before we get into such a situation. Convictions need to develop in our lives so that when pressure comes, we'll know what to do.

What are the boundaries in your life? How far will you go in a business deal to make a little extra money when you know in your heart you're violating something deep within your own soul? Do you have a set of convictions that you've thought out clearly so you'll know what to do when temptation comes?

The Power of Living Water

"He who believes in Me, as the Scripture has said, out of his heart will flow rivers of living water." But this He spoke concerning the Spirit.

John 7:38–39

The greatest danger to any ancient city during a time of siege was not the enemy without; it was the lack of resources within. More often than not, when an army like the Assyrians attacked a walled city like Jerusalem, they would simply surround the city and wait for it to run out of food and water. Then, when the people were weak and desperate, the city could be taken almost without a fight. But Hezekiah made sure that would not happen to Jerusalem. He rerouted a spring of water outside the city walls so it flowed inside the walls of the city.

Interestingly, Jesus referred often to the Holy Spirit as the living water given by God to the believer, that constitutes a secret, powerful resource in times of trouble. When you have the Holy Spirit living inside of you, you possess a resource that can give you abundant life through the longest siege of the enemy. The enemy can camp at your doorstep for an indefinite period of time, and it won't matter to you. The Holy Spirit is your indwelling source of life.

Faith Grows

We . . . thank God always for you . . .
because your faith grows exceedingly.
2 Thessalonians 1:3

"If faith dispels worry, anxiety, fear, and depression, then why am I worried, anxious, fearful, and depressed?" asked Jamie. "Why do I react so suddenly to life's punches? Why can't I trust God more?"

If you've ever asked such questions, you're in good company. Take the disciples, for example. They trusted Christ enough to leave their homes and livelihoods, to follow Him despite persecution and opposition. Yet when they faltered during the storm, He bemoaned their "little faith" (Matthew 8:26).

Fast-forward a few years. Those same disciples were braving prison, beatings, and death to take the gospel of the kingdom to the ends of the earth. Their faith had grown strong.

The simple fact is that faith is a growing thing. Paul said, "Faith grows" (2 Thessalonians 1:3). It grows as we find and claim specific promises during times of need. It grows as we ask God to increase our faith and as we advance in our understanding of the trustworthiness of our Lord.

Remember, it's not great faith you need—but faith in a great God.

Put God First

To You I have cried out, O Lord,
And in the morning my prayer comes before You.
Psalm 88:13

I remember reading about a great prayer warrior, Andrew Murray, who said that sometimes he had so much to do that he had to add an extra hour to his prayers. As a flawed human being, I have often rushed through my day trying to accomplish my work without taking time to pray. Those are the times I get to the end of the day fatigued, frustrated, and with a sense of failure.

But if I push my work aside and refuse to tackle it until I have met with God, my work is energized. I don't know how it happens, but it does. More things happen in less time. Better things happen that would not happen otherwise. I'm not a mystic, nor am I trying to read something into this that isn't there. I'm just saying that when you put God first, God takes care of you. He takes care of the things you need.

Imitators of God

Therefore be imitators of God as dear children.

Ephesians 5:1

President Calvin Coolidge invited some people from his hometown to dinner at the White House. When the time came for serving coffee, the president poured his coffee into a saucer. As soon as his guests saw it, they did the same. Next, the president poured some milk and added a little sugar to the coffee in the saucer. The home folks did the same. They thought that surely the next step would be for the president to take the saucer with the coffee and begin sipping it. But the president didn't do so. He leaned over, placed the saucer on the floor, and called the cat.

Although you may never find yourself in the position of imitating the president at a dinner in the White House, you are called to be imitators of God every day. The story in Genesis tells of humans being created in God's image, and we are to be reflectors of Him to the world. How have you reflected His image to the world recently?

When you make decisions based on the Bible and prayer, when you love your neighbor as yourself, when you strive to lead a life that is pleasing to Christ in all that you do, then you are truly being an imitator of your Maker.

Never Tired

Have you not known? Have you not heard? The everlasting God, the Lord, the Creator of the ends of the earth, neither faints nor is weary.

Isaiah 40:28

Everything that you and I do takes energy from us and causes our energy level to reduce. While there are some people who seem to have unlimited energy, nobody really does.

The older we get, the more we realize we can't do some of the things we did when we were younger. But the power of God is never diminished. When He exercises His great power on behalf of anyone or anything, all of His power is still at the same level. He is never tired.

Isaiah said, "Have you not known? Have you not heard? The everlasting God, the Lord, the Creator of the ends of the earth, neither faints nor is weary." You don't need to wait and give God a chance to rest up. You can go to God at any time and know that all of His power is available to you.

Whirlwind of Wisdom

Then the Lord answered Job out of the whirlwind.

Job 38:1

Missionaries Martin and Gracia Burnham, seized by guerrillas in the Philippines in May 2001, were held captive for 376 days. Just before a military raid led to Martin's death and Gracia's freedom, Martin said, "The Bible says to serve the Lord with gladness. Let's go out all the way. Let's serve Him all the way with gladness."

How can someone talk of joy while in deadly peril? Of serving the Lord with gladness while in captivity? It's because of God's wisdom. His infinite brilliance looks at everything with perfect understanding. God's wisdom is revealed in the Bible and imparted to us by the Holy Spirit as we study His Word.

This was the wisdom Job discovered. Overwhelmed with life, he had tried to sort out his troubles, aided by three friends whose insights were even more misguided than his own. But after human wisdom was exhausted, God spoke to Job out of a whirlwind: "Where were you when I laid the foundation of the earth?" God demanded. "Who laid its cornerstone?" (Job 38:4, 6).

We may not have all the answers to life, but the Lord does. We can defer to His wisdom and trust Him to understand things that make no sense to us.

God Works All Things for Good

And we know that all things work together for good to those who love God, to those who are the called according to His purpose.
Romans 8:28

When President Roosevelt was in office, a madman once took a shot at him, wounding the president in the arm. A steel glasses case, which the president kept in his breast pocket, deflected the bullet and saved his life. The funny thing is, President Roosevelt hated that glasses case. It was heavy and burdensome, and he had often complained about it. But in the process of God's providence, the thing he hated saved his life.

Joseph's is a similar story. Though at times Joseph may have hated his situation and wondered about God's purposes, eventually his life was an example of the rule of God's providence. God took the darkest events and used them as stepping stones to move Joseph into position. Even when Joseph couldn't understand what God was doing, the Lord was still at work. God had been arranging the situation, even when it seemed like He was far away. In the end, Joseph realized God had worked all things out for good.

Joseph had it all in perspective. He saw that God was using even the evil things of this world to illustrate His providential work in the lives of men.

My Rock and Refuge

I will say to God my Rock,
"Why have You forgotten me?
Why do I go mourning because of
the oppression of the enemy?"
Psalm 42:9

In 1174, the Italian architect Bonnano Pisano began work on what would become his most famous project: a separately standing bell tower for the cathedral of the city of Pisa. There was just one "little" problem. Builders quickly discovered that the soil was much softer than they had anticipated, and the foundation was far too shallow to adequately hold the structure! Sure enough, before long the whole structure began to tilt . . . and it continued to tilt . . . until finally the architect and the builders realized that nothing could be done to make the "leaning tower" straight again.

If only the tower had been built on the right foundation. What is the foundation of your life? If it isn't God, chances are you're tilting one way or another. Isaiah 33:6 says, "He will be your sure foundation, providing a rich store of salvation, wisdom, and knowledge. The fear of the Lord is the key to this treasure" (NLT).

Make God the rock and foundation that your life is built upon.

Memorials of God's Faithfulness

This is My name forever; and this is My memorial to all generations.

Exodus 3:15

God wants us to have memorials so we won't forget. He preserved Noah and his family through the flood and then gave them the memorial of the rainbow. From that day on, we can look into the sky at a rainbow and remember how God delivered Noah and has promised never again to destroy the earth by water.

God gave the Israelites the ark of the covenant that they carried with them. Inside the ark were the Law that God had given to Moses on Mt. Sinai, the stone tablets to remember when God had given His people a code of conduct by which to live, and a little jar. The Bible says that inside that jar was some of the manna God had fed the people during their forty years of wandering. Why manna? It was another memorial to the fact that God can feed people right there in the desert where there were no restaurants.

The Lord was wise. He instituted memorials. Why? Because we have a tendency to forget. We need to remember that we have a God who has worked in the past, and because He has worked in the past, He is willing to work in the present.

The Risky Business of Reconciliation

Blessed are the peacemakers, for they shall be called sons of God.

Matthew 5:9

Novelist John Grisham recalled a conversation with a friend who died of cancer at the age of twenty-five. When told of the diagnosis, Grisham asked, "What do you do when you are about to die?" The sick man replied, "You get right with God, spend time with those you love, and settle up with everybody else." Then he said, "Really, you ought to live every day like you have only a few more days to live."

It's one thing to "settle up" with others when facing death. But for most people, living with the possibility of rejection is a formidable burden to consider carrying the rest of their lives. Reconciliation is a risky business. Where there has been a rift in a relationship, there are no guarantees as to how the other party might respond to your efforts; that person might still be angry, hurt, and nonresponsive. On the other hand, that person may embrace you fully and the relationship may be restored.

The only way the distance between two people can be bridged is by someone taking the first step. If needed, be a peacemaker and close the gap between yourself and another.

Reconciliation is a form of investing in the future. The greater the risk, the greater the reward.

God's Beauty Treatment

Charm is deceitful and beauty is passing,
But a woman who fears the Lord,
she shall be praised.

Proverbs 31:30

Americans spend billions of dollars every year on cosmetics, but the best beauty treatment isn't found in a bottle, but in a book—the Bible. First Peter 3:3–5 says, "Do not let your adornment be merely outward—arranging the hair, wearing gold, or putting on fine apparel—rather let it be the hidden person of the heart, with the incorruptible beauty of a gentle and quiet spirit, which is very precious in the sight of God. For in this manner, in former times, the holy women who trusted in God also adorned themselves."

Little is said of the physical qualities of the woman in Proverbs 31, though we assume she had a pleasant appearance. It is her character that's emphasized—her trustworthiness (v. 11), her hard work (v. 13), her business instincts (v. 16), her generosity (v. 20), her creativity (v. 22), her initiative (v. 24), and her strength (v. 25).

It's not the makeup on her face but the makeup of her heart that makes her beautiful. We can't all be fashion models, but we can all be fashioned by grace as models of our Lord Jesus Christ.

Praise Today

Enter into His . . . courts with praise.

Psalm 100:4

Is there a sequence to follow in prayer? Prayer should be a natural conversation between us and our Father, and no specific order is required. On the other hand, prayer is our highest activity, and we shouldn't do it thoughtlessly. Would you enter the presence of a king and just start babbling?

Isaac Watts, the father of English hymnody, once wrote a little poem about the order of prayer:

Call upon God, adore, confess,
Petition, plead, and then declare
You are the Lord's, give thanks and bless,
And let Amen confirm the prayer.

Begin prayer with adoration and praise. Some people use a hymnbook and begin their time with the Lord by singing. Others keep a "praise list" in their prayer journal.

You might develop the habit of pausing as you leave your house to gaze into the sky and thank God for the beauty of that day. How often do you see the blue sky, the gentle rain, or the rising sun without acknowledging His creative genius? Other people begin the day by reciting: "This is the day the Lord has made; [I] will rejoice and be glad in it" (Psalm 118:24).

However you do it, praise God today.

The Danger of Procrastination

Blessed are those servants whom the master,
when he comes, will find watching.

Luke 12:37

Jesus tells a story of two slaves who work for an absentee master. One slave is good and faithful, and the other is evil and faithless. The good slave represents believers who will be on the earth before the Lord's return, while the evil servant represents unbelievers. Every person in the world holds his life, his possessions, and his abilities in trust from God, and they will all be held accountable to the Lord for what they have done with that trust. In the case of this evil servant, the dominant attitude is one of calloused procrastination. He doesn't believe the master is going to come back anytime soon, so he has no motivation to cease doing evil. Christ's words warn him to be careful because he doesn't know the schedule.

A man told me not long ago that he wanted to become a Christian, but it wasn't convenient for him right now. Well, because it wasn't convenient for that man to accept Christ, it won't be convenient for him to get into heaven.

There is going to be a day when that decision has to be made or it will no longer be available. If you haven't trusted Him yet, why don't you do it today? Receive Him as your Savior and your Lord.

Heaven on Earth

For the things which are seen are temporary, but the things which are not seen are eternal.

2 Corinthians 4:18

Do a survey of today's local newspaper, or pay close attention to the evening news broadcast on television. Here's what you'll likely find: stories on the U.S. economy, ongoing military efforts against terrorism, medical and technological advances, and other such stories. Here's what you will likely not find: news reports about heaven.

Let's face it: the world we live in is not focused on heaven. Atheists, agnostics, and pagans aren't concerned with heaven at all, and we can understand their inattention. The surprising reality is that many Christians hardly give heaven a second thought either. We live as if this world is the real thing, that which defines who and what we are.

In fact, just the opposite is true. This world is a very temporary parentheses in the eternal plan of God. Christians' citizenship is heavenly, not earthly. While on earth, the way we keep our eyes focused on heaven is to live in the presence of God through continual worship and communion with Him.

Though the media is full of news, don't let it distract you from the good news of the gospel.

A Parent's Impact

And he arose and came to his father. But when he was still a great way off, his father saw him and had compassion, and ran and fell on his neck and kissed him.

Luke 15:20

One writer I read said that the way parents treat their children in daily living has more impact on their children's spiritual development than the family's religious practices, including having a family altar, reading the Bible together, and attending church services regularly.

Parenting is a difficult job. But we need to remember that when the rebellious son in Luke 15 came to himself, he found a loving father waiting for him at home. That father had probably made mistakes in his parenting, but he did not stop loving either of his two sons—and the younger son, at least, knew it.

Sometimes the stress of parenting makes us want to stop loving and leave. But if we remain and continue to love, we do more to negate the chances of rebellion in our children than anything we could ever do. May God help us to love our children as He loves us.

Put Down the Hammer!

Put on the full armor of God so that you can take your stand against the devil's schemes.

Ephesians 6:11 NIV

In her "Autobiography in Five Short Chapters," Portia Nelson wrote:

> Chapter 1: I walk down the street. There is a deep hole in the sidewalk. I fall in. It isn't my fault. It takes forever to find a way out.
>
> Chapter 2: I walk down the same street. There is a deep hole in the sidewalk. I pretend I don't see it. I fall in again . . . but it isn't my fault. It still takes a long time to get out.
>
> Chapter 3: I walk down the same street. There is a deep hole in the sidewalk. I see it is there. I still fall in. . . . My eyes are open. I know where I am. It is my fault. I get out immediately.
>
> Chapter 4: I walk down the same street. There is a deep hole in the sidewalk. I walk around it.
>
> Chapter 5: I walk down another street.

Satan has his schemes and tactics, and we need to devise ours to defend ourselves from his temptations. If you know there is a temptation down one street, take a different one!

Clothing yourself in the armor of God is step one in devising strategies to resist the devil's schemes.

Like Riding a Bike

Blessed are all those who put their trust in Him.

Psalm 2:12

Do you remember learning to ride a bicycle? It was a trust issue—nothing more, nothing less. There came a time when you had to take the training wheels off, place your feet on the pedals, and allow that bike to take flight down the street.

No textbook, no parental word of advice would accomplish the mission. But once you made the leap of faith, you never again lost the aptitude for bike riding. Why? Trust.

To experience the fullness of worship, we must trust the One we worship. And to trust Him, we must know Him. Have you ever felt as if you knew all the facts about God but your prayers never passed the ceiling? Have you ever sung a hymn without being able to bring the words to life? Have you ever realized that your morning devotions have become a dry Bible study rather than a warm visit with your heavenly Father?

We need truth, and we need sound theology. The right information is essential. But above all else, we need relationship. Once we've come into His powerful and loving presence, we'll never struggle to trust Him again any more than we'll have to take a refresher course in bike riding.

I'd Rather Be a Dog

And when He had given thanks . . .

John 6:11

Rev. William Biederwolf once shocked his audience by saying, "I'd rather be a dog with gratitude enough to wag his tail . . . than to be a man with a soul so contemptibly mean as to sit down at the table three times a day and gulp down the food God has provided and never once lift my heart in thanksgiving."

We might not put it like that, but the point is well taken. When Jesus told us to pray, "Give us this day our daily bread," He was teaching us dependence upon Him for daily provision (Matthew 6:11). Even our Lord paused to give thanks before breaking the bread in John 6.

"Saying grace" shouldn't be a perfunctory act, and we shouldn't use the same words each time. Try praying an original prayer at each meal. At breakfast: "Lord, thanks for giving someone enough wisdom to invent high-fiber cereal." At lunch: "Lord, thanks for this food, but keep me from eating too much of it." And at supper? Well, you could say, "Lord, I'd rather be a dog than fail to thank You for this meatloaf."

Whatever words you use, learn to thank God for giving you this day your daily bread.

The Compassion of God

By You I have been upheld from birth;
You are He who took me out of my mother's womb.
Psalm 71:6

We have the theology for prosperity down pat, but sooner or later our prosperity will give way to adversity. If you don't have your theology finely tuned for that part of your life, you won't do well. Unexpected, unannounced, uncharted, unplanned—adversity comes to everyone.

Every believer should be able to review the compassion of God. Stop and think about all the paths God has led you down like a shepherd throughout your spiritual life. God has been faithful to you! Is there any reason you have to doubt His faithfulness now? As the psalmist says, from our mother's womb God took us, and He has upheld us from our birth.

Even if we have been a believer for only a matter of days or weeks, the grace of God has brought us life and health and strength. God's past faithfulness and compassion toward us is a heritage upon which we build our faith in the future.

God's Estate Plan

I pray also that the eyes of your heart may be enlightened in order that you may know the hope to which he has called you, the riches of his glorious inheritance in the saints.

Ephesians 1:18 NIV

The reading of a deceased person's will is a stereotypically comic event seen less often in real life than in the movies. The deceased is absent, the heirs are nervous and competitive, and the content of the will is unknown. Not a happy scene—and totally removed from the joy of a Christian's spiritual inheritance.

Christians are heirs of God and joint heirs with Jesus Christ (Romans 8:17). And there is great joy in heaven whenever one lost soul turns to God and receives his inheritance (Luke 15:10). God, the benefactor, has joy. Christians, the heirs, have joy as well.

Our inheritance is clearly spelled out. But the joy of our inheritance extends beyond this age to the "ages to come" (Ephesians 2:7). God's "estate plan" makes provision for us to enjoy Him, and for Him to enjoy us, forever. Never doubt whether there is anyone who longs to be with you. God does, and He plans to spend eternity with you, His heir.

Being an heir of God means that the Benefactor, heir, and inheritance are not separated but united in mutual joy forever.

Plug in to His Power

God is my strength and power, and
He makes my way perfect.

2 Samuel 22:33

I have little power, but God has all power. If it is going to be, it is going to be up to Him. He has the power not only to bring things into existence but to keep them out of existence as well. I have conceived a lot of things in my mind that God, in His wisdom and by His grace, has kept me from having. He has the power to do both.

So every day I need to end my prayer saying, "Lord, I know that, first of all, You are in control. Thank You. My life may seem out of control, but You are not. You are in control." The throne in heaven is not empty. God is there, seated and in sovereign control. He said a word and the worlds were made. He spoke and the moon and stars were flung out into space. He's an awesome, almighty, powerful God.

And my prayer links me with Him. I don't have to get up every morning and psych myself up for the day, because God's power is always there. All I've got to do is plug in to Him.

Fearing Fear Itself

For God has not given us a spirit of fear, but of power and of love and of a sound mind.

2 Timothy 1:7

The Great Depression began in October 1929, and began to turn around with the inauguration of Franklin D. Roosevelt as president in 1933. In his inaugural address, FDR lifted the spirit of America with these words: "Let me assert my firm belief that the only thing we have to fear is fear itself—nameless, unreasoning, unjustified terror which paralyzes needed efforts to convert retreat into advance."

God says, "Fear not" (Isaiah 41:10)—don't fear anything. The Christian has no fear that faith cannot cancel (Luke 8:25). Fear paralyzes. It stops us in our tracks and halts the advance of the kingdom of God into the kingdom of Satan, the kingdom of light into the kingdom of darkness (Colossians 1:12–14).

Satan wants nothing more than to paralyze God's saints—to halt their progress in holiness and to stop the spread of the gospel. If you are paralyzed by fear, ask God to deliver you. Say, "Lord, I'm afraid! Deliver me from evil. Deliver me from all my fears."

Power, love, and the mind of Christ advance the kingdom of God; fear turns advance into retreat.

Diligent in All Things

The desire of the lazy man kills him,
For his hands refuse to labor.

Proverbs 21:25

Billy Graham tells this of his upbringing: "I was taught that laziness was one of the worst evils, and there was dignity and honor in labor. I could abandon myself enthusiastically to milking the cows, cleaning out the latrines, and shoveling manure, not because they were pleasant jobs, but because sweaty labor held its own satisfaction."

Through godly rearing, Billy Graham developed the valuable character quality of diligence. A diligent man is one who works hard at every task, no matter how important or how menial. He uses his time efficiently and always puts forth his best work. Though he may feel sluggish at times, he refuses to be a sluggard. He is a man ruled by discipline, not feelings.

Against the backdrop of people who avoid work, cut corners, and do halfhearted jobs, a diligent man stands out. Practicing diligence is an excellent way to stand out for Christ at home, in the workplace, and even at church. Today, complete each one of your tasks, however big or small, with diligence.

Staying Spiritually Solvent

As iron sharpens iron,
So a man sharpens the countenance of his friend.
Proverbs 27:17

On February 26, 1995, Barings Bank, England's oldest, declared bankruptcy after losing nearly one billion dollars. How could such a thing happen? Lack of accountability. A twenty-eight-year-old Barings trader in Singapore had been given too much authority—like letting a schoolboy grade his own tests. He lost money in stock trades, and no one knew about it—until all of the bank's money was gone.

If that trader had been surrounded by associates who were closer to him, his failures might have been caught before they turned into a freefall. It's hard to overestimate the positive influence that good and godly friends, mentors, and role models can have on our lives—or the negative results that accrue when we have a "lone ranger" mentality. Not only can friends keep us from going astray, they can move us in the right direction as well.

Surveys have shown that in our disconnected culture, most people have few, if any, close friends. How about you? Don't be a stranger! Be a good friend, and you'll have good friends who can help you find, and stay on, the right path.

Peer pressure can have a negative or positive effect. Make sure your peers are of the positive kind.

Still Waters

In quietness and confidence shall be your strength.

Isaiah 30:15

Have you ever felt like a goldfish swimming around in a blender full of water—with someone's finger on the "high" switch? Many of us are altogether too busy, running on overdrive, overextended in our schedules and underdeveloped in our souls. Instead of green pastures and still waters, we're accustomed to clogged freeways and blaring cell phones.

King Solomon is a good example of a man who was so busy in the work of God that he neglected his walk with God. The result? He developed a great empire and a lean soul. The Lord is more concerned with our relationship with Him than with our productivity for Him, and the wise person knows that a healthy soul requires a certain amount of "quiet" and "still" and "rest."

"Come aside by yourselves to a deserted place and rest," Jesus told the disciples in Mark 6:31. "Be still and know that I am God," advises the Lord in Psalm 46:10.

Is something in your life consuming you, pulling you away from intimacy with God? Are you too busy for your own good? A man had a plaque installed on his dashboard that read "Beware the Barrenness of Busyness." Why not take a deep breath, get away from all distractions, open your Bible, and commune with Him right now?

Benefits of Boundaries

. . . having predestined us to adoption as sons by Jesus Christ to Himself, according to the good pleasure of His will.

Ephesians 1:5

In *Knowledge of the Holy*, A. W. Tozer illustrates freedom and boundaries: an ocean liner leaves New York bound for England, piloted by a captain and crew who will not be taken off course. The passengers are free to roam the giant boat and do whatever they like—within the confines of the ship. They exercise their freedoms while all the time being moved toward an ultimate destination.

God's adoption of Christians into His family reflects the same two dynamics: freedom of movement within safe boundaries, while moving toward an ultimate destination. The word *predestination* in Scripture has the idea of boundaries in its meaning. When God predestined us to adoption as His children, He set boundaries around us that gradually conform us to the image of His Son (Romans 8:29). Like children, we may chafe at times against the boundaries of our spiritual family, but they are for our good. Think how much safer you feel now than when you were lost and without hope in the world (Ephesians 2:12).

God's boundaries tell us we are on His ship, heading for a heavenly port. Without boundaries, we would be lost forever.

God's Road Map

I have led you forty years in the wilderness. Your clothes have not worn out on you, and your sandals have not worn out on your feet.

Deuteronomy 29:5

If we are honest, most of us will admit that we can deal with things that have a precedent, but walking into uncharted territory provokes fear. It is awesome to consider the thoughts that can fill our minds as we look into a future for which we have no road map. There were some things that God used to strengthen His people, and these things are available to us today as we face our challenges as well.

The people of Israel, standing on the bank of the Jordan River, had one sure thing. They had the record of God's performance on their behalf in the past.

For forty years, God's people had been wandering in the desert, yet God wonderfully and miraculously cared for them. First, they got into the wilderness through the miracle of walking through the Red Sea, and then God gave them a guidance system. Each day, for forty years, they were led by a pillar of cloud. At night they were led by a pillar of fire. They were wandering, but God was leading them. God spoke through Moses, "I have led you forty years in the wilderness. Your clothes have not worn out on you, and your sandals have not worn out on your feet."

Only a Gypsy Boy

Not many noble, are called.

1 Corinthians 1:26

Some are still around who heard the inimitable preacher Rodney (Gipsy) Smith. He was born among the gypsies in England. His mother died when he was young; and his father, Cornelius, was imprisoned for debts. But after his release, Cornelius took his children to Latimer Road Mission, where, as worshipers sang "There Is a Fountain Filled with Blood," Cornelius suddenly fell to the floor. Soon he jumped up, shouting, "I'm converted! Children, God has made a new man of me!" Young Rodney ran from the church terrified.

But at age sixteen, Rodney himself asked Christ into his heart. Someone nearby whispered, "Oh, it's only a gypsy boy." Undeterred, Rodney acquired a Bible and began preaching. Thus began seventy years of worldwide evangelistic work. He became one of the greatest preachers of his age.

Don't worry if you don't have a lot of education, a fistful of money, or a prestigious background. God takes us as we are and makes us what He wants us to be. He uses the weakest people to do His greatest work, "that no one may boast before him" (1 Corinthians 1:29 NIV).

Joy Does Not Depend on Circumstances

Finally, my brethren, rejoice in the Lord.

Philippians 3:1

Happiness is the world's cheap imitation of Christian joy. Happiness is dependent on happenings, on "hap," which is another word for "luck." Someone who is hapless is luckless.

When we have "joy," it can be our constant possession because it does not depend on the circumstances of the day. Paul said, "Rejoice in the Lord!" This philosophy made it possible for him to endure all kinds of problems and still move forward in his walk with Christ. When he wrote his second letter to the church at Corinth, he listed just a few of the things he had endured. Now we know how he endured them. He had the strength of genuine joy in his life.

How could any one man experience all these things and still have the spirit of joy? Paul understood what most modern men do not—that joy and pain are often compatible emotions.

Follow the Leader

For to this you were called, because Christ also suffered for us, leaving us an example, that you should follow His steps.

1 Peter 2:21

You show up bright and early for the first day of your new job and sit down with your boss to review your job responsibilities. Everything looks good—meet deadlines for reports, monitor departmental budget, supervise junior staff—until you get to the last item: "Suffer extreme persecution, harassment, and loss of some privilege for the sake of the company."

Whoa! Are they serious? Not many people in today's world would agree to a job that required them to suffer for the sake of the company. Yet, in a manner of speaking, that's what Christians are asked to do. For instance, when Paul met the Lord Jesus Christ on the Damascus road, Jesus said He was about to show Paul "how many things he must suffer for My name's sake" (Acts 9:16). And Paul never wavered throughout his life.

We are not promised deliverance from every hardship in this life. In fact, we are told that we will suffer. How often are you surprised at the suffering you experience in this life?

Following Jesus means imitating His example in all things—even suffering for the sake of the gospel.

The Gift of Fame

He Himself gave some to be apostles, some prophets, some evangelists, and some pastors and teachers, for the equipping of the saints for the work of ministry.

Ephesians 4:11–12

To many people, fame is nearly as desirable as wealth. This is because acceptance is one of our basic needs, and there's nothing like seeing your name in bright lights to make you feel accepted and admired. Some come to fame because of exceptional talent or brilliance. Others just happen upon it, being at the right place at the right time. Artist Andy Warhol once predicted that, due to expanding TV technology, we'll all experience fame at some point in our lives, even if for just ten or fifteen minutes. Fame is fleeting, as they say, but elusiveness only adds to its enticement.

Christians should avoid the allure of fame. It can seduce us away from our foremost desire to serve God. Paul tells us that the Holy Spirit gives us gifts. We are to discover our gifts and be diligent with them, using them for God's glory. Because of the nature of certain gifts, some of their beneficiaries may incidentally become famous. But the real purpose of spiritual gifts is to lead the church to a more meaningful relationship with the Lord.

The Expressing of Grace

Having then gifts differing according to the grace that is given to us, let us use them.

Romans 12:6

When David Livingstone volunteered as a missionary with the London Missionary Society, they asked him where he wanted to go. He replied, "Anywhere, so long as it is forward." After he had reached Africa, he recorded his impressions, saying that he was haunted by the smoke of a thousand villages stretching off into the distance. David Livingstone had the heart of a missionary.

Should every Christian have the heart of a missionary? Yes and no. In the sense of being as sure of one's calling as most missionaries are—willing to sacrifice and endure hardship—absolutely yes. But in being an actual missionary who goes to a foreign land for a lifetime of service—only if God clearly directs.

Scripture is clear that the grace of God is expressed differently through different members of the body. We do not all have the same gifts and calling. But we all do have the grace of God, which is sufficient to carry out our particular ministry with a Livingstone-like vision and commitment. What is the measure of God's grace you have received?

Zealous ministry for God is nothing more than the expression of the powerful grace of God deposited in us.

Satan Is Doomed

The weapons of our warfare are not carnal but mighty in God for pulling down strongholds.

2 Corinthians 10:4

The ultimate victory has been won at Calvary, but it will be implemented in the future. The sentence has been passed; now it needs to be enforced. The enforcement is in the hands of the church. The tool that enforces Satan's defeat is the tool of prayer. "For the weapons of our warfare are not carnal but mighty in God for pulling down strongholds, casting down arguments and every high thing that exalts itself against the knowledge of God, bringing every thought into captivity to the obedience of Christ" (2 Corinthians 10:4–5). One person praying on earth can move angels in heaven.

Christians need to learn the power of prayer against Satan, for he will be defeated in his work. We are not engaged in the warfare if we are not praying against Satan. The judgment that was effected at the cross and is enforced through prayer will be completed. Satan is doomed. Satan is on a leash, and he is only free on earth to the length of his chain. He cannot go beyond God's permission. But if we don't enforce His judgment in our own lives, we will be victims instead of victors.

Confession Is Good for the Soul

If I regard iniquity in my heart,
The Lord will not hear.
Psalm 66:18

In pre-Revolution Russia, one of the most influential people in Czar Nicholas II's court was a wandering Orthodox monk named Grigori Rasputin. Empress Alexandra fell under Rasputin's spell and his doctrine of immorality—that it is the believer's responsibility to sin with abandon in order to experience the joy of repentance. The greater the sin, the greater the joy.

Rasputin clearly had not read Romans 6:1–2: "What shall we say then? Shall we continue in sin that grace may abound? Certainly not! How shall we who died to sin live any longer in it?" And had he read Psalm 32:3–4, he would have discovered that David found no pleasure in sin: "My bones grew old through my groaning all the day long. For day and night Your hand was heavy upon me; my vitality was turned into the drought of summer." The Bible is clear that sin is what separates us from God. Choosing not to confess our sin and turn from it is like cutting the communication lines with God.

Confession means to say the same thing about our sin that God says about it. And agreeing with God is always good for the soul.

The Spirit's Witness

The Spirit Himself bears witness with our spirit that we are children of God.

Romans 8:16

In Romans 8:16, Paul told the Romans, "The Spirit Himself bears witness with our spirit that we are children of God."

Wherever I travel across this country, people ask me, "How can I have assurance of salvation? How can I know that I really belong to Christ?" There are many scriptures to which we can point, but the bottom line is this: if you have the Holy Spirit living within you, that Spirit testifies with your spirit that you are a child of God. It is the inward witness of your faith.

Most of us have had the experience of saying to people, "I don't know exactly how to explain it, but I know I'm a Christian."

"Well, how do you know?"

"I just know inside."

We know inside because the Spirit of God is there, witnessing to our assurance. Somewhere within us, a voice whispers, *You are Mine. You are not your own. You belong to Me.*

How Did We Know?

The Lord has appeared of old to me, saying: "Yes, I have loved you with an everlasting love; therefore with lovingkindness I have drawn you."

Jeremiah 31:3

Comedian Jonathan Winters said in an interview that his life was scarred by the cruel things his parents said to him in childhood. "I'm no crybaby, but I remember things with almost total recall—there's a lot of pain there." His father once told him, "You're the dumbest kid I know."

When he joined the marines and went off to the South Pacific during World War II, Jonathan felt no support from his mother. When he came back home, he discovered that she had given away the precious, personal things he had stored in the attic. He was upset, but her response was, "How did we know you were going to live?"

Many people have scars caused by people's words. If that has happened to you, there's another voice you should hear. The Lord's words are stronger than anyone else's. He has words of love and life, words of affirmation. "I have loved you with an everlasting love," says the Father.

God loves you so much, and He desires a deep and delightful relationship with you. Don't be discouraged by the words of others. You are special in God's eyes.

A Sacrifice of Praise

By Him let us continually offer the sacrifice of praise to God, that is, the fruit of our lips, giving thanks to His name.

Hebrews 13:15

In the month that lies before you, you'll have countless opportunities for sacrifice. Think of that person at work whom you struggle to love. What if you visualize yourself placing that relationship upon the altar as an offering of praise to God?

Your marriage needs to be offered up as a sacrifice every day. So does the way you spend your free time. If you begin to make a list of the things you could offer up in sacrifice, you might never stop writing. You see, the truth is that when your life becomes a temple, a home for Jesus, you begin to see His face in the faces of all those who surround you. You begin to treat them as you would treat Him. You begin to realize that all ground is holy ground because God is there. You begin to see every situation as a potential act of worship, a time to magnify the name of the Lord.

Solitude. Service. Struggles. And ultimately, the one that encapsulates them all: sacrifice. Worship in the midst of these. When that happens, be prepared to throw open the doors of your life. The world is waiting to see the person you will become when you live every moment in the wonder of worship.

The Job of Thanksgiving

Heman and Jeduthun . . . were designated by name, to give thanks to the Lord.

1 Chronicles 16:41

Perhaps you've never heard of these two men; they're among the Bible's more obscure characters. Yet their role was paramount. In the great worship choirs of King David, they were appointed to give thanks. Jeduthun and Heman "were under the authority of the king," says 1 Chronicles 25:6. And they were designated by name to give thanks. It was their job!

Giving thanks is our job too. We're under the authority of a King who commands: "Be thankful" . . . "Offer to God thanksgiving" . . . "Come before His presence with thanksgiving" . . . "Enter into His gates with thanksgiving" . . . "In everything give thanks; for this is the will of God in Christ Jesus for you" (Colossians 3:15; Psalm 50:14; 95:2; 100:4; 1 Thessalonians 5:18, respectively).

This is one of God's commands for healthy living. The Creator of the soul is the Master Psychologist. He knows that thanksgiving is not only appropriate but therapeutic. It's hard to be both thankful and, at the same time, grumpy, cantankerous, critical, or ill-tempered.

Be a Heman. Be a Jeduthun. We are appointed by the King to praise His name and to thank Him every day.

Look Above for Help

With God nothing will be impossible.

Luke 1:37

Over and over again in the Old Testament, God is described as the Maker of heaven and earth. The Hebrews' worldview was based on the fact that their God was the Maker of all things, and as such He had the power and strength to meet all their needs. Therefore it was part of the continual confession, almost as a reminder, that their God (who is also our God) made all things—nothing was too hard for Him.

God created all things, and by Him all things are held together. If God holds the entire universe together, is it not reasonable to assume that He can hold the different aspects of your individual life together as well? He created us for the journey and sustains us through the journey as well.

So when you arrive at a place on your journey and you don't know what to do and you say, "Lord, I need help," remember this: the One to whom you are praying is the One who made heaven and earth. He can help you! The God who created us for life is the One who can help us with life.

Childlike Faith

So the Lord said, "If you have faith as a mustard seed . . ."

Luke 17:6

A man approached a Little League baseball game one afternoon while strolling through a park. He stopped and asked a boy in the dugout what the score was. The boy responded, "Eighteen to nothing—we're behind."

"Boy," said the spectator, "I'll bet you're discouraged."

"Why should I be discouraged?" replied the little boy. "We haven't even gotten up to bat yet!"

What a difference an optimistic attitude makes! As Christians, we have the ultimate comfort that we are blessed with the ultimate win—eternal life in heaven with God. But until then, how are we supposed to face the discouragements of this world? Job 16:5 says, "But my mouth would encourage you; comfort from my lips would bring you relief" (NIV).

God is our great encourager. He reminds us that with His help, anything is possible. It is a matter of perspective that determines the productivity of our actions. Childlike faith is the way to success in this world. Do you believe that the Lord will be faithful to provide for your needs and your desires? He is waiting to hear and see your enthusiasm for life; He is waiting to bless a childlike faith.

There's No Substitute for God's Word

We through the patience and comfort of the Scriptures might have hope.

Romans 15:4

The Bible is filled with encouraging truths. There's no need to find substitutes from other sources. God's Word is filled with truth, given to us for the sole purpose of encouraging our hearts. In Romans 15, Paul reminds us that one of the purposes of the Old Testament was to provide encouragement for us today: "For whatever things were written before were written for our learning, that we through the patience and comfort [encouragement] of the Scriptures might have hope" (v. 4). Everything from Genesis to Malachi was written for our learning so that we, through the encouragement of the Scriptures, might have hope. If you don't get your encouragement from God's Word, you may find its benefit sadly temporary.

In the New Testament, the theme of encouragement is everywhere, especially in Paul's writings. When Paul wrote to Timothy and Titus, he reminded those young pastors of the critical importance of using God's Word as a tool of encouragement. "Preach the word! Be ready in season and out of season. Convince, rebuke, exhort [encourage], with all longsuffering and teaching" (2 Timothy 4:2).

Believe Me When I Say

So will the Son of Man be three days and three nights in the heart of the earth.

Matthew 12:40

A little boy walked up to a lady sitting under an umbrella on the beach and asked, "Are you a Christian?" "Yes, I am," she replied. "Do you read your Bible every day?" "Yes, I do." "Do you pray often?" Yes, again. "Well," the lad concluded, "will you hold my quarter while I go swimming?"

Trustworthiness is developed by telling the truth and, more importantly, never failing to do what has been promised. It only takes one unkept promise or one lie to destroy credibility and become an untrustworthy person.

Take the resurrection of Jesus, for instance. Many times during His three-year ministry on earth He foretold that He would be killed but would rise from the dead after three days. And that's exactly what happened! That may be the most astounding self-fulfilled prediction ever made. The fact that Jesus was raised from the dead exactly as He foretold gives us confidence in everything else He said.

If there is anything Jesus said that you are tempted to question, remember the Resurrection. He proved His word is good.

To be trustworthy in the hardest thing is to be trustworthy in everything.

Redirected Faith

Not everyone who says to Me, "Lord, Lord," shall enter the kingdom of heaven, but he who does the will of My Father in heaven.

MATTHEW 7:21

Many people believe they will be welcomed into heaven because they've lived a good life, or they come from a religious family, or they've attended church all their lives.

My challenge is to help them see that they are placing faith in themselves—their works, their heritage, their personal standards of ethics and morality, or some other man-made qualification. They haven't understood that to become a Christian, they must redirect their faith from themselves to Jesus Christ. They must stop trusting in themselves, their parents, their heritage, their morality—and begin trusting in Jesus Christ. They must "bet" their eternal life on Christ alone. They must take Him at His word that He alone is able to save them.

The Reason We Serve

And whatever you do in word or deed, do all in the name of the Lord Jesus, giving thanks to God the Father through Him.

Colossians 3:17

Josh McDowell, who has spoken to millions of university students worldwide and authored scores of books, began his lifetime of service to Christ in a more humble fashion. His first assignment at the headquarters of Campus Crusade for Christ was scrubbing the main entryway floor. He wasn't meeting with the ministry's leaders; he was scrubbing up the dirt from their shoes.

Biblically, Josh's introduction to ministry was the equivalent of the guy in the Old Testament who carried the tent pegs when they moved the tabernacle from place to place. That is not exactly a high-profile task. Without a proper perspective on and motivation for ministry, it would be easy to get our feathers ruffled when given a lowly assignment.

So how do we stay motivated about serving God? By the promise that we will one day reap what we sow. God has promised to reward our faithful service at the judgment seat of Christ. If you are serving God, keep your heart focused on faithfulness instead of prominence.

When it comes to our rewards, motive will be determined by how much of what we did was for Jesus' sake.

Angels Must Never Receive Worship

Let no one cheat you of your reward, taking delight in false humility and worship of angels, intruding into those things which he has not seen, vainly puffed up by his fleshly mind.

Colossians 2:18

A desire for angels that is greater than a desire for the Creator will lead to trouble. One reason why angels are invisible to humans may be that, if they were seen, they would be worshiped. Man, who is so prone to idolatry as to worship the works of his own hands, would hardly be able to resist the worship of angels were they before his eyes.

Twice in the book of Revelation, John was confronted by an angel and tried to worship him. Both times the angel told him not to worship the angel but to worship God. Karl Barth once wrote that it is inappropriate for people to talk of angels independent of their experience of God in Christ. While God may send you angels, gratitude must always be directed to God, the God we know in Christ.

It is wrong to "ask your angel" something. We are never told to pray to angels. We pray to God, and He sends the help we need.

Defense Against Distractions

Above all else, guard your heart,
for it is the wellspring of life.
Proverbs 4:23 NIV

Perhaps they didn't get enough sleep the night before; maybe they were worn out from a hard day's work. Or maybe the clock ticked "bedtime." We've all been victims of drowsiness, so we shouldn't be surprised the three young men fell asleep. But we are! We're shocked because it was such an important night. This night, more than any other, required disciplined vigilance.

Jesus, about to begin His journey to the cross, asked the disciples to pray for Him. Imagine His disappointment when He found Peter, James, and John sleeping instead. Victims of drooping eyelids, the disciples missed an opportunity to encourage and strengthen Jesus in His moment of greatest need. And they missed the opportunity to strengthen themselves through prayer as well.

Satan knows if he can keep us from worship, he can keep us from spiritual power. He is the master distracter, able to deter us from worship with his tactics. How many times have we been distracted from our private worship by the TV, the telephone, a messy house, our to-do list, a wandering mind, or heavy eyelids?

When we prepare our hearts for personal worship, we must remember to guard our hearts from the distractions of Satan.

We Can Go Anywhere with Jesus

This Book of the Law shall not depart from your mouth, but you shall meditate in it day and night, that you may observe to do according to all that is written in it.

Joshua 1:8

Most of us read the Bible casually and carelessly. We read the Word of God, and it has no effect on us. That's why the Word of God has become so insipid in our lives; it has no power over us. The greatest thing we can do in reading God's Word is to understand that the Lord has given the book to us as our marching orders. We are to read it, study it, and then do it. Our prayer before reading the Bible should be, "Lord, show me in Your Word today what You want me to do! Show me the things in my life that are not in conformity with Your will, for I commit myself as I open this book that whatever You say to me here, I'll do it."

With Jesus with us we can go anywhere—into Canaan with its walled cities and giants everywhere, and into the days of the year ahead, where every day poses a mystery and a challenge. We all will face giants in our futures, but know this: if He is with us, we are sufficient to win in the power of our Lord and Savior, Jesus Christ.

The Right Look

As water reflects a face,
So a man's heart reflects the man.
Proverbs 27:19 NIV

You can tell a lot about a man by the way he dresses. Consider the family portrait. Each family member spends hours in front of the mirror trying to look just right. Then, in front of the camera, they are all on their best behavior with their largest smiles across their faces.

What if someone followed you around every day with a camera? It would make an impact, but it is up to you what kind of impact. Charles Spurgeon once said, "A man's life is always more forcible than his speech. When men take stock of him, they reckon his deeds as dollars and his words as pennies. If his life and doctrine disagree, the mass of onlookers accept his practice and reject his preaching."

Does your appearance reflect the transformation that Christ has done in your heart? First Peter 3:3–4 says, "Your beauty should not come from outward adornment. . . . Instead, it should be that of your inner self . . . which is of great worth in God's sight" (NIV).

Hold your head up high, and make the spiritual family portrait more beautiful from the inside out.

Frozen in Sin

[The wicked man] shall die for lack of instruction,
And in the greatness of his folly he shall go astray.
Proverbs 5:23

The story is told of an eagle perched on a block of ice just above Niagara Falls. The swift current carried the ice and its majestic passenger close to the edge of the great precipice. Other birds warned the eagle of the danger ahead. But their words were unheeded. "I have great and powerful wings," he boasted. "I can fly from my perch at any time."

Suddenly the edge of the falls was only a few feet away. The eagle spread his powerful wings to mount up over his impending doom only to discover that his claws had become frozen to the block of ice.

Scripture warns those who think they are immune to sin to be careful! They are on the verge of falling (1 Corinthians 10:12; 1 Timothy 3:6). "I never thought it would happen to me" are words that have hounded many a person until their dying day (Proverbs 5:11–14). Every Christian needs to know that yielding to temptation can happen—and will, unless the instruction of wisdom is embraced.

Wisdom says, "Hear me clearly: the road to immorality is the road to destruction."

Comprehension

For we are not ignorant of his [Satan's] devices.

2 Corinthians 2:11

There's nothing wrong with eating a piece of bread, but Jesus, seeing through the devil's scheme at the Temptation, refused to partake. He said, "It is written, 'Man shall not live by bread alone, but by every word that proceeds from the mouth of God'" (Matthew 4:4).

There may be nothing wrong with repeating that story, attending that play, making that purchase, or saying those words. But sometimes there is something wrong with doing those things if we'll just have the discernment to recognize it.

One of Satan's oldest tricks is to confuse our values so that good appears to be evil, and evil appears as good. He is the deceiver, and his deadliest tools often appear to be innocent pleasures. The Bible tells us to "put on the whole armor of God, that you may be able to stand against the wiles of the devil" (Ephesians 6:11).

Where do we find the needed wisdom to spot Satan's ploys? Only a close walk with God, a deep study of Scripture, and an intense prayer life will supply the special discernment to see through his devices.

Ask God for wisdom. Ask Him to guard your mind, your mouth, and your morals. Ask Him to open your eyes and to deliver you from evil. And keep your armor on!

Rader of the Lost Souls

Your ears shall hear a word behind you,
saying, "This is the way, walk in it."
Isaiah 30:21

Evangelist Paul Rader had often spoken to a certain banker in New York concerning his soul, but to no avail. One day God seemed to speak to Rader, urging him to go immediately and once again seek out this individual. Obediently, he caught a train and went to the banker's house. As he approached the house, he saw the banker standing in the doorway. "Oh, Rader," the banker said, "I'm so glad to see you. I wrote a letter begging you to come, but I tore it up."

"That may be so," replied the evangelist, "but your message came by way of heaven." Under deep conviction of sin, the man was impressed by Rader's special effort to reach him with the gospel. Consequently, that very hour he accepted the Lord. In his newfound joy he exclaimed, "Rader, did you ever see the sky so blue or the grass so green?" Suddenly the banker leaned heavily against Rader, then with a gasp fell into his arms—dead! He had been saved on the very brink of eternity. What if Paul Rader had delayed to come, taking the promptings of the Lord with less urgency? Let us always be keenly sensitive to the Lord's leadings.

Staying Power

A new commandment I give to you,
that you love one another.

John 13:34

A cartoon in a national magazine showed a couple standing before a minister during their wedding. The minister, looking at the bride, said, "The correct response is 'I do'—not 'It's worth a try.'"

Love—in marriage and in other relationships—requires dogged commitment on our part. Contrary to popular opinion, love doesn't come naturally for us humans. Love is others-centered and self-sacrificing. We are self-centered; and, in our own natural selves, we care little about sacrifice unless powerfully motivated.

In fact, the Bible teaches that only someone who really knows God through Jesus is capable of the kind of love the Bible describes. John wrote, "Love comes from God. Everyone who loves has been born of God and knows God. Whoever does not love does not know God, because God is love" (1 John 4:7–8 NIV).

Paul taught that God's love is "poured out in our hearts by the Holy Spirit" (Romans 5:5), and Jesus said that the world would recognize that we are Christians by our love (John 13:35). Love grows as we nurture it. It develops as we feed it. It expands as we persist in it. That kind of love has staying power.

The Spirit's Instruction

Now we have received, not the spirit of the world, but the Spirit who is from God, that we might know the things that have been freely given to us by God.

1 Corinthians 2:12

Years ago, I remember hearing Campus Crusade founder Bill Bright teaching on the Holy Spirit. In his message, he told about a man to whom he'd been witnessing. One of this man's problems with the Christian faith was that he'd tried again and again to read the Bible but couldn't make any sense of it.

Then the man received Jesus Christ and came back to visit Dr. Bright a week later. He had an amazing story to tell. During that week's time, he said, it was as though somebody had rewritten his Bible. Suddenly the Scripture came alive to him. Understanding broke into his thoughts like quick lightning strikes.

How had it happened? The Teacher had taken up residence within him. What had once been obscure and confusing now pulsated with meaning, encouragement, and hope.

Paul wrote, "Now we have received, not the spirit of the world, but the Spirit who is from God, that we might know the things that have been freely given to us by God." That means that Christians, who have the Spirit of God living within them, have an inward interpreter who helps them to understand what the Bible means.

The Queen's Fast

Fast for me . . . And so I will go.

Esther 4:16

There may be times in life when we must say no to our physical desires so we can focus on spiritual needs. Fasting can express our fervency in prayer and therefore prepare us to meet challenges.

Esther's life provides a good example of the importance of fasting, especially when approaching an important moment. In Esther 4:4–16, Queen Esther became so deeply distressed about the fate of her people that she stopped eating or drinking and told all the Jews not to eat or drink for three days. The king had been tricked into signing an order for the annihilation of the Jewish nation. Knowing that it could mean her death, the queen approached the king to plead for the lives of her people. Instead of killing her, the king offered her half his kingdom because "she found favor in his sight" (5:2).

Esther prayed and fasted to save her people, and God saved them. If you are facing a critical decision, practice the spiritual discipline of fasting. Your single-mindedness will help you focus on earnestly seeking God.

Waiting Out of Control

Abram fell on his face, and God talked with him, saying, "As for Me, behold, My covenant is with you, and you shall be a father of many nations."

Genesis 17:3–4

We learn from reading about Abraham that hope is necessary because often waiting is uncontrollable. Did you know God didn't tell him how long he would have to wait? He just said, "Here's the hope. You just wait."

God's promise to Abraham was not to be fulfilled for many years. And in some respects that promise was not totally fulfilled even in his lifetime. You and I are the fulfillment of that promise. According to Galatians, we are the children of Abraham. We are the result of God having blessed Abraham, Isaac, and Jacob; having blessed the nation of Israel; and then, through Israel, having blessed all of us. We are blessed because of Abraham. But Abraham never saw all of that. He saw enough, but he had to wait.

Hope is the ingredient that keeps us going between the promise and the fulfillment. Hope is the thing that gets us up in the morning when we know that God cares but we haven't seen any evidence of it in the last few days. Hope drives us onward when we want to stop and quit. Hope keeps our dreams alive while we are waiting. And we need hope because we can't always control the timetable.

Giving Credit Where It's Due

I am the Lord, that is My name; and My glory I will not give to another.

Isaiah 42:8

Evangelist Billy Graham is well known for his humility. Despite worldwide fame, he still finds it difficult to say no to anyone approaching him, he is unfailingly pleasant to strangers, and he always credits God with the success of his ministry. His guiding verse on the subject of personal humility has been Isaiah 42:8: "I am the Lord . . . My glory I will not give to another."

Tragically, success often changes people. We see it especially in the athletic world. Someone gets to the top, makes the starting team, and experiences fame. Suddenly he changes. His humble, submissive attitude is gone.

Can you be humble in the face of success? Humility doesn't imply a lack of self-confidence, nor does it make us a doormat for others to walk on. It isn't having a low self-image or thinking poorly of oneself. Humility means not thinking of oneself very much at all, but thinking of Jesus Christ more and more.

Whatever we accomplish is due to His blessings. Whatever we gain comes from Him, for "every good and perfect gift is from above" (James 1:17 niv). Remember to give Him the glory, honor, and praise for any success that comes your way.

Awestruck

Who shall not fear You, O Lord, and glorify Your name? For you alone are holy.
Revelation 15:4

The primary meaning of the word *holy* is "separate." It means "to cut." A holy person is cut apart from the rest. God is holy in that He is totally, in His person, separate from all of us. So much so that it is almost a foreign subject to talk of Him. He is so awesome and so overwhelming in His person that there is nothing in human language or in human experience to which we may compare Him.

Some years ago, a German scholar named Rudolf Otto tried to determine in a scientific way what happened to people when they came in contact with that which they believed to be holy. He observed that there is something extra in the experience of the Holy, something you can't describe in human terms. The clearest sensation a human being has when he experiences the Holy is an overwhelming sense of creatureliness. When we meet the Absolute, we know immediately that we are not absolute. When we meet the Infinite, we come in contact immediately with our own finiteness. When we meet the Absolute Holy, we become aware that we are not like that.

Freedom to Love

Love does no harm to a neighbor; therefore love is the fulfillment of the law.

Romans 13:10

The famous nineteenth-century preacher Charles H. Spurgeon was fond of smoking cigars. Because this was before the days of research into the effects of tobacco, he saw nothing wrong with the practice. Until, that is, he passed a tobacco shop with a sign advertising a particular cigar for sale: "The cigar smoked by C. H. Spurgeon." That was the last day Spurgeon ever smoked a cigar.

Charles Spurgeon recognized that something he had a right to engage in might be viewed as a vice by other believers. He didn't want his actions to be a stumbling block for others; his love for people was greater than his love for cigars.

Spurgeon learned this spiritual lesson in love from the apostle Paul, who counseled first-century Christians to be self-sacrificing in their love for one another. While "all things are lawful," he wrote, "all things are not helpful" (1 Corinthians 6:12). Freedom in Christ does not mean we have the right to do anything we want. Rather, it means we have the power to do everything we ought.

If there is any right you love more than a brother's or sister's progress toward holiness, it is a right that is best left unexercised.

JULY

Therefore, having been justified by faith, we have peace with God through our Lord Jesus Christ.

—Romans 5:1

Offering of Peace

Peace I leave with you, My peace I give to you.
John 14:27

Christ offered His peace to the disciples during an unbelievably difficult period in His own life. He was enjoying the peace of God, but He knew the disciples were about to be sorely tested and would need God's peace as well. Anyone can have peace when things are going well at home, with finances, and with regard to health. Even the world can manifest a semblance of peace when everything is going smoothly.

It is in the context of difficulties that God wants us to experience His peace and manifest it to the world. Jesus offered His peace to the disciples at exactly the time it would be needed most: a time when their own sense of peace and calm would likely disappear. He wanted His disciples—and He wants us—to be at peace during the most difficult hours of our lives.

Believers in Christ can live in a world where seemingly irrational and indiscriminate things happen without warning but not be undone by worry and fear. We can have peace knowing that God is in control of our lives. While it may appear that things are out of control in the world, we can know that we are eternally protected and watched over by God's sovereign and loving care.

When Giving Equals Living

For the love of money is a root of all kinds of evil.

1 Timothy 6:10

The Italian city of Pompeii was destroyed by the eruption of the volcano Mount Vesuvius in AD 79. When modern excavators began digging in the ruins, among the many bodies found frozen in time was that of a woman whose feet faced the city gate but whose hand was reaching back for a bag of pearls. Her effort to save her wealth was rewarded with death.

Perhaps the woman dropped the pearls when fleeing the city, or perhaps the pearls had been dropped by another. In any case, she wanted them. Two people died that day: a person who loved life and a person who loved wealth. In her case, wealth won and life lost.

If we pursue righteousness and greed together, our destination is disaster (Matthew 6:24). The Pharisees discovered this when they refused to support their own parents by claiming that all their funds had been dedicated to the Lord's work (Mark 7:9–13). The idea that God would be pleased with such hypocrisy shows how little the Pharisees knew of Him. Greed will make hypocrites out of the pseudorighteous before they have time to say, "I wanted to give more but . . ."

The righteous live and give the same way. Make sure you don't lose something eternal while grasping for something temporal.

Worship Courageously

I will praise You with my whole heart;
Before the gods I will sing praises to You.
Psalm 138:1

David was not ashamed of his God. He would boldly praise the God of Israel in the presence of false gods without worrying what anyone said or thought of him. Are you willing to do that today?

I can remember when it was very common to see families and others in restaurants bowing their heads and joining hands to worship and thank God before their meal. Our family does that, but I don't see as many today as I used to. It is a wonderful way to encourage other families. People who are not ashamed to pray publicly to their God stand out in an age when it is common to be ridiculed for your faith.

I see some people who sort of bow their head, or look like they're looking for their napkin, or scratch their forehead—trying to pray before their meal without looking like they're praying. Who are they fooling? David said, "I will praise my God before all the pagan gods." He praised God courageously.

Revive Us Again

Will You not revive us again,
That Your people may rejoice in You?
Psalm 85:6

Only a revival of biblical proportions can restore America to moral decency and spiritual strength. Don't think that such a revival is impossible; it has happened before, and it can happen again. God often sends revival when times are at their worst.

The mood of America was grim during the mid-1850s. In New York City, a layman named Jeremiah C. Lanphier announced a series of noontime prayer meetings to begin September 23, 1857, at the Old Dutch Church on Fulton Street. When the hour came, Lanphier found himself alone. Finally, one man showed up, then a few others.

The next week, twenty came. The third week, forty. Other churches opened their doors. The revival spread to other cities. Offices and stores closed for prayer at noon. Newspapers spread the story, and even telegraph companies set aside certain hours during which businessmen could wire one another with news of the revival. The revival, sometimes called the Third Great Awakening, lasted nearly two years, and between five hundred thousand and one million people were said to have been converted.

Ask God to revive us again, and let it begin with you.

Caring for Single Saints

Now all who believed were together, and had all things in common, and sold their possessions and goods, and divided them among all, as anyone had need.

Acts 2:44–45

I want to address a word to single parents—and to those in the churches they attend. I know of no greater need for a ministry of support and encouragement than to those who are handling the pressures and responsibilities of vocation and childrearing alone. Single parents are fighting battles that no one else in the church is facing.

God can use our resources to help meet the needs of the single parents in our churches. He wants to use people to meet the needs of people in our churches today—especially the needs of all our single saints.

Are you a single Christian? Then do what you can to express a desire for ministry and a desire to be ministered to. If you are a leader in your church, do what you can to raise the priority and resources given to ministry to singles. This growing segment of the church must no longer feel as though they are outsiders. They must be as welcome as the most famous single person of all time—Jesus Himself.

Presidential Prayers

I exhort first of all that supplications, prayers, intercessions, and giving of thanks be made for all men, for kings and all who are in authority.

1 Timothy 2:1–2

On January 20, 1953, the newly sworn-in president, Dwight D. Eisenhower, surprised America by opening his inaugural address with prayer. "My friends," he said, "before I begin . . . would you permit me the privilege of uttering a little private prayer of my own? And I ask that you bow your heads."

He then prayed, "Almighty God, as we stand here at this moment, my future associates in the executive branch of government join me in beseeching that Thou will make full and complete our dedication to the service of the people in this throng. . . . Give us . . . the power to discern clearly right from wrong, and allow all our words and actions to be governed thereby."

Have you prayed today for your national, state, and local leaders? Presidents, prime ministers, and leaders everywhere need our prayers. Our senators, representatives, governors, mayors, and aldermen can be guided and influenced by prayer. Take a page from Eisenhower's speech, and ask God to give our leaders the ability to discern right from wrong—and to choose the right.

Spiritual Liberty

God has not given us a spirit of fear, but of power and of love and of a sound mind.

2 Timothy 1:7

We have been released from the spirit of fear by the Holy Spirit, who has placed us in the body of Christ. We have received the Spirit of adoption. This adoption provides for every believer release from the bondage that he once knew. The picture that Paul uses is the contrast between slavery and sonship. Slavery, with its fear and isolation, stands for our old lives before knowing Christ. We are told by the writer of Hebrews that Christ died that He might destroy the one who had the power of death and release those who were subject to a fear of death (Hebrews 2:14–15). The perfect love of God has cast out the fear to which we were once enslaved (2 Timothy 1:7; 1 John 4:18).

Anything that involves a believer in fear of bondage cannot possibly be the work of the Holy Spirit of God. It must come either from his own heart of unbelief or as a temptation of the evil one. Our sonship implies perfect spiritual liberty and the absence of all legal features that would bring us once more under the law.

FREEDOM!

If the Son makes you free, you shall be free indeed.
JOHN 8:36

John Witherspoon, one of the signers of the Declaration of Independence, had been a Presbyterian leader in Scotland when called to become president of the College of New Jersey (now Princeton). Despite his wife's terror at crossing the ocean, they accepted the call and arrived in America in 1768.

In May 1776, as the United Colonies readied for war, Witherspoon gave a famous sermon entitled "The Dominion of Providence," saying, "This is the first time of my introducing any political subject into the pulpit." He insisted the cause of freedom was just and God-blessed, but most of his message begged his hearers to give their hearts to Christ.

While independence is important, he said, the eternal state of souls is even more so. "There can be no true religion till there be a discovery of your lost state by nature and practice, and an unfeigned acceptance of Christ Jesus, as He is offered in the Gospel. Unhappy are they who either despise His mercy or are ashamed of His cross. Believe it, there is no salvation in any other."

We thank God for our freedom today. But are you "free indeed"? Have you received eternal life in the Lord Jesus Christ?

Boast About God

My soul shall make its boast in the Lord.

Psalm 34:2

When I feel afraid, I'm prone to pull the blanket over my head and hope it goes away. Or I nurse my fears. The adversary of our souls loves to get our attention focused on ourselves and not on the resources of our God.

What will happen when you praise and worship God? Your praise makes God big in your heart and mind. Soon, your problem falls into perspective. When I worship God, sometimes even with the tears coming down my face, my spirit is renewed as I praise God. My problem doesn't go away, but all of a sudden I see it in relation to the One who is in charge of everything.

It's interesting what we boast about, isn't it? At the last party you went to, what did you boast about? Put the spotlight on the Lord, and focus on Him. When we get together with friends, let's just brag on Jesus. So many good things are happening in our lives as individuals, in our families, and in our churches that we ought to boast on the Lord all the time.

LET FREEDOM RING!

And you shall know the truth, and
the truth shall make you free.
JOHN 8:32

We hold these truths to be self-evident, that all men are created equal, that they are endowed by their Creator with certain unalienable Rights, that among these are Life, Liberty, and the pursuit of Happiness." So states America's Declaration of Independence. A foundational truth, being watered down in history textbooks with every succeeding generation, is that America's Founding Fathers saw liberty as a God-given right.

America is not the symbol of liberty to the whole world by accident. This nation was designed to reflect, corporately and individually, a principle found only in the Bible—that man was created to be free. Nothing was to hinder the creature's relationship with his Creator—not kings, or governments, or tyranny, or the will of man. In a day when American soldiers are defending our right to live free from terrorism, it is incumbent upon us to thank God for a land in which freedom's bell has rung for more than two hundred years. Will prayers of thanksgiving for freedom be heard in your home today?

Those who take freedom for granted are also in danger of taking for granted the Author of freedom Himself.

Keep the Faith

It is required in stewards that one be found faithful.

1 Corinthians 4:2

God places a high premium on the quality of faithfulness. He says to us by way of Paul in 1 Corinthians 4:2, "It is required in stewards that one be found faithful." We are all stewards of the grace of God. God has given Christians an opportunity to administer part of His kingdom on this earth on His behalf.

If there is anything at all we need in our churches, it is this quality of faithfulness. Sometimes described as fidelity, sometimes defined as steadfastness, it always means the determination to stay by your word and complete your commitment.

How we need the quality of faithfulness in our world today. Contracts mean nothing. Commitments mean nothing. We don't mean what we say. Sooner or later, like everything else, that kind of thing begins to creep into the body of Christ. We have lost the characteristic of faithfulness.

God is teaching us that we are to be faithful no matter what. What a freeing thing that is! God has given all of us something to do, and He says to us, "Here's what I want from you in this assignment. Be faithful."

Worship the King

The Lamb will overcome them, for He is Lord of lords and King of kings.

Revelation 17:14

People often ask why the audience stands during the singing of the "Hallelujah Chorus" portion of Handel's *Messiah*. The custom dates back to the 1740s, when England's King George II heard the presentation for the first time. He was so moved by the "Hallelujah Chorus" that he stood to his feet in honor of the King of kings and Lord of lords. Since no one remains seated when royalty stands, the rest of the audience stood as well—and audiences have stood ever since.

In the ancient Near East, the superlative form of an adjective or adverb was not described in one word, as it is in English (such as *best*, *brightest*, or *funniest*). The best song was "the song of songs," and the greatest king was "the king of kings." Artaxerxes, king of Persia, referred to himself as the "king of kings" (Ezra 7:12), and God gave Nebuchadnezzar of Babylon the same title (Ezekiel 26:7).

A day is coming when the whole world will recognize the true "King of kings," Jesus Christ. If He is not the king you worship, wouldn't now be the time to worship Him as the King of kings?

Whether standing or bowing, worship is due the King of kings.

Jesus' Final Warning

Take heed to yourselves and to all the flock, among which the Holy Spirit has made you overseers, to shepherd the church of God which He purchased with His own blood.

Acts 20:28

If AT&T could establish a direct phone link between earth and heaven on a given Sunday morning and Jesus spoke simultaneously via satellite to congregations all over the world, what do you think He would say? You're sitting there in your pew, your heart beating fast. What will His instructions be? "You shall be witnesses to Me . . . to the end of the earth" (Acts 1:8). And after He said that, I think He would certainly repeat the words He spoke to Peter: "Feed My sheep" (John 21:17).

In other words, "Brothers and sisters in the church, you live in a time of terrible demolition. My eyes miss nothing. I have seen it all. But even while precious things all around you are being torn down and dismantled, you can be in the process of building. Build up My church! Take care of My sheep. Feed them. Tend them. Love them . . . as I have loved you."

We don't need a direct phone line, do we? We don't need a satellite connection to heaven. He has given us His inerrant Word, which is a light to our feet and a lamp to our path. He has given us His Holy Spirit to dwell within us, illuminating the pages of Scripture, reminding us of everything Jesus taught.

Freedom and Security

But seek first the kingdom of God and His righteousness, and all these things shall be added to you.

Matthew 6:33

Compare the oyster and the eagle. The oyster has a rock-hard home to protect it from predators and opens its shell whenever it wants nourishment. The eagle resides on freezing and exposed mountain crags and flies through miles of dangerous weather in search of food. The oyster is completely secure, while the eagle is completely free. Which did America choose as its national symbol?

Animals don't choose their lifestyles; they just follow their God-given instincts. So we can't be too critical of one over the other. But all too often, we see humans who choose worldly security over spiritual freedom. They invest all their time and talent in laying up treasures on earth. Security against the unexpected becomes their obsession.

There's nothing wrong with security, of course. The question is, where do we seek it: in God or in the things of this world? Do a security check in your own life. Wherever you find some insecurities, look at them against the backdrop of God's great resources, not your own.

Oysters may be secure and eagles may be free, but Christians are both secure and free when they live in dependence on God.

The Spirit of Encouragement

The Helper, the Holy Spirit, whom the Father will send in My name, He will teach you all things, and bring to your remembrance all the things that I said to you.

John 14:26

The Holy Spirit's other name is Comforter. That is my favorite name for the Holy Spirit. The word *comforter* is a Greek word, *paraclete*, and it is the same word that is translated "encourager."

The Holy Spirit is my Encourager. He comes and puts His arm around me when I am discouraged, and He encourages me.

Yes, there are times when this pastor loses his perspective a little and becomes discouraged. I may have actually slipped into depression once or twice (not recently, thank the Lord). It's the same with anyone in leadership; sometimes you feel as though there is hardly anywhere to run. You just have to get alone with your Bible, get down on your knees in prayer . . . and then the Spirit of God comes to bring encouragement to your heart. I've had that experience time and again. It is almost (almost!) worth experiencing the dark and heavy times because the encouragement of God's Spirit is so sweet. I praise God that the Holy Spirit is my Comforter and Encourager and Helper.

Guard and Guide

And the Angel of God, who went before the camp of Israel . . . gave light by night.

Exodus 14:19–20

It was the Lord Himself—a pillar of fire—who ushered the Israelites through the Red Sea. His presence cast darkness on the Egyptians but light on the children of Israel. What a perfect description of our Lord Jesus, who gives light to those who trust Him; but to those who reject Him, utter darkness. He comforts the one and confounds the other. He is a Savior to the one and a Judge to the other.

For His children, the Lord is both guard and guide. He precedes us and protects us. He is simultaneously our shepherd and shield. He is Alpha and Omega, the first and the last, the One who goes before and the One who goes behind, gathering up our debris and our failures, blessing us, and leaving a blessing behind us for others.

When you feel the enemy on your heels, remember that He who is a pillar of fire goes with you. He's "a very present help in trouble" (Psalm 46:1).

Trials in the Believer's Life

Deliver me in Your righteousness,
and cause me to escape;
Incline Your ear to me and save me.

Psalm 71:2

When in the hospital during my bout with cancer, I awakened in a morphine-induced grogginess with the thought to read Psalm 71. I recall noting the hour—3:00 a.m.—but could not remember who, prior to coming to the hospital, had encouraged me to meditate on that particular psalm. I reached for my Bible and began to read the words of the psalmist, who wrote concerning a dark night he had been through. The words of that psalm were a bright light in a dark night in my life—and can be for you as well.

Regardless of the name of the author of this psalm, we do know this about him: he was thoroughly familiar with the ways and words of God. It is a compilation of truths about God's deliverance of His saints during times of trouble.

It is not the absence of suffering but the response to suffering that makes Christians unique. Believers are not exempt from trials in life, but we can be exempt from failure in those trials.

Don't Leave Home Without Him

For through Him we both have access
by one Spirit to the Father.
Ephesians 2:18

Competing credit-card companies love to one-up each other by announcing the remote, exotic, or unique places on earth where their card is accepted—and where the competition's is not. A credit card becomes like a universal economic passport. Meet a merchant in an out-of-the-way place who accepts your credit card, and you are family! You are united by financial bonds that cross all cultural and geographic boundaries.

Well, maybe not family—but that's how the companies want us to think of ourselves if we use their cards. Go anywhere, meet anyone, buy whatever you want—your credit card is your link to the world. That may be true, but it's a shallow form of unity: an inch deep and a world wide.

A much deeper sense of belonging is provided by another type of identity: possession of the Holy Spirit. Travel anywhere in the world, meet a fellow believer in Christ, and there is instant fellowship. Next time you make a new Christian friend, skip the formalities and polite introductions—you're family!

To be filled with the Spirit as you travel through life gives access to the most meaningful network on earth: the body of Christ.

Doing the Right Thing

Wisdom is the principal thing;
Therefore get wisdom:
And in all your getting, get understanding.
Proverbs 4:7

My favorite secular definition of *wisdom* is, "Doing the right thing without precedent." That means you know what to do in a situation even though you've never experienced it before.

In his book *Knowing God*, J. I. Packer offers a helpful illustration for understanding wisdom using the metaphor of a railroad or subway system. He said some people think of wisdom as if they're sitting in the control room looking at a giant board on which the movement of all the trains is tracked. You can see everything that's going on in the city's rail system at one time; you have a total picture of everything. Some people think the wiser they become, the greater grasp they will have of the mysteries of God—how everything in the universe works and how all the pieces fit together. But that is not what biblical wisdom is all about.

I have found the opposite to be true. The more knowledge of God I get (that is, the wiser I become), the more I realize how much I don't know, and will never know, about God and His ways.

The Meyer Method

Envy is rottenness to the bones.

Proverbs 14:30

Everyone is vulnerable to jealousy. The famous Bible teacher F. B. Meyer, who struggled with it, found only one solution. Meyer often preached at D. L. Moody's Bible Conference in Northfield, Massachusetts, where he was popular and drew large crowds. But one day another well-known Bible teacher, Dr. G. Campbell Morgan, was invited to preach at Northfield.

To Meyer's consternation, Morgan's audiences were larger. Meyer confessed to his friends that he was tempted to feel envious of Morgan, but he said, "The only way I can conquer my feelings is to pray for him daily, which I do."

Why is it we feel a secret inner cringing when our close friend wins a free trip to Hawaii? When our coworker gets a raise? When our buddy wins the MVP trophy? When our best friend's child gets the starring role in the play?

Envy isn't just an inner emotion; it's a sinful attitude. Mark tells us that the chief priests handed Jesus over to be crucified "because of envy" (Mark 15:10). If you're envious of someone today, try the Meyer method—pray for that person. It's hard to envy someone while asking God to bless him!

No Ministry Apart From Service

As each one has received a gift, minister it to one another, as good stewards of the manifold grace of God.

1 Peter 4:10

Ministry and *service* are from the same Greek word and mean essentially the same thing. There is no ministry apart from service. No one can have an impact in ministry who is not also willing to serve or to be a servant.

There is always a price tag attached to service. It might be health; it might be convenience; it might be aggravation; it might be humility. Whatever the cost, it is what adorns the neck of those who minister.

Ministry in the church is like being a parent. The most successful parents are those who learn to sacrifice for their children. And while we parents think our children are never going to realize what we have sacrificed in service to them, they eventually do. And what we have sacrificed for them comes back to us as the fruit of a close and intimate relationship with them. And it's the same way in ministry in the church. The more we give of ourselves in ministry to others, the more we will get back in return. I heard the speaker John Maxwell say once, "If you are going to go up, you have to give up." There is no way to advance in ministry without giving of ourselves.

Don't Fumble Your Faith

Be sober, be vigilant; because your adversary
the devil walks about like a roaring lion,
seeking whom he may devour.

1 Peter 5:8

Running back Rashaan Salaam won the Heisman Trophy in 1994 as the best player in college football. But in his rookie season with the NFL's Chicago Bears, he fumbled the ball nine times. To prevent future fumbles, the coaches fixed a tether to the football. When Salaam ran with it in practice, someone ran behind him jerking on the tether, forcing Salaam to grasp the ball more tightly. As his grip grew stronger, his fumbles grew fewer.

The Bible is clear that God does not tempt anyone to sin (James 1:13). But it is also clear that God allows us to be tempted. Have you ever wondered why? Just as having someone try to jerk the ball out of his hands caused a star football player to stop fumbling, so God allows Satan to attempt to steal our faith so we'll learn to grasp it tighter. Often we don't realize the value of something we have until someone attempts to steal it from us. Your faith is a treasure delivered to you for safekeeping by God. Hold it tight regardless of how hard you're hit by the opposition.

View temptations as your heavenly Coach's way to keep you from fumbling your faith.

Are You Good?

Why do you call Me good? No one is good but One, that is, God.

Matthew 19:17

A person who is a good person is an individual of lofty ideals, noble purposes, strong character, reliable conduct, and trustworthy integrity. The only one who truly embodies all of those characteristics is Jesus Christ.

We come to understand the word *goodness* as we see it alongside the word *righteousness.* Someone has said that justice is what God gives to us that we deserve. Goodness goes beyond that and is that which God gives us beyond what we deserve.

The great characteristic of goodness as it is found in relationship with righteousness is generosity. It is what a person gets that isn't deserved. It is what God gives to a person that could never be earned. Goodness in its relationship to righteousness teaches us about generosity.

You don't have to be rich to be generous. But what do you do with what you have? We need to take a good, long look at our lives and ask God how our attitudes have been to the needs around us. If we've been protective and closefisted, we need to say, "God, by the grace You will give me, I will change." Begin to bear fruit in your life, the fruit of a generous spirit.

The Power of the Word

And daily in the temple, and in every house, they did not cease teaching and preaching Jesus as the Christ.

Acts 5:42

Alexander Smith was the sole survivor of the band of mutineers who took the English ship *Bounty* from its captain, William Bligh, in 1787. The community of natives for which Smith found himself responsible on Pitcairn Island were defeated, diseased, and despondent—until he discovered the *Bounty's* Bible, which he began to teach them. Twenty years later, a visiting ship found a thriving Christian community, the fruit of the Word of God.

Because the Word of God is living and active (Hebrews 4:12), and because it never fails to accomplish the purposes for which it was given (Isaiah 55:10–11), we should not be surprised when we read stories like that of Alexander Smith. Multitudes of lives throughout history—including yours?—have been transformed by responding to the teaching of Scripture. Some Christians have the spiritual gift of teaching, but all Christians are responsible for knowing God's truth and communicating it to others as the Spirit gives opportunity.

God has chosen preaching and teaching the Bible as the means for announcing the good news of salvation. How shall people otherwise hear (Romans 10:14)?

Prayer Circles

Be anxious for nothing, but in everything by prayer and supplication, with thanksgiving, let your requests be made known to God.

Philippians 4:6

One of the best ways I know to remember how to commit things to God in prayer is by remembering three circles. One is the worry circle, in which I keep nothing. Second is the prayer circle, in which I keep everything. Third is the gratitude circle, in which I keep anything. So when I pray, I am anxious for nothing, prayerful for everything, and thankful for anything (Philippians 4:6).

We feel foolish asking God to help us with some of the things in our lives. But remember, "In everything by prayer and supplication, with thanksgiving, let your requests be made known to God." You just need to write out every one of your concerns before they turn into worries and commit them to God. He does care about each of them. If you take them back, just give them back to Him in prayer again. Day by day, as you get more and more practiced at committing the affairs of your life to Him, you will begin to leave them with Him. Your trust in Him will grow, and you will stop grabbing back what you have given Him.

Accept One Another

Therefore receive one another, just as Christ also received us, to the glory of God.

Romans 15:7

Author and Nobel laureate Elie Wiesel worked in New York City after World War II as a correspondent for a French newspaper. His travel permit expired, and he was told at the French consulate that he would have to return to France to have it renewed, which he could not afford to do. At the U.S. immigration office, an official kindly said to him, "Why don't you become a U.S. resident and apply for citizenship?" So he did. Years later, when offered French citizenship, Wiesel declined. When he needed a homeland, it was America that had offered him one.

People often gravitate to where they are accepted. When we were lost, "having no hope and without God in the world" (Ephesians 2:12), it was God who "accepted [us] in the Beloved" (Ephesians 1:6). Once accepted by Him, we remain because of the riches of grace He bestows upon us. Millions of wandering souls have found welcome refuge in America, but millions more have found welcome acceptance in the kingdom of God. If you know people who are looking for acceptance, why not model God's acceptance by extending them yours?

Accepting people as they are is the first step toward helping them find out who they can become.

Footprints

Fear not, for I am with you.

Isaiah 43:5

While stranded on a deserted island, Daniel Defoe's character Robinson Crusoe salvaged a Bible from the shipwreck, read it, and was converted. He grew into a devout Christian. His life, though missing human companionship, was peaceful and prayerful.

But one day he found a footprint in the sand and realized he wasn't alone. Knowing the cannibalism of the local tribes, he grew into a fearful man, looking over his shoulder with every step. He no longer slept peacefully. He altered his habits. He visualized himself being captured and devoured. "That former confidence in God . . . now vanished, as if He that had fed me by miracle hitherto could not preserve, by His power, the provision which He had made for me by His goodness."

Crusoe had to go back to his Bible, repent of anxiety, and be strengthened again in his faith. He eventually learned the great lesson of faltering Christians: the things we most fear are likely, in the providence of God, to be most used for our good. In the end, those footprints led to his deliverance.

God has planned out our future from eternity past and guaranteed it with His promises. We can trust Him.

The Benchmark of Our Faith

And if Christ is not risen, then our preaching is empty and your faith is also empty.

1 Corinthians 15:14

The Christian apologist and author C. S. Lewis made an interesting observation about Jesus' practice of saying to people, "I forgive you." It is natural for us to forgive people for things they have done to us. But what would you say if someone cheated you out of ten dollars and I said, "That's all right; I forgive him"?

When a person goes around forgiving people who haven't done anything to harm that person, something seems amiss. The Pharisees caught the problem immediately when they once said to Jesus, "Hold on there—who are you to say, 'I forgive you'? No one but God can forgive sins" (Mark 2:7, paraphrased). Exactly. So Jesus was saying He was God.

Now, anyone could make that claim, and many have. What's needed is something to back up those claims. Jesus did many such things, all of which led up to the greatest proof of all: His resurrection from the dead. There are some things only God can do—like forgiving sin and conquering death. And Jesus did them all. The Resurrection is the ultimate, historical benchmark for your faith. Jesus is God—the Resurrection proves it.

Your faith can remain full because Jesus' grave remains empty.

A Sure Hope

Christ in you, the hope of glory.
COLOSSIANS 1:27

Though World War II did not officially end until 1945, it can be safely said that it was over on June 6, 1944. That was D-day, when 176,000 Allied troops stormed the beaches of Normandy in France. Eventually three-quarters of a million troops assembled in France to liberate Europe from the Axis powers led by Adolf Hitler. Many fierce battles followed D-day before the Axis armies were defeated. But the die was cast on D-day when hope came once again to the free world.

The same may be said of our Christian experience. Though the day is yet in the future when evil will be eradicated from earth completely, we know it will happen because of the death and resurrection of Jesus Christ. By His death, Christ freed believers from the debt of sin. And by His resurrection, death, the last great enemy, was conquered so we might live again and forever. Are you in a battle or skirmish today with the world, the flesh, or the devil? Don't wish things were different. Instead, put your hope in the fact that with the invasion of Christ into this world, victory was won. True hope is available to all allies of the conquering Christ. True hope is not wishful thinking; it is faith in fact.

Sundays

Continuing daily with one accord in the temple,
and breaking bread from house to house . . .
Acts 2:46

Evangelist Vance Havner wrote, "My father was faithful to the house of God. When he felt like it and when he didn't, when the preaching was good and when it wasn't, my father was there."

Today's crowd isn't quite so faithful, nor is our society very helpful. A group of churches in New Jersey issued an appeal to public and private sports leagues to refrain from scheduling games before noon on Sunday. Fewer and fewer families were in church because of children's sporting events.

A congregation in Andover, Massachusetts, conducted a marketing survey to find out when people could attend church. The most common response: Saturday at 5:00 p.m., because their Sundays were booked.

We need to be in church for many reasons, not the least of which is the mutual fellowship we have with other Christians. The body of Christ is a family whose members are involved with each other—encouraging and building up one another. The early Christians couldn't seem to be together enough. They continued daily with one accord in the temple and from house to house.

Be in church this Sunday.

God's Hat Trick

A man's heart plans his way,
But the Lord directs his steps.
Proverbs 16:9

Richard Storrs and Gordon Hall were students at the same theological seminary. One Saturday near the end of the semester, Hall was preparing to go to Braintree, Massachusetts, to preach, hoping that he might receive an invitation to become their pastor. That afternoon, as he was splitting some wood, his hat fell beneath the axe and was destroyed. He didn't have the money to replace it and the weather was bitter cold, so he asked his friend to take the assignment. Storrs preached and was offered the job. He accepted it, and he remained the minister of that parish until his dying day—a period of more than half a century!

Hall, although disappointed, sought other outlets for his talents. He went to India and became the first American missionary to Bombay. He was quite influential in the Indian missions movement. No one who believes in divine providence will for a moment doubt that God stationed Storrs at Braintree and Hall in India. By means of that ruined hat, the courses of two lives were changed. Nevertheless, in God's divine will, the good news was proclaimed.

Rules or Relationships?

For the kingdom of God is not eating and drinking, but righteousness and peace and joy in the Holy Spirit.

Romans 14:17

Bible scholars have attempted to count all the laws and commandments given by God in the Old Testament—635 is one such suggested total. Regardless of the exact number, life under the Law was a life of rules and regulations. Worship, food, sacrifices, clothing, diseases, marriage . . . every aspect of life was the subject of a rule.

God's rules were given for a purpose—they paved the road to a relationship. Paul says that "the law was our tutor to bring us to Christ" (Galatians 3:24). God gave rules to show us our need for Jesus. When it became apparent over centuries of trying that Israel couldn't keep God's rules by herself, God unveiled a relationship with Jesus the Messiah. That relationship offered what rules never could: "righteousness and peace and joy in the Holy Spirit." Rules can establish boundaries for a relationship, but they cannot be the soul of it. If you tend to focus on rules, it might explain the absence of peace and joy.

Rules are like the skeleton, and relationships are like the heart. Both are important, but life depends on one more than the other.

Set Free

He made Him who knew no sin to be sin for us, that we might become the righteousness of God in Him.

2 Corinthians 5:21

I once heard someone say that of all men who ever lived, Barabbas should have the best understanding of vicarious substitution. Somebody died in his place. This murderer and thief walked out a free man, the crowds cheering his release. At the same time, an innocent Jesus was sentenced to die.

But Barabbas isn't the only one who can say that Jesus died in his place. We can all say that Jesus Christ died on that cross for us, just as He did for Barabbas. In the words of 2 Corinthians 5:21, "For He made Him who knew no sin to be sin for us, that we might become the righteousness of God in Him." Jesus died that we might live. He was bound that we who are in bondage to sin might be set free.

When word of Barabbas's freedom came, he had to walk out of that cell to be truly free. Through Christ, the cell door has sprung open. All we have to do is say, "I accept what Christ did for me, and I will now live in the light of that truth."

Photos of Forgiveness

Forgive us our debts.

Matthew 6:12

Some people don't pray as they should because they feel unworthy to come before a pure and holy God. But Jesus taught us to include confession as a part of our prayers: "Forgive us our debts." When we pray in obedience, we must confess our sins; and when we pray in faith, we must trust God to fully forgive.

If you're having trouble with this, utilize some Bible visuals. Isaiah 1:18 tells us that when God forgives us, we are whiter than snow. Micah 7:19 says He casts our sins into the depths of the sea. Psalm 103:12 says He removes them as far from us as east from west.

Isaiah 38:17 says God casts our sins behind His back. In Matthew 18:21–35, Jesus compared our sins to a great debt canceled by a gracious king. Psalm 51 talks about being washed and cleansed, and about God's hiding His face from our sins and blotting out our transgressions.

God provided this assortment of images because we need to visualize the vast, many dimensions of His grace. So when you pray, confess your sins specifically and claim God's forgiveness. Then go on and pray as one who is righteous in God's sight through the grace of our Lord Jesus.

He doesn't want you to continue feeling guilty. He wants you to pray.

July 18

Worship Intelligently

I will . . . praise Your name
For Your lovingkindness and Your truth;
For You have magnified Your word
above all Your name.
In the day when I cried out, You answered me.

Psalm 138:2–3

David notes three things for which we are to praise God when we are in trouble. These make a great outline for praying in times of trouble.

1. Praise Him for His mercy and truth. God is perfectly balanced in mercy and in truth. When you come to Him, His truth is tempered by mercy and His mercy is illumined by truth.
2. Praise Him for His magnified Word. When you read God's Word and read of His loving-kindness and truth, you can know that the integrity of God and His name are behind those words.
3. Praise Him for His mighty provision. Whatever His answer, it gives us strength that makes us bold. And boldness allows us to face troubles without fear. We face trouble with confidence and strength, knowing that God is with us and will see us through. That kind of perspective keeps us from cowering in the corners of life and gives us the confidence to face each day unafraid of what it might bring.

A Heart Like God's

I have found David the son of Jesse, a man after My own heart, who will do all My will.

Acts 13:22

Imagine that you purchased a house and the previous owner gave you keys to all the rooms except one; he reserved the right to come and go as he pleased in that one room. That brings to mind how the founder of the Salvation Army, William Booth, answered Queen Victoria when she asked the secret of his ministry: "I guess the reason is because God has all there is of me."

Robert Boyd Munger wrote a famous tract titled *My Heart, Christ's Home*, in which he likened his heart to the rooms in a house. If your heart were divided into rooms, is there any one to which you would not give Christ the key? Or, like William Booth, does He have all there is of you?

When God chose a man to succeed Saul as king of Israel, He chose David. And the primary reason given in Scripture is that David was a man after God's own heart. That means that God would be just as comfortable in the house of David's heart as in His own. No surprises, no dark corners, no hidden passageways not revealed to the light. Our goal should be to create the kind of heart-home that Jesus would love to come to—a heart like God's own.

God is still looking today for hearts that are loyal to Him (2 Chronicles 16:9). Has He found yours?

The Strong Tower

The name of the Lord is a strong tower;
The righteous run to it and are safe.
Proverbs 18:10

On January 25, 1934, German clergyman Martin Neimoller confronted Adolph Hitler face-to-face in the name of Christ. As a result, Neimoller was later seized by the Gestapo and held in solitary confinement.

On the morning of his trial, he was led from his cell by a green-uniformed official. As the two men walked through eerie underground passageways, Neimoller felt overwhelming fear.

Suddenly he heard a whispered voice: "The name of the Lord is a strong tower. The righteous run to it and are safe." It was the guard, speaking under his breath.

With those words, Neimoller's fear vanished. It was replaced by an indescribable peace that didn't leave him, even during the dark days to come.

The Bible warns that prior to Christ's return the days will be perilous (2 Timothy 3:1). But even when things seem to be in chaos around us, the name of our Lord is a strong tower. The righteous run to it and are safe. God's purpose will guide us, His promises will sustain us, and His providence will keep us.

An Encouraging Promise

Jesus answered him, "Where I am going you cannot follow Me now, but you shall follow Me afterward."

John 13:36

An observer asked a foreman overseeing a demolition crew if he had to hire highly skilled men to tear the building down. "Not really," the foreman replied. "I just need strong men—men who can tear down in a matter of days something that took years to build." It never takes as long to destroy something as it took to put it together.

Jesus Christ spent three years building up a group of twelve disciples. They had high hopes and expectations that He would bring in the kingdom and rule of God to restore Israel to her former glory. While they grew steadily in their understanding of who Jesus was, it was harder for them to understand fully that He had to suffer and leave them before God's kingdom would be established on earth. Had Jesus not prepared the disciples for His going away, He could easily have crushed their spirits and undone all He had built into their lives. He chose to encourage them before the fact, not just after.

If you know someone who is about to face a potential disappointment or challenge, build him or her up beforehand with a preparatory word of encouragement. Encouragement in anticipation of disappointment may keep the latter from ever happening.

Forgiveness in Marriage

If you have anything against anyone, forgive him.

Mark 11:25

It's impossible to have a good marriage without learning how to forgive because it's impossible to have a marriage without hurting one another. Why? Because both partners are flawed human beings. Someone has said that the six most important words in a marriage are, "I admit I made a mistake." Do you know how hard it is to say those words?

Forgiveness is at the very core of relationships within the home and within the church. Whether someone has something against us or we have something against another, we are to be the proactive ones and forgive, restoring the relationship. In an ideal world, when there has been some discord or hurt in a marriage, a husband and wife ought to run into each other as they are both going to seek the forgiveness of the other, restoring harmony in the relationship.

Can you imagine a marriage that would not prosper if it were built on communication and conversation that is trustworthy, gentle, open, kind, and forgiving? While staying married is a worthy goal, a better goal is to be married—and happily so!

Nehemiah the Thanksgiver

So I . . . appointed two large thanksgiving choirs.

Nehemiah 12:31

Nehemiah is the Bible's great wall builder. His Old Testament book tells of the masterful way in which he prayerfully led his people to repair Jerusalem's broken-down defenses despite danger, discouragement, and insufficiency. At the dedication of the rebuilt walls, Nehemiah appointed two great thanksgiving choirs, made up of Levites having both musical skills and grateful souls (Nehemiah 12:8, 31). They were appointed to "praise and give thanks, group alternating with group" (v. 24). They were armed with strong voices, and with "cymbals and stringed instruments and harps . . . [and] trumpets" (vv. 27, 35).

Positioned on opposite walls, these thanksgiving choirs burst into praise and thanksgiving at the appointed moment, "for God had made them rejoice with great joy . . . so that the joy of Jerusalem was heard afar off" (v. 43).

There's a thanksgiving choir inside you. Look around at the beauty of God's creation, the power of His promises, and the record of His care over your life. Lift up your heart, and let the strains of thanksgiving pour forth from the ramparts of your soul.

Absolute Love

Rejoice with the wife of your youth.

Proverbs 5:18

How do you recover a lost love? Go back to the beginning of the relationship, and ask yourself, "What was I doing then that I'm not doing now?" and do it. Take her some flowers. I guarantee she will like it. She'll feel better because you did it, and you'll feel better too.

If you aren't all the way gone, if it's not too late for you, if there's any hope at all, you'll discover all kinds of things that you feel better for doing. The love that should be in your heart toward the woman who is your wife will begin to develop according to your loving activities. We husbands are responsible to be the leaders in love in our families. That's what it means to be the head. We are to be like Christ.

When we try to love our marriage partners realistically, sacrificially, purposefully, willingly, and absolutely, we begin to come into God's plan. And without thinking of it or planning for it, we find our own needs being met too. Our realistic, sacrificial, purposeful, willing, absolute love comes back to us from our partners, and that is the payoff. Even though Christ has not promised us lives of ease without struggle or pain, He has promised us joy.

The Art of Healthy Living

Revive me according to Your word.

Psalm 119:25

The Bible . . . is a book in which [a person] may learn from his Creator the art of healthy living," said Swiss physician Dr. Paul Tournier.

Hymnist Fanny Crosby gave this testimony: "This Book is to me God's treasure house. It is my bread of life, the anchor of my home, my pillar of fire by night, my pillar of cloud by day. It is the lantern that lights my pathway to my paradise home."

Missionary Amy Carmichael wrote, "Have you noticed this? Whatever need or trouble you are in, there is always something to help you in your Bible, if only you go on reading 'til you come to the word God specially has for you."

Doctors tell us that many lung diseases are caused by shallow breathing. We don't open up our lungs and deeply inhale the life-giving oxygen God has placed in our atmosphere. In the same way, many spiritual and emotional diseases are caused by shallow reading. We skim over favorite passages, but we don't set aside the necessary time to dig deeply into God's Word.

The Lord has given us the Bible to help us through the challenges of life. Breathe deeply of its oxygen. Feast richly on its truths. Read, study, memorize, and meditate on its verses. There you'll find the art of healthy living.

The Power of a Mother

His mother kept all these things in her heart.

Luke 2:51

The person who most influenced John Wesley, the founder of Methodism, was likely his mother, Susanna. She was fiercely devoted to the ten of her eighteen children who survived infancy, spending time with a different child each night of the week to school him or her in matters of the faith. In a letter to his mother as an adult, Wesley said, "Oh, Mother, what I'd give for a Thursday evening!" When John and Charles Wesley consulted their mother before going to America as missionaries in 1735, she said, "If I had twenty sons, I should rejoice if they were all so employed, though I should never see them more."

It has been suggested that the discipline and love of Susanna Wesley's household was formative in shaping the structure of early Methodism through her influence on John and Charles. How powerful is the influence of a mother! The bond between mother and child seems to be God-designed, the perfect union of potential and the power to make it spring forth. The simple, daily influences of prayer, persuasion, and promoting of godly values are the most powerful tools a mother can use to unleash the potential of her children.

The Strength of the Church

You also, as living stones, are being built up a spiritual house, a holy priesthood.

1 Peter 2:5

Whenever we hear about earthquakes in underdeveloped nations, the loss of life seems dis-proportionately large. Disaster experts usually cite a primary cause: the quality of building materials. It doesn't take much of a quake to bring down buildings made out of poor-quality bricks, mortar, and concrete.

Good mortar, often lacking in poorer parts of the world, has to have several ingredients to be strong: lime, cement, sand, and water. Often, small pebbles or steel bars are put in the mortar for added reinforcement. To the degree any of these elements are missing, the strength of the building is compromised.

Likewise, the "living stones" of the church need a mix of elements in order for the body to be edified, or strengthened: love, encouragement, love, correction, love, wisdom, love, service . . . and don't forget love. These, and more, make up the mortar that binds living stones to one another to withstand the assaults of the "gates of Hades" (Matthew 16:18). Make sure you add something to the mix this week to build up a brother or sister in Christ.

Dying to self is the only way living stones can strengthen one another.

Patience, Anyone?

For this reason I obtained mercy, that in me first Jesus Christ might show all longsuffering, as a pattern to those who are going to believe on Him for everlasting life.

1 Timothy 1:16

You've probably heard the great American prayer: "God give me patience, and I want it now!" We are constantly being reminded that everything can be done in a hurry, yet God says He wants to teach us to wait.

God wants to develop within us a quality of being patient and longsuffering. Someone has defined *longsuffering* as a long holding out of the mind before it gives way to action or passion. It is the power to see things through.

If there is any quality we need in our lives today, it is patience. It is the hardest of all the qualities for us to learn today because we think everything has to be done quickly. But it is the virtue I believe is closest to the heart of God. God is a God of longsuffering, patience, and forbearance.

A person who has the fruit of longsuffering is patient with people who nag. He or she does not criticize and irritate when criticized and irritated. This person does not disappear when frustrated or angered. Longsuffering knows how to sit still and wait its turn. It is slow to retaliate and does not seek to get even. It waits patiently with joy.

Riches Untold

The blessing of the Lord makes one rich.

Proverbs 10:22

The cost of refurbishing Michelangelo's painted ceiling in the Sistine Chapel was $4.3 million. Not many of us can afford a ceiling like that. But God has placed an ever-changing fresco over our heads every day. The sky-blue ceiling and the star-spangled heavens are priceless yet free.

Van Gogh's *Portrait of Dr. Gachet* brought $82.5 million at Christie's, but God gives us His beautiful world to enjoy at no charge. Have you paid your water bill recently? Your electric bill? The Lord gives us the warmth of His sunshine, the cool of His breezes, the irrigation of His rain without cost. At a political fund-raiser, VIPs who gave $4,000 each had their pictures taken with the president. But the King of kings welcomes us into His presence anytime, free of charge.

Charles Spurgeon said, "Scripture is the bank of heaven. You may draw from it as much as you please, without interference or hindrance." God cares about our needs, and He is interested in the "little things" of our lives. He wants to give us a life that's abundant, and He wants us to share abundantly with others. He wants us to freely receive and freely give. Trust Him with your needs, and learn to appreciate the riches of His grace.

A Paid Friend

You also may have fellowship with us;
and truly our fellowship is with the Father
and with His Son Jesus Christ.

1 John 1:3

A famous British playwright was leaving Liverpool by ship. He noticed that the other passengers were waving to friends on the dock. Just before the ship was to leave, he rushed down to the dock and stopped a little boy. "Would you wave to me if I pay you?" he asked the boy. "Of course," he agreed. The writer gave him a few shillings, then ran back aboard and leaned over the rail. Sure enough, the boy was waving to him. The playwright disliked solitude and loneliness so much that he had gone so far as to create an artificial friend. To him, even the semblance of friendship was better than the crushing loneliness he felt.

The key to assurance in life is fellowship. Fellowship with people locks out the grim feelings of loneliness. And fellowship with God keeps away the threat of eternal solitude.

In this epistle, John wanted to make it clear to his readers that they could fellowship with God through Jesus Christ. He stressed the importance of love: since Christians have experienced the love of God in their lives, they have no need to fear either in this life or in the life to come.

How to Miss a Blessing

They immediately left their nets and followed Him.

Matthew 4:20

When writer, congresswoman, and ambassador Clare Booth Luce was seventy-five, she was asked whether she had any regrets. She said, "Sometimes I wake up in the middle of the night, and I remember a girlhood friend of mine who had a brain tumor and called me three times to come and see her. I was always too busy, and when she died, I was profoundly ashamed. I still remember that after fifty-six years."

Is there anything you have been putting off that, once the opportunity has passed, you will regret not having done? Procrastinating about service to others is a double-edged sword: not only do we fail to extend a blessing, but we miss the blessing that comes with being a blessing! Instead of a double blessing, procrastination results in no blessings at all.

When Jesus was calling His disciples, the original twelve left "immediately" to follow Him. Later, others said, "Let me first go and [do this or that important thing]" (Luke 9:59, 61). Guess who ended up changing the world and being blessed in the process? If God has put an opportunity for service in front of you, don't fail to take it—to bless and be blessed at the same time.

Remember, today is the day you thought about yesterday when you said, "I can do that tomorrow."

Suffering to Bless Others

Do not lose heart at my tribulations
for you, which is your glory.
Ephesians 3:13

Sometimes we discover that a major reason for our suffering has been because of what God intended to do in someone else's life. That may not be obvious to us. But Paul said that his sufferings were for the glory (or means of blessing) of others (Ephesians 3:13).

"But I want you to know, brethren, that the things which happened to me have actually turned out for the furtherance of the gospel, so that it has become evident to the whole palace guard, and to all the rest, that my chains are in Christ; and most of the brethren in the Lord, having become confident by my chains, are much more bold to speak the word without fear" (Philippians l:12–14).

We do not always see the realization of God's purposes. None of us has the ability to interpret God's perfectly wise purpose in the sufferings of our fellow believers (or of ourselves, for that matter). But in order to encourage them, we need to have some awareness of what God may be doing. By sharing the biblical teaching on what God does in our lives through suffering, we may encourage others to serve God in it.

But in Everything by Prayer

Be anxious for nothing, but in everything by
prayer and supplication, with thanksgiving,
let your requests be made known to God.

Philippians 4:6

Do you have a prayer list? One young girl knew the power of specific prayer when she faced death head-on. In the midst of her sickness, she went to her pastor and asked what more she could do for Jesus in the short time she had to live. He suggested that she make a list of people in their small town who needed Christ and pray that they would find salvation. She took his advice and prayed often for each person.

Sometime later, God began to stir a revival in the village. Only after the girl died was her prayer list with the names of fifty-six people found under her pillow. All had put their faith in Christ—the last one on the night before her death.

Such is the power of definite, specific, fervent prayer. When we actively seek the Lord in prayer, He will answer. James 5:16 reminds us, "The prayer of a righteous man is powerful and effective" (NIV). Do not doubt the power of prayer in your life—it is truly a great adventure with God that is meant to bring you closer to Him.

Father–Son Talks

The fear of the LORD is the beginning of knowledge,
But fools despise wisdom and instruction.
PROVERBS 1:7

Mark Twain is given credit for the following remark: "When I was a boy of fourteen, my father was so ignorant I could hardly stand to have the old man around. But when I got to be twenty-one, I was astonished at how much the old man had learned in seven years." If that was a true record of a young man's awakening to wisdom, Mark Twain would not be the first to whom it happened. Many a young man has listened to advice from his father and discounted it—until the day he needed it. Then it turned out to be more wisdom than advice.

One of the oldest father–son talks in history is recorded in the book of Proverbs. Solomon, the world's wisest man in his day (and likely in ours), used his throne as king of Israel to dispense his wise sayings to his subjects and to those who came from afar to sit at his feet and learn. Solomon was known throughout the surrounding nations for possessing uncanny wisdom, discernment, and insight.

The principles of wisdom will work for anyone who puts them to use. But it is only those who fear the Lord who will want to practice them over a lifetime.

The Deity Is in the Details

Put my tears into Your bottle;
Are they not in Your book?
Psalm 56:8

An apocryphal story is told about the filming of the legendary movie *The Bridge on the River Kwai.* The director was preparing for the epic shot of a locomotive and train falling from an exploding bridge into a river gorge below. Three cameras were assigned to shoot the scene. After the shot, the director radioed each camera operator. "Sorry, sir—my camera jammed," said the first. "Left my lens cap on," said the second. The director nearly fainted when the third said, "Ready when you are, sir!"

With one-time opportunities, details matter. Not even enthusiasm can make up for a lack of attention to details. Modern culture likes to say "the devil's in the details." Wrong! It is our God who is at work in even the smallest parts of life.

Daniel the prophet discovered this when God showed him a preview of world history: "There shall be seven weeks and sixty-two weeks" (Daniel 9:25). Not eight and sixty-three or six and sixty-one. God knows every detail of the past, present, and future of the world—and of your life. He counts your tears and knows the number of hairs on your head. How comforting to know our God has overlooked nothing.

Because God is in the details, He is always ready when you are.

God's Plan for the Home

There is neither Jew nor Greek, there is neither slave nor free, there is neither male nor female; for you are all one in Christ Jesus.

Galatians 3:28

Galatians 3:28 makes it absolutely clear that men and women stand equal in privilege and position before God. In God's sight, there is no male and female; there are only those created in His image who are redeemed and placed into the body of Christ. In the Church of Jesus Christ, we all submit to one another—bond or free, Jew or Gentile, male or female. That is the clear intention of God, for there is one Lord over all in the church to whom we submit.

But when it comes to the functioning and the operation of the Christian home, God has given guidelines so that the home will work according to order and according to His plan. He has said, "I'm going to give you the joy of personal relationships within the context of a loving environment called the home," which He established in the Garden of Eden. And He said, "Here's how I want this to work. I want the husband to be the lover and the learner and the leader, and I want the wife to be supportive and submissive in that relationship. When you do that, there will be blessing, joy, and honor, and it will be an exciting experience."

Tiny Causes, Huge Effects

Let the words of my mouth and
the meditation of my heart
Be acceptable in Your sight,
O Lord, my strength and my Redeemer.

Psalm 19:14

In 1996, Manila, capital city of the Philippines, suffered an outbreak of cholera due to a proliferation of flies and cockroaches. The mayor announced a bounty on the bugs, dead or alive, and thousands were brought in by citizens who were paid on the spot. Health officials knew that huge problems could be prevented by dealing with tiny causes.

Stopping that cholera outbreak was an example of the law of the harvest: sow a tiny cure and reap a huge benefit. Just as removing tiny bugs saved a city, so a tiny thought in our minds can have huge results. That's why Proverbs says to "keep your heart with all diligence . . . [and] put away from you a deceitful mouth" (4:23–24).

Thoughts and words are powerful. What we meditate on and speak can do great good or great harm. In the Bible, the Christian has access to the most powerful living words ever written, words that can renew the mind. Make sure this week that you spend time sowing seeds in your mind that will bear godly fruit in your life.

History's worst acts began with a tiny, unguarded thought that yielded an ungodly harvest of destruction.

STRENGTH!

I pray that out of his glorious riches he may strengthen you with power through his Spirit in your inner being.

EPHESIANS 3:16 NIV

From one end of the Bible to the other, we read of God's strengthening His people. When the Israelites passed through the Red Sea, they praised the Lord, saying: "The LORD is my strength and my song" (Exodus 15:2 NIV).

Deuteronomy 33:25 says: "As your days, so shall your strength be." Nehemiah 8:10 says, "Do not sorrow for the joy of the LORD is your strength." Psalm 27:1 declares, "The LORD is my light and my salvation. Whom shall I fear? The LORD is the strength of my life; of whom shall I be afraid?" Psalm 46:1 avows, "God is our refuge and strength, a very present help in trouble."

Isaiah said, "Trust in the LORD forever, for in YAH, the LORD, is everlasting strength" (26:4). Isaiah 40:31 promises that "those who wait on the LORD shall renew their strength; they shall mount up with wings like eagles, they shall run and not be weary, they shall walk and not faint."

The apostle Paul told us to "be strong in the Lord and in the power of His might" (Ephesians 6:10). "I can do all things through Christ who strengthens me," he said in Philippians 4:13.

Throughout the Bible we find a simple formula: when the Word goes in, praise goes up, faith goes out, and God goes forth to strengthen His people.

Fourteen Hundred Pennies

Let your requests be made known to God.
Philippians 4:6

In his book *Master Secrets of Prayer,* Cameron V. Thompson says we should pray specifically. He wrote that when his daughter, Joy, was a small child, she set her heart on a certain present. Asking her sisters how many pennies it would take to buy it, she prayed for fourteen hundred pennies. A few days later, some friends came by with a jar of coins they had been saving. It contained slightly more than fourteen hundred pennies.

"Vague praying is lazy praying," said Thompson.

We must let our requests be made known to God and then remember to thank Him when the answers come. Toward that end, many Christians keep a prayer list or devotional notebook to record their prayer requests. Others use the flyleaf of their Bibles for this, though one soon runs out of room.

Make specific requests to God for your husband or wife, your children, your financial needs, your job, your friends, and for those who don't know Christ. Pray specifically for our local and national leaders. Pray in detail for the needs of overseas missionaries. As Philippians 4:6 says in the Phillips version: "Don't worry over anything whatever, tell God every detail."

There Is Only One Builder

Unless the Lord builds the house,
They labor in vain who build it.

Psalm 127:1

If you are going to be successful in building a family, you have to place God at the head of your home. The psalmist says in Psalm 127:1, "Unless the Lord builds the house, they labor in vain who build it." This is the most important truth in building a home. It's saying if God doesn't build it, it isn't going to work. There is only one builder in the home, and that builder is God. God, who had the idea of the home, is the One who wants to be at the head of the home. Until God is at the center of your home, all your attempts at making family life what you want will be attempts in frustration. Unless you let Him build the home, you're going to do it in vain.

We communicate our values where they really are. The best thing we could do before we install God at the head of the home is to install Him at the head of our life. Then we can ask Him to live that out little by little in our families.

Getting Back on the Altar

I beseech you therefore, brethren, by the mercies of God, that you present your bodies a living sacrifice, holy, acceptable to God, which is your reasonable service.

Romans 12:1

Genesis 22 contains one of the most famous stories in the Bible—indeed, in all of literature. It is the account of God commanding Abraham to offer his son Isaac as a sacrifice. This was the supreme test of Abraham's obedience, and he did not hesitate. Because of his obedience, Isaac was spared moments before the sacrifice was completed.

Consider this: What if God had told Isaac to take himself up to Mount Moriah; to build an altar; to climb upon the altar; and, with his own knife, to offer himself as a sacrifice to God? The Old Testament sacrificial rituals prepared people to offer animals as sacrifices; a sacrifice was something other than yourself. That tradition did not prepare the early church for what Paul instructed them to do: offer yourself as a living sacrifice to God.

Living sacrifices don't die physically, but they must die spiritually every day. As someone has well said, "The problem with living sacrifices is they keep crawling off the altar."

Look around—if you're standing on the ground, it's time to get back on the altar.

Peace, Please

Therefore, having been justified by faith, we have peace with God through our Lord Jesus Christ.

Romans 5:1

True peace gives not only a calm exterior but a very quiet inside as well. Peace seems to be an elusive quality that everyone chases after and few people find. Romans 5:1 says, "Therefore, having been justified by faith, we have peace with God." What does that mean? Is God my enemy? Have I been at war with God? God is holy and humans are sinful. They are on different sides. As creatures apart from God, we are at enmity with God.

But the Bible says God provided Jesus Christ that we might have peace with God. I see that picture so beautifully illustrated by the cross itself. Pointing up to heaven, it pictures that Jesus Christ, the God-man, reached up and took the hand of the Father. Pointing down toward earth, it pictures that Jesus Christ, the Son of man, reached down and took hold of fallen human beings. With one hand in the hand of God and the other hand in the hand of man, the only unique personality who was God and man brought the two together and made peace between God and man. He is our peace. He is the Prince of Peace because He is the One who solved the enmity between us and God. Accept Him and you have peace with God.

Holes in the Carpet

Teach me Your way, O Lord.

Psalm 27:11

The village of Clifton Springs is situated in the Finger Lakes district of New York, known for its rolling hills and tranquil waters. In 1849, Dr. Henry Foster, a dedicated Christian, arrived there, looking for a place to practice medicine. He felt that many sick and exhausted people could be restored to active living through a combination of physical and spiritual treatment. From around the world, people trekked to his Clifton Springs Sanitarium to regain their health.

After Dr. Foster's death, visitors to the sanitarium would often ask one of his coworkers for the secret of the man's life and wisdom. Dr. Foster had exhibited an unusual grip on God's will and ways. The coworker would take the visitors upstairs to Dr. Foster's former office and, pointing to two ragged holes in the carpet worn out by the doctor's knees, say, "That, sir, was the secret of Henry Foster's power and wisdom in the things of God and man."

God often imparts His will to us in an atmosphere of prayer. Guidance doesn't usually come on the run. We must wait before the Lord until He teaches us His marvelous ways.

Gaining Perspective

Faith comes by hearing, and
hearing by the word of God.
Romans 10:17

It's impossible to have faith unless the mind embraces that information that comprises the Gospel message. There are specific facts that must be embraced. Faith is not just a warm feeling that comes over you on a bright, sunny day. How would anyone in Seattle or Alaska ever get saved? No, faith is more than a warm feeling. It is the appropriation of certain facts about a man named Jesus.

Gaining perception means you have perceived something. And that "something" are the facts of the Gospel message—objective, quantifiable, expressible information. The Bible speaks about false gospels, which means someone has the facts wrong, purposefully or accidentally. So the truth is what has to be perceived and received as "step one" in gaining faith. And that truth comes by hearing the Word of God.

First Things First

All things are lawful for me, but all things are not helpful. All things are lawful for me, but I will not be brought under the power of any.

1 Corinthians 6:12

A godly seminary professor once told his students about spending the summer in Jerusalem working on a new Bible translation. While the students were envious of such a spiritual assignment, they were shocked to hear the professor say it had been one of the most unfruitful and carnal summers he had ever experienced!

How could studying and translating the Bible result in carnality and spiritual frustration? The professor reported that their scholarly efforts became mechanical and academic. In the midst of their dictionaries and texts, they lost sight of the One they were there to serve.

Christian service is important, but it can actually draw us away from the Savior if we let it. We can become so focused on meeting goals and achieving objectives that we don't notice ourselves drifting away from the Lord. Like Paul, we need to differentiate between the good, better, and best. Is there anything—even a good thing—that is keeping you from the Best?

Just because something can be done is not enough of a reason that it should be done.

AUGUST

These things I have spoken to you,
that My joy may remain in you,
and that your joy may be full.

—John 15:11

God Deserves Attention

I will meditate on Your precepts,
And contemplate Your ways.
Psalm 119:15

Most of us don't spend a lot of time thinking about God. We go to church on Sunday and we sing the songs and we talk the way Christians talk, but we don't give God the attention He deserves. We don't give Him the concentrated attention of someone who is trying to get to know and get close to another person. But a relationship with God is similar to a relationship with a person. If we want to have a meaningful relationship, we must spend time getting to know that person. We must spend time talking with and listening to that person. We can't be close to someone if we don't know who they really are.

God tells us in the Bible who He is. Not only that, but He tells us how much He wants us to know Him.

The more you know God, the more you will love Him. And the more you know and love Him, the more you can celebrate Him in the way He deserves.

An Encouraging Pardon

Then He said to Thomas, "Reach your finger here, and look at My hands; and reach your hand here, and put it into My side. Do not be unbelieving, but believing."

John 20:27

While we say, "There's no such thing as a stupid question," we don't always act that way. Who hasn't found himself wanting to ask a question but feeling too afraid? We think everyone else already knows the answer (they usually don't) and that everyone else will make fun of us (they probably will).

Among Jesus' disciples, there was one man who wasn't afraid to ask: Thomas. In fact, history remembers him as "doubting Thomas" because of his refusal to believe that which he hadn't personally proven to be true. He was as discouraged as the rest of the disciples about Jesus' death, but eight days after the Resurrection, he still wouldn't take their word for it. (He was absent on Resurrection evening when Jesus appeared to the group.)

When he finally met Jesus face-to-face, Thomas found the Lord forgiving, not belittling. He allowed Thomas to come to faith in his own way and at his own pace. Jesus does the same with us. If you have a question, ask Him—you'll see.

Thankfully, Jesus makes fun of no one—even those of shaky faith.

He Stretches Out His Hand

Though I walk in the midst of trouble, You will revive me;
You will stretch out Your hand
Against the wrath of my enemies,
And Your right hand will save me.

Psalm 138:7

David spent most of his life in trouble. Before he was king he was running from Saul; as king he was warring with his neighbors. And toward the end of his reign, his house rose up in rebellion against him. David walked most of his life in the midst of trouble. Yet David said in Psalm 23, "Yea, though I walk through the valley of the shadow of death, I will fear no evil; for You are with me; Your rod and Your staff, they comfort me" (v. 4). David was confident of God's protection, just as David's sheep had been "confident" of David's protection when he was their shepherd in the Judean hills.

Does that mean we will never be injured? Apparently not, for David says God will "revive" him when needed. But it does mean that God will proactively stretch out His hand in our behalf. He will protect us.

Careless Words

*Let no corrupt word proceed out of your mouth,
but what is good for necessary edification.*
Ephesians 4:29

It's right there on page sixty-four. A filthy word that occurs in a children's book entitled *The Canning Season*, along with quite a few other profanities and obscenities. And this isn't just an obscure book for kids. *The Canning Season* was glowingly reviewed in the *New York Times Book Review*, and it won the 2003 National Book Award for Young People's Literature.

Is there anything more out of place than profanity in a children's book?

Yes. Profanity in the mouth of someone who claims to follow the Lord Jesus Christ. The Bible warns that we can grieve the Holy Spirit by the words we say. Paul wrote that we should avoid filthiness, foolish talk, and coarse jesting. Our mouths should be full of thanksgiving instead (Ephesians 5:4–5).

Have you allowed some careless words to slip into your vocabulary? Have you grown used to hearing profanity on television, in novels, and, yes, even in today's children's entertainment? Rededicate yourself to obedience in this area, and let no corrupt communication proceed from your mouth.

Prayer Is Hard Work

Epaphras, who is one of you, a bondservant of Christ, greets you, always laboring fervently for you in prayers, that you may stand perfect and complete in all the will of God.

Colossians 4:12

Fiercely is the right English word to convey Paul's meaning here. He says Epaphras labors fervently in prayer, and the word *laboring* is sometimes translated as "wrestling." The image is that of Greek athletes who competed fiercely to win a perishable crown of an olive leaf garland. And in our modern day, how many athletes devote years of their lives to preparing for the Olympic games? The sacrifices they endure and the prices they pay are almost inconceivable to the non-Olympically inclined among us. They train and compete fiercely, pushing themselves beyond the limits of endurance.

One of the greatest revelations I've had in recent years is that prayer is hard work. Prayer requires labor, striving, continuance, endurance, wrestling, and faithfulness. I've heard people say, "I would pray more, but it's so hard." At least they understood the nature of prayer. It is indeed hard work. Sometimes it helps to begin our prayers by confessing we don't feel like praying—and ask God to help us with our preference to be doing something else. Be honest with God and ask Him to give you a willingness to do the work of prayer.

One-Time Rewards

And whatever you do, do it heartily, as to the Lord and not to men.

Colossians 3:23

Years ago, a popular auto product commercial on television said, "You can pay me now, or you can pay me later." The idea was that it makes more sense to pay for an oil change now than to pay to have the whole engine rebuilt later.

There is an aspect of that theme that is consistent with Jesus' teaching on rewards for faithfulness in the spiritual life. In essence, He said, "You will be rewarded for the spiritual acts you undertake, but you'll only be rewarded once. You can either do your acts for men and get your rewards from them, or do your acts for God and get your rewards from Him." In other words, "Get your rewards now or get your rewards later—your choice."

Why would anyone choose to forego the eternal riches of God's rewards for the temporal rewards of man? Praise, notoriety, glory, and prominence—these are powerful and tempting inducements to work for man and be rewarded immediately. But a greater motivation for working only for God is the idea of being rewarded by Him alone with rewards that will never fade away.

Remember, we only get rewarded once. Choose the rewards that will last the longest and mean the most—those that come from God.

Need a Friend?

A friend loves at all times,
And a brother is born for adversity.
Proverbs 17:17

I believe God intends relationships and friendships to be the context in which He does some of His most important work in our lives. Life is difficult from any perspective, and everyone needs friends to help them through the difficult times. Those who have close friends know they couldn't live without them. Friends love you enough to confront you when you are wrong and to stand by you through thick and thin. These are friends who act toward you like a marriage partner is supposed to—for better or for worse. If you have a friend like that, you are rich. If you have more than one, you are wealthy beyond measure.

In today's world, many people do not take time to cultivate committed friendships, and they are the poorer for it. But the need for committed friends doesn't mean we should rush out and try to accumulate them on a wholesale basis. Many things in life are not left to our choosing, but friendships are. The choice of friends is more than a right, however—it is a responsibility.

Makeover Priorities

For the Lord does not see as man sees; for man looks at the outward appearance, but the Lord looks at the heart.

1 Samuel 16:7

America has gone "makeover" crazy! You can't watch prime-time television very long on a weeknight without seeing a commercial for a makeover show—they're even making over houses. Whether the focus is on a person's body or home, the idea is the same: the exterior is all-important. Tear down the old, build up the new, and life will be better.

While exterior makeovers probably bring happiness to some, success isn't guaranteed. Studies have discovered a high degree of depression in post-makeover women because their plastic surgery didn't bring them the happiness they thought it would.

Isn't it great that we don't have to have a physical makeover to be attractive to God? The prophet Samuel said that God looks on the heart above all (1 Samuel 16:7), Jesus said it's what's on the inside of a person that's most important (Matthew 15:11), and Peter said wives are most attractive when they have a beautiful spirit (1 Peter 3:1–6). If you've been thinking about a makeover lately, start with the heart. Beauty on the interior can make us more attractive than rearranging the exterior.

A surgeon can make over the body, but only God can make over the heart.

Righteousness Is a Free Gift

For Christ is the end of the law for righteousness to everyone who believes.

Romans 10:4

Christ did in His perfect flesh what the flesh of mortal man could never do—keep the law of God. There is nothing wrong with the law; it is just and holy and good (Romans 7:12).

The problem is sinful human flesh. We have no ability to keep God's holy law. And if one is going to establish his own righteousness, it means keeping 100 percent of God's requirements according to the law. To break the law in one point is to break it all (James 2:10). Therefore Christ came into the world to do what we could not do—satisfy the requirements of the law in order to win righteousness for those who would receive it as a free gift instead of trying to earn it themselves.

Christ is the end of righteousness for all who believe. Are you one who has believed? If so, let your life become an "I love You" to God, thanking Him for what Christ has done for you.

Freedom Not to Sin

Having been set free from sin, you became slaves of righteousness.
Romans 6:18

In *The Grace Awakening*, Charles Swindoll recounts the first time his father let him take the family car out by himself for two hours. He thought of all the things he could do with his freedom—speeding, a quick trip out of town, showing off for his friends—and did none of them. Out of respect for his father's trust, he drove around safely and returned home early.

What would you do if you were granted unlimited freedom from any consequences for your actions? And how often do you find yourself angry with someone who has taken away your freedom (freedom to peace and quiet, freedom to a parking space, freedom to spend your money as you like)? It's easy, living in the "land of the free," to misunderstand the true meaning of spiritual freedom.

When we are born again through faith in Christ, we are given the power to be freed from the destructive compulsions and tendencies that can hurt us and others, and we are given new power to do what is best in life. We're given power to do those things that God created us to do, power to deny the demands of our old sin nature.

If there is a sin you're having trouble saying no to, ask God to give you a fresh glimpse of what it means to be free.

Are You a Joyless Christian?

The kingdom of God is . . . righteousness and peace and joy in the Holy Spirit.

Romans 14:17

If you're a Christian and you don't have joy, here are some very basic things you need to understand about what it means to have the joy of the Lord in your life. Receiving Christ, submitting to the Spirit, reading the Bible, and praying don't sound very original. But there isn't anything more original than the Word of God. That's the bedrock simplicity of what it means to have joy in Christ. Here is why: if joy is in Christ, then everything that has to do with joy has to be centered on Christ.

As the Holy Spirit indwells and controls us, and as we read the Bible, we will come to prayer time and into fellowship with Jesus. As we spend time with Him, we come to love, adore, and praise Him, and Jesus becomes literally the focus of our lives. That is how we have joy in God.

Christian joy isn't always laughing and having a good, hilarious time. Christian joy is the deep, settled peace that comes to live within your heart when you know that the really important things are all right. Life can be taken from us, but we are going to live somewhere for eternity. You can have joy in your heart when you know everything is all right with you forever.

Asking for Directions

Whoever gives heed to instruction prospers,
and blessed is he who trusts in the Lord.

Proverbs 16:20 NIV

An old sailor repeatedly got lost at sea, so his friends gave him a compass and urged him to use it. The next time he went out in his boat, he followed their advice and took the compass with him, but he still got lost.

Finally, he was rescued by his friends. Disgusted and impatient with him, they asked, "Why didn't you use that compass we gave you? You could have saved us a lot of trouble!" The sailor responded, "I didn't dare to! I wanted to go north, but as hard as I tried to make the needle aim in that direction, it just kept on pointing southeast." The old sailor was so certain he knew which direction was north that he stubbornly tried to force his own personal persuasion on his compass. Unable to do so, he tossed it aside as worthless and failed to benefit from the guidance it offered.

God's Word is your compass. Use it on a daily basis to check in, to make sure that you are going in the right direction. Stubbornness and busyness can take you off course, but God's Word is right there waiting for your return. Don't be afraid to ask God for directions.

Eternal Protection

Having now been justified by His blood, we shall be saved from wrath through Him.

Romans 5:9

The story is told of a man who had been condemned by a Spanish court to be shot. Because he was an American citizen and of English birth, the consuls of the United States and England decided to intervene. They declared that the Spanish authorities had no power to put him to death. Their protest went unheeded, and the Spaniards proceeded to prepare the firing squad.

At the time the execution was scheduled to take place, the consuls boldly approached the accused man, already tied and blindfolded, and wrapped him up in their flags—the Stars and Stripes and the Union Jack. Then they shouted, "Fire a shot if you dare! If you do so, you will bring the powers of our two great empires upon you." There stood the prisoner, unharmed. One bullet could have ended his life, but protected by those flags and the governments they represented, he was invulnerable.

The Lord Jesus takes the soul of the sinner who believes in Him and covers the guilty one with His blood. Thus wrapped and sheltered by the Savior, he is safe.

The Hands of Jesus

Now God worked unusual miracles by the hands of Paul.

Acts 19:11

After World War II, a group of German students volunteered to rebuild a severely damaged cathedral. A large statue of Jesus, with outstretched arms and the words "Come unto Me" inscribed on it, was missing both hands. Since it proved impossible to reattach the hands, they decided to leave them off. And they changed the inscription to read, "Christ has no hands but ours."

The most well-known metaphor used by the apostle Paul for the followers of Jesus was "the body of Christ." First, though Jesus' literal body is absent from the earth, He is still ministering through the corporate body of His followers. Second, a body has many unique parts, which the New Testament writers compared to individual Christians. Some are ears, some are hands, some are feet—all working in harmony to do the work of Jesus in the world.

If you are a follower of Jesus, you have been given grace (a spiritual gift), through the Holy Spirit, to do something that Jesus would do if He were here personally. Through you, the hands of Jesus are ministering daily to others.

The person touched by Christ's follower is being touched by Christ Himself.

God's Training Process

He who is faithful in what is least
is faithful also in much.

Luke 16:10

Joseph was cooperative with God's process of training. Joseph had to go through thirteen years of schooling so that he could experience eighty years of ministry. Throughout all that training, Joseph focused on the Lord. In slavery, in the pit, and in prison, he worked to become a strong, disciplined man of God. There was no complaining, simply a desire to obey the Lord and do his best.

If we are God's people, we will be obedient to Him no matter what our situation. Joseph was faithful in every circumstance, and the Lord blessed him. He proved himself faithful in a home, and God put him in charge of a prison. He proved himself faithful in a prison, and God put him in charge of a nation. God used Joseph because he was cooperative with God's training process, and the Lord is still looking for cooperative men and women today.

When Criticism Comes

Each one should test his own actions.
Then he can take pride in himself, without
comparing himself to somebody else.

Galatians 6:4 NIV

The Chinese Christian Watchman Nee died for his faith in a Communist prison. During his lifetime, he was roundly criticized by the government. Smear campaigns were employed to discredit him, but he never responded to critics and never defended himself. Asked about it, he said, "Brothers, if people trust us, there is no need to explain; and if they don't trust us, there is no use in explaining."

The apostle Paul said about his critics: "It matters very little to me what you think of me, even less where I rank in popular opinion. I don't even rank myself. . . . The Master makes that judgment" (1 Corinthians 4:3–4 MSG).

How do we respond to unfair criticism and unkind words? Our natural reaction is to feel indignant and defensive, to try to straighten everyone out. But we need thick skin, soft hearts, and an absolute trust in the Lord to give us favor in the sight of God and man as He chooses. There may be times to defend ourselves or offer an explanation, but we must guard against taking criticism too seriously. We're responsible for our character, but we can leave our reputation in His hands.

A Hunger for God

O God, You are my God; . . .
My soul thirsts for You;
My flesh longs for You.
Psalm 63:1

It is amazing that with no knowledge of eternal life, no knowledge of a sacrificial Savior, no knowledge of the resurrection—all the things we know well in the New Testament era—Old Testament saints like David had such a longing for God. They had a sense of His presence with them that few Christians seem to enjoy in our day.

David must have already learned that even the royal trappings of kingship could not provide what his heart needed, that only God could slake his thirst and satisfy his longing. He had lived long enough to know that none of what the world offers, whether in the desert or the palace, could satisfy the longings of his heart.

Someone has said that Satan knows nothing of true pleasure and satisfaction, that he is an expert only in amusements. David had learned the difference, and we would do well to imitate him. True pleasure comes from knowing God, being known by God, and being at rest in His presence.

Mother's Sacrifice

Let your father and your mother be glad,
And let her who bore you rejoice.
Proverbs 23:25

A teacher asked a boy this question: "Suppose your mother baked a pie and there were seven of you—your parents and five children. What part of the pie would you get?" "A sixth," replied the boy. "I'm afraid you don't know your fractions," said the teacher. "Remember, there are seven of you." "Yes, Teacher," said the boy, "but you don't know my mother. Mother would say she didn't want any pie."

One of the most amazing character traits of a mother is her willingness to sacrifice her own desires for her family. The word *sacrifice* means forfeiture of something highly valued for the sake of one considered to have a greater value or claim. Whether it's a piece of pie or valuable time, all mothers give up what they want for the benefit of their children. But the giving of themselves is not done in vain; there are great rewards. Having a servant's heart is a theme throughout the entire Bible.

There is no greater reward than reaping the benefits of sacrificing personal needs for those of others. A mother's commitment, sacrifice, and prayer can be the foundation that directs her children into a lifelong journey with God.

God Forgives

If we confess our sins, He is faithful and just to forgive us our sins and to cleanse us from all unrighteousness.

1 John 1:9

What happens when we fail? What happens when we do not take God up on His promise? Reading this verse in view of the faithfulness of God puts it in a whole new light. We may feel our sin is too bad to be forgiven. But this Scripture says that when we confess, God forgives. If you refuse to believe that, it's an affront to the faithfulness of God who cannot and will not and shall not lie. God says if we confess it, He will cleanse it. And He risks His faithfulness on that promise.

When asked, "What does the faithfulness of God make you think of first?" many people reply that it makes them think of their own unfaithfulness and the way they fail Him. But Scripture goes on record as saying that, even when we fail, God does not. "If we are faithless, He remains faithful; He cannot deny Himself" (2 Timothy 2:13).

You can say you don't deserve the faithfulness of God. None of us does. That isn't the issue. The issue is that even when we are faithless, He is faithful.

The Wolf of Death

Then they will call on me, but I will not answer;
They will seek me diligently, but they will not find me.

Proverbs 1:28

One of Aesop's fables is about a shepherd boy who was watching a flock of sheep. Wanting to play a trick on the villagers, several times he cried out, "Wolf! Wolf!" and then laughed at the villagers who rushed to his aid. When a wolf actually came to attack his flock, the boy cried out in earnest but was ignored. His game-playing proved his undoing when death was at his door.

Picture the shepherd boy as the nominal religious person of our day and the villagers as the God of Scripture. Some people are going through life treating it as a game, playing at religion, believing that when the day of judgment comes, God will save them from destruction. They think about the Gospel in their idle moments or when small crises occur, but they never really commit themselves to a saving relationship with Christ.

If you have been living life on the periphery of faith, don't wait until the last day. Call out for Christ by faith before it is too late. Better to call out for Jesus while you have your breath than in the day you lose it.

Discover God's Work for You

We are His workmanship, created in Christ Jesus for good works, which God prepared beforehand that we should walk in them.

Ephesians 2:10

So often in the past I have concentrated on this goal and that goal. I'm really into goals, objectives, and plans—both in my personal life and as the pastor of a church. But I believe that people should not concentrate so much on the goal as on the power. And as we pray, we may discover that what we thought were great and lofty goals are pale and puny alongside His goals for our life and ministry.

Let us ask God to make us faithful as people of prayer, and let us pray that God will do His work through us. Then, whatever God wants to do, let's be open to it!

I have no idea what God is up to in your life and mine, but as He works through His mighty Spirit, we are about to find out! I promise you, it will not be on anybody's chart. You are not going to find a framed copy of it hanging on the wall of some office. God is going to do it in His own way—in startling, unexpected ways—through us as we trust Him and as we pray.

Seeking Godly Counsel

Listen to advice and accept instruction,
That you may gain wisdom for the future.
PROVERBS 19:20 RSV

Automaker Henry Ford asked electrical genius Charlie Steinmetz to build the generators for his factory. One day the generators ground to a halt, and the repairmen couldn't find the problem. So Ford called Steinmetz, who tinkered with the machines for a few hours and then threw the switch. The generators whirred to life. Then Ford got a bill for $10,000 from Steinmetz. Flabbergasted, the rather tightfisted carmaker inquired why the bill was so high when it took so little time. Steinmetz's reply: "For tinkering with the generators, $10. For knowing where to tinker, $9,990." Ford paid the bill.

Obtaining wisdom and godly advice is priceless and hard to find in today's society. There are plenty of people who want to give their opinion, but the Bible is the ultimate guidebook on wisdom. One place you might not have thought of is your local church. Most churches offer mentoring programs, counseling, and the chance to meet one-on-one with the pastor.

Take this into consideration the next time you are making big decisions or are confused about an issue. Proverbs 15:22 says, "Plans fail for lack of counsel, but with many advisers they succeed" (NIV).

Blind Hope

By faith Abraham obeyed when he was called to go out to the place which he would receive as an inheritance. And he went out, not knowing where he was going.

Hebrews 11:8

Hope is necessary in our lives today because often the way is unknown. God came to Abraham and said, "I want you to go to a place that I have charted out for you. I want you to leave your home and your family and go there." He didn't give Abraham a map. He just said, "Go," and Abraham pulled up everything and he left.

God came to Abraham and said, "I am going to bless you with a son, and out of that son is going to be a nation. In fact, you are going to have so many descendants that they will be like the sands of the sea and the stars of the sky because you won't be able to number them. I'm going to bless you, and I'm going to bless your son, and I'm going to bless the whole nation that comes from this promise."

What a wonderful promise—except that when Abraham got those words he was already in his nineties and didn't have a son. It was the hope that Abraham had in his heart that helped him get through the way he didn't know. Abraham woke up every morning not knowing what God was up to, but his hope helped him hold on to what God had told him.

Forgiveness That Heals

Be kind and compassionate to one another, forgiving each other, just as in Christ God forgave you.

Ephesians 4:32 NIV

A Spanish father and son had become estranged after years of fighting. The son ran away, and the father set out to find him. He searched for months to no avail. Finally, in a last desperate effort to find him, the father put an ad in a Madrid newspaper. The ad read, "Dear Paco, meet me in front of this newspaper office at noon on Saturday. All is forgiven. I love you. Your father." On Saturday, eight hundred Pacos showed up, looking for forgiveness and love from their fathers.

People are not perfect. That is why God sent His Son to earth—to forgive us of our sins. But forgiveness doesn't stop there; it is just the beginning. Matthew 6:14 says, "For if you forgive men when they sin against you, your heavenly Father will also forgive you" (NIV). The act of forgiveness is not easy, but the Bible calls us to put aside our pride and forgive one another.

Is there someone in your life who needs your forgiveness? Is there a family member or friend who needs to forgive you? There is no better time than right now to make those relationships right.

You Can't Know All God's Secrets

The secret things belong to the Lord our God.

Deuteronomy 29:29

We would be less than honest if we denied the tension that exists between God's sovereignty and man's responsibility. God is in control, but man is responsible. An old Puritan preacher had a wise perspective on the dilemma. He said that he just preached both God's sovereignty and man's responsibility as hard as he could. In Luke 22:22, Jesus said, "And truly the Son of Man goes as it has been determined, but woe to that man by whom He is betrayed!" Do you see both parts of the tension in this verse? It was determined by God that Jesus should be betrayed—but "woe to that man" who does the betraying.

A key verse in all these matters is Deuteronomy 29:29: "The secret things belong to the Lord our God, but those things which are revealed belong to us and to our children forever, that we may do all the words of this law." The secret things are God's determined, sovereign purpose. Our problem is wanting to know all God's secrets. But our responsibility is to take what God has revealed and work to understand it and implement it with all our heart—and leave everything else to God.

Deleting the Virus of Sin

A little leaven leavens the whole lump.

Galatians 5:9

Almost weekly we hear about a new computer virus that is spreading around the world—deleting files, crashing hard drives, and souring attitudes. Software viruses act like their biological cousins—they spread from one computer to another. The surest way to prevent them from infecting other computers is to delete them as soon as they're discovered.

Hitting the Delete button on a computer is a simple and effective way of staying virus-free. But the language of the New Testament pictures staying sin-free as a little more involved. Paul describes sin almost like a virus. He calls it leaven, the bacteria that makes bread dough rise. Once leaven gets in a lump of dough . . . well, getting it out takes some effort.

It's far better never to let sin get into our lives to begin with. But if it does, what do we do then? First, we must repent—that is, make up our minds to go a different way. Then we confess—agree with God about what we've done, and receive His forgiveness. Finally, we put on the armor of God: faith, righteousness, and the Word of God. Don't let the virus of sin multiply in your life.

It is far better to deal with our own sin than to have God deal with it for us.

Our Gigantic Secret

These things I have spoken to you, that My joy may remain in you, and that your joy may be full.

John 15:11

The Bible shows that joy is present in all of the major events of the Christian life. There is joy in salvation, in baptism, when we read the Word of God, and in prayer. In fact, Christian joy is so unique that the Bible teaches us that it comes even at times of discouragement—even when we are dying.

G. K. Chesterton wrote that "joy is the gigantic secret of the Christian." I believe he's right. This kind of joy is not known anyplace else in the world except in the life of a person who knows Jesus Christ in a personal way.

Jesus said, "These things I have spoken to you, that My joy may remain in you, and that your joy may be full" (John 15:11). The center of joy for the Christian is Christ. The joy is Christ's joy. It is simply the life of the Lord Jesus Christ being lived out in an individual. Christian joy is letting Christ live His life out through you so that you become what He is. There are other kinds of joy found in other places in the world, but there is no place where you can find Christian joy except in Christ.

Rejection

The stone which the builders rejected
Has become the chief cornerstone.

Psalm 118:22

Miriam's heart sank as she stood by her locker reading a letter her school counselor had just handed her. She'd been rejected by the university she wanted to attend. Across the hall, Martin was experiencing the same feeling, having been cut from the high school basketball team. His buddy, Thomas, had stayed home from school that day, literally sick because his girlfriend had broken up with him.

Rejection is one of the hardest burdens we're ever called on to bear. It undercuts our self-confidence and damages our sense of well-being. But it helps to remember that our Lord Himself understands the pain of rejection. Isaiah 53:3 says, "He is despised and rejected by men, a Man of sorrows and acquainted with grief. And we hid, as it were, our faces from Him." Jesus said, "The Son of Man must suffer many things, and be rejected" (Luke 9:22).

Because He was rejected, we can be accepted. Ephesians 1:6 says that it is God's grace "by which He made us accepted in the Beloved."

If you're facing the pain of rejection today, remember that Jesus Himself understands, He cares, and He is waiting to embrace your hurts and encourage your heart.

The Great Divide

Between us and you there is a great gulf fixed, so that those who want to pass from here to you cannot, nor can those from there pass to us.

Luke 16:26

The gulf between Hades and Paradise is fixed—immovable. The gulf is not going to be taken away. What you do in this life fixes forever where you will spend eternity. If you reject Jesus Christ in this life, you will remain in hell forever. There is no crossing back, no second chance, no coming back and starting over.

Thankfully, the decision you make for Jesus Christ in this life fixes your eternal salvation forever as well. The point is that the gulf, the divide between heaven and hell, is a fixed divide. Therefore, whatever decision you make in this life—for or against Jesus Christ—is a decision that you will live with for eternity. No one knows what the next minute, hour, day, or year will bring. The decision you die with is the decision you will live with forever.

Amazing Mercy and Grace

Therefore, I urge you, brothers, in view of God's mercy, to offer your bodies as living sacrifices.

Romans 12:1 NIV

A young Englishman wanted to be a seafaring man like his father, but the British Royal Navy would not have him. He ended up in West Africa working for a slave trader, a "wretched man," as one writer called him, begging for food to stay alive. Escaping Africa, he was washed overboard in a storm and nearly drowned at sea. After being rescued, the words of Thomas à Kempis's *Imitation of Christ* came to him, and he cried out to God for salvation. Years later, John Newton wrote a hymn in praise of the "amazing grace" that saved a wretch like him.

Not all of us have experienced the depths of wretchedness John Newton did before being saved. Or King Nebuchadnezzar, for that matter. He lost his dignity and sanity—and fortunately, his pride—before coming to his senses (Daniel 4:33–37). Whether we come from a background of wickedness or willfulness, our sin merits the same response in God's sight: condemnation. It is only God's amazing mercy and grace that can save us from ourselves.

Recipients of God's grace are easy to spot—they're the ones with the grateful looks on their faces and words of thanks on their lips.

Meditate on the Lord

I remember You on my bed,
I meditate on You in the night watches.
Psalm 63:6

Many people spend their nights tossing and turning when they face difficult circumstances. But not David. When he lay on his bed at night, he simply meditated on the Lord. He remembered the many ways in which God had been faithful to him in the past.

Are you losing sleep over a situation or circumstance in your life? As you think about the past, the present, and the future, meditate upon it from God's perspective. Keeping hope alive is partly based on reliving the memories of the good things we have experienced as a child of God and the difficult things God brought us through.

Think of what David must have meditated upon. David stood before that mountain of a man with three things: a sling, a bag of stones, and faith in the power of God to give him victory. And that was all he needed—the battle was his. Never forget what God has done for you in the past. Those victories will fuel your faith in victories yet to come.

No Exceptions

Therefore show these men the proof of your love and the reason for our pride in you, so that the churches can see it.

2 Corinthians 8:24 NIV

One evening Pastor Bill Hybels stopped by his church to encourage those rehearsing for the spring musical. He didn't intend to stay long, so he parked next to the entrance.

The next morning he received this note: "A small thing, but last night you parked in the 'No Parking' area. One of my crew (who did not recognize you) said, 'There's another jerk in the "No Parking" area!' We try hard not to allow people—even workers—to park anywhere other than the parking lots. I would appreciate your cooperation too. Signed, a member of maintenance."

What an example from a leader! No one is exempt from church rules or God's rules. That night Bill realized the employee didn't want him to be labeled "I'm an exception." Exemplary conduct means encouraging others to imitate us, even in small matters. Whether the leader of a church or a member of the clean-up crew, we are all to be held accountable so that we are an example of God's love.

Be aware throughout the day of the example God gave us through His Son, Jesus. And be aware of your actions and how they affect others. Be an example God would be proud of.

Decide to Love

This is My commandment, that you love one another as I have loved you.

John 15:12

Agape love is God's special kind of self-giving. *Agape* describes a love that comes from and is rooted in God. It is totally selfless love. It delights in giving, even though the loved one may be unkind, unlovely, and unworthy. Agape love continues to give.

Agape determines to do whatever is best for the loved one. It willingly sacrifices itself for another's good. Agape gives when it gets nothing in return. It does not even think of getting something back.

Do you think love is just a feeling? It is not a feeling. Love is a decision. The Bible says God is love. God is not a feeling. The Bible says we are commanded to love. We don't have any option.

Maybe you don't feel like loving. Do it anyway. God commands you to love. Maybe you think you can't love. Then find out whatever it is you are supposed to do when you love somebody and do all those things. Depend upon God to do His part. When we do what we're commanded in obedience to God, we discover that grace begins to develop in our lives.

Need a Miracle?

This beginning of signs Jesus did in Cana of Galilee, and manifested His glory; and His disciples believed in Him.

John 2:11

A couple sits on opposite ends of the couch, each of them lonely. What was once a vital marriage has digressed into something neither of them ever intended. They love each other, but they both know restoring the marriage they once had would take a miracle.

Fortunately for them, and the millions like them, a miracle is not a far stretch for our God. In fact, Jesus' first miracle recorded in Scripture was performed in a home at a wedding (John 2:1–11). He came by invitation to the very ceremony where marriage is established—a reminder to us that God cares very deeply for families.

If we aren't careful, we might think God had abandoned the institution of marriage and the importance of the home altogether. Browbeaten with statistics of marital failure, many couples forget who authored the marriage relationship in the first place.

Does your home need a miracle? Invite Christ into every room. Make Him the foundation of each relationship that is built within its walls. Like the water turned to wine at the wedding in Cana, Christ's power can transform hurt into harmony.

To Know the Lord, Wait

I wait for the Lord, my soul waits,
And in His word I do hope.

Psalm 130:5

There is a sense in which we have to wait before God for Him to reveal Himself to us so we can learn more about Him. The reason has to do with how we learn anything. We learn things in the human realm by acquiring a new piece of knowledge and comparing it to something we already know. But with God, since He is beyond our finding out, we have nothing to compare Him to.

We can never know God completely because we don't have enough common ground to associate who He is with what we know. And so we are consigned to waiting before Him as He reveals more of Himself to us. If that seems strange to us, it is because we are not used to thinking of God in the truly transcendent terms in which He exists. As we grow in our experience and knowledge of God, we develop more and more common ground with Him by which we can learn even more. Therefore, knowing God is a process, and waiting before Him in worship is the means to knowing Him better.

Secret of Contentment

Not that I speak in regard to need, for I have learned in whatever state I am, to be content.

Philippians 4:11

A man named Agur once prayed a prayer that most moderns would find curious: "Give me neither poverty nor riches—feed me with the food allotted to me; lest I be full and deny You, and say, 'Who is the Lord?' Or lest I be poor and steal, and profane the name of my God" (Proverbs 30:8–9).

Most people today want to avoid poverty (though not for Agur's reason), but who in our materialistic day prays to avoid riches? Agur knew something that people today have missed completely: riches have the potential for being a trap and a source of ruin.

The apostle Paul knew what Agur knew; he had learned the secret of contentment. Paul was comfortable with having little and with having a lot because he believed that God was his provider. Because his eyes were fixed on heavenly things, he could be content with whatever earthly things God gave him.

The next time you lose your material contentment, remind yourself of who owns it all and how He's promised to provide. Contentment is an excellent indicator of what we think about God and His will.

Yield to God

He who calls you is faithful, who also will do it.

1 Thessalonians 5:24

Pastors and ministers struggle with the temptation to get "stressed out" as much as any other Christian. Sometimes I can let the expectations of the members of my church become so many separate circles of responsibility that I begin to be stressed about meeting all those expectations. Pastors are expected to visit everyone who goes to the hospital, counsel everyone who has a problem, go to see every new visitor, and preach dynamic messages three or four times each week. Any pastor who tries to do all those things will find himself burned out in a matter of weeks, months, or years—and many have.

The only way I survive as a pastor of a large church is to know that the very best thing I can do for our church is to do the will of God. God loves each person in our church, and I know if I am following His plan and will for me, the congregation's needs will be met. I constantly have to bring myself back under His authority and learn from Him how to stay focused on His will for my life.

Persistence in Prayer

The effective, fervent prayer of a righteous man avails much.

James 5:16

A devout Scottish preacher named John Welsh used to kneel at his bedside and pray for the members of his church before retiring for the night. His wife was known to say, "Come to bed, John; it's too cold." His response to her was always the same: "But, dear, I have the souls of three thousand people to answer for, and I do not know how it is with many of them."

It is one thing to pray, but it is altogether another to pray without giving up until the answer to your prayers is received. Jesus taught the disciples a parable about a widow who wouldn't give a judge any peace until she got what she needed. The lesson? That people "always ought to pray and not lose heart" (Luke 18:1–8). He easily could have told them the story of Daniel who prayed for twenty-one days before he received an answer from heaven—an answer delayed by spiritual warfare in the heavenlies (Daniel 10:1–11:1).

What if Daniel had given up praying after a week? After two weeks? No wonder God blessed Daniel with an understanding of mysteries revealed to no one else. If you are praying and waiting on an answer, don't stop! The answer may be just another prayer away.

The surest way not to get an answer to prayer is not to pray!

Seek to Serve Our Redeemer

Having been set free from sin, you became slaves of righteousness.

Romans 6:18

As familiar as many of us are with the Passover and Exodus, one aspect of that great event is often overlooked: God redeemed His chosen people from bondage to Pharaoh for the purpose that they might become slaves to Him. Freedom for the sake of absolute freedom from all responsibility was never God's purpose. The children of Israel, once they came out of Egypt, did not suddenly scatter to the four points of the compass to do whatever they wished. God's desire was that they might walk in His will and invest their freedom from bondage in obedience to His will. Why? So He might bless them! When they failed to obey Him, He did not revoke their redemption and send them back into bondage—but they did miss out on the temporal blessings of continued obedience.

The parallel between the nation of Israel in the Old Testament and the individual believer today is inescapable. We should invest our freedom from slavery to sin, not in indulging the whims of the flesh, but in seeking to serve the God who redeemed us.

Trusting God

They said to Joshua, "Truly the Lord has delivered all the land into our hands, for indeed all the inhabitants of the country are fainthearted because of us."

Joshua 2:24

When Joshua sent the spies into Jericho, he must have recalled what had happened to the twelve spies forty years earlier. This time Joshua chose men with trusting, faithful hearts who would take God at His Word and not panic. Despite a narrow escape, the explorers returned with a good report.

The Lord is still looking for people who will trust Him. Too many of us get upset and angry in the face of pain and problems. Such reactions, though natural, are unhealthy. A recent study found hostility a bigger predictor of coronary heart disease than high cholesterol, smoking, or obesity. Those who respond to adversity with anger or acute anxiety may trigger such conditions as cardiac arrhythmia.

Faith, however, calms us. It was the inhabitants of Jericho, not the spies, who were fainthearted in this story. How wonderful to say, "With God, we can be victorious."

How wonderful to live by faith, not by fear.

Transformation Power

I was formerly a blasphemer, a persecutor, and an insolent man; but I obtained mercy.

1 Timothy 1:13

The great glory of the story of the apostle Paul is knowing what he had been before seeing what he became. The greatest enemy of the Lord Jesus Christ in the first century became His greatest servant, most trusted apostle, and a faithful friend. The same hand that wrote out indictments of heresy against the early church was the hand that wrote the letters upon which the early church was based and ultimately spread. The heart that rejoiced when Stephen was stoned to death became a heart that rejoiced at the privilege of suffering for Christ's sake. The noble statements of theology in Romans, the sweet lyrics of Christian love in 1 Corinthians 13, and the desire to reach the regions beyond with the gospel all came from the former persecutor of Christ and His church.

If ever there was any evidence of the transforming power of the gospel, it is seen in the life of Saul the persecutor who became Paul the apostle. Hopefully that same gospel has transformed you as well. If so, like Paul, may you ask the Lord today, "What do You want me to do?"

Onward Christian Soldier

And whoever does not bear his cross and come after Me cannot be My disciple.

Luke 14:27

Entering boot camp for basic military training used to mean being stripped of all your identity. Everything was taken from you—including your hair!—and you were given back only what you would need to be a good soldier. You were even told what to think. "When I want your opinion," the drill sergeant would bark, "I'll give it to you!"

Not to compare the Christian life with the military . . . but wait—even Paul drew that comparison (2 Timothy 2:3). There is discipline, training, and especially sacrifice in both the military and the Christian life. When Jesus was recruiting and training His own kingdom soldiers, He told them they would only need one thing in order to follow Him: a cross.

He didn't say to bring your checkbook, your 401(k) retirement portfolio, your dreams and aspirations, or your hobbies. He just said to take up your cross and follow Him. The point of that drastic charge was simple: following Jesus means giving up everything in order to receive from Him so much more in due time and in His way.

The Christian soldier carries only one possession into battle: the cross of self-surrender to Jesus.

Christ's Communication

These are written that you may believe Jesus is the Christ, the Son of God, and that believing you may have life in His name.

John 20:31

Jesus was not only victorious over death, but He reached out to all those around Him. He desperately wanted to communicate with those who had been closest to Him. He used His scars with Thomas, His voice with Mary, the breaking of bread with two disciples, and a repeated fishing adventure with the other disciples because He loved them and wanted to reveal Himself to them.

He still has that passion today. We are so blessed to have the precious Word of God, the record of all the Lord did to reveal Himself to people. By it He has communicated to us, asking us to believe so that we may have life.

He continues to reach out to people today, through His church, through radio and television messages, through books and tapes, and through the personal witness of those who know Him as their personal Savior. He keeps on reaching to us with the message that He is alive, and because He lives, we may live also.

Lost Love Sought

If it is possible, as much as depends on you, live peaceably with all men.

Romans 12:18

Elizabeth Barrett Browning's parents so disapproved of her marriage to Robert Browning that they disowned her. For ten years, Elizabeth wrote love letters to her parents seeking reconciliation, but with no reply. Then a large box arrived in the mail from her parents. Excitedly she opened it, only to find all of her letters to her parents unopened and unread.

We know Elizabeth Browning's love letters today as some of the most beautiful in all of classical English literature. They would have been even more famous if they had stirred the reconciliation with her parents that she longed for. Given Elizabeth's experience, some might say, "See, what's the use? All that work and no results." But if only one letter out of the hundreds had been read, and it had healed the relationship between daughter and parents, all her labor would have been repaid.

Restoring relationships is not easy. It requires death to oneself, obedience to God, and love for others—just what Christ displayed when He reconciled us to the Father. Be Christlike today, and restore a lost love.

No one ever said reconciliation was easy—just desirable, possible, and much more joyful than the alternative.

Trust in the Giver, Not the Gifts

He who trusts in his riches will fall,
But the righteous will flourish like foliage.
Proverbs 11:28

Proverbs' primary principle on the governance of money is found in 11:28: "He who trusts in his riches will fall, but the righteous will flourish like foliage."

There is nothing wrong with obtaining riches, but there is a great deal wrong with trusting in them instead of trusting in the One who gives them—and who can take them away. We are warned against greed and against putting our trust in transitory things like wealth so that nothing comes between us and God.

Money is not given to us as a permanent possession, and therefore should never be the object of trust. God, on the other hand, is permanent and eternal, the perfect object for our trust. Therefore, we are to trust the Giver, not the gift, when it comes to material prosperity.

If we manage what God has given, we will have enough money to give away.

Faith versus Fate

Yet who knows whether you have come to the kingdom for such a time as this?

Esther 4:14

The Confederate general Thomas "Stonewall" Jackson had an unswerving confidence in the plan and protection of God. Once, during a battle, he sat down to write out a message to send to a subordinate. A Union cannonball struck a large oak tree above where he sat, showering him with bark and wood chips. He brushed off his paper and continued writing, focused on his task.

Jackson might have echoed the words of Esther from the fifth century BC in Persia: "If I perish, I perish" (4:16). When Esther spoke those words, she didn't speak fatalistically; she spoke faithfully. Esther was a Jewess who was the wife of the Persian king. When she learned of a plot by a Persian official to destroy all the Jews in Persia, she took her life in her hands by daring to approach the king to save her people from destruction. Persian law said that anyone approaching the king without permission—even his wife—would die unless the king granted a pardon. Your faith in Christ may not be a life-or-death issue, but if it were, would your faith let you risk dying in order to do the will of God?

When your faith is in God, the chips can fall where they may without taking you from the task at hand.

God's Beautiful Creation

The earth is full of the goodness of the Lord.
Psalm 33:5

God loves to bring about blessings in our lives. We can see the goodness of God not only by how He provides for us in our own lives, but also by looking at the beauty that He built into the universe He created. The psalmist says, "The earth is full of the goodness of the Lord." Arthur W. Pink wrote that the goodness of God is seen in the variety of natural pleasures that He has provided for us. God could have satisfied our hunger without worrying about our taste, but He gives us taste buds and gratifies them with good-tasting food. God could have made the earth fertile without its surface being so delightfully beautiful. We could have lived without beautiful flowers and the music of birds. But the source of all this loveliness and charm leads us back to the goodness of God.

We have a beautiful world, and every time we have a chance to visit the greatness and goodness of God in His provision of this beauty for us, we ought to stop and praise His name. He has cared so wonderfully for us as His creatures.

Honor and Blessing

Honor your father and your mother, that your days may be long upon the land which the Lord your God is giving you.

Exodus 20:12

There is widespread agreement that the custom of standing during the "Hallelujah Chorus" of Handel's *Messiah* began with King George II of England. When the king stood, everyone in the room stood.

Showing respect for authorities, women, the elderly, parents, and others is fast disappearing in modern cultures. In ancient cultures, a failure to show respect could have a serious impact on one's lifespan. The fifth of the Ten Commandments promised long life in the Promised Land to Israelites who honored their parents.

Theologians refer to this law as the "law of filial obedience," and violation of this law could lead to the death of a rebellious child. Children of all ages have a biblical responsibility to honor their parents in appropriate ways and the expectation of God's blessing upon their "filial obedience."

Honoring one's parents translates to "the fear of the Lord" (Proverbs 1:7) as we honor our own heavenly Father.

Overcoming Peer Pressure

Do not be deceived: "Evil company corrupts good habits."
1 Corinthians 15:33

One of my favorite television shows over the years was *Candid Camera.* I especially enjoyed the segments when the situations illustrated peer pressure. In one sketch, there was an elevator full of actors all facing the back of the elevator. When the doors opened and the unsuspecting "guinea pig" stepped in, he was the only one facing the correct way. But eventually the camera showed him turning around the wrong way as well. He couldn't take the pressure of being the only one doing the right thing.

The pressure to conform is at its very greatest during the years when a young person is moving from childhood to adulthood. During that time in our lives we want to be accepted so badly that we are very vulnerable to group pressure. And don't think this pressure doesn't impact Christian young people. Whether it's drugs being passed around a car, a party where alcohol is available, or a slumber party where sexual exploits are discussed, there is immense pressure on young people to conform to society's standards. Peer pressure among young people today is one of the strongest forces for ruining lives. And it's time we as parents and young people get on top of the problem and begin to develop a strategy to overcome it.

Courageous Faith

Be strong and of good courage, do not fear nor be afraid of them; for the Lord *your God, He is the One who goes with you. He will not leave you nor forsake you.*

Deuteronomy 31:6

When Martin Luther stood before his accusers at the Diet of Worms in Germany on April 18, 1521, he epitomized courage. "My conscience is captive to the Word of God," he declared. "I cannot and will not retract anything, since it is neither safe nor right to go against conscience. I cannot do otherwise; here I stand; may God help me. Amen."

Martin Luther's courage and resolve were like those of Daniel, who found himself captive in Babylon. As a teenager, Daniel was put on a "fast track" to become a scholar in Nebuchadnezzar's court. When given Babylonian food to eat, he took a stand. The food violated Israel's dietary standards and had probably been offered to idols before being served. Fortunately, he suggested an alternative diet that increased his health and his reputation for wisdom.

When your convictions are challenged, suggest a creative alternative. But before you do, make sure you have the courage to back it up—in case the answer is no.

If you are going to have courage, you must first have a conscience nurtured by conviction.

Pray at All Times

He spoke a parable to them, that men always ought to pray and not lose heart.

Luke 18:1

Here is something I have learned about prayer that I have not seen mentioned in books on prayer I have read: prayer is meant to be preventative more than remedial. We usually treat prayer as remedial, meaning we pray when we have a need or are in trouble. But in Luke 18:1, Jesus says that at all times we "ought to pray . . . and not lose heart." In other words, prayer isn't the last thought; it's the first thought. It is preventative, not remedial. Also, instead of praying when we are tempted, Jesus says we should pray that we may not "enter into temptation" (Matthew 26:41). When we are not under pressure and stress, we should be praying so that we might be shored up and defended against the pressures that will come.

Until we come to the place of prayer, we will never find release from stress. If we treat prayer as just a religious ritual or option, then we are not truly living in dependence upon God. Prayer is the soul of man crying out in inadequacy to a God who is adequate, a God who is able to do what man cannot.

Our On-Time God

Your eyes saw my substance, being yet unformed.
And in Your book they all were written,
The days fashioned for me,
When as yet there were none of them.

Psalm 139:16

In June 1926, Raymond Edman, a young missionary in Ecuador, fell ill with typhus fever. When he was finally seen by a doctor, his condition was pronounced as incurable, and funeral plans were made. Back in Boston, a friend interrupted a prayer meeting with a burden to pray for Ray Edman. Years later, in 1967, Dr. Raymond Edman, president of Wheaton College, finished addressing the student body in chapel and collapsed in death.

Raymond Edman's first brush with death was just forty-one years too soon; God had a college He wanted Edman to run before coming home to heaven. God's timetable, especially in matters of life and death, is the Christian's greatest security.

No one discovered that more than the friends and family of Lazarus. When Jesus did resurrect Lazarus, it was to the glory of God. No one but God could raise a corpse that had been dead four days (John 11:39). If you're facing a life-or-death crisis, remember: God is never early or late.

When your timetable doesn't match God's, someone is either early or late. And guess who has never been either?

Father, thank You that Your schedule is perfect, that You are always on time.

Divine Direction

May the Lord direct your hearts into the love of God and into the patience of Christ.

2 Thessalonians 3:5

The nineteenth century was the period of westward expansion as wagon trains rolled across the Great Plains toward California. By the 1850s, some of the most sought-after people in America were the frontier scouts. Men like Kit Carson and Jim Bridger, who had spent years exploring the western regions, were hired to lead the pioneers safely to their destination. They alone knew the dangers and how to avoid them. They couldn't move the Rocky Mountains, but they knew the way through them.

When the apostle Paul prayed that God would "direct" believers, he was praying that God would go before them and remove the obstacles in their way—the literal meaning of the word *direct*. God doesn't just point and say, "Go there." Like a frontier scout, He leads the way and removes the obstacles and dangers that would keep us from growing in maturity in Christ. But be careful if you pray Paul's prayer! What you count as a possession—a relationship, a material idol, a secret sin—God may see as a problem and remove it.

Life is filled with obstacles to maturity. Only God can remove them, helping us grow up before we grow old.

Positive Changes

He changes the times and the seasons.

Daniel 2:21

A cartoonist in the *New Yorker* drew a picture of a small-town general store with this banner in the window: "Going Out of Business, Slowly but Surely." Many churches and organizations go out of business slowly but surely because they resist change.

You might not like change, but I'll bet you can think of something worse—stagnation! "Stagnation can befall any kind of organization," warns consultant Jeanie Daniel Duck.

Stagnation can also befall people. We have to remember that while not all changes are good, changes from God are very good. "Wherever the Lord's Spirit is, there is freedom," wrote the apostle Paul. "As all of us reflect the Lord's glory with faces that are not covered with veils, we are being changed into His image with ever-increasing glory. This comes from the Lord, who is the Spirit" (2 Corinthians 3:18 GW).

What a mess we'd be in if we couldn't change our sinful lives, if we couldn't grow or improve, if we couldn't learn or advance. Don't be afraid of change, and don't be afraid to change. Just make sure you're changing for the better.

Speak Softly

A soft answer turns away wrath,
But a harsh word stirs up anger.
Proverbs 15:1

The mouth of the righteous is a well of life (Proverbs 10:11) and is as valuable as silver (v. 20). The words of the righteous are wisdom; they are like food for those hungry to know how to live (vv. 21, 31). And most of all, the lips of the righteous are discerning, knowing what is acceptable to say (v. 32). I believe the sensitive, Spirit-led Christian can depend upon the Holy Spirit to give him freedom to speak or freedom not to speak, depending on whether the words are appropriate in the given situation.

Perhaps the most underutilized word of healing that Proverbs discusses is the "soft answer [that] turns away wrath." It takes two people to have a heated, angry argument. If one of them decides to use a soft answer and not participate in the shouting match, the heated argument must, by definition, come to a halt. If you enter a situation where an angry argument is taking place, you can diffuse the tension and lower the decibel level by your soft words.

It is a blessing beyond description to see the spirits of a person rise, the life restored to their eyes, as a result of a healing word from your own lips.

Be Honest With Yourself

Let no one deceive you.

Ephesians 5:6

A well-known defense attorney named Charles A. Peruto Jr. was asked about the admission by Pete Rose, after fourteen years of denial, that he bet on baseball while managing the Cincinnati Reds. Peruto replied dryly, "So now 100 percent of the population knows he bet on baseball. The only person who didn't know before he confessed was him."

It's odd how easy it is to deceive ourselves. Is it possible that your husband, your wife, or your best friend has a better grasp of your strengths and weaknesses than you do? Is it possible that you're in denial about a particular weakness, insisting you don't have a problem, though it's perfectly obvious to everyone else that you do?

Those who work with addictions say that denial and self-deception are our greatest enemies. We insist we don't have a problem when it's readily apparent to everyone else that we're in deep trouble. It isn't just addictive disorders, of course. All sin is self-deceiving.

Ask God to show you if there is an area in your life that needs correction. Pray in these words from an old hymn: "Search me, O God, and know my heart today! Try me, O Father, and know my thoughts, I pray."

Robin Hood and Little John

If when we were enemies we were reconciled to God through the death of His Son, much more, having been reconciled, we shall be saved by His life.

Romans 5:10

Anyone who knows the story of Robin Hood will recall the first time the celebrated thief encountered Little John. Both men were traveling through the forest heading toward each other. They first saw each other at the opposite ends of a bridge that was designed to hold just one man at a time. Each was too proud to let the other pass first, so they both started across. They met at the middle, exchanged insults, and began to fight. As the story goes, both men fell into the waters below. Later, as they recovered on the banks of the river, they began to laugh at themselves. Subsequently, they became the best of friends. Not only had these adversaries settled their differences; they had gone a step further, becoming good friends.

Before we became Christians, we were in effect opposed to God. Our surrender to Him didn't lead to a mere master-slave relationship. As Paul says, Jesus Christ's act of love has made us His friends.

Do I Have Faith?

Now faith is the substance of things hoped for, the evidence of things not seen.

Hebrews 11:1

The African impala is one of the most powerful and graceful animals in Africa. It can jump to a height of more than ten feet and cover a distance of more than thirty feet in one jump. In spite of its great ability, an impala can be kept in an enclosure with a solid fence no more than three feet high. Impalas will not jump if they can't see where their feet will land. Impalas walk by sight, not faith.

Don't laugh—there are many Christians who walk the same way. Faith is "the evidence of things not seen," not the evidence of things seen. As a believer, if we are willing to take steps in life only when we can see exactly what's on the path, we don't have biblical faith.

Abraham was a man who had true faith. God called him from his home in Mesopotamia and directed him to he knew not where. Abraham just obeyed God, left his home, and walked one step at a time. Eventually he arrived at his destination—not because he saw Canaan but because he saw the will of God for his life.

The future can only be faced in two ways: with faith or with fear. How small is the enclosure that has you penned in? If you have to see the next step before you'll move ahead, you're trusting your sight instead of your Savior.

THE UNTAMED TONGUE

Every kind of beast and bird, of reptile and creature of the sea, is tamed and has been tamed by mankind. But no man can tame the tongue.

JAMES 3:7–8

James says we are able to control every kind of beast and animal, yet we have not learned how to control the tongue. After God created man, he was to rule over the fish, birds, cattle, and every creeping thing (Genesis 1:26). When Noah came out of the ark, God reiterated His purpose: "And the fear of you and the dread of you shall be on every beast of the earth, on every bird of the air, on all that move on the earth, and on all the fish of the sea. They are given into your hand" (9:2).

Today, the nature of the animal has been tamed by the nature of man. We have dancing bears, trained seals, talking dolphins, acrobatic birds, charmed snakes, dogs jumping through hoops, and lions with their mouths open wide and the trainer's head inside. We have elephants that march in line behind one another with riders perched on top. All of these creatures have been tamed, but the tongue is untamed and untamable without God's help.

Sharing God's Word

Those who fear You will be glad when they see me,
Because I have hoped in Your word.

Psalm 119:74

In 1631, an English Bible printer made a serious error: he forgot to include the "not" in one of the Ten Commandments. His version of Exodus 20:14 read, "Thou shalt commit adultery." His edition of the Bible became known as "The Wicked Bible." He was fined £300, and all the copies of his Bible were destroyed.

The moral of the story? It's wonderful to share the Bible with others, but make sure you share it accurately! Jesus compared the Word of God with seeds sown in the soil. The condition of the soil, the depth of the soil, and environmental factors will determine whether seeds spring up and ultimately bear fruit (Matthew 13:3–23). And the same is true of the Word of God. Many factors are beyond our control, but what we can control is whether the Word of God is shared with others.

Christians as well as non-Christians need the Word, so it is not just a matter of evangelism. It is a matter of being a person who speaks the Word and wisdom of God to others to address the critical needs in the world today.

When people with receptive hearts discover that your words are God's words, not the words of man, they will rejoice when they see you.

In-Your-Face Forever Friends

As iron sharpens iron,
So a man sharpens the countenance of his friend.
Proverbs 27:17

Proverbs 27:17 suggests, "As iron sharpens iron, so a man sharpens the countenance of his friend." An in-your-face friend is one who will tackle the tough issues of life with you—someone who is not offended if you disagree with him and someone who is not afraid to disagree with you. You both have higher goals than agreement.

Proverbs 17:17 says, "A friend loves at all times, and a brother is born for adversity." The best way to determine who your "forever friends" are is to go through a crisis. Adversity is like a filter—it separates those who are loyal from those who are not. You cannot tell your true friends until adversity appears. Your friends may not even know whether they are loyal friends until they are asked to identify with your suffering. It is easy to be a friend when things are good and pleasant. But the number of people who will stand beside you decreases as the temperature of your crisis goes up.

How does one get that kind of friend? By being one. Proverbs 18:24 says, "A man who has friends must himself be friendly." How many times have you proven yourself to be a forever friend by sticking close to someone through their time of trouble and adversity?

Strife or Life?

If it is possible, as much as depends on you, live peaceably with all men.

Romans 12:18

Hercules, according to legend, grew increasingly irritated by a menacing animal that kept blocking his path. He angrily struck the animal with his club, killing it. As he continued on his path, he kept encountering the same animal, each time more menacing than before. At last, a friend warned Hercules to stop his furious assaults. "The monster is Strife, and you are stirring it up," said the messenger. "Just let it alone, and it will shrivel and die."

Our newspapers are full of stories about strife. We read about nations disrupted by civil strife, athletes upset by team strife, companies suffering labor strife, of homes troubled by marital strife.

The Bible uses the word *strife* many times. Solomon said, "Better is a dry morsel with quietness, than a house full of feasting with strife" (Proverbs 17:1). And Paul said, "Let us walk properly, as in the day, not in . . . strife and envy" (Romans 13:13).

Are you stirring up strife? We're not responsible for the actions and reactions of others, but we are responsible for our own. Put on the Lord Jesus, evict strife from your life, forgive that grudge, and seek to live peaceably with all.

SEPTEMBER

My God shall supply all your need according to His riches in glory by Christ Jesus.

—Philippians 4:19

A Pattern of Life

I will bless the Lord at all times;
His praise shall continually be in my mouth.

Psalm 34:1

It has been said that too many Christians worship their work, work at their play, and play at their worship. What we do on Sundays we call "worship," but is it really? For many people the subject of worship is an enigma. They come to services and sing, but they sense something is missing. They pray and talk with God each day, but find themselves wondering if perhaps there is something they failed to learn about their life with God.

When you begin to read the Scriptures and study the people of the Old Testament, you cannot read far before you begin to understand that worship was the pattern of their lives. The Lord Himself designed the first worship center. He was very specific; it took seven chapters to describe how He wanted it built. He made it portable and designed it to be a visual aid for the worshiping Israelites. The tabernacle was the center of the encampment of God's people. It was a way of showing that God was to be at the center of His people in worship as a way of life. Worship is at the top of God's priority list.

Eight O'Clock

The prayer of a righteous man is powerful and effective.

James 5:16 NIV

Howard Cadle started drinking at age twelve and was soon in the grip of every kind of addiction. He also became caught up in a sprawling Midwest crime syndicate. His worried mother could do nothing but pray. "Always remember, son," she said, "that at eight o'clock every night I'll be kneeling beside your bed, asking God to protect my precious boy."

One evening in a rampage, Howard pulled a gun on a man and squeezed the trigger. The weapon didn't fire, and someone knocked it away. It was exactly eight o'clock. Shortly afterward, Howard made his way home, penniless and ill. "Mother," he said, "I've broken your heart. I'd like to be saved, but I've sinned too much."

His mother, using Isaiah 1:18, led him to the Lord. Howard Cadle went on to become a successful businessman, Christian leader, and one of America's pioneer radio evangelists, preaching on Cincinnati's powerful WLM. "Until He calls me," Cadle once said, "I shall preach the same gospel that caused my sainted mother to pray for me."

Don't forget to pray for your children, and never give up. The prayers of a righteous parent are powerful and effective.

Emptying the Nest

Therefore a man shall leave his father and mother and be joined to his wife, and they shall become one flesh.

Genesis 2:24

As our kids become older, we notice that, little by little, we are losing control. That's what parenting is all about: the gradual loss of control. That's when we find out how well we've done.

Ultimately all of us must say good-bye to our kids. Yet sometimes I find myself thinking angry thoughts about the process of emptying the nest. It just doesn't seem fair to invest twenty prime years—the best years of my life—in four kids, only to see them walk away one by one and leave me for their own lives.

Whose idea was this anyway?

Let me answer that question from Genesis 2:24: "Therefore a man shall leave his father and mother and be joined to his wife, and they shall become one flesh." The Bible makes it clear that this whole leaving thing was God's idea. As sad as we sometimes feel, as much as we grieve, as often as dread creeps into our lives when our kids move into their high school years, we need to remember this: the empty nest was God's idea.

Picture of Encouragement

I am sending him to you . . . that he may know . . . and comfort your hearts.

Colossians 4:8

Edward Steichen, who eventually became one of the world's most renowned photographers, almost gave up on the day he shot his first pictures. At sixteen, young Steichen bought a camera and took fifty photos. Only one turned out. Edward's father thought that was a poor showing. But his mother insisted that the one photograph was so beautiful that it more than compensated for forty-nine failures. Her encouragement convinced him not to quit. Steichen stayed with photography for all his life, but it had been a close call.

What tipped the scales? His mother's vision. She saw excellence in the midst of failure. That's what God does for us. He is our most persistent encourager, and He often uses others to encourage us.

A word of encouragement can be used of God to help a fellow believer reach spiritual success. Jesus prepared His discouraged followers with the promise that He would send them another Comforter.

Perhaps today God will direct you in being an encourager. First Thessalonians 5:11 tells us, "Comfort each other." There is no greater joy than to know the Comforter can work through you to comfort others.

Promises and Predictions

Look up and lift up your heads, because your redemption draws near.

Luke 21:28

In 1949, the magazine *Popular Science* predicted, "Computers in the future may weigh no more than 1.5 tons." In 1977, Ken Olsen, founder of Digital Equipment Corporation, said, "There is no reason anyone would want a computer in their home." Bill Gates said in 1981, "640K ought to be enough for anybody."

Making predictions is risky business—unless you are God! According to John Wesley White, the coming again of Christ and the end of the age occupies some 1,845 scriptural verses, and each one offers sure and certain hope for the Christian. Just consider these promises: "For the Lord Himself will descend from heaven with a shout, with the voice of an archangel, and with the trumpet of God. And the dead in Christ will rise first" (1 Thessalonians 4:16). "I will come again and receive you to Myself; that where I am, there you may be also" (John 14:3). "Behold, I am coming quickly!" (Revelation 22:7).

Vance Havner said, "We are not just looking for something to happen; we are looking for Someone to come! And when these things begin to come to pass, we are not to drop our heads in discouragement or shake our heads in despair, but rather lift up our heads in delight."

Who and Whose You Are

For whom the Lord *loves He corrects,*
Just as a father the son in whom he delights.
Proverbs 3:12

Individual birth certificates are so important that state governments keep a copy in case the original is lost or destroyed. Your birth certificate proves two things about you: who you are (your name, date, and place of birth) and whose you are (your parents' names). You can't get married, obtain a passport, or receive a driver's license without a birth certificate.

For the Christian, there is a different kind of proof that tells who and whose you are, spiritually speaking: the loving discipline of a heavenly Father. In Scripture, discipline is more akin to child training than to punishment. Just as an earthly father employs numerous methods of training in raising his children, so does God in raising us as His spiritual children.

In fact, the Bible says we are illegitimate children, not really God's, if we don't experience His hand of training in our lives. God's discipline is proof that we belong to Him. Treat God's discipline in your life with as much care as you do your birth certificate.

When God's training stretches you beyond your comfort zone, be thankful that it proves who and whose you are.

Cling to God

The salvation of the righteous is from the Lord;
He is their strength in the time of trouble.
Psalm 37:39

Here's a way for you to think about this the next time trouble comes: if you and God are standing apart from one another, and trouble comes between you, it can drive you farther apart. But when you see trouble coming and cling to God with all your might, you never let trouble come between you and God—then you have the victory. In fact, the pressure of the trouble will push you closer and closer to God. It will only serve to strengthen your relationship with Him. People tell me all the time, and I can testify as well, that they never experience the nearness of God as much as they do when they are in the desert places of life. That happens by not letting trouble come between you and God.

Prayer is a way to cling to God. You reach out to Him and communicate with Him with the words of your heart. You pour out your praises and your petitions, and you stay in an attitude of prayer until deliverance comes.

Look and See

For since the creation of the world His invisible attributes are clearly seen, being understood by the things that are made, even His eternal power and Godhead, so that they are without excuse.

Romans 1:20

During the early years of the space race in the 1960s, a Soviet cosmonaut proclaimed to the world that he had proved there was no God because he had looked around in space while circling the earth and couldn't find Him. (One humorist suggested that the cosmonaut would have met Him promptly if he had just opened the hatch of the capsule!)

Several years later, on December 24, 1968, another message was boldly proclaimed by American astronauts James Lovell, Frank Borman, and William Anders as they circled the moon: "In the beginning, God created the heavens and the earth." Had our astronauts seen God in person to verify their claim? No—but they had seen evidence of Him.

The Bible tells us that one of the chief ways we know of God's existence and His love for us is by the marvels of His creation. Whether we step back and look at the way our solar system works, or step forward and look at the intricacies of nature and the miracle of human life, we see evidence of God.

The next time you need reassurance of the presence of God, venture outdoors and open your eyes wide!

A Living Example

The things which you learned and received and heard and saw in me, these do, and the God of peace will be with you.

PHILIPPIANS 4:9

The Philippian believers were instructed to practice the things they had heard, seen, learned, and received from Paul. The items on that action list included:

- Loving more
- Having greater discernment
- Being sincere and without offense
- Being filled with the fruits of righteousness
- Having conduct worthy of the gospel
- Standing fast in one spirit
- Striving together for the gospel
- Being like-minded, of one accord
- Esteeming others better than themselves
- Working out their own salvation in fear and trembling
- Doing all things without complaining and disputing
- Holding fast the Word of Life

When Paul spoke of the things learned and received, he was talking about careful exhortation. When he spoke of those things heard and seen, he was referring to concrete example. Paul was a living example of the conduct he expected from the Philippians.

In Tune with God

O Lord, do good to those who are good,
whose hearts are in tune with you.

Psalm 125:4 NLT

Some years ago, musicians noted that errand boys in a certain part of London all whistled out of tune as they went about their work. It was talked about, and someone suggested that it was because the bells of Westminster were slightly out of tune. Something had gone wrong with the chimes, and they were discordant. The boys did not know there was anything wrong with the peals, and quite unconsciously they had copied their pitch.

We tend to copy the people with whom we associate; we borrow thoughts from the books we read and the programs to which we listen, almost without knowing it. God has given us His Word, which is the absolute pitch of life and living. If we learn to sing by it, we shall easily detect the false in all of the music of the world.

Being in tune with God and fellow believers is the most beautiful music you can make. When you find yourself out of tune, go back to the Word, and He will put a song in your heart.

How to Build Up Others

Encourage one another and build each other up, just as in fact you are doing.

1 THESSALONIANS 5:11 NIV

We say, "I'm going to sit down and figure out how I can build others up." That's fine, but how do we build others up? How do we know what to do?

Paul gave this advice in Acts 20:32: "So now, brethren, I commend you to God and to the word of His grace, which is able to build you up and give you an inheritance among all those who are sanctified."

How do we get built up enough to build up somebody else? My friends, it's the Bible. Read the Bible. The Word of God is the fuel to help us be builders. In 1 Peter 2:2, we are told, "As newborn babes, desire the pure milk of the word, that you may grow thereby."

One New Testament passage, Jude verses 20–21, talks about building ourselves up: "But you, beloved, building yourselves up on your most holy faith, praying in the Holy Spirit, keep yourselves in the love of God, looking for the mercy of our Lord Jesus Christ unto eternal life."

What does Jesus want us to do? I think He wants us to be builders—edifiers—men and women who are committed to strengthening the body. Let us build one another up!

GIANTS

Why will you discourage the heart of the children of Israel from going over into the land?

NUMBERS 32:7

In the Book of Numbers, the twelve spies returned from searching out Canaan. Two of them were upbeat, saying that with the Lord's help they could take the land. But the other ten discouraged the Israelites, planting seeds of doubt and pessimism. They worried about the giants in the land and about the fortified cities. As a result, the people's morale collapsed.

One of the problems with being discouraged is that we also become discouraging. When we fail to trust the Lord with our giants, we're telegraphing a message to others: "The Lord can't help you with your giants either." Discouragement becomes as contagious as smallpox.

Discouragement was one of Paul's concerns when he was persecuted. He was afraid his imprisonment would discourage his converts. Writing to the Thessalonians, he said, "We didn't want any of you to be discouraged by all these troubles. You knew we would have to suffer, because when we were with you, we told you this would happen" (1 Thessalonians 3:3–4 CEV).

If you're facing a difficulty now, may the Lord help you respond to it so that others will be encouraged to trust Him too.

The Poison of Gossip

He who covers a transgression seeks love,
But he who repeats a matter separates friends.

Proverbs 17:9

For many Christians, the indoor sport of choice is gossip. Only we don't call it gossip—we say we are "sharing prayer requests." The book of Proverbs speaks volumes about the poison that can be spread by the tongue: "He who repeats a matter separates friends" (17:9; see also 16:27–28; 18:8; 26:18–22).

A story is told of a woman who learned this lesson the hard way. She gossiped extensively about another woman, only to discover that all she had been repeating was not true. She sought the advice of her pastor on how to make things right. He told her to take a feather pillow, cut a hole in it, and go around town sprinkling the feathers everywhere she went.

The next day he told her to go back through town and collect each of the tiny feathers. The woman realized that she could no more retract the damage done by her words than she could collect thousands of tiny feathers scattered by the wind.

No Day Like Today

Behold, now is the accepted time; behold, now is the day of salvation.

2 Corinthians 6:2

On December 28, 1908, a devastating earthquake struck Messina, Italy, killing eighty-four thousand people. Just hours before the earthquake, local authorities passed a number of ordinances reflecting their ungodly character. In fact, the Christmas Day issue of the local paper had contained a parody actually daring God to make Himself known by sending an earthquake! And He obliged.

It is not wise to refuse the grace of God. Jesus gave such an opinion in a parable about some evil tenants (Matthew 21:33–41). They refused to give their landowner his rightful share of their harvest, even after he made numerous requests. They killed the landowner's messengers, even his own son, in their arrogant rejection of the landowner. So the landowner rejected them and gave the vineyard to others.

Many people have the mistaken notion that God is infinitely patient, that the rejection of His offers of salvation do not offend Him. But parables such as this warn us not to reject the grace of God when it is being offered. If you have heard the offer of God's salvation but have not responded, receive it while it is still being made.

Of all the days suitable for salvation, none is better than today.

KEEP BUILDING THE CHURCH

Each of us should please his neighbor
for his good, to build him up.
ROMANS 15:2 NIV

I will never forget the process of building the worship center for our church. It was exciting, a vision taking shape before our eyes. Even now I can visualize every step of the process: from the time the backhoe dug the first scoop of dirt until the carpet was laid in the finished building.

We get excited about buildings and seeing them take shape. However, the New Testament is much more concerned about building people. Build up the body of Christ. That, I believe, is what you and I are to be about as the last days come upon us.

With all my heart, I want every year of my life to be a building year. I'm not speaking of physical buildings, though some may be built. I'm referring to the building of God's people. I want to build up the body of Christ until He comes or calls me home. Join me, please.

Vanguard of Victory

Now when they began to sing and to praise, the Lord set ambushes against the people of Ammon.

2 Chronicles 20:22

When King Jehoshaphat faced the combined armies of Moab, Ammon, and Edom, he proclaimed a national fast and begged for God's help. "We have no power against this great multitude . . . ," he prayed, "nor do we know what to do, but our eyes are upon You" (2 Chronicles 20:12). A prophet named Jahaziel gave this reply: "Do not be afraid nor dismayed because of this great multitude, for the battle is not yours, but God's" (v. 15).

It was then that Jehoshaphat realized he had a secret weapon. He appointed choirs to go before the armies of Judah. With all their hearts, these royal musicians sang and praised God for His assured victory. As this unlikely vanguard neared the battlefront, the Lord threw their enemies into confusion, and Judah won the battle—not with soldiers, but with songs.

How often we need to echo Jehoshaphat's prayer! Sometimes there are problems we can't solve. Sometimes our pressures are beyond us. "Oh Lord," you can pray, "I don't know what to do, but my eyes are on You."

Praise is the Christian's secret weapon. Satan is allergic to praise; he just can't remain where God is being glorified.

The Words of God

That which was from the beginning, which we have heard, which we have seen with our eyes, which we have looked at and our hands have touched— this we proclaim concerning the Word of life.

1 John 1:1 NIV

It was the ancient Greeks who first sent representatives to conduct official business on behalf of their government. Today, ambassadors speak with the full authority of their governments, and embassies are considered inviolable territory. In short, how a nation treats another nation's ambassador and embassy is a good indication of the esteem in which it holds the foreign nation as a whole.

The idea of identifying and valuing two entities as equals is a biblical concept. For two people in covenant, to harm one was to harm the other (1 Samuel 18:1–4). And to disregard a person's word was to disparage the person himself (Luke 6:46). Therefore, how we value the Living Word of God, Jesus Christ, is a good indicator of how we value the written Word of God, the Bible. What conclusions would someone draw about your love for the Savior after observing your relationship to the Scriptures for a few weeks? Since both the Bible and Jesus Christ are the Word of God, it's impossible to value one and not the other.

A proven way to grow closer to God is to grow closer to God's Word.

Rocky or Rock Solid?

Marriage should be honored by all.

Hebrews 13:4 NIV

Researchers at the University of Washington claim they can predict with 87 percent accuracy which newlyweds will divorce and which will stay together for a lifetime. Their predictions are based on how a couple talks to each other. Those expressing fondness and love to each other had marriages that tended to last. Those who were always rude and seemed unable to say good things often divorced.

At the dawn of history, God created a man named Adam and allowed him to experience loneliness, to feel incomplete and unfulfilled. The animals of the field and the birds of the air didn't satisfy Adam's physical and emotional needs. So the Lord created a woman—not a child, a son or daughter, or another man, but someone like Adam yet different. Bringing Adam and Eve together, the Lord established the ordinance of marriage with these words: "Therefore a man shall leave his father and mother and be joined to his wife, and they shall become one flesh" (Genesis 2:24).

When the writer of Hebrews later said that marriage should be "honored" by all, he used a word meaning "to view as valuable, of great worth, priceless."

Your marriage is God designed and priceless. Take care of it.

What, Lord?

Our hope for you is steadfast, because we know that as you are partakers of the sufferings, so also you will partake of the consolation.

2 Corinthians 1:7

During stormy weather, when the strong winds blow, the roots of plants actually dig down deeper. Then when the calm days return, the new roots provide a deeper foundation for new growth. That is the way it should be with us. What we receive from disruptive moments depends upon how we respond.

The right question is never, "Why, Lord?" It is always, "What, Lord? What do You want to teach me through this disruptive moment? Take me around and through the bend in the road as my Teacher. Don't let me miss anything that You want me to see and learn."

Dear friend, if you face a disruptive moment with any other perspective than that, it will just be a bump in the road that bounces you all over the highway. When it is over you will just be sore, and you won't be any better. Purpose now, before you get to the bends in the road, that you will respond in a way that produces more of God's will in your life.

Set Free to Serve

But beware lest somehow this liberty of yours become a stumbling block to those who are weak.

1 Corinthians 8:9

At the 1994 National Prayer Breakfast in Washington, D.C., Mother Teresa of Calcutta was the keynote speaker. Only four and a half feet tall, she could barely see over the podium. But when she spoke, the president and other dignitaries heard a stinging rebuke: America had become a selfish nation, losing the meaning of love because of our practice of aborting unborn children.

America, the beacon of freedom for the rest of the world, has at times misapplied the meaning of the word. True freedom and liberty are experienced when we find the courage and power to serve the weak, the immature, the less fortunate than ourselves.

Like Mother Teresa, the apostle Paul had words of rebuke for Christians who cared more about their personal rights and freedoms than the spiritual needs of the less mature. Yes, Christians are free, not bound by rules and regulations. But if we use our freedom to offend another, we have become abusers, not servants. What freedoms have you set aside lately in order to serve someone who needed your strength?

The freest person in the world is the one who makes himself a voluntary servant of others.

The Outcome Is Confirmed

Thanks be to God, who gives us the victory through our Lord Jesus Christ.

1 Corinthians 15:57

On September 11, 2001, the United States of America was attacked by hostile forces. The destruction wrought by terrorists in New York City and Washington, D.C., was the first time anyone in modern times had brought so serious an attack within the continental boundaries of America.

U.S. President George W. Bush interpreted the attacks as acts of war and immediately declared war on terrorism. The declaration itself was evidence of the changing face of warfare in the modern era. For the first time, war was being declared by America not on an offending nation, but on an ideology—the ideology of terrorism.

The weapons of war were new. Diplomatic strategies, embargos, financial tools, trade, and social strategies would be used to isolate and ostracize nations in the world community that did not eagerly join the worldwide fight against terrorism. Finally, the military would be employed.

Unlike military conflicts in this world, the outcome of our spiritual warfare is already confirmed: Satan will be defeated and believers in Jesus Christ will reign triumphantly with Him forever.

Let's Roll!

And we know that all things work together for good to those who love God, to those who are the called according to His purpose.

Romans 8:28

In her book *Let's Roll: Finding Hope in the Midst of Crisis,* Lisa Beamer wrote about her feelings on the morning of September 11, 2001. "In that dark moment, my soul cried out to God, and He began to give me a sense of peace and a confidence that the children and I were going to be okay. But even that comfort didn't take away the wrenching pain or the awful sense of loss I felt."

Every person who lost a loved one in the 2001 terrorist attacks went through, and still lives with, heart-wrenching loss. But for the Christian, there is hope. Even Todd Beamer, one of the heroes of Flight 93, turned to God in the midst of his own trial. With a telephone operator, he prayed the Lord's Prayer and recited the Twenty-third Psalm, and was heard to whisper, "Help me, Jesus," several times before calling his fellow passengers to action: "Let's roll!"

Those with a sure confidence in God's purposes and plans are never frozen by fear. Todd Beamer was not. Lisa Beamer is not. And you will not be, through faith in the goodness of God.

The fact that God has a plan, not your knowledge of the plan, is the basis of your peace and hope.

Victorious Warriors

Whatever is born of God overcomes the world. And this is the victory that has overcome the world—our faith.

1 John 5:4

The Bible says that Satan's purpose is to blind sinners and beguile Christians, and to hurt and discourage those who belong to God. He will do anything to disturb the mind, deceive the heart, and defeat life. He is actively involved in the world today, and if you read your Bible, you'll find he has always been active: he led Lot into Sodom, got Peter to deny Christ, made Ananias and Sapphira lie to the church, and even dared attack Jesus Christ. If he isn't afraid to attack the Lord of glory, you should not be surprised to discover that he is willing to attack the most mature Christian. He wants to bring division into the church today, paralyzing its ministry and scandalizing its leaders.

Yet the Word of God tells us that this warfare is one for which we can prepare. We can walk into a hostile environment and do warfare for God and not be defeated. Our Commander in Chief has already won the war, and He is waiting for us to get in on the victory. God can help us to learn how to be victorious warriors in the great spiritual battle.

Where to Find Wisdom

If any of you lacks wisdom, let him ask of God, who gives to all liberally and without reproach, and it will be given to him.

James 1:5

Forbes magazine is one of the longest running and most respected business publications in the world. Its pages profile the wealthiest, most innovative, and most successful business leaders in the world. Yet in the midst of all its worldly wisdom, the magazine includes an acknowledgment of the true source of wisdom. The headline of the editorial page features a quote from Proverbs 4:7: "With all thy getting get understanding" (KJV).

The complete admonition from Solomon says, "Wisdom is the principal thing; therefore get wisdom. And in all your getting, get understanding." Why is this a good message for business leaders—and for every person? Because it's so easy to get caught up in getting what this world has to offer: power, position, and prestige. But wisdom and understanding do not flow from these things; they flow only from God. It's easy for the average Christian to think that powerful people need that lesson. But all of us are subject to the same temptation: to value man's wisdom over God's.

Remember, with all your getting, make sure you get—and keep—true wisdom from God.

Trust God to Fulfill Your Needs

My God shall supply all your need according to His riches in glory by Christ Jesus.

Philippians 4:19

Paul reminded the Philippians that the God who had cared for his needs through their loving concern would also care for their needs as they trusted Him! This promise is often taken out of context. It was given to encourage those who were sacrificial in response to the needs of God's work. There is another promise very similar to this one that is also found in the middle of some strong teaching on stewardship: "And God is able to make all grace abound toward you, that you, always having all sufficiency in all things, may have an abundance for every good work" (2 Corinthians 9:8).

Paul had been rejoicing in the fact that the Philippians had supplied his need. Now he told them that God would supply their need. His promise to them was personal: "my God." It was positive: "shall supply." It was pointed: "all your need." It was plentiful: "according to His riches in glory." And it was powerful: "by Christ Jesus."

This is a consistent principle in the working of God with men. "Give, and it will be given to you: good measure, pressed down, shaken together, and running over will be put into your bosom. For with the same measure that you use, it will be measured back to you" (Luke 6:38).

The Whole Duty of Man

I devoted myself to study and to explore.
ECCLESIASTES 1:13 NIV

What an enigma Solomon was—the wisest man on earth yet the most foolish. Scottish preacher Alexander Whyte said, "If ever ship set sail on a sunny morning, but all that was left of her was a board or two on the shore that night, that ship was Solomon."

In his Book of Ecclesiastes, Solomon applied his God-given wisdom to the pursuit of meaning in life. He explored every avenue, seeking satisfaction. He tried education, money, public works, fame, creative writing, sensual pleasure, and religion. But nothing satisfied.

Are you exploring, experimenting, and seeking satisfaction in similar things? Tennis star Boris Becker said, "I had won Wimbledon twice before, once as the youngest player. I was rich. I had all the material possessions I needed. . . . It's the old song of movie stars and pop stars who commit suicide. They have everything, and yet they are so unhappy. I had no inner peace."

In Ecclesiastes 12:13, Solomon finally reached the conclusion of the whole matter: "Fear God and keep his commandments, for this is the whole duty of man" (NIV).

Only a life devoted to God through Jesus Christ satisfies the heart.

Refreshing Friends

Ointment and perfume delight the heart,
And the sweetness of a man's friend
gives delight by hearty counsel.
Proverbs 27:9

Proverbs 27:9 says that "hearty counsel," or the kind of advice that comes from a good friend, is as pleasant as "ointment and perfume." Good, strong advice from a good, strong friend is a delight to receive. It shows that a person really cares about you and wants your best. "Hearty counsel" builds you up and strengthens you and helps you face difficult things.

These words, attributed to George Eliot, define a fortifying friend: "Oh, the inexpressible comfort of feeling safe with a person, having neither to weigh thoughts nor measure words, but pouring them all right out, just as they are, chaff and grain together, certain that a faithful hand will take and sift them, keep what is worth keeping, and then, with the breath of kindness, blow the rest away."

The Bible contains a wonderful example of a fortifying friendship between two men, David and Jonathan. In spite of circumstances that would make their friendship an unlikely one, they forged a bond that fortified each of them. Their relationship stands as a testament to what true friendship can endure and accomplish.

A Foundation for Giving

And all the tithe of the land, whether of the seed of the land or of the fruit of the tree, is the Lord's.

Leviticus 27:30

Every good citizen . . . should be willing to devote a brief time . . . to the making up of a listing of his income for taxes . . . to contribute to his Government, not the scriptural tithe, but a small percentage of his net profits." So said U.S. Representative Cordell Hull in the House of Representatives on April 26, 1913.

Note that in 1913, the biblical tithe was well-enough understood in American culture to be used as a standard of comparison in public discourse. Note also that income taxes were suggested to be less than 10 percent! Today, however, a common reference to the "scriptural tithe" would bring blank stares from many in our culture.

Tithe is the English word meaning one-tenth, and it describes that portion of every Israelite's property and harvest that was set apart for the Lord. The tithe is not replaced in the New Testament but serves as a foundation upon which the overflow of giving by grace can continue.

Do you set aside for the Lord at least one-tenth of all you receive from Him? Doing so reflects an obedient and trusting heart.

Prayer Attack

Continue earnestly in prayer, being vigilant in it with thanksgiving.
Colossians 4:2

During World War I, the French decided to take one of the enemy's strategic strongholds. But the enemy's lines were so defended by trenches, parapets, and barbed wire that it was virtually impossible for the infantry to get through.

But the attacking general had amassed a large amount of powerful artillery. He began to fire round after round of the most explosive shells at them. With this excessive strength, a continuous fire was kept up for more than five hours, until all the trenches were covered, palisades thrown down, and wire entanglements blown to pieces. The infantry was then able to enter and capture the base with ease.

This incident is analogous to spiritual warfare. There are positions of the adversary that cannot be stormed or starved. There are defenses that seem impregnable. But with a barrage of constant prayer, the defenses can be lowered, and souls will be ready to surrender to the Lord. Let us be productive soldiers in the battle against sin and Satan.

What's in a Name?

No longer shall your name be called Abram, but your name shall be Abraham; for I have made you a father of many nations.

Genesis 17:5

A married couple named their new son "Foolish One." The name stuck; and by the time Fool was a grown man, he had lived up to his name. Once, he was befriended by a stranger but incurred the stranger's wrath when he failed to acknowledge his kindness. His wife, who was wise, did the right thing and settled Fool's debt—the shock of which caused Fool to have a stroke. A fool from birth, in ten days Nabal was dead.

That's right—Nabal of the Old Testament (1 Samuel 25) bore a name that, in Hebrew, means "fool." Why would parents burden a child with such a negative name? Naming is a powerful tool in the hand of a parent or any authority figure. When we name someone, we exercise a certain power over his or her life. That person believes us—why shouldn't he?—and thinks of himself in those terms. Just think: which would a Little League slugger rather hear from a parent in the stands: "Way to go, champ!" or "Way to go, chump!"?

Regardless of your legal name, if you're a believer in Christ, you have a new name: Christian, meaning "Christ one" or "little Christ." That's a name worthy of living up to.

Names are word pictures. Paint them ever so carefully.

Now Is the Time to Obey

You do not know what will happen tomorrow. For what is your life? It is even a vapor that appears for a little time and then vanishes away.

James 4:14

We discover from the Old Testament that the destructive practice of procrastination has been around for a long time (Proverbs 3:27–28; Isaiah 56:12). But the Bible has written the word *NOW* in large letters in the gospel message. "Behold, now is the accepted time; behold, now is the day of salvation" (2 Corinthians 6:2). The time for obedience is now! We cannot count on tomorrow, so we must take advantage of today. In business terms, yesterday is a canceled check. Tomorrow is a promissory note. Today is the only cash you have.

According to James, knowledge and responsibility work together. To sin ignorantly is one thing, but to sin in the face of known truth is quite another. Statements from our Lord and the apostle Peter confirm the truth that James presents in verse 17: We are held accountable for what we know but fail (or choose not) to do (Luke 12:47–48; 2 Peter 2:21). Sins of omission are just as serious as sins of commission. To omit God from the planning processes of our lives, knowing that we should include Him, is sin.

Prayers to Be Reckoned With

My . . . prayer to God . . . is that they may be saved.

Romans 10:1

By intercessory prayer," wrote Oswald Chambers, "we can hold off Satan from other lives and give the Holy Ghost a chance with them."

A woman in Colorado told of a daughter who had been deeply ensnared in demonism, witchcraft, and the occult. "When she came back to the Lord," said the woman, "she credited my prayers and those of my friends. 'I didn't have a chance against your prayers, Mom,' she told me."

J. Sidlow Baxter points out that our loved ones may "spurn our appeals, reject our message, oppose our arguments, despise our persons, but they are helpless against our prayers."

Are you heavy-hearted because your child is away from the Lord? Your spouse? Your parents? Are you burdened for relatives or friends who don't know Christ? James said the prayer of a righteous person is "something powerful to be reckoned with" (James 5:16 msg).

If you don't know what to pray, try turning the first verses of Psalm 40 into a prayer: "Lord, please pull my friend from the miry clay. Set his feet on a rock, and put a song of praise in his mouth." It may take awhile, but keep on storming heaven. After all, someone once prayed like that for you.

Jesus: Man of His Word

Let not your heart be troubled; you believe in God, believe also in Me.

John 14:1

A young boy was out in the country, climbing among a row of cliffs. He yelled from the top of one, "Hey, Dad! Catch me!" The father turned around to see his son joyfully jumping off a rock straight at him. The dad became an instant circus act, catching his son, causing them both to fall to the ground.

When the father found his voice, he gasped in exasperation, "Son, can you give me one good reason why you did that?" He responded with remarkable calmness: "Sure . . . because you're my dad." His whole assurance was based on the fact that his father was trustworthy.

As Christians, we can throw ourselves into the arms of Jesus because He is trustworthy. We can stake our lives upon His promises because He is a Man of His Word. If doubts assail us, we must simply look at the convincing evidence—His perfect track record! For instance, He said He would die and He did (Matthew 20:18). He said He would rise from the dead on the third day and He did (v. 19). He said He would return to His Father and He did (John 7:33).

Because Jesus is a Man of His Word, we can be assured He will keep His future promises as well. He said He will return for us and He will (14:3).

Living or Dying

For the wages of sin is death, but the gift of God is eternal life in Christ Jesus our Lord.

Romans 6:23

An aged Scotchman, while dying, was asked what he thought of death. He replied, "It matters little to me whether I live or die. If I die, I will be with Jesus, and if I live Jesus will be with me."

When you really consider life and death, is your attitude similar to the aged Scotchman? Sometimes it is easy to get caught up in the drudgery of everyday routines. But what makes life worth living is our hope in Jesus Christ. The Christian life is a commitment that always looks toward eternity.

Perhaps one of the greatest joys that comes with age is realizing that your relationship with God deepens and continues to reach new and amazing levels. Celebrate this joy by sharing the good news with younger generations. By being a living example of the hope you have in Christ, you are able to reach out to others with His amazing love.

Whether you die at the end of this day or live—Jesus will be with you! Everyone must face death, but you can face it with Jesus by your side. Focus on the future of eternity with Jesus, so that every day you are alive is a reflection of Him.

His Wonderful Presence

You shall worship the Lord your God,
and Him only you shall serve.
Matthew 4:10

God exists everywhere, but He is not always manifest everywhere. His manifest presence comes to us when He is praised. C. S. Lewis once wrote that "it is in the process of being worshiped that God communicates His presence to men . . . even in Judaism the essence of the sacrifice was not really that men gave bulls and goats to God, but that by their so doing God gave Himself to men."

Perhaps you have experienced the wonderful presence of God during a special time of worship. As you were singing, praying, praising, and worshiping the Lord, you felt His presence closer to you than ever before! Worship causes the presence of God to be felt and experienced by His people. If you really want God to be in your church meetings, praise Him as best you can.

Satan tempted Jesus by asking for His worship, not His service: "All these things I will give You if You will fall down and worship me" (Matthew 4:9). Satan understands the correct order—the one you worship is the one you will serve. And keep in mind Christ's response in verse 10: "You shall worship the Lord your God, and Him only you shall serve."

Jesus Sees You

For the Lord your God . . . knows your trudging through this great wilderness. These forty years the Lord your God has been with you; you have lacked nothing.

Deuteronomy 2:7

What parent has not exhorted his teenager to behave properly "because God is watching"? From childhood, we are taught that God sees and knows everything—and so He does. But there's a flip side to that truth. While it's true He sees our failings, it is even truer that He sees our successes—and our struggles.

Family experts tell parents, "Instead of trying to catch your kids doing something wrong, catch them doing something right!" More often than not, when we are being faithful to obey the Lord and find it difficult, we think He is nowhere around. But that's not true. God is ever watchful, which means He sees our struggles when we're trying to serve Him faithfully. And He comes to us with aid in His time just like He did with the disciples when they were obediently rowing across the Sea of Galilee in a storm. Jesus was alone on a mountain praying, but "He saw them straining at rowing" and "He came to them" (Mark 6:48). If you are struggling in a storm, don't worry—Jesus sees you.

Knowing that Jesus is aware of our needs is a comfort beyond measure.

The Power of the Word

For the word of God is living and powerful,
and sharper than any two-edged sword.
Hebrews 4:12

A young German monk desperately wanted to find relief for his tormented soul. He prayed, studied, and even went on a pilgrimage to Rome, but he still found no peace. Finally, when studying Paul's letter to the Romans, the eyes of his heart were opened: "The righteous will live by faith" (Romans 1:17 NIV). Martin Luther, the father of the Protestant Reformation, finally found the assurance he had sought for so long.

Because the Word of God is alive (Hebrews 4:12), it is able to bring about changes of all sorts. Whereas Martin Luther was able to find assurance of salvation through faith alone, another person may find freedom from anxiety through knowledge of God's sovereign control over life. The Word of God is used by the Holy Spirit to probe the deepest parts of the human heart and bring illumination. Perhaps there is an area of life where change has eluded you. If you will search the Word of God, you will discover the truth the Holy Spirit can use to satisfy your deepest longing (Proverbs 2:1–5).

The Word of God will bring forth the will of God in the life of the willing child of God.

Saying Thank You

For God so loved the world that He gave His only begotten Son, that whoever believes in Him should not perish but have everlasting life.

John 3:16

A medieval monk announced he would be preaching the following Sunday evening on the love of God. As the shadows fell and the light ceased to come in through the cathedral windows, the congregation gathered. In the darkness of the altar, the monk lit a candle and carried it to a statue of Christ on the cross. First of all, he illumined the crown of thorns; next, the two wounded hands; finally, the marks of the spear wound. In the hush that fell, the monk blew out the candle and left the chancel. There was nothing else to say.

The greatest example of God's love for us is that He gave His only Son so that we could have the chance to live with Him in eternity. How do you say thank you for the ultimate gift? By worshiping and honoring God in everything you do. Live like every action is a thank-you note to Him—while washing the dishes, driving your car, singing at church. Every moment you live is another opportunity to say thank you. By becoming involved in your local church and supporting other believers with your talents and offerings, you are opening up for God to work through you.

When you say thank you to God with your life, He will bless you.

Safe in the Will of God

You have need of endurance, so that after you have done the will of God, you may receive the promise.

Hebrews 10:36

When we have trials in our lives, we always have three choices:

We can endure our trials. Of course, some people make us endure their trials with them. We ask them how they're doing, and they're more than happy to tell us. But when we merely endure our troubles, we run the risk of becoming bitter.

We can just escape. Run! Leave! Get out of there! When we do that, we get away from where we are. But if God hasn't told us to leave, we leave the place where God can help us.

We can enlist our troubles. This is the right thing to do. In other words, we can let God use the crises in our lives to make us better, to help us grow in His way. We can step up on our trouble and move to a higher level.

We all have a natural "flight syndrome" that causes us to think, *If I could just run away!* But when we do that, if we're not careful, we make matters worse instead of better. No matter how difficult our circumstances, the safest place for us is always in the will of God.

Carry Them to Jesus

Do not cease to cry out to the Lord *our God for us, that He may save us.*

1 Samuel 7:8

Just as the four men in Mark 2 carried their sick friend on a bed to Jesus, we can carry our friends to Jesus on a stretcher of prayer. We bring them to Jesus as we intercede for them and as we plead for their salvation. He can heal them, He can forgive them, and He responds to our faith.

For many years, Cathy Crawford, missionary to France, prayed earnestly for her father's salvation. In time, she developed some health problems and was diagnosed with multiple sclerosis. She was able to continue her missionary work. While home on furlough, she had trouble traveling from church to church, so her retired father offered to drive her. As a result, he not only repeatedly heard her missionary testimony, but he heard biblical sermons almost every night of the week from the host pastors. By the end of the summer, he was won to Christ.

"I can be thankful for my illness," Cathy said, "for God used it to answer the greatest prayer in my heart, the one for my dad's salvation."

Do you have a friend or loved one for whom you're burdened? Don't cease to cry out for God to save that person, though the case is hard. Follow Jesus' advice: we "always ought to pray and not lose heart" (Luke 18:1).

Finding Friends

Faithful are the wounds of a friend,
But the kisses of an enemy are deceitful.
Proverbs 27:6

Some friends are willing to wound you in order to help you: "Faithful are the wounds of a friend, but the kisses of an enemy are deceitful" (Proverbs 27:6). Consider the last part of the verse—the characteristics of an "enemy." Essentially, what to be on the watch for is the flattering lips of a deceiver.

A person who constantly compliments you may not be a faithful friend. The wise person will quickly ask, "Why is this person saying all these nice things?" Sometimes that person has a hidden agenda. Perhaps they want something or are so insecure that fawning over people is the only way they know to find a friend.

So how do you find a faithful friend without being taken in by a flatterer or deceiver? Faithful friends edify, but they don't flatter (Romans 15:2). They are humble and demonstrate love (Ephesians 4:2). They don't always tell you what you want to hear. Instead, they are willing to rebuke you if necessary out of love for you (Proverbs 9:8).

Everyone needs to be close to someone who will ask them the hard questions about their lives. A faithful friend will ask those questions and not rest until he gets the right answers.

Dare to Be a Daniel

Daniel purposed in his heart that he would not defile himself with the portion of the king's delicacies, nor with the wine which he drank.

Daniel 1:8

A Roman emperor once said about the eloquent preacher John Chrysostom, "What in the world can you do with a man like that?" Chrysostom wouldn't be silenced. He disregarded threats and kept preaching whether imprisoned, banished, bound, or free.

How like Daniel. As Daniel functioned in his culture, we don't see him being a wild-eyed radical fundamentalist, as some call believers today. By outward appearances, he was as professional in that corporate culture as he could be. But inside, he was a radical subversive for the kingdom of God. His wisdom and integrity provoked envy and anger on the part of everyone around him.

Daniel performed his job with such excellence that he kept being promoted to the top. His critics followed him around, watching him everywhere he went, but they found no fault in him. Their only valid accusation was in his faithfulness to the law of his God.

Daniel's life glorified God, vindicated his faith, and changed history. Dare to be the same. The world just doesn't know what to do with people like that!

Defining the Gospel

I delivered to you first of all that which I also received: that Christ died for our sins according to the Scriptures, and that He was buried, and that He rose again the third day.

1 Corinthians 15:3–4

Duncan McNeil, the Scottish evangelist, once said that in school he had a seminary professor who insisted on opening his theology classes with a question. No one could ever anticipate what the question would be. One day he said to his students, "Gentlemen, can someone give me a definition of the gospel?"

A student rose and read John 3:16: "For God loved the world so much that he gave his only Son so that anyone who believes in Him shall not perish but have eternal life."

The professor said, "That is a good gospel text, but it is not a definition of the gospel." Another student read 1 Timothy 1:15: "How true it is, and how I long that everyone should know it, that Christ Jesus came into the world to save sinners—and I was the greatest of them all." Again the professor declined to accept it; he waited for what he wanted. Finally, a student stood and read 1 Corinthians 15:3–5, much to the professor's delight. It was evident that he had the reply he desired; he said, "Gentlemen, that is the gospel. Believe it, live it, preach it, and die for it if necessary."

Here's How

The excellence of the knowledge of
Christ Jesus my Lord . . .
Philippians 3:8

How can we get to know the holy God? If He is so pure, so infinite, so high, and so lifted up, how can we approach Him, and how can we grow more intimately acquainted with Him?

First, we must come to Him by simple faith in Jesus Christ. Second, we must study our Bible and learn all we can about Him. Third, we must turn our knowledge about Him into knowledge of Him.

How can we do that? In his book *Knowing God*, J. I. Packer gave the formula. "The rule for doing this," wrote Packer, "is demanding but simple. It is that we turn each truth that we learn about God into a matter of meditation before God, leading to prayer and praise to God."

Packer defined meditation as "the activity of calling to mind, and thinking over, and dwelling on, and applying to oneself, the various things that one knows about the works and ways and purposes and promises of God."

It is this activity of holy thought, this practice and pattern of letting our minds dwell on Him, that helps us become more deeply and intimately acquainted with the Holy One, who is our life.

Deo Volente

You ought to say, "If the Lord wills, we shall live and do this or that."

James 4:15

If you have read letters exchanged between Christians a hundred years ago, you may have noticed the postscript "D.V." These two letters stand for the words *Deo Volente*, which is Latin for "if the Lord wills."

Submission to the will of God is James's proposed alternative to the presumptuous lifestyle of the businessman: "Instead you ought to say, 'If the Lord wills, we shall live and do this or that'" (James 4:15). This would be an acknowledgment that the planners wanted God's direction and approval and would do nothing without it.

Christians generally agree that three basic issues are involved in knowing the will of God. First, there must be a willingness to do God's will when we find it. Second, we must realize that God's will is always in harmony with His Word. And third, we must come to Him earnestly in prayer seeking guidance. These steps will lead us directly into the will of God.

Shocked by the Bible

All Scripture is given by inspiration of God, and is profitable for doctrine, for reproof, for correction, for instruction in righteousness.

2 Timothy 3:16

A professor at a major university asked her class to write a short essay on the Sermon on the Mount (Matthew 5–7). At first, she was shocked at her students' responses: "a hoax . . . strict . . . no fun . . . perfectionism . . . extreme, stupid, unhuman." Then it dawned on her: this is how Jesus' original audience responded! The Bible is offensive. God's perspective on life is a wake-up call to those familiar only with the world's ways.

When Jesus says calling your brother a fool is as serious as murder and lusting is equal to adultery, do His statements seem narrow-minded? It's easy to get comfortable with the routines of Christianity—going to church and Sunday school, serving on a committee, giving of our money, helping a neighbor—without continuing to grow in a deep understanding of God's character through studying His Word.

If you are no longer "shocked" by what God expects and requires, it may be because you have stopped delving into the details. There is no substitute for reading the Bible when it comes to learning to think God's thoughts after Him.

To avoid shock when reading the Bible, read it more, not less!

Ignorant Worship

You worship what you do not know; we know what we worship, for salvation is of the Jews.

John 4:22

As a pastor, I have come to realize that worship is the ultimate priority for which all of us were created. What does it mean to worship?

When Jesus was talking to the Samaritan woman in John 4 about worship, He said, "You worship what you do not know." How can you truly worship something without knowing what it is? How do you worship a God you don't know? Paul calls that ignorant worship.

Last Sunday, churches across the country were filled with people who walked in to worship something they did not know. People engaged in ignorant worship, and nothing really happened in their church or in their lives. They went through the external motions without ever really understanding the internal working, and nothing happened because God does not accept ignorant worship.

Worship is knowing God and worshiping Him, and if we do not know God, we cannot worship Him. Make it a priority to know God.

The Glory of Fatherhood

The glory of children is their father.

Proverbs 17:6

Whatever happened to the idea that a father knows best? In a few short decades, we went from a television show called *Father Knows Best*, in which the father was a wise, strong, and loving head of his home, to the film *Father of the Bride*, in which comedian Steve Martin played a lovable doofus of a dad, always being corrected by his unflappable and all-together wife.

There seems to be little glory left in fatherhood in the modern world. Television shows (especially commercials) and movies have stereotyped fathers as either absent physically or absentminded. As usual, the culture has it all wrong. The term *father* is applied with honor to a host of biblical heroes: God Himself, prophets, priests, male parents, grandfathers, great-grandfathers, ancestors, and leaders such as Abraham and Paul. Those are big shoes for modern fathers to fill, but strong fathers are God's will.

Dads, don't succumb to the cultural demotion of fatherhood. Let your practice produce the honor that your position deserves.

Fortunately, every earthly father has a role model in God the Father. Being honored as a father begins with honoring your heavenly Father.

The Strength of Tenderness

Husbands, likewise, dwell with them with understanding, giving honor to the wife. . . . Be tenderhearted.

1 Peter 3:7–8

In every survey I have seen asking women what is the main thing they need from their husbands, it's always been the same: tenderness. In our John Wayne and Rambo-inspired culture, men are encouraged to maintain a macho-type persona where tenderness and emotion are not to be displayed. In varying degrees and places, tenderness—not to mention tears—has been viewed as a sign of weakness. But from God's perspective nothing could be further from the truth.

Perhaps the greatest impediment to tenderness for men, especially when it comes to praying and pursuing spiritual interests together, is the presumption of weakness. We don't like to see ourselves as helpless, totally dependent on God. And yet often, the greatest sign of strength that a wife is looking for in her husband is the evidence that he is totally dependent on God and not afraid to confess his own need for Him. His vulnerability in that area is what frees his wife to confess her needs, her fears, and her dependence on God as well.

A marriage that is led by a man who loves his wife authentically, sacrificially, deliberately, and unconditionally will be a prosperous marriage, one that mirrors the relationship between Christ and His Church.

Imperfections Made Perfect

And He said to me, "My grace is sufficient for you, for My strength is made perfect in weakness." Therefore most gladly I will rather boast in my infirmities, that the power of Christ may rest upon me.

2 Corinthians 12:9

J. Stuart Holden tells of an old Scottish mansion close to where he had his summer home. The walls of one room were filled with sketches made by distinguished artists. The practice began after a pitcher of soda water was accidentally spilled on a freshly decorated wall, leaving an unsightly stain. At the time, noted artist Lord Landseer was a guest in the house. One day when the family went out to the moors, Landseer stayed behind. With a few masterful strokes, that ugly spot became the outline of a beautiful waterfall, bordered by trees and wildlife. He turned that disfigured wall into one of his most successful depictions of highland life.

Just as the artist turned a stain into a waterfall, so Jesus can turn your pain and problems into a beautiful picture of His all-knowing love. When you pray to God, ask to see the problems in your life in a new way. Romans 8:28 tells us, "And we know that all things work together for good to those who love God, to those who are the called according to His purpose."

When you meditate on this truth, you will begin to sense the Holy Spirit working on your attitude. With God, imperfections can be perfected.

Fueled by Prayer

[Pray] always with all prayer and supplication in the Spirit.

Ephesians 6:18

I once borrowed a car and as a favor to the owner filled it with gas. That big Oldsmobile station wagon had an ornament on the hood that said "diesel," a sticker on the rear gate that said "Oldsmobile Diesel," and a note on the fuel gauge reading, "Diesel Fuel Only." So naturally I put diesel fuel in the tank. Big mistake, since the owner had recently converted it to gasoline. When it broke down on the main street of a town in New York, I had to explain why I had put diesel fuel into a vehicle with a gasoline engine.

I don't think I'll ever live that down, so I use it as the perfect illustration of Christians. We are human beings, and we have "Human Being" written all over us, but we've been converted into something else. If you try to run your new spiritual self on the old kind of fuel, it won't work. There are a lot of Christians who haven't figured that out yet. The fuel for the Christian life is prayer. Prayer is the energy that makes it possible for the Christian warrior to wear the armor and wield the sword.

You cannot fight the battle in your own power. No matter how talented you are, if you try to fight the spiritual battle in your own strength, you will be defeated.

Knowing Our Place

That none of you may be puffed up on behalf of one against the other.

1 Corinthians 4:6

NBC news commentator Tim Russert described a meeting he had with Pope John Paul II. The pope put his arm around Russert and said, "You are from NBC. They tell me you're a very important man." Taken aback, Russert said, "Your Holiness, there are only two of us in this room, and I am certainly a distant second." The pope looked at him and said, "Right."

A degree of humility can keep us from stumbling in social settings. Humility is not only key in social settings but in spiritual service as well. As the writer of Proverbs said, "Pride goes before destruction" (16:18). Christians have been given the inestimable privilege of receiving gifts of grace from God—spiritual enablements that make it possible for us to serve Him in carrying out the ministry of Jesus.

And if that isn't enough, someday we'll be given rewards in heaven for using those gifts faithfully! God provides the gifts, the power to use them, and the rewards. Where is the room for pride in such a plan? Our place is to humbly receive and employ what God has graciously given.

The Christian who knows his place is the one whose place God will make known.

Repent Where You Are

Remember therefore from where you have fallen; repent and do the first works.

Revelation 2:5

Perhaps we walked with God early in life, or even got all the way through college with our faith intact. But then, through small concessions in our lives, our walk with the Lord began to erode. Little by little, we slipped away from the things that once had been important to us.

What should we do today? How do we get back? We must remember from whence we have fallen. Repent where we are. Go back and repeat the first works. Confess our sin. Acknowledge who we are. And then remember that God loves us.

The good news of the Gospel, my friend, is that before the prodigal ever turned his heart toward home, the father had been praying and waiting for him, thinking of what it would be like to embrace him again in his arms.

God will not force Himself upon us. He will not come and drag us out of our situation. But if we will return, He will love us all the way back home.

The Purpose of Suffering

It is good for me that I have been afflicted,
That I may learn Your statutes.

Psalm 119:71

After spending thirty-five years in a wheelchair following a diving accident that left her paralyzed at age seventeen, Joni Eareckson Tada said, "I think that we all want to know Christ, that we want to know the power of His resurrection. But not many of us want to share in the fellowship of His sufferings, and nobody wants to become like Him in His death."

The apostle Paul said in Philippians 3:10 that "being conformed to [Christ's] death" is how we know "the power of His resurrection, and the fellowship of His sufferings." We are conformed to His death by dying to our old sinful nature. And that hurts!

God, motivated by His goal of having us become like Jesus (Romans 8:29), brings us face-to-face with that which is least like Christ. Maybe it's our impatience, our anger, our love of creature comforts, our fear of the future, our desire to do things our way. Dying to those things is the only way we will become like Christ, which is God's ultimate plan for us. If God is showing you, perhaps painfully, something that needs to go—let it go!

The power of Jesus and fellowship with Jesus are realized when we learn to embrace suffering like Jesus.

Getting a Grip

Giving all diligence, add to your faith virtue, to virtue knowledge, to knowledge self-control.

2 Peter 1:5–6

Most of us would agree that when it comes to the battle for the right kind of living, the biggest enemy is not out there. The biggest enemy is right here—ourselves. That's why the principle of self-control is so very vital. It is that quality that makes it possible to achieve the goals God has set before us.

In the Greek, the word *temperance* is *kratain*. It means "to grab hold of, to grasp." I believe it's the concept from which we get the idiom "Get hold of yourself," which we use when we're talking to someone who is getting too emotional. The word is used only seven times in the New Testament. In almost every situation, it is used to describe the importance of gaining control and reigning over our passions and desires.

The matter of self-control is a battle fought in the mind. The mind controls the passions. The battle is fought in the world of thought. There is no conflict so severe as the conflict one goes through to subdue oneself.

I'd like to suggest that the best way to deal with the struggle for control over your thoughts and passions is focusing your mind upon Jesus Christ.

Restore Such a One

Brethren, if a man is overtaken in any trespass, you who are spiritual restore such a one in a spirit of gentleness.

Galatians 6:1

In his book *Returning to Your First Love*, pastor Tony Evans tells how his younger brother, after rebelling against their father's authority, was sent packing, suitcase in hand. Twenty minutes later, the banished one returned home, asking to be reinstated to the family. He had been put out in order to learn respect and was taken in when he learned it.

That's how church discipline works (1 Corinthians 5:1–13). But what happens when the one who has sinned repents? Paul says, "You should . . . forgive and comfort him, otherwise such a one might be overwhelmed by excessive sorrow" (2 Corinthians 2:7 NASB). How frustrating it would be for someone to say, "I'm sorry," only to find his cries landing on deaf ears!

Can you imagine God turning a deaf ear to a repentant sinner? As we are to forgive the same way God does, we are to restore and accept anyone who has accepted a measure of discipline for his sins (Ephesians 4:32). If there is anyone who has sinned against you, be sure you "restore such a one in a spirit of gentleness"—just as God restores you.

The surest sign of a person accepting his own forgiveness is the freedom with which he extends forgiveness to others.

Who Prays?

Confess your trespasses to one another,
and pray for one another.
James 5:16

The ancient historian Eusebius portrayed James as a Nazarite, an Israelite wholly devoted to God (Numbers 6:1–23), whose times of prayer for his nation were frequent and prolonged.

Most of us find it very hard to identify with a man like James. Who do we know who prays so much that he develops knots on his knees? Perhaps the better question might be, "Who do we know who prays—really prays?" That's not an unfair question, nor is it calculated to instill guilt. It reflects the surveys that have been taken by both Christian and secular researchers. It seems Christians today are too busy to pray!

One of the New Testament's strongest passages on prayer is contained in James's final words to his fellow Jewish believers. In James 5:7–12, the word for patience is used seven times. In this passage, the word for prayer occurs seven times. When patience is required, prayer is the key.

The Right Path

Be wise,
and set your heart on the right path.
Proverbs 23:19 NIV

How does a worm get inside an apple? Perhaps you think the worm burrows in from the outside. No, scientists have discovered that the worm comes from inside. But how does he get in there? Simple! An insect lays an egg in the apple blossom. Sometime later, the worm hatches in the heart of the apple and then eats his way out.

Sin, like the worm, begins in the heart and works out through a person's thoughts, words, and actions. All humans have a sinful nature, and we are capable of self-serving, self-centered, sinful behavior. Romans 5:12 says, "Through one man sin entered the world, and death through sin, and thus death spread to all men, because all sinned." How you are inside will reflect out to the world through your actions.

If not for the mercy and grace of God, our entire lives would resemble the apple that might look good from the outside but is rotten and bruised on the inside. Guard your walk with the Lord. Stay in fellowship with Him in order to keep on the right path.

From the Inside Out

The heart of the righteous studies how to answer.

Proverbs 15:28

For many years following the assassination of President John F. Kennedy, people would ask one another, "Where were you when Kennedy was killed?" Now another date and event has replaced all others in the modern era as the subject of the "Where were you?" discussions: September 11, 2001. More than any other event in our day, the terrorist attacks on New York and Washington, D.C., have redefined life for most people. And many people have come to fear that definition.

The only silver lining in this dark cloud of tragedy is that people are asking questions for which only the Bible has answers: "What is our world coming to?" "Why do people do such things?" "What can we do to keep terror at bay?" The answer that every Christian has discovered and every non-Christian needs to know is this: The world cannot be changed, but people can be. When someone asks you the post-9/11 questions, encourage them with the words of a first-century converted terrorist named Paul: the Gospel is the power of God for salvation (Romans 1:16).

The only way the world will be changed is the same way individuals are changed: from the inside out.

Speak, Lord

Do not be like the horse or like the mule,
Which have no understanding,
Which must be harnessed with bit and bridle,
Else they will not come near you.

Psalm 32:9

A certain harbor in Italy can be entered only through a narrow channel bounded by dangerous rocks and shoals. To keep ships in the center of the channel at night, three beacons stand on poles in the water. When all three lights are lined up perfectly so they appear as one, a ship's captain knows he is in the center of the channel. To enter when the lights don't shine as one is to risk certain calamity.

How foolish would a ship's captain have to be to enter that harbor while one of the lights was out of line with the other two—and especially if all three were visible? God has given the Christian three divine lights that, when aligned in one direction, give certainty concerning His will: a divine standard (the Bible), a divine witness (the Holy Spirit), and divine circumstances (the providence of God). He may, or may not, provide all three at once. But to ignore any, or all, of these guiding lights when they are given is to risk being outside of God's will.

God's guidance is seen most clearly by those who live in eager anticipation of receiving it.

OCTOBER

You are in Christ Jesus, who became for us wisdom from God—and righteousness and sanctification and redemption.

—1 Corinthians 1:30

Jesus: Man About His Father's Business

And He said to them, "Why did you seek Me? Did you not know that I must be about My Father's business?"

Luke 2:49

Have you ever come home from church and discovered you left a child behind? As your family gathers around the dinner table, your eyes fixate on the empty chair. "Where's Johnny?" you ask. Blank stares and shrugged shoulders reveal the worst—Johnny got left behind.

When Jesus was just twelve years old, He, too, was left behind at the temple. His parents returned to find Him and discovered Him sitting among the teachers, asking questions. Greatly distressed, His mother asked Him why He had done this to them. He replied, "Did you not know that I must be about My Father's business?" Even at a young age, Jesus knew He had a unique mission to accomplish. Convinced of this, He did not allow people or circumstances to deter Him.

What unique mission has God called you to? Has He commissioned you to a special assignment at home, work, or the church? Whatever it may be, pursue it with all of your heart. Then at the end of your life, you may say as Jesus did, "I have finished the work which You have given Me to do" (John 17:4).

Father Abraham

Take now your son . . . whom you love, and . . . offer him.
Genesis 22:2

Abraham is one of history's most famous fathers. Not only was he Isaac's father, but he was the father of the entire Jewish nation (Luke 1:73). Furthermore, Paul considered him the father of all who believe in Christ by virtue of his example of being justified by faith (Romans 4:11–12).

What was Abraham's greatest trait as a father? The quality of his fathering stemmed from his supreme love for God. In Genesis 22, God tested Abraham, commanding him to offer his beloved son, Isaac, as a burnt offering. This command implied the possibility that Abraham might have become more devoted to his earthly son than to his heavenly Father. Abraham passed the test. Despite his deep love for Isaac, the Lord came first.

Is it possible to love your children too much? No, but it is possible to love your Lord too little. Jesus warned, "He who loves father or mother more than Me is not worthy of Me. And he who loves son or daughter more than Me is not worthy of Me" (Matthew 10:37).

We'll love our children with a holier and healthier love if Christ comes before anything—or anyone—else in our hearts.

Your World Needs Kindness

Be kind to one another, tenderhearted, forgiving one another, just as God in Christ forgave you.

Ephesians 4:32

The world needs kindness. But let's narrow the scope even further. Your world needs kindness. Your home needs kindness. Where people are living in close proximity, kindness sometimes gets lost.

In the New Testament, the language given to the church is given to the home. The church met in the home. When Ephesians 4:32 says, "Be kind to one another, tenderhearted, forgiving one another, even as God in Christ forgave you," that's also directed at the home.

We need to be tenderhearted, kind, and forgiving. The fruit of the Spirit is tested in that laboratory we call the family. If you can make it work there, it will work anyplace on the face of the earth.

Accountable

You are a pleasure-crazy kingdom, living at ease and feeling secure, bragging as if you were the greatest in the world! You say, "I'm self-sufficient and not accountable to anyone!"

Isaiah 47:8 NLT

Have you noticed how many business, professional, and leadership books have the word *accountable* in their titles? One bestseller, for example, is *The Oz Principle: Getting Results Through Individual and Organizational Accountability.*

Accountability is important for the Christian too. Sinful habits can be pleasurable and desirable, and they can be hard to break. It's tough to do it on our own; we sometimes need to be accountable to others.

That's why the New Testament is so full of "one another" passages—pray for one another, encourage one another, confess your sins to one another, love one another, and admonish one another. If you're struggling with a sinful habit, covenant with a friend to be held accountable. Ask him or her to be your personal encourager and to monitor your progress.

Solomon said, "Two are better than one. . . . For if they fall, one will lift up his companion. But woe to him who is alone when he falls, for he has no one to help him up" (Ecclesiastes 4:9–10).

God Encourages; You Should Too

Blessed be the God . . . the Father of mercies.

2 Corinthians 1:3

In the New Testament, each member of the triune God (God the Father, God the Son, God the Holy Spirit) places a priority on encouragement.

Paul wrote to the Corinthians, "Blessed be the God . . . the Father of mercies [encouragement]" (2 Corinthians 1:3). In one of his letters to the Thessalonians, Paul reminded his readers that Jesus Christ is also, at the very core of His ministry, an encourager (2 Thessalonians 2:16–17).

And what can we say about the Holy Spirit? "Encourager" is one of His names! The King James Bible says of the Holy Spirit (in John 14 and 16), "However when He the Comforter is come. . . ." The title "Comforter" translates the word *paraklete*, which means "to encourage." When we encourage people, we live out the ministry of the third Person of the Trinity. He is the Encourager.

God the Father encourages. God the Son encourages. God the Holy Spirit encourages. We need to be encouragers because encouragement is one of the primary ministries—in fact, it's a priority of our triune God.

Consume with Care

Flee also youthful lusts; but pursue righteousness, faith, love, peace with those who call on the Lord out of a pure heart.

2 Timothy 2:22

Shipwreck victims, adrift on the ocean without water, have died after consuming salt water in desperation. Because salt water contains seven times more salt than the human body can digest, the body begins to demand more water to flush out the salt. So the more salt water one drinks, the thirstier one gets. The body finally succumbs, consumed by its own desires.

Wise is the person who remembers the line from Samuel Taylor Coleridge's "The Rime of the Ancient Mariner": "Water, water everywhere, nor any drop to drink." And wise is the person making his way through this world who remembers the same thing with regard to the lusts and desires of the flesh. Just as the body has a natural desire for water, so the soul has natural desires as well: for intimacy, recognition, or achievement.

But any one of those legitimate desires can lead to spiritual death if too much of the wrong thing is consumed in pursuit of gratification. That's why Paul told Timothy to "flee also youthful lusts," and why he told the Roman Christians to "make no provision for the flesh, to fulfill its lusts" (Romans 13:14).

Meeting a legitimate need in an illegitimate way is a good way to be consumed by your own desires.

Choose Not to Be Lonely

They should seek the Lord, in the hope that they might grope for Him and find Him, though He is not far from each one of us.

Acts 17:27

There is a fundamental emptiness in every human being that can only be filled by the presence of God Himself. It is interesting to note that the only time Jesus Christ cried out in loneliness was from the cross, when the Father forsook Him and allowed Him to die as a sacrifice for the world.

Without the presence of God, the most agonizing loneliness will afflict even the strongest person. No person should search for a solution for his loneliness without solving the basic issue of separation from God.

Accepting Jesus Christ, and being filled by His Spirit, is the first step toward overcoming the negative dimensions of loneliness.

Seeing Like Jesus Sees

And He was moved with compassion
for them, and healed their sick.
Matthew 14:14

Are you old enough to remember the 3-D craze of several decades ago? Using cardboard glasses with red and blue lenses, you could read comic books drawn and printed in a certain way and—*voilà!*—the flat, lifeless pages sprang to life in three dimensions. The 3-D glasses were even available for certain movies.

Wouldn't it be interesting to suddenly be able to look at the world through "Jesus-colored lenses"—that is, to be able to see the world as Jesus sees it? There must be a radical difference between what He sees and what we see simply because we don't always act like He did. For instance, what He saw evoked compassion on numerous occasions. Sick people, demonized people, lost people, hungry and homeless people . . . these were not just the froth on the wake of a fast-moving society. These were real people with real needs.

When Jesus looked at life, He always did the same thing—He gave. He gave of His time, His power, His wisdom . . . and ultimately, He gave His life. What do you see when you look at the world—and what do you do in response? The closer we get to Jesus, the more we'll see what He saw.

Seeing the world like Jesus means giving to the world like Jesus.

God Is in Control

Oh, the depth of the riches both of the wisdom and knowledge of God! How unsearchable are His judgments and His ways past finding out!

Romans 11:33

The greatest minds of history have wrestled with the issue of the sovereignty of God versus the free will of humankind. Someday in eternity we may discover how the track of God's sovereignty and the track of our responsibility finally come together. But the way we should look at this is so simple we sometimes miss it: let God take care of His sovereignty, and let us take care of our responsibility. God's sovereignty explains things that humans cannot possibly fathom.

The sovereignty of God in our lives, from our perspective, is like looking at a weaving from the wrong side. We see all the various threads and knots and strands sticking out. We see it from the back side because we do not have the perspective that God has. But someday in eternity, God will take that patchwork we have looked at and haven't understood, and He will turn it around. We will see the beautiful tapestry that has been woven out of our lives. We can spend all our lives trying to figure out why God does this and why God does that. Sometimes we just have to fall back on the fact that God is sovereign and in control. We can rest secure in that truth.

Reasons to Be Content

Do we have no right to take along a believing wife, as do also the other apostles?

1 Corinthians 9:5

If you need a new appliance, where do you start looking? You probably do an Internet search to find the best combination of value, price, and warranty. That same mindset has caused matchmaking and dating-service websites to be the fastest-growing segment of online business. Singles are shopping for mates the same way they'd shop for a toaster.

Marriage partners have become a commodity in our culture—something to be used up and discarded as tastes, desires, or circumstances dictate. The existing standard seems to be: if you're tired of being single, get married; if you're tired of being married, get single. The state most people seem to be most discontent with is the state they're in.

While it's true that God told Adam it was not good for him to be alone (Genesis 2:18), that statement was tied more to the procreative function of humans to fill the earth than to Adam's constitution as a single person. Every human being, single or married, should find his or her ultimate contentment in God.

Whether we are married or single should not determine our contentment in life. The way we live our lives is an expression of contentment with God.

The Greatest Bargain in the World

You are in Christ Jesus, who became for us wisdom from God—and righteousness and sanctification and redemption.

1 Corinthians 1:30

The Bible tells us that when we become Christians, we are immediately equipped with the righteousness of Christ. Paul told the Corinthians, "You are in Christ Jesus, who became for us wisdom from God—and righteousness and sanctification and redemption" (1 Corinthians 1:30). When Jesus Christ came down to this earth as the perfect Son of God, He went to the cross and died for you.

As He hung upon the cross, two major things happened. First, He took our sin upon Himself. The Bible says He became sin for us. All the sins of the world were crucified on that cross with Jesus. Second, He imparted righteousness to us. So when we give our lives over to Him, when we put our trust in Him for eternal life, Christ not only forgives our sin but gives to us His righteousness. We become righteous in Christ Jesus.

You know, that is the greatest bargain the world has ever known. You give up your sin, and you get His righteousness in return. It is the greatest opportunity anybody has ever had, to get rid of your sin and get the righteousness of Christ imputed to your account in return.

Zacchaeus: A Walking Testimony

Let your light so shine before men, that they may see your good works and glorify your Father in heaven.

Matthew 5:16

The famous London preacher Charles Spurgeon and his wife would not give away the eggs their chickens laid but would sell them—even to close relatives. As a result, some labeled the Spurgeons stingy and greedy. But when Mrs. Spurgeon died, it was revealed that the egg money had been used for years to support two elderly widows. The Spurgeons endured the criticism in silence, knowing that time would validate their actions.

Another man's crafty financial dealings brought him far less praise when they were revealed. Zacchaeus was a Jewish tax collector in league with the Romans and hated by his fellow Jews. Tax collectors grew wealthy by charging citizens more than was due and pocketing the excess. But when Zacchaeus met Jesus, he immediately changed his ways. He confessed what he had done and purposed to pay back all he had stolen and more. Jesus validated Zacchaeus's change of heart: "Today salvation has come to this house" (Luke 19:9).

It's good to talk about your salvation, but it's even better to let your actions speak louder than your words. The world is waiting to meet Christians whose talk is drowned out by their walk.

Christ the Rock

For they drank of that spiritual Rock that followed them, and that Rock was Christ.

1 Corinthians 10:4

You've probably heard this guideline for health and safety: a human being can go forty days without food, four days without water, and four minutes without oxygen. Generally speaking those are good outside limits to keep in mind—under ideal circumstances. If you've just run a marathon, you'll need oxygen in less than four minutes. And if you're wandering across the desert in 110-degree heat, four days without water will seem like an eternity. That's exactly what it felt like to the children of Israel on their way to the promised land.

When they ran out of water, they accused Moses of bringing them out of Egypt to kill them. God told Moses to take the same rod with which he parted the waters of the Red Sea and strike a large rock where they were camped. From that rock flowed water for all of Israel, and they were saved. Centuries later, the apostle Paul said "that Rock was Christ." Indeed, it was He who offered living, spiritual water to all who would believe and be saved (John 4:14). How long can you go without continuing to drink from the Rock that is Christ?

It takes more than an initial drink to survive life's deserts. Drink deeply from Christ the Rock today.

Marks of a Servant

Nevertheless we . . . endure all things lest we hinder the gospel of Christ.

1 Corinthians 9:12

Philip Pillsbury had an international reputation as a connoisseur of fine foods. But to his employees, he was one of the troops. He bore the unmistakable mark of a journeyman grain miller—the tips of three of his fingers were missing. He would not allow his wealth and prestige to separate him from the workers he led, and he had the factory scars to prove it.

The term *servant leader* describes leaders who serve those whom they lead—leaders whose main task is to remove the obstacles that might keep their followers from succeeding. Jesus Christ was certainly a servant leader, as was the apostle Paul. In fact, Paul confessed that he would rather do anything than hinder the spread of the Gospel. So he gave up his rights in order that none would be confused about his motives. He adapted himself to the lifestyle of those he sought to win to Christ. And he bore in his body the telltale marks of a follower of Jesus (Galatians 6:17).

What marks do we bear that reveal our willingness to serve those we are called to lead? Commitment to a cause is measured by the self-denial we're willing to endure to see it accomplished.

Unconditional Love

A new commandment I give to you, that you love one another; as I have loved you, that you also love one another.

John 13:34

Francis of Assisi was terrified of leprosy. And one day, in the narrow path that he was traveling, he saw a leper! Instinctively, his heart shrank back, recoiling from the contamination of that loathsome disease. But then he rallied and, ashamed of himself, ran and cast his arms about the sufferer's neck and kissed him and passed on.

How many of us recoil from those who are different? When we meet someone who looks different, belongs to a different class, believes in a different religion, clashes with our personality, or is on a different intellectual level, we automatically withdraw. Rather than looking at these differences as an opportunity to show love, we allow the differences to separate us.

When you come in contact with those who are different, how do you respond? Do you reach out with arms of love, or do you shrink back? Determine today, with God's help, to love others unconditionally, accepting their differences. If this seems especially difficult, remember that God loves you unconditionally! There are no restrictions on His love.

Will You Hear Me Now?

My son, pay attention to my wisdom;
Lend your ear to my understanding.

Proverbs 5:1

Does anyone really listen anymore? Are you frustrated by shallow conversation with the people you deal with from day to day? If so, you might want to check your newspaper. A woman once placed an ad in a suburban newspaper offering to listen to anyone talk for thirty minutes for five dollars. The next thing she knew, her phone was ringing off the hook! People were hungry to be heard, and they were more than willing to pay someone to listen to them. Listening intently with one's mouth firmly shut is an elusive grace.

Not being heard in relationships is equal to not being valued. We can't always offer a potential masterpiece in our relationship conversation, but we can always respond to others as though it were just that. When Jesus came to visit Mary and Martha, they responded in very different ways. Mary sat at the Lord's feet and listened to His words, while Martha busied herself in the kitchen.

There is a time and place for everything, but the highest priority with each other should be the willingness to listen. In Luke 10:41–42, Jesus responded to Martha, "You are worried and upset about many things, but only one thing is needed. Mary has chosen what is better" (NIV).

Choose what is better: choose to listen.

Life-Changing Wisdom

Incline your ear to wisdom,
And apply your heart to understanding.
Proverbs 2:2

Some years ago, I was at a men's retreat. The speaker issued a challenge to the group, which he said would change our lives: read one chapter of the book of Proverbs each day for a year. Since there are thirty-one chapters in Proverbs, reading a chapter a day would equal reading the whole book each month (reading two chapters on one day in the months with only thirty days). Reading the entire book of Proverbs twelve times in a year, he said, would change our lives.

Well, I accepted his challenge. In fact, I did it more than once. And I remember the incredible impact it had on my life. Almost without fail, I would read a verse in the morning that would have some bearing on an event that took place during that day. The Proverbs of Solomon are the most practical, hands-on truths one could ever hope to find. And to saturate my mind with those truths day after day for a year turned out to be a powerful tonic for my spiritual life.

Anyone who takes seriously the wisdom of the book of Proverbs will experience these blessings, and many more, as a result.

In the Arena

The things which happened to me have actually turned out for the furtherance of the gospel.

Philippians 1:12

Missionary Isobel Kuhn wrote a book entitled *In the Arena*, in which she described great difficulties she had faced, showing how each had become an arena in which her influence for Christ was magnified.

After they were thrown into the fiery furnace, the three Hebrews in Daniel 3 were promoted, and their reputation was enhanced. It was his imprisonment that allowed Paul to evangelize Rome's Praetorian Guard and that spurred the early church to action.

It was after Charles Colson had served time in a federal penitentiary for his role in the Watergate scandal that he became a prominent spokesman for the faith, establishing an effective ministry to men and women in prisons across America.

It was after his arm was amputated from cancer that the world began listening to the testimony of baseball player Dave Dravecky.

It was after months of uncertain captivity by the ruling Taliban in Afghanistan that Dayna Curry and Heather Mercer emerged to tell their stories and glorify God for His deliverance.

Are you in a season of suffering? God will use it to magnify your influence for Him. Trust Him, and be faithful.

Courageous in Any Crisis

I will go to the king, which is against the law; and if I perish, I perish!

Esther 4:16

When your course is righteous, your courage will be reinforced. Esther had the righteous cause. She was to stand before the king and plead for the life of her people. Was she afraid? Undoubtedly.

Courage is not the absence of fear. Courage is persevering in spite of the fear. Courage doesn't mean being oblivious to danger. People who wait for all the courage they need before they act will never act. But those who take the first little step in the process of courageous activity will be given greater strength by God.

The challenges of life will not get much bigger. But building your faith in God can grow you into a giant able to be courageous in any crisis. We build our faith by doing the things that seem hard to us at the time so that we can gain strength to do the really hard things that come to us in the future.

A Prideful Heart

So they come to you as people do, they sit before you as My people, and they hear your words, but they do not do them; for with their mouth they show much love, but their hearts pursue their own gain.

Ezekiel 33:31

In the summer of 1986, two ships collided in the Black Sea off the coast of Russia. Hundreds of passengers died as they were hurled into the icy waters below. News of the disaster was further darkened when an investigation revealed the cause of the accident. It wasn't a technology problem like radar malfunction—or even thick fog. The cause was human stubbornness.

Each captain was aware of the other ship's presence nearby. Both could have steered clear, but according to news reports, neither captain wanted to give way to the other. Each was too proud to yield first. By the time they came to their senses, it was too late.

Pride gets in the way of good intentions. The Bible calls believers to have a humble heart, to watch out for one another. In your life journey, are you aware of those around you?

Watch out for the other hearts that are cruising along the sea of life, and love the way you want to be loved. Practice humility.

Choose One Chair

Whoever therefore wants to be a friend of the world makes himself an enemy of God.

James 4:4

When Luciano Pavarotti was a boy, his father introduced him to the wonders of song. He urged Luciano to work very hard to develop his voice. Taking his father's advice, Luciano because a pupil under Arrigo Pola, a professional tenor. He also enrolled in a teachers college. On graduating, he asked his father, "Shall I be a teacher or a singer?" His father replied, "If you try to sit on two chairs, you will fall between them. For life, you must choose one chair."

Luciano chose one. After seven years of study, he made his first professional appearance. After another seven years, he reached the Metropolitan Opera. He went on to say, "Now I think whether it's laying bricks, writing a book—whatever we choose—we should give ourselves to it. Commitment, that's the key. Choose one chair."

In regard to your spiritual life, you must also make a choice. Will you serve God or the world? You cannot be faithful to both. For if you choose to be a friend of the world, you automatically become an enemy of God. There is no room for split alliances, no room for a divided heart. You must choose one chair.

Suitably Submissive Spouses

Be filled with the Spirit . . . submitting to one another in the fear of God.

Ephesians 5:18, 21

After a church service in which the pastor preached a sermon on wives submitting to their husbands, a man told his wife, "From now on, things are going to be different around here. I'm going to call the shots. I'm the boss, and you're nothing!" "Big deal," his wife countered. "Boss over nothing!"

We might laugh in that case, but sadly neither the husband's rule nor the wife's response was commendable. We smile nonetheless because we know how prickly the subject of submission in marriage can be. Paul did indeed say that wives are to submit to their husbands (Ephesians 5:22). But that is not all he said about submission. In the preceding verse, he implied that submission to one another is an evidence of the filling of the Spirit.

In other words, submission is not primarily a wifely duty; it is a Christian duty. Further on, Paul pictures Christ as One who submitted Himself to suffering for the benefit of His bride, the church. True strength is seen in submitting rather than in forcing submission.

The strongest marriages are those built out of complementary stones held fast by the mortar of mutual submission.

The Return of George Lucas

Dear friends, never avenge yourselves.
Leave that to God, for he has said that
he will repay those who deserve it.
Romans 12:19 TLB

The third movie in the Star Wars series was originally titled *Revenge of the Jedi.* Several months prior to the release of the film, many promotional materials were sent to movie theaters and chains across the country. Then someone suggested to director George Lucas that if the Jedi knights were indeed agents of goodness and peace, they would not be motivated by revenge.

Lucas thought about it, then agreed. Even though a title change would mean a substantial cost in redesigning film titles and replacing promotional materials, Lucas retitled the film *Return of the Jedi.*

In our culture, vengeance is not an uncommon concept. When someone does us wrong, our immediate reaction is to want to get back at them. If we are to be Christlike, though, we must give up our vengefulness.

God the Surgeon

For the wages of sin is death, but the gift of God is eternal life in Christ Jesus our Lord.

Romans 6:23

Dr. Evan O'Neil Kane was a pioneering physician who believed most surgeries should be performed with local, not general, anesthesia. To prove his point, he decided to operate using only local anesthesia. But where would he find a patient willing to be the test case for a new medical theory? Having performed nearly four thousand appendectomies, Dr. Kane applied a local anesthetic to himself and removed his own appendix—and made medical history.

Jesus said, "Greater love has no one than this, than to lay down one's life for his friends" (John 15:13). In a sense, God did for the human race what the good doctor did for his patients. God operated on Himself by sending Jesus Christ, the second Person of the Godhead, to die for the sins of mankind. God assumed the risk and endured the pain when He placed the sins of the world upon the shoulders of His one and only Son. If the love of a doctor is seen by making himself a patient, how much more is the love of God seen by making Himself a sacrifice?

God performed the heart surgery that gave us new life.

Get Busy for God

Therefore, brethren, stand fast and hold the traditions which you were taught, whether by word or our epistle.

2 Thessalonians 2:15

Paul says, "Therefore, brethren, stand fast and hold the traditions which you were taught, whether by word or our epistle" (2 Thessalonians 2:15). The daily news can discourage us. But in the midst of it all, there is Jesus and His encouragement. We need to cultivate our relationship with Him until He is not just one of the things in our life; He is the one thing in our life—the focus of who we are.

"Comfort your hearts and establish you in every good word and work," Paul goes on to say. This is not the time to wear a white robe, sit on a fence, and passively wait for the Lord's return. This is a time to use the powers and energy you have and get busy for God.

The most simple objective of Christians is not only to go to heaven but to take as many people with us as we can. Share the Gospel, teach children, build up one another, strengthen one another, encourage those who are fallen, and reach out to those who are hurting.

In every good work, "occupy till I come" (Luke 19:13 KJV), said the Lord. This is no time for idleness. This is a time for us to seek the truth and live it out every day.

In God We Trust

Some trust in chariots, and some in horses;
But we will remember the name of the Lord our God.
Psalm 20:7

Before his 1971 fight with Joe Frazier, Muhammad Ali said, "There's not a man alive who can whup me." (He jabbed at the air with his blinding left.) "I'm too smart." (He tapped his head.) "I'm too pretty." (He showed the cameras his profile, like a bust on a pedestal.) "I am the greatest! I am the king! I should be on a postage stamp—that's the only way I'll get licked!" Then Ali lost to Frazier.

When confidence in one's abilities and resources changes to pride and then becomes arrogance, there's trouble ahead: "Pride goes before destruction, and a haughty spirit before a fall" (Proverbs 16:18). So how do we find the balance? Simply by remembering that every gift, ability, talent, and resource we have comes from God.

There's nothing sinful about recognizing and confessing what God has provided, but the difference between self-confidence and Christ-confidence is found in who gets the credit. A good way to keep this thought at the forefront of our life is to practice the art of thanksgiving. It's hard to be too self-confident when we acknowledge we are nothing without God.

Live confidently—as long as your confidence is in Christ.

Rejoice in Your Children

Let her who bore you rejoice.

Proverbs 23:25

There's great joy in children. Almighty God meant for children to be blessings, not burdens. They are our future. We invest in them everything we are and everything we have, and they carry into future generations who we are.

It isn't true that when a person dies, he really dies, because he lives on—not only in the presence of the Lord if he is a Christian but in the children who live after him. And if those children are born into the family of God, they will carry that influence with them throughout their lives and through their children's lives after them.

God gives us children as blessings, as benedictions, and as graces to life. In fact, the more children you have, the more potential you have for happiness. I know some don't believe that, but it's true.

We need to remember that children are a gift from God. They are God's blessing upon us. That's the truth of the Word of Almighty God.

When Faith Overlaps Faith

And teach [these things] to your children and your grandchildren.

Deuteronomy 4:9

Manasseh became king of Judah at age twelve and was a horribly wicked king until he came to know the Lord late in life. Manasseh's son Amon took over the throne at age twenty-two and was likewise wicked. But when Amon's son Josiah took the throne, he was one of Judah's most godly kings. How do you explain the change?

Josiah's righteousness was probably influenced by his first six years overlapping with his grandfather's last six years. When Amon was assassinated after only two years as king, Josiah took the throne at age eight. Therefore, his first six years were under the godly influence of his grandfather, Manasseh. In Hebrew culture, it was the responsibility of grandfathers to teach their children and grandchildren the righteous standards of God.

Every parent knows that children look at their grandparents as sources of wisdom and security. Linking the latter years of one with the early years of the other is a perfect way to pass on a love for the Word of God.

Grandparents are in a perfect position to build faith in young hearts by declaring the precious promises of God.

Live Today

God said to Moses, "I am WHO I am."
Exodus 3:14

No one ever sank under the burdens of today; but add yesterday and tomorrow to today, and it can capsize your life. Jesus said, "Sufficient for the day is its own trouble" (Matthew 6:34).

Dr. Osler, a famous physician of years past, made a helpful observation. He noted how oceangoing vessels were able to seal off various sections of the boat so that a leak could be contained in only one part of the ship. Though damaged, a ship could still make it to safety.

Just so, he suggested, we need to develop the capacity for sealing off the yesterdays and tomorrows that fuel the fires of worry. We need to learn to live in the compartment of today alone.

God is the great "I AM" (Exodus 3:14), not "I WAS" or "I WILL BE." The Christian who lives with Him today, in the present tense, is the one who will be free from worries about yesterday, today, or tomorrow.

Your Neighbor Needs You

You shall not take vengeance . . . but you shall love your neighbor as yourself.

Leviticus 19:18

During the American Revolution, a man named Michael Wittman was sentenced to die for treason. A pastor who had been an object of Wittman's hatred walked seventy miles to plead with General George Washington for Wittman's life. Washington refused until he discovered Wittman was the pastor's enemy, not his friend. Because the pastor had shown such love for an enemy, Wittman was released and became the pastor's fast friend.

One of Jesus' best-known parables was about two religious men, a priest and a Levite, who failed to show mercy and love to a dying man. Only when an enemy of the man, a Samaritan, came along was love revealed and the man saved (Luke 10:30–37). Jesus told this story to illustrate the true meaning of the command to "love your neighbor."

The willingness to love one's neighbor was first revealed by God when He sent Jesus to die for us, His enemies (Romans 5:8, 10). As Christ loved us, so we are to love others (1 John 4:11). The good Samaritan changed his world with love. Is there a neighbor in your world whose life could be changed by your love?

Who is your neighbor? Your neighbor is anyone who has a need that you have the ability to meet.

Love's Attitude

Paul, a bondservant of Jesus Christ, called to be an apostle, separated to the gospel of God.

Romans 1:1

When we meet people for the first time, frequently in addition to stating our name we will identify our occupation or profession. Our identity is closely linked to what we do.

Paul introduced himself in the book of Romans by stating, "Paul, a bondservant of Jesus Christ, called to be an apostle, separated to the gospel of God."

Paul saw everything in his life through the lens of his slavery to Christ. Outwardly he wrote as a slave of Caesar, but inwardly he considered himself a bondslave to Jesus Christ. To Paul the term *servant* was a title of dignity and humility. There was no greater position than to be a servant of Jehovah God.

We all would do well to remember that God did not save us to become sensations, but rather to become servants.

A Happy Marriage

That their hearts may be encouraged, being knit together in love, and attaining to all riches of the full assurance of understanding, to the knowledge of the mystery of God, both of the Father and of Christ.

Colossians 2:2

On her golden wedding anniversary, a grandmother revealed the secret of her long and happy marriage. "On my wedding day, I decided to choose ten of my husband's faults which, for the sake of our marriage, I would overlook," she explained. A guest asked her to name some of the faults. "To tell the truth," she replied, "I never did get around to listing them. But whenever my husband did something that made me hopping mad, I would say to myself, 'Lucky for him, that's one of the ten.'"

No one is perfect. So marriage is the union of two imperfect people, with their individual faults, bad habits, and undesirable qualities. As Christians, marriage should be a place to practice grace. When you can look past the faults of your spouse and concentrate on encouraging him or her, you will find satisfaction and peace. If you choose to turn his or her faults into the only things you can see about your spouse, you will find yourself in a lonely marriage.

A Christian marriage demonstrates love through grace and forgiveness, and it stands as an example for others to follow.

Our God of Order

You are complete in Him, who is the head of all principality and power.

Colossians 2:10

It appears from the information in the Bible that Michael is the protecting and fighting angel and Gabriel is the preaching or announcing angel. Each of them has his own job description and carries out God's will in perfection.

Our God is a God of order and organization. That characteristic of God is reflected in the angelic realm. God has set up an authority structure within the universe, within the church, within the family, within human government; and all these lesser authorities are in submission to the greater authority of Christ Himself. The Bible tells us we are complete in Him, "who is the head of all principality and power" (Colossians 2:10).

God is able to respond to our needs and the challenges of our lives because He is a God of power and order. He is able to do what is necessary, and His angels are set up to respond to His every directive.

Get Back to Work

[Peter] said to Him, "Yes, Lord; You know that I love You."

John 21:15

Peter blundered a lot, but he passionately loved Christ; and in the end, that made the difference. Like Peter, we all have a set of personal regrets. All of us would do things differently if we could relive life, but we can't change the past. Instead, the Lord tells us to confess our sins, accept His forgiveness, and learn from our blunders.

There's a well-known story of an employee who made a mistake that cost his company a million dollars. His boss called him in, saying, "I'm not going to fire you, for I've just invested a million dollars in you. The secret of making a million dollars instead of losing a million dollars is making good decisions. And the secret to good decisions is learning from bad ones. Now get back to work!"

That was Jesus' approach to Peter—and to us as well. If you're suffering a load of regret, confess your sins to God. Trust His pardon to wash away the guilt, and depend on His providence to bring good out of bad. Like Peter, passionately love Christ and learn from your mistakes.

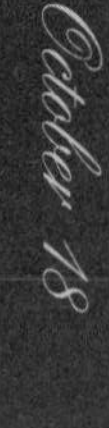

The Dedication of One

If you remain completely silent at this time . . .
you and your father's house will perish.
Yet who knows whether you have come to
the kingdom for such a time as this?
Esther 4:14

It is hard to believe that one person can make a difference in the course of human events. But if you subtract Esther from the Old Testament, there is no Jewish nation, there is no Jesus Christ, there is no Bible, and there is no hope for humankind because Esther was the link that preserved the Jewish nation.

She was one who consecrated her life to God and did what God wanted her to do. God used Esther to turn the events of the world around.

He may choose to use you in a significant way as well. The dedication of one can make the difference for many.

Right or Righteous?

Woe to you, scribes and Pharisees, hypocrites! For you pay tithe of mint and anise and cumin, and have neglected the weightier matters of the law: justice and mercy and faith.

Matthew 23:23

Theologian Jack Deere wrote about a period in his life when he was more concerned about being right than anything else. He was a scholarly professor at a well-known seminary, and he prided himself on knowledge and biblical correctness more than anything—until God did a work in his heart.

If anyone scored an A+ on being right in Jesus' day, it was the Pharisees. They knew the Law backward and forward. They tithed their herbs and made up laws about what was allowed on the Sabbath. And one of the things that was most certainly not allowed was the "work" of healing. So when Jesus healed a man born blind from birth, and did it on the Sabbath . . . well, that just wasn't right.

The Pharisees were too busy being right to rejoice with the man who could see for the first time in his life. They didn't have time for the righteousness, peace, and joy of the kingdom of God (Romans 14:17). Which is the greater priority in your life: rightness or righteousness?

Righteousness means being right in the eyes of God, not men.

Seeking Solid Role Models

Receive him therefore in the Lord with all gladness, and hold such men in esteem.

PHILIPPIANS 2:29

When Raphael was painting his famous Vatican frescoes, a couple of cardinals stopped by to watch and criticize. "The face of the apostle Paul is too red," said one. Raphael replied, "He blushes to see into whose hands the church has fallen."

No one needs to remind us that we live in an age of fallen heroes. But maybe instead of spending so much time analyzing our failures, we ought to seek out some solid role models to emulate and then determine to become the same for the generation that is looking to us.

Paul introduces three such people in the last half of Philippians 2. We learn that Paul himself is an example of selflessness. Paul then presents his spiritual son, Timothy, as an example of service. Finally, we are introduced to Epaphroditus as an example of suffering. Paul was an apostle, Timothy was a pastor, and Epaphroditus was a layman. While it is true that Jesus Christ is the Christian's model, these men are presented as model Christians. Jesus poured Himself out in service to God. These men poured themselves out as servants of Jesus Christ!

The Golden Rule

And he who reaps receives wages, and gathers fruit for eternal life, that both he who sows and he who reaps may rejoice together.

John 4:36

When you hear phrases like "Land of a Thousand Lakes," "Sunshine State," "Famous Potatoes," and "Big Sky Country," you'll probably think of license plates and state slogans. What about "Golden Rule State"?

In the spring of 2003, State Concurrent Resolution 1006 was passed, designating Arizona as the "Golden Rule State." In part, the resolution says, "Living and practicing the Golden Rule will have a powerfully positive effect on each individual and the society in which we all live."

Applying the golden rule to everyday life is contagious even in the secular world. But as Christians, we should treat others the way we want to be treated, not just because it's a decent creed to live by. Matthew 7:12 tells us to "treat people the same way you want them to treat you" (NASB). That's a tall order! But start out by taking it one day at a time—even one minute at a time.

Think about how you can affirm a loved one or a co-worker right now. If you would like to receive attention and encouragement, make sure you are giving them out.

Don't Give the Devil a Foothold

Do not . . . give place to the devil.

Ephesians 4:26–27

It's easy to allow the devil entry into our lives. The King James Version of the Bible translates Ephesians 4:27 as, "Neither give place to the devil." Better is the New American Standard's, "Do not give the devil an opportunity."

But perhaps the most graphic is the New International Version's, "Do not give the devil a foothold." The *American Heritage Dictionary* says that a *foothold* is "a firm or secure position that provides a base for further advancement." All we need do is give the devil a foothold—a little place where he can bide his time and wait for the opportunity to advance further—to ultimately find ourselves in big spiritual trouble.

Unconfessed bouts of anger, pride, deceit, lust, envy—or any sin—may seem small to you, but they are just what the devil is looking for. If need be, confess them now, and purpose to leave no place for the devil to get a foothold in your life.

The Job of an Evangelist

Bondservants, obey in all things your masters according to the flesh, not with eyeservice, as men-pleasers, but in sincerity of heart, fearing God.

Colossians 3:22

In 1990, following a televised Monday-night game, eight players from the San Francisco 49ers and eight from the New York Giants knelt together at midfield to pray. The practice was criticized by *Sports Illustrated* magazine, and NFL officials indicated they might stop it—which they didn't. The practice continues today.

Being a witness for Christ means two things: making your faith a matter of public record and making sure your work style is consistent with the Gospel. What would it do to the credibility of the Gospel if an NFL player used abusive language, took cheap physical shots, and argued disrespectfully with referee rulings . . . and then knelt down to pray as a Christian after the game? Such a lifestyle in the workplace of a football player would significantly discredit the Gospel.

The workplace can be a challenge to our spirituality. But Scripture says the way we work and honor our employer brings credit, or discredit, to Jesus Christ.

The job of an evangelist is to do his work so well that he is invited to explain what makes him different.

Righteousness Through Propitiation

He Himself is the propitiation for our sins, and not for ours only but also for the whole world.

1 John 2:2

This word *propitiation* is one of the great words of the Bible even though it appears only four times in the entire New Testament. The Greek word for *propitiation* translated the Hebrew word that described the mercy seat, the cover of the ark of the covenant, which sat in the Holy of Holies. God was believed to dwell above the ark, between the outstretched wings of the two cherubim at either end of the mercy seat. The ark contained the stone tablets on which were written the Ten Commandments, the Law that man continually broke. But once a year, the high priest would enter the Holy of Holies and sprinkle the blood of a sacrifice over the mercy seat to cover the broken Law. In this act, he made propitiation for the sins of Israel.

As a result of the covering of the mercy seat with blood, God no longer saw the broken Law, but saw instead the blood of the sacrifice. Propitiation was made. In the same way, John wrote, "If anyone sins, we have an Advocate with the Father, Jesus Christ the righteous. And He Himself is the propitiation for our sins, and not for ours only but also for the whole world" (1 John 2:1–2).

THE HARDEST QUESTION IN THE WORLD

Forgive us our debts, as we forgive our debtors.

MATTHEW 6:12

Greg Anderson learned that cancer would likely take his life in thirty days. Desperate for healing, he decided to forgive everyone against whom he held a grudge, including a man at work with whom he had developed a feud three months earlier—a man who was also diagnosed with cancer. Greg asked for and received the man's forgiveness. Years later, as a wellness crusader, Greg Anderson counts that act of seeking forgiveness as the turning point in his healing.

Doctors agree that bitterness and unforgiveness can lead to illness. With that kind of risk, it's amazing that anyone would hesitate to seek and offer forgiveness. Yet "Would you please forgive me?" has to be one of life's most difficult questions. And waiting for the answer may be a hard place to be—but it's a good place to be.

Saying, "I was wrong" or "It was my fault" is a good start on the road to forgiveness, but it's not a good finish. If you've hurt another person, humble yourself and ask to be forgiven.

Why? Because "God resists the proud, but gives grace to the humble" (James 4:6). Which would you like Him to do to you?

Errors in Judgment

We all must appear before the judgment seat of Christ, that each one may receive the things done in the body, according to what he has done, whether good or bad.

2 Corinthians 5:10

The Judgment Seat of Christ is not about the judgment for your sin. The Bible tells us that judgment already took place at the cross of Jesus Christ. There is nothing anyone can ever do to you about your sin because God did it to His Son in your behalf. Christ was condemned for us. That is what we read in Galatians 1:4: "Who gave Himself for our sins, that He might deliver us from this present evil age."

One of the most commonly asked questions about this is, "How can someone have his sins forgiven and still have his works reviewed at the judgment seat of Christ?" Forgiveness is about justification, while rewards are about the things we do as justified people. These are not works that are done for justification. Because each believer must stand before the Judgment Seat of Christ, we have no right to judge the work of other believers. We do not even know the rewards we're going to receive, so how in the world would we know what rewards anybody else would receive? We do not know enough about anyone else's motive of heart or faithfulness to know what they would even deserve. And I promise you, when it all comes out, there will be a lot of surprises!

If You're Happy and You Know It

For I wish that all men were even as I myself. But each one has his own gift from God, one in this manner and another in that.

1 Corinthians 7:7

When Margaret Achorn retrieved a large package from the post office one Christmas, she didn't recognize the sender's name. She became suspicious: what if it was a bomb? After the police bomb squad opened it, the only thing left in the debris was the warranty card for the new stereo. She never found out who sent such a nice gift, or why.

Sometimes Christians act suspicious about the gifts God has given them. While they may know the giver is God, they are hesitant to enjoy the gift, wondering what strings might be attached. A little-known reference to spiritual gifts in the New Testament is when Paul uses the Greek word *charisma* to refer to the inclination to be married or remain single (1 Corinthians 7:7).

Some unmarried Christians are fully content being single but get the idea from the world (and sometimes the church) that they shouldn't be—that marriage is always better. If you are single and content, stay that way, and use your gift for the glory of God.

Singles can build up the body of Christ with their gift only if the church recognizes the grace of God at work in their lives.

The Decree

[God] canceled out the certificate of debt consisting of decrees against us and which was hostile to us; and He has taken it out of the way, having nailed it to the cross.

Colossians 2:14 NASB

There are two decrees in the book of Esther: the decree of death and the decree of life. One of the things we learn in studying the Bible is that God has a way to save sinners. You can't go to heaven by your own good works. You can't ever be good enough to go to heaven.

The Bible says, "You must be born again" (John 3:7). The reason you must be born again is because a decree has been written that the wages of sin is death. The decree has been written that no one can go to heaven with his sin.

God will not overturn that decree. We violate God the day we are born because of our own sin that we inherited. But the good news is that, just as the decree in Persia was overruled by another decree, God has given us another decree. That decree is that if we believe on the Lord Jesus Christ, we will be saved.

Be Prepared

Then Hezekiah and all the people rejoiced that God had prepared the people, since the events took place so suddenly.

2 Chronicles 29:36

Golfing coach Bill Hartman insists that great golfers are made, not born. "I've seen great athletes play at all levels in a number of sports," he said, "and you know what separates the 'greats' from the 'good'? Their level of physical preparation."

The Lord is our heavenly Coach, preparing us for all the events of our lives as well as for the work He plans for us to do. He knows the future as well as He knows the past, and He is fully capable of preparing us for all that lies ahead. We mustn't disdain the preparation time.

Think of the eighty years He prepared Moses before sending him to liberate the children of Israel from Egypt. Think of David's years in the wilderness, running from King Saul and living as a fugitive. It was God's way of preparing him for the throne. Think of Jesus' hidden years in Nazareth and Paul's silent years in Arabia.

Ephesians 2:10 indicates that God is preparing us for the work that He is planning for us to do. The courage and confidence you'll have in the future will come from the preparation and practice you're experiencing right now.

Fellow Workers for Christ

I considered it necessary to send to you Epaphroditus, my brother, fellow worker, and fellow soldier, but your messenger and the one who ministered to my need.

Philippians 2:25

Epaphroditus was a fellow worker in the body of Christ, which is another reason why Paul was so fond of him. Paul was without question a worker, and he was attracted to others who gave their all to the advancement of the Gospel.

In the spirit of love, I must ask you the same thing I ask myself and those whom I pastor in my church: are you a worker? If you are a Christian, I know you are a brother or sister. But I want to know if you've moved beyond that point and become a worker for Christ. Unfortunately, many in the body of Christ today are looking for the church that offers them the most services. Who do they think provides all those services if not workers just like themselves? If they do find a church offering what they are seeking, then they conclude, "This church is large and has everything all together. They don't need me to do anything." That perspective reflects a definite lack of knowledge about the church of Jesus Christ and its needs.

Every church needs its members to be workers.

Prayer That Never Stops

Pray without ceasing.
1 Thessalonians 5:17

If you have suffered from the flu, you know the symptoms: achiness, chills, fever, headaches, stuffy head—and that persistent, hacking cough that just won't stop. If you've had the flu—especially the cough—then you know what it means to be a spiritual warrior who prays without ceasing.

Paul wrote in 1 Thessalonians 5:17 that believers should "pray without ceasing." To make his point, he used *adialeiptos*, an adverb meaning "incessantly, constantly." It has been found in historical Greek documents to refer to a persistent, hacking cough—a flu-like cough, in modern terms. When you suffer from that kind of cough, you can't get rid of it; it's with you wherever you go and whatever you do. You're interrupted by it when you speak and you wake up with it in the night. You become one with your cough.

That's how prayer should be with the Christian—not the irritating, annoying part, but the persistent part. Praying without ceasing means to live in a continual state of God-consciousness, communicating with Him about everything. Stay well, and practice the presence of God wherever you go.

To lose one's consciousness of God's presence is to lose the ability to pray without ceasing.

What About Doubt?

Lord, I believe; help my unbelief!

Mark 9:24

Why do you doubt? Have you been influenced by a book? A professor? Another believer? A non-believer? Identifying your doubts and their source will help you understand what you need answers for and why.

Think of the people in the Old Testament whom God greatly used who had doubts when they heard His plans for them—Sarah, Moses, Gideon, and Jeremiah, just to name a few. These people were approached by God Himself and they still doubted!

God knew their doubts just as He knows yours and mine. We don't turn our doubts into prayers to God in order to inform God of our doubts. We tell God what we are thinking and feeling about our faith. That makes it more understandable to us as we try to figure out what is going on in our lives.

Go to God with your doubts. He is waiting to hear from you.

Patience, Please

As for God, His way is perfect.

Psalm 18:30

Nothing is harder than praying and waiting. But God answers prayer and fulfills promises in His time, not in ours. Our times are in His hands. One man earnestly prayed for his child about a certain matter involving a phone call, but the Lord allowed the exact opposite of what he had requested. He was bewildered and angry, but that morning's Bible reading took him to Psalm 18, and God gave him verse 30: "As for God, His way is perfect." The Lord was working in His own way, on His own timetable.

Ruth Graham once said, "How often has God said no to my earnest prayers that He might answer my deepest longings, give me something more, something better."

The great church father Augustine came to the Lord after years of waywardness. His mother, Monica, prayed for him unceasingly, once begging God not to let Augustine go to Italy. Augustine went anyway—and there he was saved. Augustine later wrote, "Thou, taking Thy own secret counsel and noting the real point of her desire, didst not grant what she was then asking in order to grant to her the thing that she had always been asking."

Don't grow discouraged. Keep praying. Your times are in God's hands, and His ways are perfect.

The Focus of Evangelism

The Lord added to the church daily
those who were being saved.
Acts 2:47

Pastor Charles Swindoll tells about what was, at one time, the greatest evangelistic outreach center in the metropolitan Boston area—a gas station in Arlington. Bob, the owner, had a vision for his work being part of his faith. He provided such honest and dependable service that cars would often be lined up just to buy gas and be serviced at his station. There were no "Jesus Saves" banners, religious sayings, or "fish" symbols in sight. Just Bob—a committed Christian who led dozens of people to faith in Christ because of his Christlike life.

Rebecca Pippert has said, "Christians and non-Christians have something in common: We're both uptight about evangelism." People found Christ at Bob's gas station because Christ, not evangelism, was what they encountered. When evangelism, the church, or even Christianity takes the place of Christ, everybody gets uptight. What is your "gas station"? Wherever you encounter non-Christians, ask God to show you how to make Christ, not evangelism, the focus.

Every Christian is a lens through which the world is trying to catch a glimpse of Jesus.

Renovation

Therefore, if anyone is in Christ, he is a new creation; old things have passed away; behold, all things have become new.

2 Corinthians 5:17

London businessman Lindsay Clegg told the story of a warehouse property he was selling. The building had been empty for months and needed repairs. Vandals had damaged the doors, smashed the windows, and strewn trash around the interior. As he showed a prospective buyer the property, Clegg took pains to say that he would replace the broken windows, bring in a crew to correct any structural damage, and clean out the garbage. "Forget about the repairs," the buyer said. "When I buy this place, I'm going to build something completely different. I don't want the building; I want the site."

Compared with the renovation God has in mind, our efforts to improve our own lives are as trivial as sweeping a warehouse slated for the wrecking ball. Ephesians 4:22–24 says, "You were taught, with regard to your former way of life, to put off your old self, which is being corrupted by its deceitful desires; to be made new in the attitude of your minds; and to put on the new self, created to be like God in true righteousness and holiness" (NIV).

When we become God's, the old life is over. He makes all things new. All He wants is the site and the permission to build.

Compassion for the Hurting

Rejoice with those who rejoice, and
weep with those who weep.
Romans 12:15

Babe Ruth, one of the most famous baseball players of all time, finished his career in a slump. According to a legendary story, he was ridiculed mercilessly one game as he made his way back to the dugout. The fans continued to boo and yell obscenities until a little boy jumped the fence and ran to Babe's side.

The child threw his arms around Babe's legs, crying as he fiercely hugged him. Moved by the young boy's display of affection, Ruth gently lifted the boy up into his arms. As they walked off the field, the man and boy cried together.

This young boy demonstrated the true nature of compassion—he sympathized with the sorrows of another. His example reminds us that a compassionate man does not stand detached from the sufferings of others. Rather, he steps into the world of the hurting and feels the pain and anguish of the one suffering. And he expresses his compassion through a sincere concern, through a listening ear, a shed tear.

The world is full of hurting people, many who are longing for a compassionate friend. Will you be that friend?

Disconnect to Reconnect

So He Himself often withdrew into
the wilderness and prayed.

Luke 5:16

Henri Nouwen, theologian and professor, once left his busy schedule to live for six months in a monastery. His life had become a paradox. As much as he felt burdened by the demands of his busy life, he lived in fear of the absence of activity. He had become dependent on the "compulsions and illusions" of his world and decided to seek out "the quiet stream underneath the fluctuating affirmations and rejections" that had become his security. That quiet stream, of course, was God Himself. But to find Him, Nouwen had to leave the noise and activity of his life behind and face the quietness and solitude of God alone.

In this age of wireless this and mobile that, we have become addicted to noise. By computer, cell phone, MP3 player, radio, or laptop, we have created umbilical cords that keep us tied to that which we believe affirms our existence. We are afraid to sit in silence, since silence suggests we are disconnected from affirmation.

Solitude is a periodic necessity—even for family members who are together 24/7. Find a time and a place to unplug and disconnect so you can reconnect with God.

Being alone with God is to hear His voice above all others.

Rare Objectivity

Then the king said to me, "What do you request?" So I prayed to the God of heaven.

Nehemiah 2:4

Charles Swindoll once called wisdom "the God-given ability to see life with rare objectivity and to handle life with rare stability."

Swindoll wrote, "When we operate in the sphere of the wisdom of God . . . we look at life through lenses of perception, and we respond to it in calm confidence. There's a remarkable absence of fear. . . . We can either lose our jobs or we can be promoted in our work, and neither will derail us . . . because we see it with God-given objectivity, and we handle it in His wisdom."

That's the missing factor in many lives today. We're so busy with our problems that we don't pause to seek God's wisdom in handling them, as commanded in James 1:5. But praying for wisdom doesn't always take that long. In Nehemiah 2, King Artaxerxes noticed that Nehemiah seemed troubled, and he asked the reason. "So I prayed to the God of heaven," Nehemiah later recorded. "And I said to the king. . . ." It was an urgent arrow of prayer, shot silently to heaven in the middle of a momentous conversation—and it got the job done.

If you're facing a challenge today, take time to seek God's wisdom.

Lifted by Song

It is good to sing praises to our God.

Psalm 147:1

The Great Depression hit a man named J. C. Penney particularly hard, endangering his very health. Anxious and desperate because of huge financial losses, he felt he had nothing to live for. Even his family and friends shunned him. In the hospital one night, he grew so demoralized he expected to die before morning; but he heard singing coming from the little hospital chapel. The words of the song said, "Be not dismayed whate'er betide; God will take care of you."

Entering the chapel, Penney listened to the song and to the Scripture reading and prayer. He later wrote, "Suddenly—something happened. I can't explain it. I can only call it a miracle. I felt as if I had been instantly lifted out of the darkness of a dungeon into warm, brilliant sunlight." From that day, J. C. Penney was never plagued with worry, and he later called those moments in the chapel "the most dramatic and glorious twenty minutes of my life." When he died at age ninety-five, he left behind 1,660 department stores in his name.

Music is therapy for the soul. Today, lift up your heart in song; it is good to sing praises to our God!

God Is With Us

Lo, I am with you always, even to the end of the age.

Matthew 28:20

Christ is the only Savior of the world. But the Bible tells stories of leaders who, with God's help, "saved" their people. Moses led his people out of Egypt, where they were miserable and enslaved. But after he brought the Ten Commandments down from the mountain where God had given them to him, he saw his people sinning. He had spent days there with God only to return to find the Israelites had not listened to him or to God. As a savior he was alone, and it was his sole duty to bring his people back to God. With God's help Moses was a savior, and he, too, felt lonely.

Joseph saved the Hebrew people from famine by giving them food that Egypt had stored. Joseph had spent many years alone because his brothers sold him into slavery, and Joseph was also jailed for an offense of which he was not guilty. Joseph, too, had saved the Israelites by following God's orders. But his path was not an easy one; it was often a lonely one.

Christ bore His burden alone on the cross so that He could obtain victory over death for us. Since Christ bore all the agony, loneliness, and sin of the world, we do not have to fear God's forsaking us. God will always be with us, even unto the end of the age.

Prayer Patrols

All kinds of prayers . . .

Ephesians 6:18 NIV

An urban church in Bristol, England, developed an interesting response to the high crime rate in its neighborhood. It developed "prayer patrols" that take place three times daily. Volunteers walk through the streets, knocking on doors, collecting prayer requests, and praying with the inhabitants. Police officials say that the number of robberies has been reduced by 51 percent, and burglaries are down by 21 percent. City officials say that prayer has broken the siege mentality that had gripped the neighborhood as a result of gang warfare.

There are many different ways and times to pray, and sometimes we get in a rut. Try walking through your neighborhood, praying for the families in the homes you pass. Try praying for the churches you pass on your drive to work. Try praying over your newspaper, interceding to God for the events of the day. Try praying out loud. Try writing out your prayers. Try composing a hymn of prayer to God.

The Bible says, "Pray in the Spirit on all occasions with all kinds of prayers and requests. With this in mind, be alert and always keep on praying for all the saints" (Ephesians 6:18 NIV).

Getting to "Yes" the Hard Way

Whom the Lord loves, He chastens.

Hebrews 12:6

Until we are faced with the consequences of what we do wrong, we won't even admit it to ourselves. We are the most marvelous people at rationalizing wrongdoing.

In our culture, absolutes are almost gone. We face a major problem in the church today with people doing what is absolutely wrong and thinking they have a good case for why it is not so bad. Until we face the penalty for our wrongdoing, we often won't be honest with ourselves.

I think Jonah probably thought he had a good case for not being the right man for the Assyrian job until the gastric juices started working on him in the belly of the fish. Then he started to say, "Well, maybe I am the right man for the job after all."

Some people think that this type of foxhole decision isn't genuine. But just because we say yes to God under pressure doesn't mean we aren't being honest. It means we had to get to "yes" the hard way, but we got there all the same.

Endless Possibilities

With men it is impossible, but not with God;
for with God all things are possible.

Mark 10:27

Dr. Billy Graham is reported to have had a conversation with the former chancellor of West Germany, Konrad Adenauer. The chancellor asked Dr. Graham, "Do you believe Christ rose from the dead?" "Yes, I do," replied the evangelist. "Do you believe He is in heaven now?" "Yes, I do." "Do you believe He will return and reign over the earth?" "Yes, I do." "So do I," the chancellor concluded. "If He doesn't, there is no hope for this world."

The famous German leader had come to the same conclusion that millions throughout history have: the only one who can save the earth is God Himself. The world's problems continue to be addressed by many trying to help those who hurt. Others have resigned themselves to man's ultimate self-destruction and have insulated themselves from suffering with barriers of materialism and pleasure.

Both are right about one thing: man has created a world incapable of saving itself. And that is exactly the kind of world God is able to save—one in which man's possibilities are totally limited but God's are unlimited.

God can best demonstrate Himself when man has reached the limits of himself.

Selfless Love

Now abide faith, hope, love, these three;
but the greatest of these is love.
1 Corinthians 13:13

Paul tells us that the secret to all of life is love. A love that cares, that goes out of its own way to find what it can do to minister, makes a difference. Love in a kitchen. Love on the football field. Most of all, love selflessly. I have seen people ministering in churches who get no credit for what they do, and yet, behind the scenes, they serve, minister, and work. They have love—love for children, love for the church, and love for the Lord. There are many Christians who give sacrificially. They do it because love in their hearts makes them want to turn away from their own needs and wants and give of themselves and their substance back to God. That is where joy is to be found.

There is one thing I can tell you about selfless love: if you ever get close to it, you will know it because it feels so good. You won't have to tell anybody about it, and if you do, you might lose it in the process. But if you experience it, you will know the joy of it.

Never Too Old

Now also when I am old and grayheaded,
O God, do not forsake me,
Until I declare Your strength to this generation,
Your power to everyone who is to come.

Psalm 71:18

Sometimes an elderly Christian isn't sure what his or her role is at church. That wasn't true of two saints named Simeon and Anna. Simeon spent all his time at church involved in Bible study and prayer, and Anna, a godly widow in her eighties, worshiped, fasted, and prayed day and night. As it turns out, they were the first two people to pronounce blessings upon a baby boy named Jesus.

Somehow Simeon and Anna missed the "retirement" message. Instead, they continued serving the Lord as they always had. As it worked out, their faithfulness was rewarded. They both recognized Jesus as the promised "Consolation of Israel," the Messiah, when His parents brought Him to the temple to be offered to the Lord as the firstborn son (Luke 2:25). Simeon and Anna declared His identity to all who were in the temple, and offered prayers and blessings over Him. Whatever your age today, plan on remaining faithful and active your entire life. If you're available, God will use you to bless someone.

The only aged saints who don't get used by God are those who have removed themselves from service.

NOVEMBER

Rest in the L*ORD*, *and wait patiently for Him.*

—PSALM 37:7

Beautiful Heaven

Then I, John, saw the holy city, New Jerusalem, coming down out of heaven from God, prepared as a bride adorned for her husband.

Revelation 21:2

I read a story once about a little blind girl whose idea of the beauty of the world was based solely on what her parents had told her. A surgical procedure was developed that would allow her to regain her vision, and she regained her eyesight. After her convalescence, the day came for the bandages to be removed from her eyes. The first person she saw was her mother, and after embracing her she went immediately to the door to look outside. For the first time she saw the beauty of creation. She turned to her mother and exclaimed, "Mama, why didn't you tell me it was so beautiful?"

Of course, her mother had done her best to describe the world in the most colorful ways possible, but the fact is, a picture is worth a thousand words. And I think someday when we get to heaven, we are going to have the same reaction that little girl did—"John, why didn't you tell us it was going to be so beautiful?" I do not know that anyone, in the limited space in which John the apostle wrote, could have described heaven any better. But one glimpse of heaven will outstrip all of his words.

Change Is Good

I have been crucified with Christ; it is no longer I who live, but Christ lives in me; and the life which I now live in the flesh I live by faith in the Son of God, who loved me and gave Himself for me.

Galatians 2:20

John Wesley described his revelatory conversion to Christ this way: "In the evening I went very unwillingly to a society in Aldersgate Street where one was reading Luther's preface to the Epistle to the Romans. . . . While he was describing the change which God works in the heart through faith in Christ, I felt my heart strangely warmed. I felt I did trust in Christ, Christ alone, for salvation."

Notice what caught Wesley's attention: the change that comes through genuine conversion. Wesley realized he had been devoutly religious but had never been changed. But after that night, John Wesley became a different person, changing his world through the power and person of Christ living in his heart.

Abraham and Sarah had to learn this lesson as well. They wanted to live in the past, walking by sight; but God wanted them to walk by faith. Have you experienced the changed life that only comes with knowing Christ? No one can meet Christ and stay the same; the old life is nothing like the new.

Conversion is one instance in which change is not only good; it's required.

God's Enduring Mercy

Oh, give thanks to the Lord, for He is good!
For His mercy endures forever.

Psalm 106:1

God's mercy is a recurring theme in the Scriptures. God's grace is God giving us what we do not deserve, and God's mercy is withholding from us what we really do deserve.

Sometimes I hear even Christian people talking about getting their rights. I, for one, don't want my rights. I know what I deserve and it is not something I would like to have. I am grateful for the mercy of God.

Isn't it a matter of His goodness that when man sinned in the garden, God didn't just completely give up on humanity? Isn't it a matter of His goodness that when humankind failed (and when we fail), God didn't immediately withdraw all of the joys and privileges of life? When we wake up in this beautiful world and compare it to what we know we deserve, we should sing with the psalmist, "Oh, give thanks to the Lord, for His mercy and His goodness endure forever!"

Forgive With Feeling

And be kind to one another, tenderhearted, forgiving one another, even as God in Christ forgave you.

Ephesians 4:32

In 1982, John Hinckley Jr. attempted to take the life of President Ronald Reagan by shooting him with a handgun. Reagan's daughter, Patti Davis, later recounted what she learned from her father: "My father said he knew his physical healing was directly dependent on his ability to forgive John Hinckley. By showing me that forgiveness is the key to everything . . . he gave me an example of Christ-like thinking."

The Scriptures give Christians a clear standard concerning wrongs we experience. We are to forgive those who hurt us "even as God in Christ forgave [us]." Therefore, God's forgiveness is the model for how we are to forgive. Sometimes we dispense forgiveness like a soft drink from a vending machine—mechanically, with no feelings attached.

But Paul says two attitudes should accompany forgiveness: kindness and tenderheartedness. Why? Because that's the way God forgave us. Throughout Scripture, we find emotions such as kindness, gentleness, compassion, and tenderness—in word or by action—ascribed to God. Yes, He forgave, but He forgave with feeling. And we should do the same.

True forgiveness is as much an act of the heart as it is an act of the will.

Straight Lines

Moreover, as for me, far be it from me that I should sin against the Lord in ceasing to pray for you.

1 Samuel 12:23

Do you know someone who is heading the wrong way? Someone struggling with an overwhelming problem or temptation?

Pray—earnestly pray—for that one. The prophet Samuel told the Israelites, "Moreover, as for me, far be it from me that I should sin against the Lord in ceasing to pray for you." J. Sidlow Baxter pointed out that our loved ones may "spurn our appeals, reject our message, oppose our arguments, despise our persons, but they are helpless against our prayers."

In Colossians 4, we meet a man whose prayers for others were so powerful that he received special commendation in the Bible: Epaphras . . . "a bondservant of Christ, greets you, always laboring fervently for you in prayers, that you may stand perfect and complete in all the will of God" (v. 12).

Oswald Chambers said, "By intercessory prayer we can hold off Satan from other lives and give the Holy Ghost a chance with them. No wonder Jesus put such tremendous emphasis on prayer!"

Spiritual Synergy

And they continued steadfastly in the apostles' doctrine and fellowship, in the breaking of bread, and in prayers.

Acts 2:42

Euclid was a Greek mathematician who lived around 300 BC and is best known for his thirteen-volume treatise titled *Elements*. Two of Euclid's axioms of geometry have been revised to produce the modern saying, "The whole is greater than the sum of its parts." Another way of stating this principle is that something happens in a group that goes beyond the logic of math.

That something is called synergy, from the Greek word *sunergia*, meaning "cooperation, or working together." Spiritual synergy can develop "where two or three are gathered together" in Christ's name for Bible study (Matthew 18:20). One person's insight brings a comment from another, which reminds a third of an illustration that really clicks in the mind of a fourth.

The Holy Spirit hasn't revealed everything to anyone. Therefore, Christians have to learn together to discover truth. It's God's way of encouraging the church to meet together and function interdependently. If you're not meeting regularly for Bible study with others, consider joining a group soon.

Wisdom is being willing to share what God has taught you and being willing to learn what He has taught others.

Love in the Little Things

There should be no schism in the body,
but . . . the members should have
the same care for one another.
1 Corinthians 12:25

Courtesy is one of those things that is so simple we forget about it. Most of us want to get involved in the large, huge, loving things. But you see, courtesy isn't the great big love involvement. Courtesy is love in the little things. Courtesy is the simplicity of love.

You can take the most untutored person and put him into the highest society, and if he has a reservoir of courteous love, he will not behave unwisely. A person who is committed to God's kind of love, as simple as he may be, will know what to do and will be accepted. Carlisle said of Robert Burns that there was no truer gentleman than the plowman poet. "He loved everything, and all things great and small that God had made. So with this simple passport he could mingle with any society and enter courts and palaces from his little cottage, and be accepted."

I've known people like that. Maybe they don't have the right clothes or don't know just the right words to say, but because of their simplicity and their easiness with people and their courtesy in conversation, they seem to be accepted in any strata of society. That is the simplicity of love.

In All Things, Charity

It seemed good to the Holy Spirit, and to us, to lay upon you no greater burden than these necessary things.

Acts 15:28

There are dos and don'ts in the Bible, but we have a tendency to add to them—and to expect others to follow our lists. The church has invented lots of rules since the first century to define what it means to be a "good Christian." Over time, in our minds, these rules become traditions almost equal to Scripture. When the traditions of men become more important than God's people and God's law, they've gone too far.

Paul devoted Romans 14 and 15 to telling us that, while we must agree on the great central truths of Scripture (essential doctrines), there are many areas in which Christians may disagree (nonessential doctrines). "One person esteems one day above another; another esteems every day alike. Let each be fully convinced in his own mind" (Romans 14:5).

Have you been upset with someone who didn't agree with you on some nonessential point of doctrine? Have you been critical of someone whose opinion differed from yours? Perhaps in insisting on your list, you've forgotten the most important item on God's list: that we exhibit His love.

A Need-to-Know Basis

As the heavens are higher than the earth,
so are My ways higher than your ways, and
My thoughts than your thoughts.

Isaiah 55:9

The more I study, the more I discover I don't know—and I study all the time! I continually pray that God would give me greater capacity to learn and know about Him. But I accept the fact that I will never know it all—and so should you. There are definite limitations to what we have the capacity and intelligence to understand.

The Bible has everything you need to know in order to know God and receive eternal life, through faith in His Son. If you have other questions that are answered in the Bible, all the better. But if the Bible doesn't have the answers, don't doubt the answers the Bible does have.

There is so much about the universe and the God who made it that we simply do not know. The bottom line is that we will never understand God and all of His ways.

God's purposes, and what He has revealed to us of them, are moving ahead on His timetable. And He has told us what we need to know, to make sure we are safely on board. Let's learn to trust God with the things we do not understand.

Who's Your Teacher?

But the Helper, the Holy Spirit, whom the Father will send in My name, He will teach you all things.

John 14:26

A graduate engineer worked in his field for a number of years and then served in a ministry vocation for nearly a decade. Returning to his previous career as an electrical engineer with a leading electronics company, he found himself woefully behind the technical curve.

Because of his absence, he felt like he was starting over as an engineer. It would have been nice for him to have a tutor accompany him throughout his absence from the engineering arena, teaching him and keeping him up-to-date. Nice, but impractical.

Having such a tutor is not impractical for the Christian. God has given us a full-time teacher to live with us twenty-four hours a day, keeping us up-to-date on "the things which God has prepared for those who love Him" (1 Corinthians 2:9).

That teacher is, of course, the Holy Spirit, sent by God to open the spiritual eyes and ears of every believer, to educate us about the kingdom of God, and to give us the mind of Christ. No believer should ever lack the wisdom and knowledge of God.

The Teacher is always ready. The question is whether we have taken our seat and opened our Book.

Putting Others First

Let each of you look out not only for his own interests, but also for the interests of others.
Philippians 2:4

Theodore Roosevelt's child once jabbed, "Father always had to be the center of attention. When he went to a wedding, he wanted to be the bride. When he went to a funeral, he was sorry that he couldn't be the corpse."

Although we may find humor in this illustration, it reflects a harmful "me-first" philosophy. This philosophy can best be defined by the motto "Look out for number one." Self is enthroned as king; people, circumstances, and life are subjects that must bow down. After all, every individual deserves to be happy. Embracing this philosophy, self becomes the epicenter of the world. But according to God's Word, self is not to be the focal point of our lives. God's plan is for us to focus our thoughts, time, and energy on loving Him and others (Matthew 22:36–39).

If you were to write your life motto, what would it say? Look out for number one? Or look out for the needs of others? Ask God to help you live a selfless life.

What's Your Perspective?

As each one has received a gift, minister it to one another, as good stewards of the manifold grace of God.

1 Peter 4:10

As the last couple arrives for the potluck dinner, their hot casserole dish slides off its tray and crashes to the floor in the entryway. The sound of a crash and the accompanying groans bring the rest of the guests running to see what happened. And they instinctively take different courses of action.

A person with the gift of mercy wades through the stroganoff to hug the tearful wife who dropped the dish. A person with the gift of leadership starts assigning various clean-up tasks. A person with the gift of teaching bites his tongue just before saying that a plastic dish with a sealed lid might have prevented the disaster. A person with the gift of giving volunteers to drive to a nearby deli and pick up more food. And a person with the gift of prophecy starts explaining the spiritual lesson inherent in the mess—but then stops when he gets "the look" from his wife!

God has so gifted the members of the body of Christ that each has a unique perspective and contribution to make. Whatever your spiritual gift from God is, the body suffers to the degree you don't use it.

A gift given but unused is the same as a gift never given.

Personal Accountability to Him

On the first day of the week let each one of you lay something aside, storing up as he may prosper.

1 Corinthians 16:2

There is a rumor afoot that God holds churches accountable for how much they give. But that's all it is—a rumor. That's not the truth. In no place does the Bible even hint that God holds a church accountable for its giving. However, God does operate on an individual accountability basis. And that's very clear in Scripture.

When we give ourselves to God first, we understand that we are accountable to Him as His people. The Bible says we are to lay aside each week that which God has entrusted to us. And we are reminded over and over in the New Testament that someday we are to give an account to God for what we have done.

If I have given myself to God first, if I have said, "God, everything that I am, everything that I have belongs to You," then I don't really have to live in fear of that day of accountability. I've already had my day of accountability. I've stood before God the best I know how and said, "God, You direct me, and I'll be a channel for whatever You put in my hands. I am going to be accountable to You as You tell me in Your Word You want me to be."

Praying Parents

Simon, Simon! Indeed, Satan has asked for you, that he may sift you as wheat. But I have prayed for you, that your faith should not fail.

Luke 22:31

It's a tough job to raise children today, but one of the secrets is to put God first and to pray for our youngsters. Find a spot at the kitchen table, by your bedside, or in a spare room, and spend time every day interceding for your kids. Some parents keep a journal with a picture of a child on each page, followed by various needs and prayer requests.

Don't know what to pray? Writer Lovelace Howard says, "Jesus' prayer for His disciples and St. Paul's prayers for his converts are ones we can always use with confidence in praying for our children. When, at any age, our children face temptation and danger, we can pray for them as Jesus did for Peter, that their faith may not fail and that their Heavenly Father will keep them from the evil one."

Or adapt Paul's prayer in Philippians 1:9–10: "Lord, I pray that my children's love may abound more and more in knowledge and all discernment, that they may approve the things that are excellent."

No child is more fortunate than one with a praying parent or grandparent.

Trust God for Everything

Your heavenly Father knows that you need these things.

Matthew 6:32

When we read about the widow in Mark 12, we see a woman who trusted completely in God, who gave everything she had to Him because she knew He would care for her. Perhaps if we were to examine our own hearts, we would find that the reason we are reluctant to give is not so much a matter of treasure as it is a matter of trust. We have entrusted God with our eternal souls, but we are unwilling to trust Him with our temporal riches.

I heard about a man who complained to his pastor about not having any money left over for God after paying his bills. The pastor asked him, "Would you be willing to trust God to take care of you, tithe every month, and bring me whatever bills you can't pay?" Of course, the man quickly agreed to that plan, but that led the pastor to say, "It's strange you would trust me, an imperfect man, to care for your needs, but you will not trust Almighty God, who demonstrated His love for you by sending His Son to die on a cross." When it comes right down to it, we either trust God to take care of us, or we trust in our money.

Growing to Maturity

Do not labor for the food which perishes, but for the food which endures to everlasting life, which the Son of Man will give you, because God the Father has set His seal on Him.

John 6:27

One day following the end of World War I, General Louis Lyautey asked his gardener to plant a particular type of tree on his estate. The gardener objected that the tree, being unusually slow to grow, would take nearly a century to reach maturity. "In that case," the marshal replied, "there is no time to lose. Plant it this afternoon!"

Maturing is a long and sometimes slow process. You don't need to rely on church for your spiritual food. Rather, take in portions throughout the week—do a personal Bible study, attend a group Bible study, listen to Bible teaching on the radio or watch teaching on TV, be focused on your prayer life. As a child grows into a man, he is ready for solid foods. In the same way, when Christians mature spiritually, they crave deeper satisfaction.

It takes a lifetime of growth to become spiritually mature, but it's a beautiful and worthwhile process, just as waiting for a tree to blossom. Be patient as you work toward maturity in Christ.

Audit Your Anger

Let all bitterness, wrath, anger, clamor, and evil speaking be put away from you.

Ephesians 4:31

Anger turns into resentment, resentment turns into bitterness, bitterness turns into unforgiveness, and unforgiveness turns into a defiled conscience. Pretty soon, we have become captives of our own anger.

Anger is nothing more than a sophisticated version of a temper tantrum. Just because we can define it with eloquent speech doesn't mean it is any more justified. We are still mad that we can't get what we want. And our anger overflows out of us and defiles everyone around us.

Instead of nursing, rehearsing, conversing about, and dispersing our anger, we need to reverse our anger before it hurts us and others.

How do you reverse anger? Paul says you do it with forgiveness and loving-kindness and tenderness. You go to the person toward whom you have directed your anger, and you seek forgiveness.

Eternity-Colored Glasses

For now we see in a mirror, dimly, but then face to face.

1 Corinthians 13:12

Author and evangelist Josh McDowell tells how he once wanted to purchase a new car. He had the car picked out and had settled on all the details. He knew he should pray about it first, so he began to pray. Every day, as he continued to pray, he began to sense that God was not giving him freedom to get the car. The more he prayed about it, the less important the car became until he finally prayed it right out of his life!

What happened to Josh and his new car will happen anytime we look at the things of this life through eternity-colored glasses. Imagine what the object of your concern would look like if you could transport it to heaven and set it down in the midst of the glory of eternity.

When we take our illness, our unemployment, our financial problems, our strained relationships, our fears and worries about the future—all the things that burden us in this life—and view them from God's eternal perspective, we will see them as they truly are. And we do that through worshipful prayer.

Take the things that concern you most into the presence of God. Through worship, you'll see them in a whole new light.

Everything Comes from God

For all things come from You, and of Your own we have given You.

1 Chronicles 29:14

James 1:17 tells us that every good and perfect gift comes from the Father. It isn't earned; it's something He decides to give. That's why Deuteronomy 8:18 warns us to remember the Lord, "for it is He who gives you power to get wealth." A businessman may think he is a self-made man, but the very power to succeed came from God. As Paul said in 1 Timothy 6:7 and 17, "For we brought nothing into this world, and it is certain we can carry nothing out. . . . [It is] God who gives us richly all things to enjoy."

After one of the greatest offerings in history, King David had to actually tell the people to stop giving because they had given so much. After he had received the offering, David prayed these words, recorded in 1 Chronicles 29:14: "For all things come from You, and of Your own we have given You." I love those words, for they remind me that anything I give to God is merely a giving back of His own abundant blessing. I'm simply giving back to God what He already owns.

Operation Andrew

Andrew . . . first found his own brother Simon, and said to him, "We have found the Messiah." . . . And he brought him to Jesus.

John 1:40–42

Early in his ministry, Billy Graham wanted to mobilize local Christians to bring unsaved friends and relatives to his meetings. The Graham team devised "Operation Andrew," a simple plan whereby church members listed unsaved friends, prayed for them, and invited them to hear the gospel.

Why the name? Because every time we see Andrew in John's Gospel, he's bringing someone to Christ. He began with his brother, Peter. In John 6, he brought a lad to the Savior; and in John 12, he led a group of Greeks to Christ.

We can do the same. Years ago, a new Christian named Albert McMakin, age twenty-four, loaded his pickup truck with friends and took them each night to an evangelistic campaign in his city. You may never have heard McMakin's name; but you've heard the name of one of his passengers, a young man who was converted that week—Billy Graham.

Do you have room for someone in your "pickup"? When you walk in the footsteps of the Savior, you're walking the path of evangelism—and you never know whose life may be changed.

Speak to Your "Abba Father"

Abba, Father, all things are possible for You.

Mark 14:36

Calling God "Abba" is rooted in Jesus' agony in the Garden of Gethsemane: "He said, 'Abba, Father, all things are possible for You. Take this cup away from Me; nevertheless, not what I will, but what You will'" (Mark 14:36).

Abba was an ordinary family word of Jesus' day. It conveyed intimacy, tenderness, dependence, and complete lack of fear or anxiety. Modern English equivalents would be Daddy or Papa.

No Jew would have dreamed of using this very intimate term to address God. However, Jesus always used this word in His prayers (Aramaic *abba* or its Greek equivalent *pater*), with the exception of His cry from the cross.

And Jesus instructed His disciples to use this word in their prayers as well. We are empowered to speak to God just as a small child speaks to his father.

Determined Faith

And after my skin is destroyed, this I know,
that in my flesh I shall see God.

Job 19:26

The story of a famous man reads like this: chapter 1, he's wealthy and prosperous; chapter 2, he loses everything (even his children and his health); chapter 42, he is more prosperous than in chapter 1. Wouldn't you like to know what happened from chapters 3 through 41?

If so, you should read the story of Job, that prosperous patriarch of the Old Testament who had it all, lost it all, and got it all back in the end—doubled. You'll be blessed by reading his story in Scripture; but here's the word that summarizes Job's return to prosperity: *determination*. When Job lost everything, everyone around him tried to convince him to give up on God and give up on himself.

But Job had a determined faith—he knew God was just and fair. He wasn't about to give up on God or throw in the towel on his own faith just because he was stuck in a place he didn't understand. In the end, God met with Job, explained as much as he needed to know, and restored his health, family, and fortune.

If you're stuck in a place you don't understand right now, don't give up—on God or yourself. Faith that throws in the towel today won't have one to wave in victory tomorrow.

We Can't Fool Our Kids

A disciple is not above his teacher, but everyone who is perfectly trained will be like his teacher.

Luke 6:40

We can't fool our kids. At home, you and I are the real you and me. "Do as I say, not as I do" won't cut it. What we do is so powerful that it can destroy everything we say. We had better live out what we say we believe from the Word of God, or our words will act more like poison than fertilizer in the soil of our children's hearts.

If we don't model a real, genuine relationship with Jesus Christ, there's little chance our children will grow up to possess what we lack.

For many reasons, King David is revered by millions today, centuries after he ruled Israel. He gave his children all they needed, except an example they could follow. As we trace the pattern in David's family, we see David's children repeating the same mistakes their father made. His serious errors stripped him of the power to restrain his children.

Does this mean we have to be perfect? Of course not. But our children can see the genuineness of who we are in Christ as we trust the Lord each day.

Jesus with Us

Then Peter said to them, "Repent, and let every one of you be baptized in the name of Jesus Christ for the remission of sins; and you shall receive the gift of the Holy Spirit."

Acts 2:38

Roald Amundsen was a Norwegian explorer who was the first to discover the magnetic meridian of the North Pole and to discover the South Pole. On one of his trips to the top of the world, Amundsen took a cage containing a homing pigeon—and released it near the North Pole. When his wife saw the pigeon circling their home, she knew her husband was alive!

That is a perfect picture of how God demonstrated His love for believers in Christ—by sending the Holy Spirit. First He sent the Holy Spirit, in the form of a dove, to indicate His anointing of Jesus (Luke 3:22). Then He sent the Spirit as a gift to the church at Pentecost (Acts 2:1–4). Jesus called the Holy Spirit the *paraklete* ("one called alongside"), sometimes translated as "Helper" (John 14:16). Just as Jesus loved and encouraged His disciples by being with them, so the Holy Spirit loves and encourages Jesus' disciples by being in them.

Jesus may be absent from us physically, but His presence is within us spiritually by the power of the Holy Spirit.

The Great Physician

May your whole spirit, soul, and body be preserved blameless at the coming of our Lord Jesus Christ.

1 Thessalonians 5:23

"Is there no balm in Gilead?" asked Jeremiah. "Is there no physician there? Why then is there no recovery for the health of . . . my people?" (Jeremiah 8:22).

Gilead, a region east of the Jordan, was famous for its medicinal salve, but Jeremiah warned that not even Gilead's balm could heal the soul.

But the Great Physician can heal. He can give physical healing, and we should pray for one another to be healed (James 5:16). God sometimes heals miraculously and other times through medical science. Sometimes He doesn't grant physical healing because He has other plans and purposes for us (2 Corinthians 12:8–9).

He can give emotional healing. When Jeremiah was devastated by the terror of war, he felt like a man mangled by a lion or trapped in a tomb. But as he recalled God's unfailing mercy, hope returned to his heart (Lamentations 3:6, 10, 21–24).

The Lord can give spiritual healing. "The chastisement for our peace was upon Him, and by His stripes we are healed" (Isaiah 53:5).

Whatever your need, the Great Physician now is near, the sympathizing Jesus.

Who's the Boss?

. . . knowing that whatever good anyone does, he will receive the same from the Lord, whether he is a slave or free.

Ephesians 6:8

A group of men gathered one Saturday morning to help paint a friend's large two-story home. Toward the end of the day when the job was almost complete, a small bit of trim, which could not be seen from the ground, remained unpainted. One of the men said, "Since nobody can see that piece of trim, I guess we don't need to paint it." "Not true," said another of the crew as he went for a ladder. "God sees it."

The difference in the two approaches is the difference between working man's way and working God's way, working in light of the end of the day versus working in light of the end of life, and working for immediate rewards versus working for ultimate rewards. It's easy to get confused about whom we really work for in this life.

We go to work and interact with a human boss who makes the rules and signs the checks. We may face him at the end of the day; but at the end of the age, we will come face-to-face with the ultimate Boss, God Himself. What we got away with on the job will be made known, and what went unrewarded will be paid in full.

The best way to get high marks on our final "employee review" is to picture God as our employer each day.

Rest in the Lord

Rest in the Lord, and wait patiently for Him.

Psalm 37:7

What does it mean to rest in the Lord? Let me use a familiar illustration. When you enter your church on Sunday morning and go to a particular pew or chair to take your seat, you probably do not give one second's thought to whether that pew or chair is going to hold your weight when you sit on it. Why is that? Simply because you have grown accustomed to the fact that you do not have to worry about the seats holding your weight. Week after week, the seats in your church have been found faithful. At some point, those seats passed the test in your mind, and you have never given them another thought.

You can develop the same kind of confidence in God. By trusting and delighting in Him, you can learn to rest in Him as well. With each problem that arises, you can exercise confidence that He will be faithful to meet your needs. You, by resting, will be unmovable in your place of faith because day after day, week after week, year after year, you have entered into His presence and given over to Him the cares of your life.

If My People

If My people who are called by My name will humble themselves, and pray and seek My face, and turn from their wicked ways, then I will hear from heaven, and will forgive their sin and heal their land.

2 Chronicles 7:14

Just before his inauguration, Dwight Eisenhower invited Billy Graham to the Commodore Hotel in New York. "I'd like to quote one or two passages from the Bible in my inaugural speech," he said. Eisenhower felt one of the reasons he was elected was to help set the moral climate of America. Graham suggested 2 Chronicles 7:14.

Eisenhower prepared a speech that, to everyone's surprise, opened with what he called "a little prayer of my own." After his prayer, Ike's speech spoke repeatedly of spiritual things. "In the swift rush of great events," he said, "we find ourselves groping to know the full meaning of these times in which we live. In our quest for understanding, we beseech God's guidance." He was sworn into office with his hand resting on two Bibles, both opened to 2 Chronicles 7:14.

Take this verse as a personal mandate today—to humble yourself and pray that America might turn from any wicked way.

Renew Your Mind

Do not be conformed to this world, but be transformed by the renewing of your mind.

Romans 12:2

The only way to survive in a world that tries to slowly poison our minds is to renew our minds each day. The psalmist says in Psalm 1 that the blessed man is the one who delights in the law of the Lord, meditating on it day and night. When I open my Bible for personal devotions, I know that I'm looking at the very Word of God. It's different from everything else around me. What I'm reading is in a whole different universe. I'm getting a transfusion of heavenly culture into my system. I know that if I try to make it in this world, I'll get pulled down. I'll never be happy following the world's plan.

But when I came to Jesus Christ, the happiness of this world was ruined for me. I've got the Holy Spirit inside me, and I can never be happy unless I'm walking with Him. People can try to be happy, but they'll never achieve it apart from the Lord. Christians can try to follow the world's plan for happiness, but the only way they will find it is to let the Word of God cleanse and renew them.

Empathy

I sat where they sat, and remained there astonished among them seven days.

Ezekiel 3:15

In his book *Seven Habits of Highly Effective People*, Stephen Covey describes an experience on a subway in New York. A man and his children boarded the train, and the children were so loud and rambunctious they disrupted the entire car. The man sat down beside Covey, oblivious to the situation. Covey finally said, "Sir, your children are really disturbing a lot of people. I wonder if you couldn't control them a little more."

The man looked startled, then said, "Oh, you're right. I guess I should do something about it. We just came from the hospital, where their mother died about an hour ago. I don't know what to think, and I guess they don't know how to handle it either."

Covey's attitude instantly changed, and he later admitted that he learned a valuable lesson: seek to understand before seeking to be understood.

Sometimes people irritate or hurt us because they themselves are in pain. If they lash out at us, perhaps it's just the burst dam of personal frustration. Let's look beyond their words and see their hearts. Let's seek to understand before seeking to be understood.

Faithfulness in Ministry

You heard and knew the grace of God in truth; as you also learned from Epaphras, our dear fellow servant who is a faithful minister of Christ on your behalf.

Colossians 1:6–7

In Colossians 1:7, Paul not only calls Epaphras a dear fellow servant, but a "faithful minister of Christ." Here is another key characteristic of those God uses: faithfulness. When was the last time you heard someone in the body of Christ commended for being so faithful? We speak well of almost every other trait before we think of faithfulness. Yet, in truth, faithfulness in ministry underlies everything else we do for Christ. It's easy to be faithful in moments of crisis or great need, but I'm talking about those who labor faithfully for the Lord, day in and day out, with little notice. Faithfulness translates into persistence in ministry.

The persistent minister is the one who makes it to the finish line. Teaching Sunday school? Leading a backyard Bible club? Singing in the choir? Serving as a deacon? Faithfulness in these or any other ministry means you will take your last step as you cross the finish line—and not before. Epaphras was that kind of man—a faithful minister of Christ.

The Choice Is Yours

Therefore choose life, that both you and your descendants may live.

Deuteronomy 30:19

When most people think of America, they think of democracy—and they're partly correct. In its purest form, a democracy means "the majority rules." America's Founding Fathers, knowing that the majority is not always right, wisely established America's government as a republic so that governing officials, elected by the people, serve as a buffer between pure "majority rule" and policy.

Besides government, there is another realm in which the majority is not always right: spiritual discernment. Jesus made it clear that life consists of two roads leading to two gates: a wide road leading to a broad gate that leads to destruction, and a difficult road leading to a narrow gate that leads to life (Matthew 7:13–14). The majority travels on the wide road leading to destruction, and the minority passes through the narrow gate leading to life.

People are like sheep—they tend to move blindly in herds without a lot of choice regarding danger. Which road are you on? Which gate have you chosen? Which destiny is yours?

The larger the crowd, the greater the cause for caution—especially when it comes to eternal choices.

The Pearly Gate

We love Him because He first loved us.

1 John 4:19

Why does God love us? Not because we're lovable by nature. Deuteronomy 7:7–8 offers this remarkable answer: "The Lord did not set His love on you nor choose you because you were more in number than any other people, for you were the least of all peoples; but because the Lord loves you." Read that again! "The Lord . . . set His love on you . . . because . . . the Lord loves you." He loves us just because He loves us. His nature is to love.

Why do we love God? Not because we are loving by nature. First John 4:19 offers a remarkable answer: "We love Him because He first loved us." Our love is responsive. William Tyndale, who was later burned at the stake for translating the Bible into English, was a brilliant, winsome scholar whose life was changed by finding 1 John 4:19 in the Greek New Testament. He called it "the pearly gate through which I entered the Kingdom." Tyndale wrote, "I used to think that salvation was not for me, since I did not love God; but those precious words showed me that God does not love us because we first loved Him. No, no; we love Him because He first loved us. It makes all the difference!"

Timely Faith

Yet who knows whether you have come to
the kingdom for such a time as this?

Esther 4:14

Just before Charles Colson was to preach to three hundred inmates at San Quentin Prison, a lockdown confined the prisoners to their cells. To the few allowed to attend, he decided to go ahead and give the complete message he had prepared. Later, when he expressed disappointment that the three hundred were unable to attend, he was told, "We videotaped your message and will be showing it numerous times to all twenty-two hundred prisoners."

What if Colson had, as he first considered, just given a short devotional to the several Christians who were allowed to attend instead of the full evangelistic message he had prepared? More than two thousand needy souls would not have heard the gospel.

Being faithful in unlikely circumstances is what Esther is remembered for. As the newly appointed queen of Persia, she gained the ear of the king to plead for the safety of the Jews, who were about to be massacred. The king responded, and the Jewish people were saved.

An occasion may arise when you are the only person available to speak for God. Will you be faithful in such a moment as that? You are the most important person in the world to God when you are the one He has called to do something for Him.

The Danger of Unbelief

He did not do many mighty works
there because of their unbelief.
Matthew 13:58

Unbelief is the greatest obstacle to the expression of faith in the life of Christians. Unbelief has ruined the vision of more people than any other single characteristic. One of the reasons so many churches settle for mediocrity is because they are limited by their unbelief.

We ought to pray every day, both corporately and as individuals, that God would never limit us through our own unbelief. Sometimes we set barriers on our lives because we won't believe great things. Matthew 13:58 tells of Jesus coming to Nazareth and not doing many miracles "because of their unbelief." The greatest problem we face in churches is the problem of unbelief. Doubt creeps into the hearts of those who should be walking in faith and trusting God for His provision.

Unbelief settles into their lives like a dark cloud, wiping out God's plan and destroying the opportunity for His miracle-making power to take place. There will always be confrontation with unbelief for anyone willing to do great things for God.

Find the Way Home

For our citizenship is in heaven, from which we also eagerly wait for the Savior, the Lord Jesus Christ.

Philippians 3:20

Every year Pacific salmon, having lived five to six years in the ocean, suddenly get the urge to return to the headwaters of their birth river. Battling fishermen, bears, and giant hydroelectric dams, the fish fight their way upstream, determined to reach their home.

Scientists don't know how the salmon make their way back to the exact river in which they were born after being in the ocean for several years. Some think they can taste or smell the fresh water from their river. Others think they may use the stars to navigate. However they do it, we know they don't use charts and compasses; their journey is intuitive. They have a longing for a particular river that isn't satisfied until they find it.

And that's exactly how it is with us. God created us for heaven, and nothing in this earthly life can satisfy our longing (Ecclesiastes 3:11). We should be like salmon—being in the ocean but not being of the ocean, not being at rest until we find our way home to heaven.

If fish know when they're home and when they're not, how much more intense is that knowledge in those who bear God's image?

Pride—the Original Sin

God resists the proud, but gives grace to the humble.

James 4:6

If there is a deadly sin, one that is more wicked than any other, it has to be pride. James 4:6 tells us, "God resists the proud, but gives grace to the humble." God resists the proud. The one thing that seems to turn the power of God off in a person's life more than anything else is pride.

Pride is the original sin, if there is such a thing. It goes all the way back to when Satan was separated from God. Isaiah 14:12–14 says, "How you are fallen from heaven, O Lucifer, son of the morning! . . . For you have said in your heart: 'I will ascend into heaven. I will exalt my throne above the stars of God; . . . I will ascend above the heights of the clouds, I will be like the Most High.'"

And God said, "I have had enough of Lucifer!" Next thing we know, the separation has occurred and Satan and his demons are gone. With all of the difficulties and problems that God brings into our lives, things we would never choose for ourselves, I wonder sometimes if they are simply God's messengers to keep our feet on the ground and away from a proud heart.

Active Versus Passive Parenting

And you, fathers, . . . bring [your children] up
in the training and admonition of the Lord.

Ephesians 6:4

If you are a gardener, you know that planting a seed is only the first of a season's worth of steps. There's watering, fertilizing, weeding, and protecting the struggling plant from pests and diseases. Many flowers and vegetables require stakes, cages, or other supports to help them stand tall and bear their fruit. The gardener who does nothing but sow a seed shouldn't be surprised if plants never reach maturity.

Almost all living things in God's creation reproduce by sowing a seed: human beings, plants, birds, fish, and animals. When a plant seed is buried out of sight in the ground, there's little we can do to impact its growth. But when a new plant—and especially a new baby—enters the world, that's where the results of real husbandry and parenting can be seen.

Parents can have children, but only loving mothers and fathers actively nurture them to maturity. Feeding your child's mind, body, and spirit must be actively pursued. Passive parenting is letting a child grow on his or her own, while active parenting is bringing up a child "in the way he should go" (Proverbs 22:6).

It's true that we reap what we sow, but we also harvest fruit from what we carefully cultivate and nourish.

Paying the Piper

Be sure your sin will find you out.

Numbers 32:23

The great news of the Gospel is that we have a forgiving God. When we come to Him, open our hearts, and confess our sins, God does hear us and forgive us. He's just waiting for us to come and ask Him. God puts confessed sins behind His back as far as the east is from the west. He buries them in the deepest sea.

God forgets what He forgives. Yet there's a postscript: the Lord won't erase history. Some consequences may be set in motion while we are out of fellowship with God, and we must reap what we sow. Even when we have been restored to fellowship through the forgiveness process, sometimes we have to "pay the piper."

It is impossible to get away with sin. You can't do it. Numbers 32:23 says it this way: "Be sure your sin will find you out." Just as surely as you can't get away with sin, you can't get away from God's love. No matter how evil your conduct, God loves you. The reason you have that hurt in your heart right now is because you're God's, and He doesn't want you out of fellowship with Him.

The Enemy of God

Put on the whole armor of God, that you may be able to stand against the wiles of the devil.

Ephesians 6:11

A wealthy and godly farmer in the Middle East loses his home, his crops and livestock, his children, and his health. An Old Testament prophet prays to God for three weeks without hearing an answer to his prayers. A New Testament apostle suffers for years with a certain malady and finds no relief. These three individuals, though separated by time, were united by the common source of their problems: Satan.

In the cases of Job, Daniel, and Paul, Satan was allowed by God to enter their lives and bring pain, doubt, and discomfort. It is important for Christians to recognize that Satan is not an invention of Hollywood—he is a real being, intent on opposing God and His people at every turn.

But the Bible also clearly teaches that Satan is a troubler on a leash. He can go only as far as God allows and accomplish only that which fits and suits God's plans and purposes. While Paul explains in detail the spiritual armor of the believer against Satan's attacks, James summarizes it in just a single sentence: "Submit to God" (4:7).

The conscious choice to be under Christ's lordship is the surest defense against the devil's attacks.

Trail of Blood

The things you have heard . . . commit these to faithful men who will be able to teach others also.

2 Timothy 2:2

Long before Martin Luther "discovered" Reformation truth, John Hus was preaching it in Behemia (Czech Republic). Born about 1373 of peasant parentage, Hus became the most powerful preacher in Prague. He advocated reform in the church, which drew the displeasure of his fellow clergy. When he declared Scripture alone sufficient for Christian life and practice, he was summoned before the Council of Constance.

On July 6, 1415, Hus was found guilty of heresy, condemned, and taken to the outskirts of town to be burned. His last words were, "I have never thought nor preached except with the intention of winning men, if possible, from their sins. In the truth of the gospel I have written, taught, and preached; today I will gladly die."

It's dangerously easy to sit in church and yawn over the very truths for which earlier generations died. Our Bibles have been passed to us at great cost. Take a few moments today to thank God for the faithfulness of those who have handed down to us the Gospel, and rededicate yourself to passing it along to someone else.

The Nature of Love

You shall not take vengeance, nor bear any grudge against the children of your people, but you shall love your neighbor as yourself: I am the Lord.

Leviticus 19:18

A holy man, sitting by a stream, noticed a large scorpion struggling to get out of the swirling waters. The holy man used a stick to try to push the insect ashore, but it only struck at the stick with its poisonous tail. A friend passed by and said, "Don't you know it's the nature of a scorpion to attack?" "Yes," said the holy man, "but it is my nature to save. Why should I change my nature just because the scorpion won't change his?"

That's a good question—one every Christian should consider. If ever we strike back at someone who has attacked us, we deny the very nature of Christ, who lives in us. The apostle Paul said, "It is no longer I who live, but Christ lives in me; and the life which I now live in the flesh I live by faith in the Son of God, who loved me and gave Himself for me" (Galatians 2:20). Did Jesus retaliate and strike back at those who mistreated Him? We know He did not (1 Peter 2:21–23). If Christ lives in us, we should not retaliate either.

Nothing can quench the fires of hatred like the healing waters of love.

Judge Your Own Sin

For if we would judge ourselves,
we would not be judged.
1 Corinthians 11:31

When I was a boy, I worked at a place where I could get the autograph of some pretty famous Christians, and they would always put a favorite Scripture reference under their name. One time a man signed his name and wrote underneath it, "1 Corinthians 11:31." I didn't know that verse, so that night I found it and read the words, "For if we would judge ourselves, we would not be judged." If we take note of the sin in our lives and take the initiative to put it behind us, then the Bible says we won't be judged for that sin. But then the converse thought occurred to me: if there is unconfessed sin our lives, and we refuse to deal with it, God will have to judge that sin.

None of us can make it through this life without sinning. The road of life is rough, and there are ruts and potholes in which we can fall. But the Bible tells us how to deal with the sin in life: repent and confess it. If we do, God will bless. If we don't, God will judge. The choice is ours.

Bring an Offering

Give to the Lord the glory due His name;
Bring an offering, and come into His courts.
Psalm 96:8

In writing of her years in China, missionary Bertha Smith tells of a time when Dr. Wiley Glass, missionary educator, was kneeling during a prayer service at a large church. Mr. Wang, the church treasurer, was kneeling nearby. Suddenly Mr. Wang cried out, "Lord, have mercy on me! I've stolen! I'm a thief! I have stolen from God!" In astonishment, Dr. Glass thought, *Not you, Brother Wang; surely not you! All these years you have been such a trustworthy, devoted deacon, faithful trustee of the seminary, and upright Christian gentleman. You just could not have taken money from the church treasury!*

After a while, Brother Wang managed to explain, "I've not paid my tithe to the Lord! According to His Word, I've stolen it from Him!" The Chinese keep accurate records. Brother Wang calculated his tithe from the time he became a Christian, more than twenty years before, subtracted from it the total amount contributed to the church, and sold some land in order to pay what he felt he owed. From then on, he was aflame for Christ.

Do we love our Lord? How else can we express it except by giving? After all, God so loved us that He gave . . .

Train Up a Child

Train up a child in the way he should go,
And when he is old he will not depart from it.
Proverbs 22:6

Each child needs to know that he is unique and not like any other child God ever created. The Hebrew phrase "in the way" describes the habit or character of an individual at his own age level. The emphasis is on the importance of adjusting our training according to the ability of the child at each stage of his development. Each child has his own way, and by paying attention, we can determine what that way is.

The root meaning for the term *train up* is "palate or roof of the mouth." The Arab midwife would take olive oil or crushed dates on her finger and rub the palate of a newborn baby to create in the infant a desire to suck. A real meaning of "training" is to create a taste or desire. Our task is to develop in our children a hunger or desire for spiritual things, to cultivate an urge to follow God.

Choosing to Give Thanks

At midnight I will rise to give thanks to You.

Psalm 119:62

If you are in America on the fourth Thursday of November, there's a good chance you'll eat a big meal before the day is over. What began in 1621 as a conscious decision to give thanks to God was made a national day of thanksgiving in 1863 by President Abraham Lincoln. Today, Thanksgiving is a commercial and cultural institution in America.

Acts that are spontaneous and creative in the beginning often become formal and ritualistic. And that may be true of Thanksgiving in America. But it can also be true of thanksgiving in our personal lives. A quick way to determine whether your thanksgiving to God is creative and conscious, or rote and repetitious, is to examine when and where you give thanks to God. Is it only in church? Only during formal prayers? Only before you eat a meal? Or are there instances when you stop and give thanks to God at unplanned times?

Maybe we don't rise at midnight to give thanks like the psalmist (119:62). But we should find ourselves giving thanks to God all during the day as events unfold (Ephesians 5:20).

The fourth Thursday in November is a great day to give thanks to God—just as are the other 364 days of the year!

The Master Key to Spiritual Growth

For whoever has, to him more will be given, and he will have abundance: but whoever does not have, even what he has will be taken away from him.

Matthew 13:12

Jesus explained in Matthew 13:12: "For whoever has, to him more will be given, and he will have abundance; but whoever does not have, even what he has will be taken away from him."

This is the great principle upon which God operates in human lives today, the master key to our spiritual growth. This principle is so fundamental that it applies to other things besides spiritual truth. For instance, while I was in college, I broke both my ankles within a period of about a year and a half. After having a cast on my ankle and calf, and removing it, I discovered my calf had shrunk dramatically in size compared to the one without a cast. Why? Because the muscles in the calf had atrophied from lack of use. Everything that is not used is ultimately lost.

Jesus was giving His disciples a principle: those who have responded to what they have been given will get more and continue to grow. But those who have not responded to what they have been given will find what they have decreasing until it is removed altogether. Lack of revelation from God is due to lack of willingness to receive it.

Thanking and Speaking

She gave thanks to the Lord, and spoke of Him.

Luke 2:38

Like it or not, the holiday season is here, with all its frenzy and fun. Now is a good time to decide to be an Anna. This older saint is one of the original characters in the Christmas story—a prophetess, a widow of many years who virtually lived at the temple, awaiting the arrival of the Redeemer. She "served God with fastings and prayers night and day" (Luke 2:37).

Imagine her rapture when Joseph and Mary entered the temple, bearing in their arms the long-awaited Christ child. Somehow God assured her that this was the Messiah. Anna's reaction gives us a clue about our own attitude during the upcoming holidays: "She gave thanks to the Lord, and spoke of Him to all those who looked for redemption in Jerusalem" (v. 38).

Those are our two great obligations as we enjoy the seasons of Thanksgiving and Christmas: to thank God for Christ, and to speak of Him to others.

When was the last time you devoted more than a few seconds to thanking God for the Lord Jesus? Take some time today, and thank Him for Christ's life, His death, His resurrection, His ascension, His present intercessory ministry, and His soon return. Then speak of Him to someone else.

Eternal Profit from Our Pain

For they indeed for a few days chastened us as seemed best to them, but He for our profit, that we may be partakers of His holiness.

Hebrews 12:10

When Jacob was an old man, the Lord commanded him to move to Bethel, and Jacob finally decided to obey God. He met the Lord face-to-face, after having fought Him his whole life, and the result was that, in his old age, Jacob finally stopped resisting.

God will not spare present pain if it means eternal profit. God is more concerned with our spiritual growth than our temporal comfort, so He allows adversity to help us grow. God perseveres with us, even when we have given up on ourselves. What the Lord starts, He finishes. Jacob was an unlovely person, but God loved Him anyway. God's priority for our lives does not include a Jacob-like experience. God's will for our lives is to obey Him, not run away so that He has to discipline us.

Jacob's son Joseph learned those lessons. When he was called by God to obey, he obeyed willingly. The difference between his life and that of his father is stunning—and particularly insightful. It pays to serve the Lord.

Now Thank We All Our God

We give thanks to You, O God, we give thanks!

Psalm 75:1

Martin Rinkart pastored in Eilenberg, Saxony, during the Thirty Years War. The Swedish army surrounded the gates; and inside the walls, there was nothing but plague, famine, and fear. There was a tremendous strain on the pastors, who expended all their strength preaching the Gospel, caring for the sick, and burying the dead. One after another, the pastors themselves perished until at last only Martin was left. Some days he conducted as many as fifty funerals.

When the Swedes demanded a huge ransom, Martin left the safety of the city walls to negotiate, and there was soon a conclusion of hostilities. Knowing there is no healing without thanksgiving, Martin composed a hymn for the survivors of Eilenberg:

Now thank we all our God, with heart and hands
and voices,
Who wondrous things hath done, in whom His
world rejoices . . .

It's been sung around the world ever since and is one of our greatest thanksgiving hymns. This is a time to focus our attention on God, who is the giver of all good things, and to thank Him for what is left, not what is lost.

Today, thank your God with heart and hands and voice.

Peace in Turmoil

Let not your heart be troubled,
neither let it be afraid.
John 14:27

Jesus said, "Let not your heart be troubled." He spoke these words to His disciples on a night when He knew that, in a matter of hours, the lives of His disciples would be permanently impacted through His own terrible ordeal and death.

He told them the Holy Spirit would come as a Comforter. He told them a place was being prepared for them. He told them He would come again and receive them unto Himself. He told His disciples that they could have peace in the midst of turmoil if they would receive the peace He gives.

All too often we lose our peace in the midst of tragedy and the circumstances of life. When we do that, we have nothing to offer a watching world. If a neighbor comes to us distraught over tragedy and finds us just as undone, what testimony have we given about the peace of Christ that He promised? It is the Christians in a community who should be able to offer a word of encouragement and comfort during difficult times. But we can only do that if we possess the peace of Christ—that peace He purchased for us at the price of His own blood.

Power of Persuasion

For Christ did not send me to baptize, but to preach the gospel, not with wisdom of words, lest the cross of Christ should be made of no effect.

1 Corinthians 1:17

The late Fred Rogers of television's *Mister Rogers* once attended church with friends while in seminary. During the sermon, he made a mental list of all the mistakes he felt the elderly preacher was making. When the service was over, he was caught short by the tears running down his friend's face. "He said exactly what I needed to hear," she said.

Sometimes what seems like poor preaching from a human perspective can be greatly used by God. What makes the difference? The Holy Spirit. Scripture and tradition give us reason to believe that the apostle Paul was not a very dynamic person, humanly speaking. Yet who can deny the impact of his words? No one, apart from Christ Himself, has accomplished more by his speaking.

Paul said it was good that his words were not "persuasive words of human wisdom" (1 Corinthians 2:4), lest people look to him instead of to God as the true source of power. We would do well to examine ourselves the same way—to see whom we rely on for power in our lives: the Holy Spirit or ourselves.

It's fine to use the natural gifts God has given us—as long as they don't replace His supernatural gift of the Spirit.

With Open Hands

Give, and it will be given to you: good measure, pressed down, shaken together, and running over will be put into your bosom.

Luke 6:38

When Elijah met the widow of Zarephath, she was locked in the clutches of a handful of meal and a tiny bit of oil. That's all she had. We can sympathize with her. In fact, some of us can identify with her. And Elijah's heart went out to her.

The difference was that he knew something she didn't know. He knew that the way to have what you have and have it to the fullest is to always put God first. That's why he said, "Make me a little cake first." In other words, "Trust God by putting Him first and watch what He does."

When we first see this woman in the story, she is clutching everything she has. At the end of the story, she is releasing it all to God. The way to have what you have is to give it back to God. That is the only way you can ever possess your possessions. If you give it back to God with open hands, He will not only bless you, He will also put back what you need.

The Changed Centurion

So when the centurion . . . saw that He cried out like this and breathed His last, he said, "Truly this Man was the Son of God!"

Mark 15:39

An African woman became a Christian, which enraged her husband. He decided to get rid of her by accusing her of thievery—of stealing his keys. He threw his key ring in a river and planned to accuse her of taking it. Later that day, his wife bought a large fish for their supper and discovered her husband's keys in its stomach! When her husband came home later that night demanding to know where his keys were, she calmly handed them to him—and he was instantly converted to Christ!

While Christians are warned against walking by sight, sometimes it's true that seeing is believing. At some point, it becomes difficult to deny the evidence of the power and presence of a miracle-working God. A Roman centurion who watched Jesus suffer on Calvary—and then felt the earth shake when an earthquake accompanied His death—concluded that Jesus was truly the Son of God. Was he converted? The Bible doesn't say, but we know he was changed.

Think about how your life has changed since seeing Jesus. Seeing Jesus for who He really is always precedes seeing ourselves for who we really are.

Compared With What?

We do not care to classify or compare ourselves with some who commend themselves. When they measure themselves by themselves and compare themselves with themselves, they are not wise.

2 Corinthians 10:12 NIV

I'm always a little surprised when I hear someone comment that they cannot understand why God would do something for Mr. and Mrs. Someone and not for them. But the comment that shocks me is when they say, "It isn't fair."

The hard truth is, we ought to be asking why God would ever do anything for any of us. As Jeremiah wrote, "Through the Lord's mercies we are not consumed, because His compassions fail not" (Lamentations 3:22). The only thing we "deserve" is His wrath. Whatever talent or ability we may develop or position we may achieve, it is only because of God's great grace.

I love Paul's gentle sarcasm when he wrote: "We do not dare to classify or compare ourselves with some who commend themselves. When they measure themselves by themselves and compare themselves with themselves, they are not wise" (2 Corinthians 10:12 NIV). Today, thank Him for who you are and every blessing He has provided.

No Accidents

Now to the King eternal, immortal, invisible, to God who alone is wise, be honor and glory forever and ever. Amen.

1 Timothy 1:17

"I have lived a long time," Benjamin Franklin, age eighty-one, told the Constitutional Convention, "and the longer I live, the more convincing proofs I see of this truth—that God governs in the affairs of men. And if a sparrow cannot fall to the ground without His notice, is it probable that an empire can rise without His aid?"

Nations rise and fall; leaders come and go. But there is only one King of kings and Lord of lords, and He who ordains the flow of history and guides the sparrow's flight also carefully attends to the needs of His children.

A. W. Tozer wrote, "To the child of God, there is no such thing as accident. He travels an appointed way. . . . Accidents may indeed appear to befall him and misfortune stalk his way; but these evils will be so in appearance only and will seem evil only because we cannot read the secret script of God's hidden providence."

God is eternal, so His perspective is broad. He is immortal, having no fear of death. He is invisible and always present. He is all-wise, always knowing just what to do. Trust Him—and give Him honor and glory forever and ever. Amen.

Prayer Makes Us Better

[Give] thanks always for all things to God the Father in the name of our Lord Jesus Christ.

Ephesians 5:20

It is not new truth to many of us that prayer is a great comfort in uneasy times and a mighty warrior against worry. I am convinced, however, that we are confused about the way prayer actually works for us in such stressful and difficult days.

Does Paul's call to prayer mean that when we pray, all the things we worry about will be straightened out for us and that our trouble will be gone? Not necessarily!

If prayer does not always change our situation so that it no longer worries us, then what is the value of praying? Here is the answer! Prayer does not always change the situation and make it better, but prayer always changes us and makes us better.

Prayer, especially prayer accompanied by thanksgiving, is the perfect answer to a heart that is overridden with anxiety.

Shaping the Future

Keep this forever in the . . . heart of Your people . . .
and give my son Solomon a loyal heart to keep Your
commandments and Your testimonies and Your statutes.

1 Chronicles 29:18–19

A retired French lawyer struck a deal with a ninety-year-old widow. For a payment of $500 per month to her until she died, he bought the rights to take over the lease on her fashionable apartment. At her age, it looked like a shrewd investment. In 1995, thirty years and $180,000 later, he was still paying—when she turned 120!

The future rarely turns out the way we think it will, so our best efforts to predict it ought to be held lightly. But there is one perspective on the future that is a sure thing: God's perspective.

Consider King David, for example. The days of his kingship over Israel were coming to a close. The nation was preparing to build a great temple for God, and Solomon, David's young son, was ascending to the throne. Instead of predicting or worrying about the future, David did the right thing: he prayed about it. He prayed for the people and he prayed for his son, that God would bless them and keep them faithful.

Shape your future, and your family's future, by committing everything to God in prayer. The only future that is a sure thing is the one to which God has said yes.

Problem or Pulpit?

The things which happened to me have actually turned out for the furtherance of the gospel.

Philippians 1:12

Samuel Rutherford attended Edinburgh University as a young man and began teaching there at age twenty-three. But desiring to preach the Gospel, he assumed the pastorate in Anwoth, Scotland, in 1627, and served faithfully for ten years. In 1636, he was called before the High Commission Court to defend his Puritan views. He lost the case and was exiled from his congregation.

On July 13, 1637, he wrote to his church from exile: "Next to Christ, I had but one joy, the apple of the eye of my delights, to preach Christ my Lord; and they have violently plucked that away from me. It was to me like the poor man's one eye; and they have put out that eye, and quenched my light in the inheritance of the Lord." But all this actually furthered the Gospel. While in exile, he wrote many letters that were later compiled into one of Christian history's greatest classics, *The Letters of Samuel Rutherford*.

Whenever you experience a reversal in life, look around for an opportunity to share the gospel. Problems have a way of becoming pulpits in the overruling providence of God.

Leaders in Giving

Be an example to the believers in word, in conduct, in love, in spirit, in faith, in purity.

1 Timothy 4:12

William Wallace won the respect of his army of Scottish commoners by being on the front line of every battle they fought. The same commoners despised the fur-clad Scottish lords because they sat in the rear on horseback, never staining themselves with the soil or blood of battle.

In war or in peace—or in the life of the church—sacrifice is the admission price to the ranks of leadership. Leadership in giving must be no less sacrificial. If church leaders want members to give, they must set the example, as must parents who want their children to learn to give.

King David followed this pattern when raising money to build Israel's first temple. He gave generously from his own personal wealth; then the leaders of families, tribes, and other officials followed his example and gave. Their examples caused the Israelite people to rejoice in their own giving.

Everyone leads someone. What kind of an example of giving are you providing for those you lead? Are those you lead faithful in giving?

Before examining their habits, make sure you have examined your own. From the pattern comes the product.

DECEMBER

God is our refuge and strength.

—Psalm 46:1

ONE PLUS GOD

I sought for a man among them who would make a wall, and stand in the gap before Me on behalf of the land, that I should not destroy it; but I found no one.

EZEKIEL 22:30

When Frances Havergal, author of the hymn "Take My Life and Let It Be," was a teenager, her parents moved to Dusseldorf, Germany, where she was placed in a German school. She was the only Christian among 110 pupils. The others made fun of her, teased her, even persecuted her. Her response? "It was very bracing," she wrote. "I felt I must try to walk worthy of my calling, for Christ's sake. It was a sort of nailing my colors to the mast."

You might be the only Christian in your school, on your ball team, at your office, or in your family. What an opportunity! Christians are the "salt of the earth." It doesn't take a lot of salt to season the whole pot. The presence of even one believer can hinder sin, delay judgment, prompt conviction, and extend the kingdom of God.

Paul and his two companions were apparently the only believers on the storm-tossed ship in Acts 27. But their presence saved all 276 people on board. The odds against Elijah on Mount Carmel were 450 to one, but one plus God is a majority. The feeblest light is best seen in the thickest darkness. Don't be afraid to nail your colors to the mast.

All It Takes

For the eyes of the Lord run to and fro throughout the whole earth, to show Himself strong on behalf of those whose heart is loyal to Him.

2 Chronicles 16:9

Dwight L. Moody preached the Gospel to more people in the nineteenth century than anyone else in the world. He left home at age seventeen with the equivalent of a fifth-grade education. He was won to Christ as a teenager, and in 1873, a friend in England challenged him with the following statement: "The world has yet to see what God can do with a man fully consecrated to him." Moody's reply was, "With God's help, I aim to be that man."

That challenge certainly motivated Moody, but it wasn't altogether accurate. For the world had already seen what God would do with a man fully committed to Him. Daniel, taken from Jerusalem to Babylon by Nebuchadnezzar, immediately impressed his pagan captors. His physical appearance, his wisdom, and his unswerving commitment to his God elevated him to a place of influence—all without compromising his beliefs. Noah, Joseph, Daniel, Paul—all were ordinary people whom God used to do extraordinary things.

Will today's world see extraordinary things done for God? All it takes is a person like Daniel or Dwight L. Moody—that is, a person like you—fully consecrated to God.

The Missing Jewel

He is your Lord, worship Him.

Psalm 45:11

Once A. W. Tozer called worship the "missing jewel" of the modern church. There are too many churches, too many Christians that do not know how to worship God, or even why worship is our primary responsibility before Him. We have churches that emphasize preaching, churches that stress evangelism, and churches that highlight body fellowship, but worship is the priority commandment from God. We are called to love the Lord our God with all our heart, soul, mind, and strength, and we develop our love for Him in worship.

Our lives are changed and our spiritual walk is strengthened as we come before God and worship Him. It is the priority commandment in His Word. We will never truly know God until we worship Him, and we will never really worship Him unless we know Him. He is sitting on the throne in heaven, worthy of honor and glory and praise, awaiting our worship. He inhabits the praises of His people and can be found there with them as they worship Him. He is a great God, a King above all gods who will be gloriously worshiped throughout all eternity. And He wants you to know Him.

Keeping Christ in Christmas

*And the Word became flesh and dwelt among us,
and we beheld His glory, the glory as of the only
begotten of the Father, full of grace and truth.*

John 1:14

A survey of five thousand households, conducted in August 2003 by the Conference Board's Consumer Research Center, showed that consumers planned to spend more for Christmas that year than the previous one—in spite of continuing national economic woes. One-third of the families surveyed planned to spend $500 or more on presents in 2003.

No one knows exactly when it happened, but Christmas in America has become more about money than the manger. Certainly gift giving is a meaningful part of the Christmas celebration. After all, our gifts to one another and to God remind us of His greater gift of His own Son, Jesus Christ (Romans 6:23). But it's easy to let material gifts overshadow the greatest Gift, to think more about what we want than Whom we need, and to let money replace ministry in our attitudes toward others.

Why not begin this Christmas season, either alone or with family or friends, refocusing on the Reason for the season. Give to Christ the only gift He really wants, this and every year—the gift of your loving heart.

All the Christmas presents in the world mean nothing without the presence of Christ.

In Tragedies and Triumphs

But as for you, you meant evil against me; but God meant it for good, in order to bring it about as it is this day, to save many people alive.

Genesis 50:20

One of the greatest assets Joseph had was his sensitivity to every situation. In both his triumphs and tragedies, Joseph was able to see through his circumstances and see God at work behind the scenes.

Joseph always seems to be conscious of God in his life. He refused the invitation of Potiphar's wife because he recognized that it would be "a sin against God" (Genesis 39:9). He refused to exalt himself when interpreting Pharaoh's dream, instead insisting that "God will give Pharaoh an answer" (41:16). Now he refuses to take vengeance upon his brothers for selling him as a slave, since he now knows the Lord had it in mind all along. Joseph made God part of every aspect of his life.

If we can come to a place in our spiritual walk where we can see God at work in both our triumphs and tragedies, we'll find new peace in our souls. We don't always understand or particularly like what God arranges, but we understand the fact that He is in charge, and we bow to His sovereignty. That's called living with an eternal perspective, and it's exactly what Joseph does. He has confidence that God is at work on His master plan, regardless of how the immediate circumstances appear.

Even in the Night

Yet I will rejoice.

Habakkuk 3:18

John Newton, who penned the words to "Amazing Grace," was an eighteenth-century pastor in London who was devoted to his wife, Mary. Their relationship was one of the most tender in Christian history, and they sometimes worried that their love for each other was almost idolatrous. One day she broke the news that a famous surgeon had diagnosed her with cancer. Newton's anguish was terrible. He said he felt like a bull caught in a net. When she died fifteen months later, friends worried because he seemed inconsolable.

But then, strengthened in faith, John preached her funeral, choosing as his text Habakkuk 3:17–18: "Though the fig tree may not blossom, nor fruit be on the vines; though the labor of the olive may fail, and the fields yield no food . . . yet I will rejoice in the Lord, I will joy in the God of my salvation."

We can still focus on God in worship even when we don't understand His decisions and directions in our lives. We're caught in time and trapped in transience. God, who transcends all, is eternal and infinite. We don't always understand, but He knows. He cares.

God works things together for good. He is worthy to be praised, even in the night. We can yet rejoice in Him.

Come to Me

Come to Me, all you who labor and are heavy laden, and I will give you rest.
Matthew 11:28

Stress is the catchall disease of our day. It is blamed for medical conditions and just about anything else that people don't know how to otherwise explain. Huge sums of money are spent every year to teach people how to live with stress.

Two thousand years ago, a book was written under the inspiration of God the Holy Spirit that purports to have the answers to all of mankind's needs. Can a book written so long ago really speak to the modern age in which we live? See if Jesus' words in Matthew 11:28–30 aren't the perfect invitation to the stressed-out people of our day: "Come to Me, all you who labor and are heavy laden, and I will give you rest. Take My yoke upon you and learn from Me, for I am gentle and lowly in heart, and you will find rest for your souls. For My yoke is easy and My burden is light."

The invitation, though two thousand years old, is still valid because the basic human need is still the same: people are still weary from the process of living life without God.

Christmas Cheer

Love the Lord your God with all your heart and with all your soul and with all your strength and with all your mind"; and, "Love your neighbor as yourself.

Luke 10:27 NIV

Mamie Adams always went to a specific branch post office in her town because the postal employees were friendly. On a busy afternoon, just a few days before Christmas, she stopped by to purchase a few stamps. While waiting in the long line, a man pointed out that there was no need to wait; a stamp machine was in the lobby. "I know," said Mamie, "but the machine won't ask me about my arthritis."

The art of kindness has not been lost, but sometimes it gets tucked away, especially during the holidays. There are so many errands to run, goodies to bake, and gifts to wrap that we forget the spirit of Christmas, sharing the good news of Jesus' birth with others by showing our love and generosity.

When you take the time to encourage someone, it might be the small act that changes his or her entire life! Go the extra mile for someone in need—become involved in your community. The art of kindness is in you.

Need a Lift?

Now my head shall be lifted up above
my enemies all around me.

Psalm 27:6

Have you ever seen people with so much trouble that their heads are down? Have you felt that way? You face a confrontation and it goes wrong. You walk away from there with your head down. Very graphic, isn't it? The Bible says that when you face trouble and you worship, that worship becomes the lifter of your head. You could walk into church with the burdens of the world on you, and when you get caught up in the worship of the Lord, it's almost like God just lifts your head right up.

Worship makes God big in your heart. Is God big? Yes. He can't get any bigger than He is. I mean, God is God. But worship magnifies God; it puts awareness of who God is into your heart so you begin to sense and appreciate the greatness of Almighty God. When you see His greatness and you put your trouble in that picture, everything changes. When you measure your trouble against others, you might be depressed, but when you measure your trouble against the greatness and magnificence of God, that's encouraging. No wonder your head gets lifted!

Knowing and Doing

For if anyone is a hearer of the word and not a doer, he is like a man observing his natural face in a mirror.

James 1:23

A well-known seminary professor spent a summer studying in Jerusalem. In his apartment building lived an orthodox Jewish rabbi, with whom he studied Hebrew throughout the summer. One day the professor sat and listened to his Jewish friend recite the entire Book of Psalms, in Hebrew, without missing so much as a jot or a tittle.

The lesson he brought back was the same lesson Jesus taught in Matthew 7:24–27: It is not the hearers and "knowers" of God's Word who will be blessed, but the doers. The knowledge of God's Word is important—without it, God's people have been known to suffer (Hosea 4:6). But great knowledge can also water the root of pride in the sinful human heart (1 Corinthians 8:1).

One man said that to consume the Bible without putting it into practice is the equivalent of going into a fine restaurant and eating the menu while ignoring the meal. Which are you more focused on in your Christian life: knowing the Word for the sake of knowing it, or knowing it in order to put it into practice?

Knowing the Bible should lead to living the Bible, which leads to honoring the Author of the Bible.

Seeking, Not Just Tending

The Son of Man has come to seek and to save that which was lost.

Luke 19:10

We are all familiar with the idea of equipping the saints to do the work of the ministry (Ephesians 4:12)—and that is certainly part of our responsibility. But I think if the Lord Jesus were in the average Bible-believing church, He would want to know why we spend so much time trying to meet our own needs when there are so many lost sheep out there who don't know God.

I love the ministry of the church I pastor, and yet I sometimes wonder if our church is not doing as much seeking and saving of the lost as we should be. Sometimes we are like Old Testament armies who come upon the spoils of a battle and gorge themselves instead of sharing with others.

I think Jesus is telling us in this parable that, while it is nice to be part of the ninety-nine sheep who are already safe inside the sheepfold, we ought to keep looking for the lost ones. Remembering what it means personally to be found is a great motivation for going to find others.

God Knows the Future

Behold the maidservant of the Lord! Let it be to me according to your word.

Luke 1:38

A marble slab in a New Hampshire cemetery holds an unbelievable epitaph: "Murdered by the Baptist Ministry and Churches." Apparently the deceased was accused of lying in a church meeting. She was expelled and reduced to poverty, and the church refused to allow any outside investigation. The assassination of her character led to an early death.

It takes great faith to stand under the weight of false accusation and shame. When a teenager named Mary was approached by the angel Gabriel and told she was to be the mother of Jesus, imagine what raced through her mind: *I am not married. If I become pregnant, people will think at worst that I am immoral or at best that my husband-to-be, Joseph, and I have had relations—neither of which is true!* But then she must have thought, *Surely God knows these possibilities. If He knows what could happen and still wants me to serve Him, then I will do it.*

The next time that obeying the Lord puts you at risk for being misunderstood, remember that God knows all the possibilities—and He has planned accordingly.

Saying yes to God means believing that He knows where that response will lead.

Love Never Fails

Love never fails.

1 Corinthians 13:8

Eusebius, the "father of church history," wrote how the early Christians demonstrated love during plagues and epidemics: "Most of our brethren showed love and loyalty in not sparing themselves while helping one another, tending to the sick with no thought of danger, and gladly departing this life after becoming infected with their disease. Many who nursed others to health died themselves."

He then added, "The heathen were the exact opposite. They pushed away those with the first signs of the disease and fled from their dearest."

Philippians 2:4 gives a great definition of love: "Let each of you look out not only for his own interests, but also for the interests of others." Love is seeking the best of the one loved. It is meeting the needs of another without thought of our own. It is doing for another what we would like to have done for ourselves (Matthew 7:12).

On a very practical level, this involves a lot of little things—sharing housework with your spouse, remaining patient with your children, listening to a friend, sharing praise with a co-worker, helping a neighbor in need, or maybe just holding your tongue when you'd rather let loose. This kind of love never fails.

The Gift of Prayer

But the mercy of the Lord *is from*
everlasting to everlasting
On those who fear Him,
And His righteousness to children's children.

Psalm 103:17

One of our favorite Christmas poems says, "Over the river and through the woods, to Grandmother's house we go. The horse knows the way to carry the sleigh through the white and drifted snow." Those words convey the joy of grandparents and grandchildren spending the holidays together.

But what if the grandchildren aren't coming? Many grandparents are sad this month because they can't be with their grandchildren. Are you among them?

Why not give your grandkids a special gift of prayer? Devote extra time every day to praying for your dear ones by name. Search the Scriptures for verses to pray into their lives. When Christmas Eve or Christmas Day arrives, set aside a "sweet hour of prayer" on their behalf.

One of the things grandparents can do better than anyone else is to pray for their grandchildren. How many of us had grandparents who were prayer warriors? Who can tell how much our lives were shaped and protected by their strong and ceaseless intercession?

If you can't spend this Christmas with your grandchildren, spend it for your grandchildren. Spend it on your knees.

Listen to Others

Let every man be swift to hear, slow to speak, and slow to wrath, for the wrath of man does not produce the righteousness of God.

James 1:19–20

It is unfortunate that when we think about communication, we only think of the active aspect of communication, which is talking. We ought also to consider the important passive application of communication, which is listening. Experts tell us that it is not easy to teach people to listen, but it is a skill that can be learned. Did you know that in one day approximately 9 percent of your time will be spent writing, 16 percent of your time will be spent reading, 30 percent of your time will be spent speaking, and 45 percent of your time will be spent listening?

We spend more time listening than any other activity, yet I've never seen a Christian training seminar that teaches you how to listen. It is possible to go to almost any graduation and see people getting awards for speaking, but I have never seen anyone get an award for listening. Remember the words of James: "So then, my beloved brethren, let every man be swift to hear, slow to speak, slow to wrath, for the wrath of man does not produce the righteousness of God" (1:19–20).

It's All Good

[Barnabas] was a good man, full of the Holy Spirit and of faith.

Acts 11:24

In his book *Wind and Fire*, Bruce Larson notes characteristics of sandhill cranes, which fly great distances across continents. In flight, no bird leads all the time, and only birds that can handle wind turbulence get to lead the flock. But most important, all the time the leader is breaking the wind resistance for the others, the entire flock pours forth a constant stream of affirming honks.

Whether given in the form of honks or hugs, encouragement probably has the highest cost-to-benefit ratio of any human act. Barnabas is the prototype of an encourager; we may have the Gospel of Mark today because of him.

Once, when Paul and Barnabas went on a ministry trip, they took young Mark with them—but he deserted them before the end of their trip (Acts 13:13). Later, Paul wouldn't take Mark on a second trip, so Barnabas took Mark under his wing (Acts 15:36–40). Barnabas's forgiving and encouraging attitude toward the young leader probably saved Mark's ministerial life. Look around—do you see someone with potential whose world you could change with a little encouragement?

Whether honks, hugs, hollers, or hallelujahs—encouragement is all good.

The Goodness of God

I would have lost heart, unless I had believed
That I would see the goodness of the Lord
In the land of the living.
Psalm 27:13

I don't have to debate with you about the goodness of the Lord in the land of the living. We expect that as God's people, but sometimes we don't see it because we don't look for it. I've been keeping track of the goodness of God in the land of my living. I keep a little journal in which I write things God does. My list is growing. When I'm in trouble and my faith gets down to a flickering flame, I open up my journal and read my list, which shows the goodness of God in the land of my living. It has been a great encouragement to me.

God isn't on our time schedule. We need to remain calm when God delays. Sometimes when we pray, "Lord, help," He doesn't do it right away.

When trouble comes express, extend, experience, and enjoy your faith. When you pray in times of trouble, respond to God, rely on Him, resign to His will, and remain calm until His help arrives.

The Message of Holly

In Him we have redemption through His blood, the forgiveness of sins, according to the riches of His grace.

Ephesians 1:7

Millions of people this Christmas will go to their local garden center in search of the traditional *Ilex opaca*. Or they might even inquire about the fancier English *Ilex aquifolium*. If you can't remember the fancy Latin names, no problem. Just ask for Christmas holly, and you'll come home with the spiny green leaves and the bright red berries that have adorned wreathes and fireplaces for generations.

Over the centuries, red and green have been used as the two primary colors of Christmas. The shiny red holly berries and the bright green holly leaves are the perfect combination of the two most traditional colors. The small holly berries are thought to have originally reminded Christians of the drops of Christ's blood caused by the crown of thorns He wore on Calvary. The bright green leaves and all the evergreens used at Christmas speak of the never-ending life that the shedding of Christ's blood secured for all who believe in Him.

Even the sharp spines on the holly leaves remind us of what Jesus suffered on our behalf.

Be My Disciple

Take My yoke upon you and learn from Me, for I am gentle and lowly in heart, and you will find rest for your souls.

Matthew 11:29

There are two kinds of stress that people need to deal with. First is the stress of sin that is relieved when we come to Christ initially. But second is the stress that accumulates when we don't live our lives under Christ's lordship. That is the cause of the vast majority of the stress that Christians live with daily. To use Jesus' own words, it is the stress that comes from not taking Jesus' yoke upon us.

A yoke suggests a picture of oxen linked together pulling a common plow. That's not really what His words mean. Taking on a yoke was a rabbinical expression meaning to become a disciple of someone. Therefore, He is saying, "Come and be My disciple. Begin to let your life be patterned after the dictates of My life and My soul. Come and get involved in submission to Me in lordship. Take My yoke upon you."

Jesus, as the victorious Lord, the King of kings, is inviting us to be His disciples, to let Him rule over our lives.

Never-Ending Union

And truly our fellowship is with the Father and with His Son Jesus Christ.

1 John 1:3

From the early days of Irish Christianity, the Celtic cross has had a circle surrounding the intersection of the vertical and horizontal axes of the cross. Some believe the design originated with St. Patrick, who, upon seeing a round symbol of the moon goddess, drew a Christian cross over it, changing a Druid symbol into a new symbol for Irish Christianity.

In the same way that St. Patrick adopted a pagan circle and gave it new meaning, so other Christians adopted another circle and gave it new meaning to celebrate Christ's birth. When early Christians changed the Roman Winter Solstice celebration of the rebirth of the sun (originally on December 21) to a celebration of the birth of the "Son of Righteousness," the evergreen wreath was adopted as well—but given new meaning.

Instead of being simply a garland, the round Christmas wreath speaks of the never-ending unity and fellowship we have with God through Christ. It is a picture of what C. S. Lewis wrote: "Once a man is united to God, how could he not live forever?"

When you hang a wreath on your door or over your fireplace this Christmas, don't fail to notice that the wreath has no end. Likewise, there is no end to our union with God.

Plugged In

The Lord called Samuel. And he answered, "Here I am!"

1 Samuel 3:4

Ernest Hemingway once lamented, "I live in a vacuum that is as lonely as a radio tube when the batteries are dead and there is no current to plug into."

Not so the Christian. We have a mission and a message. God has placed us on earth for a brief time to do an urgent work. Our lives have purpose, and all our days are scheduled in His perfect will. We travel an appointed way. What is the burning vision for your life? What does God want you to do?

Ask Him to show you. Read His Word, seeking His will for your life. Tell Him you're available. Say, like Samuel, "Here I am." Find something to do and begin doing it. Find a need and begin filling it.

Perhaps it's visiting someone in the hospital or nursing home or working with children in the church nursery. Perhaps it's singing in the choir, making visits for your church, or serving as an usher or greeter on Sunday morning.

Be faithful in that smaller things, and the Lord will give you more work to do, and more and more—all for His glory. He wants to use you. He has a purpose for your life, and He alone can give you a vision of His will.

The Christmas Spirit

Bearing with one another, and forgiving one another.

Colossians 3:13

In their book *None of These Diseases*, S. I. McMillen and David Stern describe the damage we inflict on ourselves when we dislike someone or refuse to forgive him or her. "The moment I begin to hate a man, I become his slave. He controls my thoughts. He controls my feelings. He even controls my dreams. Stress hormones constantly surge through my bloodstream and wear down my body. . . . The one I hate hounds me wherever I go."

As your family gathers this holiday, perhaps there's a member you don't like or haven't forgiven. Perhaps a father-in-law or a stepchild. Maybe a brother or sister who hurt you years ago.

Remember that Christmas is all about God's love and forgiveness. Jesus left the infinite riches of the heavenly palace to sleep in an animal's food trough, choosing to live among unlovely people. He came to forgive and redeem. He can flush all the hatred from your heart if you'll only let Him.

If you're not looking forward to seeing someone in your family this Christmas, offer this prayer: "Lord, I confess that I don't like __________, and I am dreading being with him (or her). Forgive me, and help me to forgive and forbear. May the love of the Christmas Christ be funneled through me this season."

The Sin of Worry

Do not worry about your life, what you will eat; nor about the body, what you will put on. Life is more than food, and the body is more than clothing.

Luke 12:22–23

Let me begin by stating something that you may or may not agree with: worry is sin. Worry is not part of our personality; it is not something to be excused because "everybody does it." From God's perspective, worry is sin. But in order to clarify this (it's important to know when we are sinning and when we are not), let's separate worry from concern.

It is certainly right to be concerned about things that are your responsibility and over which you exercise control. God expects us to be responsible, to be concerned that we follow through on what is ours to do. But worry is concerning yourself about things over which you have no control. Worry is allowing care and concern to escalate beyond the realm of responsibility and into a realm in which you have no authority or control—God's realm. And that kind of concern, which is worry, is sin.

When we worry, we deny the faithfulness of God—and that is why worry is sin.

Life That Never Fades

The cypress, the pine, and the box tree together,
to beautify the place of My sanctuary.

Isaiah 60:13

If you selected a Christmas tree blindfolded, your chances of choosing the right kind are good. There are only two kinds of trees in the world: deciduous (those whose leaves die annually) and evergreens (those whose leaves stay green). Still, you're better off peeking when you choose. Bringing home a six-foot oak with bare limbs might get you lumps of coal in your stocking.

Evergreen. The word itself brings up images of Christmas trees in December—cedars, spruces, and firs. And the scents! Evergreen garlands cascading down banisters and flowing over mantels fill the house with an aroma we wish would last forever. The evergreen tree is certainly the most traditional of Christmas decorations—though electric lights weren't used on them until 1882. But for centuries, evergreens have represented the most everlasting aspect of the first Christmas in Bethlehem—our eternal life with Jesus Christ. Our Christmas trees, once cut, won't last forever. But what they picture will: life in heaven forever.

When you put up your Christmas tree this year, remind family and friends that, though the green of the tree will ultimately fade, the greatness of our eternal life in Christ will not.

Let It Be

Mary, you are going to be with child in a way that no one has ever been with child before, or shall ever be afterward.

Luke 1:35 (author's paraphrase)

There are several ways humans come into being. Adam and Eve were created directly by God. They did not come through the birth process. Today, we are the products of a relationship between our mother and father. But Jesus was uniquely born in the sense that He was born of His mother, but He had no earthly father. So Mary was asked, at the age of sixteen, to comprehend a concept, a birth process, that had never before occurred in the history of humanity. No wonder she was perplexed!

This is the glory and wonder of Christmas, that God could plant not only into the womb of this woman the Son of God, but He could plant in her heart the faith to believe the message that she received from the angel. Her response has always overwhelmed me with a sense of absolute submission that ought to be in the heart of every child of God. Mary said, "Behold the maidservant of the Lord! Let it be to me according to your word" (Luke 1:38).

How God Treats Us

All things work together for good.

Romans 8:28

Anger is a universal emotion. Even babies lose their temper if they don't get their way. Few of us make it through a week without fuming or fussing about something. Occasionally our anger is justified, but often we harbor an unhealthy, unforgiving spirit.

Sometimes we're just angry at life. Grace Saxe, for example, a dedicated Bible teacher of an earlier generation, had hoped to become a missionary. After her acceptance by a mission's board, she packed her bags, bade her friends farewell, and prepared to sail off; but the night before her departure, her father was seized by a life-threatening illness. She was unable to leave, and the ship sailed without her. In a day or two, her father recovered.

"Why would God treat me like this?" Grace wondered. For several days, she was angry and depressed. At the end of the week, a report came that the ship was lost at sea and everyone aboard had perished. Grace's resentment melted into understanding, then into thankfulness.

Are you resentful at life's circumstances? Is your Christmas being marred by a bitter spirit? Give it to the Lord and let Him have His way. Trust Him, for He knows just what He is doing.

Children Are Gifts From God

Behold, children are a heritage from the Lord,
The fruit of the womb is a reward.

Psalm 127:3

The Bible is clear in teaching us that our children are a gift from God. As far back as Genesis 4:1, we find Eve declaring that her son Cain had been given to her by God. Later, Abraham and Sarah had their son Isaac as a direct result of God's intervention in opening Sarah's womb. God also opened the womb of Leah, Jacob's first wife, and Rachel, also his wife. Ruth was also made a mother due to God's intervention (Ruth 4:13).

The little ones God gives to us do not come by accident or as interruptions to our lives. They come as God's good gifts to us, entrusted as a stewardship from Him. Children are not only given to receive love from their parents but to be God's teachers. What parent would say they have not learned about sacrifice, patience, priorities—not to mention learned more about God's love for us, His children—as a result of being a parent? Children are a gift for which parents should thank God every day.

Christmas Gifts

When they saw the star, they rejoiced
with exceeding great joy.
Matthew 2:10 KJV

The holiday season is one of the busiest times of the year. Who has time to take a break? But when we do slow down, we see why people are speeding around. If you visit any shopping center in the middle of December, read the newspaper advertisements, or look under the tree on Christmas Day, you will see that gifts have become the focus of this holiday.

As Christians, we know the deeper meaning of Christmas and gift giving. When we present a gift to someone, we say in a tangible way how much we appreciate him, respect him, and have concern for him. But most of all, we say how much we love him. Remember how Jesus' birth was celebrated with gifts: "And when they had come into the house, they saw the young Child with Mary His mother, and fell down and worshiped Him. And when they had opened their treasures, they presented gifts to Him: gold, frankincense, and myrrh" (Matthew 2:11).

The tradition of gift giving today is a powerful testimony to the deeper meaning of the season. Giving at this time of year is a rich and exciting experience, reflecting God's gift to us.

Do Not Seek Revenge

Repay no one evil for evil.

Romans 12:17

If you are seeking revenge, you have just opened your whole heart for Satan and his demons to take control of your life. Romans 12:17–21 teaches us what we are to do when we are tempted to revenge: "Repay no one evil for evil. Have regard for good things in the sight of all men. If it is possible, as much as depends on you, live peaceably with all men. Beloved, do not avenge yourselves, but rather give place to wrath; for it is written, 'Vengeance is mine, I will repay,' says the Lord. Therefore, if your enemy is hungry, feed him; if he is thirsty, give him a drink; for in so doing you will heap coals of fire on his head."

The Bible teaches that if we seek revenge, we are violating the principles of God and setting ourselves up for the control of Satan in our lives. When Jesus was under attack, He did not respond or seek to get even. He held Himself under control by the Spirit of God, and He serves as an example for all of us.

GIVING THE GIFT OF CHRIST

And remember the words of the Lord Jesus, that He said, "It is more blessed to give than to receive."

ACTS 20:35

The most endearing people associated with the first Christmas in Bethlehem in addition to the Christ child and His parents are the wise men. Their gifts of "gold, frankincense, and myrrh" (Matthew 2:11) suggest there were three. But their number is as much speculation as their identity, homeland, and vocation. "Magi" suggests wisdom, while "the East" suggests Arabia.

This we do know about the Magi: They went to considerable effort and expense to do something for others. Their goal was to give something to Jesus, not to receive something for themselves. In doing so, they unknowingly embodied what ought to be the spirit of Christmas for every Christian.

Studies show that Christmas can be one of the most discouraging times of the year for many people. Widows and widowers, shut-ins, singles, the elderly, those with no family nearby . . . the list goes on of people who are often lonely and forgotten in the Christmas rush. This year, spread some Christmas cheer and the love of Christ to someone who may be in need of both. It might make this your best Christmas ever—and theirs.

This Christmas, remind yourself of why it is more blessed to give than to receive.

Don't Rejoice in Sin

[Love] does not rejoice in iniquity,
but rejoices in the truth.
1 Corinthians 13:6

In Greek, the phrase, "Love does not rejoice in iniquity," literally means, "Love does not take satisfaction from sin." To rejoice in unrighteousness is to justify sin. It is making wrong appear to be right. This is what Isaiah said in Isaiah 5:20: "Woe to those who call evil good, and good evil; who put darkness for light, and light for darkness."

There is much of that going on in our world today. Men and women in the media have come to understand that bad news is good news in the sense that it makes the headlines and provides more readership and listenership, but God's love is saddened when it hears of the defeats and tragedies in other people's lives. It is easy to be glad at another person's misfortune, but God says that as Christian people we are never to rejoice in sin. When you love somebody, you cover their sins; you don't broadcast them. John puts it this way: "I have no greater joy than to hear that my children walk in truth" (3 John v. 4).

What Can You Do?

She has done a good work for Me. . . .
She has done what she could.

Mark 14:6, 8

Dr. James Kennedy tells of a Christian peasant woman living in Africa more than fifty years ago. People were bringing gifts as offerings to the Lord, but she had nothing to bring. When she appeared with a dollar to place on the altar, the missionary was suspicious of its origin, given her poverty. He inquired and discovered she had sold herself as a slave for life to a nearby plantation—for a dollar.

What this woman did for Christ shocks our modern sensibilities—and makes us squirm with shame. But it was the woman's attitude, not her act, that should be our example. The apostle Paul said there is a lack of wisdom in making carnal comparisons (2 Corinthians 10:12). We should not try to be like others in our giving. Instead, we should ask the Lord, "What can I do? What can I bring?" The Magi brought expensive gifts to Jesus because they could.

The poor woman in Africa could not copy the wealthy Magi in actions, but she could in attitude—she brought what she could. Look around and consider what God has given to you that you could give back to Him (and don't make the mistake of looking only for money).

Our goal is not to bring what God has given another but what God has given us.

The Greater Ministry

This gospel of the kingdom will be preached in all the world as a witness to all the nations.

Matthew 24:14

I remember when television first came out. Many Christians shunned it, believing it was run by the prince of the power of the air. The evil one certainly had his influence in that medium (and still does), but why not use television as a means to proclaim the good news? Why not use radio? Why not use print? Why not use the Internet? Why not use any means at hand to take the message of the Gospel and spread it throughout the whole world? The farther, the better. The faster, the better. The sooner, the better. Until He comes!

What Jesus was saying to His disciples was this: "While I was on this earth, I was localized; I could only touch individual men and women in My travels and speak to a few local audiences. But believe Me, after I am gone and the Holy Spirit comes to fill and empower My sons and daughters, then My ministry will be as far spread as Christians are."

So wherever there is a Christian, there is Christ. Wherever there is a believer, there is ministry.

Come and Coming

Blessed is he who waits.

Daniel 12:12

The prophet Daniel never put up a Christmas tree, never lit an Advent wreath, and never sang a holiday carol. But he celebrated Christmas anyway. He anticipated the coming of the Messiah, and his whole life was lived against the backdrop of Christ's appearance. It gave him daily encouragement. In Daniel 7:13, he said, "I was watching in the night visions, and behold, One like the Son of Man, [was] coming."

For us, too, the promise of His coming imparts optimism. Our attitude is that of Revelation 1:7: "Behold, He is coming with clouds, and every eye will see Him."

Imagine how excited you'd be if your loved one were returning after a tour of duty in a war zone. You'd be almost giddy with excitement, straightening the house, planning a menu, calling friends, and preparing for the long-awaited reunion.

How wonderful that Jesus came, clothed in humanity, born of a virgin, laid in a manger. How wonderful that He is coming again, clothed in triumph, descending with angels, crowned with glory.

Celebrate Christmas this year with both a backward glance and a forward look. Rejoice! Our King is coming.

A Good Conscience

Then Paul, looking earnestly at the council, said, "Men and brethren, I have lived in all good conscience before God until this day."

Acts 23:1

On August 18, 1788, as he prepared to become the first president of the United States, George Washington wrote to Alexander Hamilton, saying, "I hope I shall possess firmness and virtue enough to maintain what I consider the most enviable of all titles, the character of an honest man."

Character is to leadership what wood is to a tree—that inner "stuff" that provides its sturdiness and strength. Many a tree has blown down because it rotted on the inside. The notion that a person's personal life has no bearing on his or her leadership is an unbiblical streak of postmodern thinking that ravages not only leaders but their followers as well.

Each of us is a leader—of a group, a home, a project, a segment of God's work. We need to maintain a clear conscience and be worthy of the calling we've received. "I myself always strive to have a conscience without offense toward God and men," wrote Paul in Acts 24:16. That's important not only for ourselves but for those we're influencing.

Obeying the Coach

Then Joseph, being aroused from sleep, did as the angel of the Lord commanded him and took to him his wife.

Matthew 1:24

Earl Weaver, former manager of the Baltimore Orioles, had a rule: no base stealing without a sign from him. The great Reggie Jackson decided to steal second without a sign from Weaver. Though Jackson was successful, Weaver took him aside after the game and explained two negative ways in which Jackson's "successful" steal impacted the game. Jackson saw only his desire, while Weaver was watching the whole game.

Sometimes those in authority over us ask us to do things we don't understand. Along with our children, we ask the "Why?" question as often as not. The maturing Christian learns that God explains reasons sometimes, but other times He does not (Deuteronomy 29:29). Knowing that God sees everything provides a solid foundation for our obedience.

Think about Joseph when he learned that his betrothed, Mary, was pregnant before their wedding. As practically hard and publicly humiliating as it might have been, Joseph obeyed God's instructions to stay engaged to Mary.

When you're tempted to steal away in your own direction, remember: God is watching the whole game.

God's View of Prosperity

The keeper of the prison did not look into anything that was under Joseph's authority, because the Lord was with him; and whatever he did, the Lord made it prosper.

Genesis 39:23

Think about Joseph's circumstances. He was a slave, bound to his master. Yet the Bible says he was prosperous. We have this idea in America that prosperity is related to money and possessions, but prosperity in the eyes of God refers to character. If we are true to the Lord and His Word, we are rich. If we are in His will, we have the assurance that all things work together for good, something we certainly see evident in the life of Joseph.

It has been said that God doesn't do anything or allow anything to be done to us that we would not choose for ourselves, if we could only see things from His perspective. If we could see every event exactly as God does, we would do things the very same way. He sees the end from the beginning, how everything fits together, and how necessary some of our hurts and disappointments are. Prosperity isn't a matter of circumstances, but a matter of character. When Scripture says that Joseph was prosperous, it has little to do with how many material possessions he had, but with how much of him God had. Even though a slave, Joseph was a prosperous man.

From Why to Who

We are more than conquerors through Him who . . .
Romans 8:37

The word *why* occurs twenty-four times in the Book of Job, as the afflicted patriarch grapples with multiplied problems. "Why did I not die at birth?" he wondered (3:11). "Why have you made me your target?" he asked God (7:20 NIV).

At one time or another, many of our Bible heroes asked the question, "Why?" Trace the word through a concordance, and you'll be amazed at how frequently it's found. Even our Lord Jesus cried, "My God, My God, why have You forsaken Me?" (Matthew 27:46).

But at some point we've got to move from "Why?" to "Who?", as in, "Who loves us?" It is possible to worship God even when we don't have all the answers. We live by promises, after all, not by explanations. Sometimes we're in green pastures and beside still waters; other times we're in the valley of the shadow of death. In both cases, our Shepherd is before us, and goodness and mercy are following.

Faith is keeping our eyes on Jesus regardless of the storms and shadows. It is being fully persuaded that God has the power to do what He has promised. It's lifting our voices in praise even when our spirits are low.

Do you have unanswered questions in your life today? Trust God with your whys and focus on the Who.

Master Companion

Fear not, for I have redeemed you; I have called you by your name; you are Mine.

Isaiah 43:1

We need companionship. We need fellowship. God has built these needs into us. In those moments when we are between friends, in those dark caverns of being all alone, we have the Master Companion who stays with us through it all.

Now, thus says the Lord, who created you, O Jacob.
And He who formed you, O Israel:
"Fear not, for I have redeemed you;
I have called you by your name;
You are Mine.
When you pass through the waters, I will be with you;
And through the rivers, they shall not overflow you.
When you walk through the fire,
you shall not be burned,
Nor shall the flame scorch you.
For I am the Lord your God,
The Holy One of Israel, your Savior.
(Isaiah 43:1–3)

The prophet Isaiah reminds us that God's immediate presence in our lives is not affected by our circumstances.

A Christlike Christmas

Though He was rich . . . He became poor.

2 Corinthians 8:9

Poor, distraught Johnny. It was Christmas morning, and he had opened the last of his eleven presents. There wasn't a twelfth one, and he felt as deflated as a leaky hot water bottle. How strange that our culture has turned Christmas inside out, making it a frenzy of materialism.

Christmas, to Jesus, meant selflessness. Though "in the form of God, [He] did not consider it robbery to be equal with God, but made Himself of no reputation, taking the form of a bondservant" (Philippians 2:6–7).

Christmas, to Jesus, meant service. He came not to be catered to but to minister to others (Mark 10:45). He wasn't as interested in being given to, as in giving. He gave Himself, and in giving Himself, He gave His all.

Christmas, to Jesus, meant submission. In claiming to be "sent" from heaven, He implied His obedience to the Sender—His Father. And Christmas, to Jesus, meant sacrifice. His birth set the stage for Calvary.

God's people must reverse the trends of our culture and begin seeing our Lord's birth as He saw it. Can you think of a way in which you can be a selfless, submissive, sacrificing servant today?

If so, you've got a divine corner on Christmas.

The Greater Message

Do not rejoice in this, that the spirits are subject to you, but rather rejoice because your names are written in heaven.

Luke 10:20

I read about a group of short-term missionaries who recently held evangelistic meetings in Africa. During those meetings, these believers reported, a blind man miraculously received his sight. When the believers came back to report to the sending churches, that was just about all they could talk about. Yet during those same meetings, many embraced Jesus Christ as Savior and found eternal salvation. Many stepped out of spiritual blindness into the light of God's kingdom. But that news always seemed to receive second billing to "the miracle." If we could only view these things as God does! The message of reconciliation meets the basic needs of every man and woman, every boy and girl. In miracles, only God's power and goodness are revealed, but in conversion, God's grace is revealed—something that causes even the angels to look over the rampart of heaven in wonder (1 Peter 1:12).

The message of the saving grace of God is the greater message. The death, burial, and resurrection of Jesus Christ have given to us in this generation the greatest message that has ever been communicated to any people. Anywhere. At any time. Period.

The Pure in Heart

Rejoice, highly favored one, the Lord is with you; blessed are you among women!

Luke 1:28

Elizabeth I, queen of England from 1558 to 1603, set out to implement a full Protestant Reformation in Roman Catholic England. That movement became known as Puritanism because of its emphasis on personal regeneration and purity, household prayer, and strict morality. Those who embraced this movement were called Puritans because they wanted to purify the church of all ceremonies, vestments, and customs inherited from the medieval church.

In today's world of loose morality and liberal theology, the term *puritanical* is used negatively to refer to those who are out of step with modern thinking and progressive ways. And it is usually an accurate description, since those who desire to live as the pure in heart do find themselves in the minority.

A teenage girl in the town of Nazareth, more than two millennia ago, could be called a Puritan for all the right reasons. She had a heart that was set upon knowing and serving God, and she lived in such a way that she found favor in God's sight. Mary, the mother of Jesus, wasn't perfect or sinless, but it was her desire to serve God that attracted His attention.

Puritanical in the world's eyes may equal pure in heart in God's eyes.

The Source of Song

He has put a new song in my mouth—
Praise to our God;
Many will see it and fear,
And will trust in the Lord.

Psalm 40:3

Christianity is a religion of song. Agnosticism has no carols. Confucianism and Brahmanism have no anthems or alleluias. Dreary, weird dirges reveal no hope for the present or for the future. Christianity, however, is filled with music. Only the message of Christ puts a song in a person's heart.

When you have Christ in your heart, something changes inside of you, and a melody starts to form that you can't really control. It is unlike any other belief system.

As we read the stories of Christmas in the Gospel of Luke, we find six different songs recorded almost back-to-back: the "Beatitude of Elizabeth," when she was visited by Mary; the "Magnificat of Mary," Mary's song; the "Benedictus of Zacharias," the father of John the Baptist; the "Song of Simeon," when he was presented with the Christ child at the temple; the "Evangel Song" of the angel of the Lord over the plains; and finally, the "Gloria" of the angelic hosts. When Jesus came into the world, music was reborn.

Christmas Opportunities

Make the most of every opportunity for
doing good in these evil days.
Ephesians 5:16 NLT

Christmas gives us opportunities to do things for people we might otherwise neglect, and we must take advantage of each opportunity. As long as we're on earth, God has work for us to do. When He's finished with us here, He'll take us home.

Seventeenth-century preacher Thomas Fuller said, "God's children are immortal while their Father hath anything for them to do on earth." Missionary David Livingstone said similarly, "Men are immortal until their work is done."

The British preacher Charles Spurgeon said, "Whatever occurs around us, we need not be alarmed. We are immortal until our work is done. And amidst infectious or contagious diseases, if we are called to go there, we may sit as easily as though in balmy air. It is not ours to preserve our life by neglecting our duty. It is better to die in service than live in idleness—better to glorify God and depart, than rot above ground in neglecting what He would have us to do. Unto God belong the issues from death. We may, therefore, go without temerity into any danger where duty calls us."

There is a child, a bag lady, a prisoner, a soldier whom God wants you to touch this Christmas season. Make the most of every opportunity.

Go with Haste

Now there were in the same country shepherds living out in the fields, keeping watch over their flock by night.

Luke 2:8

Christmas is the season of twinkling lights, shiny tinsel, and cheery holiday bells. Yet within the brightness of Christmas a dark paradox looms: Christmas is not the best but the worst time of year for many people. Suicides increase, loneliness is heightened, and broken families feel the pain of separation. People reason that the other eleven months of the year aren't necessarily supposed to be filled with joy—but Christmas is.

Loneliness, financial limitations, ill health . . . many things can quench the holiday spark. If you fear the feelings that come your way at Christmas, you're not alone. Another group of "forgotten" people heard a special message from the angels that first Christmas: "Fear not"! (Luke 2:10 KJV). The angels announced the One who would dispel all fear forever—Jesus Christ. The shepherds went "with haste" (v. 16). They didn't let fear stop them from meeting the Messiah.

Just as the shepherds cast aside their fears and immediately went to find Jesus, you can do the same this Christmas. Jesus is waiting to be found.

Be an Angel

Glory to God in the highest, and on earth
peace, goodwill toward men!

Luke 2:14

By the fourth century AD, a psalm was in use in Christian churches, and it is still in use today, called *Gloria in Excelsis Deo.* Its title comes from the Latin Bible's translation of the words proclaimed by the angels as they announced the birth of Jesus to the shepherds: "Glory to God in the highest . . . we praise thee, we bless thee, we worship thee, we glorify thee, we give thanks to thee for thy great glory."

If angels do anything, they worship God. In Scripture, we find them doing many things on earth—delivering messages, guarding and coming to the aid of the saints, doing battle. But in the heavenly places, the heavenly host seems to have one primary agenda—to proclaim the glory of God forever and ever.

It is not surprising that at the birth of Jesus, the glory of God was the first thing on the angels' lips. They were not unaware, after all, of the cosmic struggle going on between Satan and man. When the Father's own Son was dispatched to earth to defeat the enemy, angels accompanied the announcement by proclaiming God's glory. Is His glory and praise the first thing on our lips this Christmas season?

Imitate the angels this Christmas by declaring the glory of God to someone who has not beheld it.

Celebrate His Love

Glory to God in the highest, and on earth peace, goodwill toward men!

Luke 2:14

In more than a few past wars, the warring nations would call a cease-fire for Christmas Day. They would agree that on Christmas Day they wouldn't shoot at each other, drop bombs, or try to destroy one another. Then, of course, the day after Christmas they would start killing each other again.

As strange as that custom has been, in a wonderful way it is a mute testimony to the purpose for which Christ came—to bring peace. That was the message the angels proclaimed.

Today, there are many places in our world where *peace* is not a word in anyone's vocabulary. Yet every Christian knows that there is coming a time when peace will reign on this earth. Each Christmas season, a kind of new hope is born in our hearts—that though the outlook may be dark, we can look beyond today. The Prince of Peace has come and with Him the faith that someday men will beat their swords into plowshares and their spears into pruning hooks and we shall be at peace.

His Name Shall Be Called . . .

But who do you say that I am?

Luke 9:20

Strange how many people feel depressed on Christmas. It's called the "Christmas blues," or seasonal affective disorder. Whatever it is, if you're down in the dumps today, stop thinking about Christmas. Think instead about Christ.

He is our Prophet, Priest, and King. He is the Master, the Bridegroom, the Good Shepherd, the Holy One of God. His name is "Emmanuel—God with us." His name was called Jesus. John introduced Him as "the Lamb of God who takes away the sin of the world" (John 1:29). The wise men recognized Him as the "King of the Jews," and even the demons called Him "the Holy One of God" (Matthew 2:2; Mark 1:24, respectively).

"Is this not the carpenter?" asked the people of Nazareth in Mark 6:3. "Could this be the Christ?" asked the woman by the well in John 4:29. Thomas called Him, "My Lord and my God" (John 20:28).

Today isn't about Christmas but about Christ. It isn't about presents but about His presence. You may or may not have family nearby, but your Father is close at hand, and your faith is more important than your feelings. He sets us free from chains we can never remove ourselves. He is our hope.

Don't worry about celebrating Christmas. Just celebrate Jesus!

The Cry of Life

And she brought forth her firstborn Son.

Luke 2:7

Life and especially history are full of all kinds of cries. There have been cries of anguish and joy, cries of victory and defeat. And yet there is probably no cry that is as touching, as tender, and as timely as the fragile first cry of a newborn babe.

If you are a parent, you know the delirious joy—indeed, relief—that came when your own babies shattered the delivery room air with their first cry. Why does a child's cry, something that normally brings concern to a parent, produce joy when it is first heard? Because it's a sign of life. The tension in the delivery room waiting on that first cry is not unlike the tension in all of creation that first Christmas Eve. When the cold silence of a Bethlehem night was broken by Jesus' first cry, it meant more than just life. It meant eternal life—spiritual life! No longer would mankind live in fear of death. Life itself had been born in Bethlehem.

History's most famous cry was that of a tiny Babe, born in a manger. Celebrate that cry of life this Christmas season. Even today, it echoes in your heart if you know Jesus Christ as a Savior.

The Joy of Christmas

Where were you when . . . the angels shouted for joy?

Job 38:4, 7 NIV

From 27 BC to AD 180, the Mediterranean world enjoyed what history calls *Pax Romana*—the Roman peace. It was a period of unprecedented peace and prosperity brought about by the dominant presence of the Roman Empire. Roads and aqueducts were built, cities were modernized, the rule of law brought stability, and religions were tolerated. Into Pax Romana the Prince of Peace was born.

Some might ask, "What need was there for a Prince of Peace when there was Roman peace throughout the land?" The peace of man is very different from the peace of God—the Pax Romana lasted only two hundred years. No wonder the angel who appeared to the shepherds said he was bringing "good tidings of great joy . . . to all people" (Luke 2:10).

The angels had been overjoyed once before when the Son of God, through whom all things were created, laid the foundations of the earth (Job 38:1–7). But now the same Son was coming to dwell upon the earth He created! The joy only the angels had known would now be a joy spread throughout the earth to all people. Have you experienced the peace of which the angel spoke?

While the peace of Rome has passed away, the peace of God endures forever.

Delight in the Lord

Delight yourself also in the Lord,
And He shall give you the desires of your heart.
Psalm 37:4

Tracing the word *delight* through the Old Testament, I was surprised to learn that the majority of its uses are in relationship to the Word of God—delighting in the Word. The psalmists delighted in God's will as expressed in His law (Psalm 40:8); delighted in His statutes (119:16); delighted in His commandments (119:35); and delighted in His precepts and law (119:69–70, 77, 92, 174).

There is a profound relationship between delighting in the Lord and delighting in His Word. Think about your relationship with a person who is the object of your affections. Your conversations, the letters you receive, the phone calls you share—their words are a reflection of who they are. So to delight in that person's words is to delight in them. And the same is true of our relationship with God. To trust in God is also to delight in Him and His promises. No Christian who delights in what God says about the future ("I will provide for you") can also be found worrying about the future.

When delighting in the Lord is your focus, everything else is brought into perspective.

Giving the Very Best

And when they had opened their treasures, they presented gifts to Him: gold, frankincense, and myrrh.

Matthew 2:11

O'Henry's famous short story "The Gift of the Magi" tells the story of Jim and Della, each of whom wanted nothing more for Christmas than to give a gift to their beloved. Della sold her beautiful hair to a wig maker to buy Jim a gold chain for his watch, while Jim sold his watch to buy Della beautiful combs for her hair. The sacrifice of their most treasured possessions showed the depth of their love.

Wanting to give the greatest of gifts to one's spouse is understandable. With each passing year of a relationship, love should deepen and gifts become more precious. But when a small group of astrologers journeyed from their distant land to bring expensive gifts to the infant Jesus, it was a remarkable act of worshipful recognition. He was just a young child, born to poor parents in the most humble of circumstances. Yet somehow they knew He deserved the best they had—and they gave it.

The Magi present to us a thoughtful question: if they who knew Jesus not at all gave to Him their best, how much more should we who know Him give?

Make a New Year's resolution to give Jesus the gift that keeps on giving—the gift of your love.

Use God's Strength

My grace is sufficient for you, for My strength is made perfect in weakness.

2 Corinthians 12:9

When we try to live our lives in our own strength, we ultimately fail. And if we don't fail, we fall very short of God's purposes for us. When we operate in the flesh, three things are always true: (1) we will always lack the power of the Spirit, and we'll suffer from fatigue; (2) we will always lack the vision of the Spirit, so we'll suffer from frustration; and (3) we will always lack the sustaining ministry of the Spirit, so we'll suffer from failure.

Do these consequences sound familiar? You will always suffer these results when you tackle life in your own strength. But when tragedy strikes—an illness, financial hardship, rebellious children—you turn to God. When you feel helpless, inadequate, and weak, the Spirit of God gives you strength. All of a sudden you realize something dynamic is going on that you have never experienced before. It's not your power; it's God's power. The apostle Paul admits that if it takes weakness to get God's power in his life, he's better off weak than strong. Because when you are weak, then you are strong.

The Promise of Fellowship

But if we walk in the light as He is in the light,
we have fellowship with one another.

1 John 1:7

The festive spirit of Christmas is captured perfectly in the beloved carol "Deck the Halls": "'Tis the season to be jolly . . . strike the harp and join the chorus . . . sing we joyous all together . . ." It's not hard to picture friends and family together enjoying fellowship while they "deck the halls with boughs of holly."

The evergreen garlands that line stairs, mantels, doors, and windows at Christmas create a festive venue that speaks of gathering together with friends at Christmas—and year-round as well. The pine and cedar boughs we use to "deck the halls" today are just another way of saying to guests that they've entered a setting of warmth and celebration. The smell of evergreen, mixed with enticing aromas from the Christmas kitchen, communicates Christmas love to those who gather in your home this Christmas season. Christmas is a perfect time to show our love for Christ by opening our homes to those who share that love.

Why not have some friends in for a post-Christmas time of sharing—while the garlands are still fresh and the cider and cookies still plentiful? Christmas fellowship is a great way to prepare for living close to those you love for the rest of the year.

Encouragement Is Urgent

Let us encourage one another.

Hebrews 10:25 NIV

I wear many hats as a parent, as all parents do. I am a provider, a leader, and a disciplinarian when necessary. But I believe my greatest responsibility is as a cheerleader. More than anything else, kids today need the supportive love, encouragement, and cheering-on of their parents. James Dobson, the family expert who spent years studying problems of adolescent behavior, once said in my presence, "Here's the distilled wisdom of all my research. Here is what you need to do if you have adolescents: just get them through it."

Just get them through it! Hang in there with them until the whitewater rapids of the teenage years are left behind.

Encouragement is an urgent need of our day. A church that does not equip its people as encouragers will soon phase out of any meaningful ministry in its community. God help us to learn how to be encouragers!

If Christ Had Not Come

The Lord Jesus Christ, our hope.

1 Timothy 1:1

Christmas isn't just an optional holiday on the calendar, but a foundational event that undergirds all we are and believe. We shudder when we realize that if Christ had not come, our Bibles would be untrue, for the story of the Incarnation fills both the Old and New Testaments.

If Christ had not come, our God would be unknown, for Christ is the image of the invisible God, the Word made flesh. He is Immanuel—God with us.

If Christ had not come, our sins would be unforgiven. The chief purpose for Christ's being born in Bethlehem was to save us from our sins. His very name—Jesus—means "Jehovah saves!" John the Baptist called Him "the Lamb of God who takes away the sin of the world" (John 1:29).

If Christ had not come, our prayers would be unanswered. Hebrews 4:15–16 says that since we do have a High Priest—namely, Jesus—we can approach the throne of grace with boldness.

If Christ had not come, our hope would be unfounded. We'd have no future, no life, no heaven, and no eternity. No reunions with our loved ones. Nothing beyond the grave.

But now, we praise God! Christmas is real, and Jesus Christ is our hope of glory.

Problems Promote Maturity

Now no chastening seems to be joyful for the present, but painful; nevertheless, afterward it yields the peaceable fruit of righteousness to those who have been trained by it.

Hebrews 12:11

The concept of gaining strength through difficulties is under assault today by those preaching success and prosperity. Some have claimed that, if we're Christians, God wants everything to be right and easy for us.

It certainly sounds spiritual to claim that those close to God ought never to experience failure or illness, but that has never been the message of the church. Rather than producing soldiers, that sort of thinking produces pampered children. There is no Bible verse, nor even an implied principle, that suggests our walk on earth should be free from trouble.

Problems are God's gifts to us to make us strong. And those who would keep us out of problems sometimes seek to short-circuit the plan of God. Problems are God's way of molding us into maturity, putting iron into our souls so that we can face the challenges ahead. Problems promote maturity.

GLORY AND JOY IN THE NEW YEAR

Therefore, whether you eat or drink, or
whatever you do, do all to the glory of God.

1 CORINTHIANS 10:31

In 1642, the English parliament abolished the episcopal system of church government in the Church of England. An assembly of 120 ministers and thirty laypersons was called to Westminster Cathedral in London to rebuild the English church. The documents coming out of the six-year Westminster Assembly are some of the most famous in church history.

The first question in the Westminster Shorter Catechism reads, "What is the chief end of man?" Answer: "Man's chief end is to glorify God, and to enjoy him forever." The implications of that question and answer, profound in their simplicity, are that to glorify God is to enjoy God, and to accomplish both is to fulfill man's ultimate purpose in life. It is a rewording of Paul's famous words: "Whatever you do, do all to the glory of God."

What are you going to do in the coming year? Are there areas of your life that are not glorifying to God, and you are therefore not enjoying? Purpose to do two things well in the new year: glorify God and enjoy Him all year long in every area of your life!

The same words that rebuilt a national church can also rebuild a personal life.

Ever-Present God

God is . . . a very present help in trouble.

Psalm 46:1

"God is . . . a very present help in trouble." God is not just present; He is very present! It's like you telling a good friend that you are available to help them if they need you. "Oh, I hate to bother you," they reply. "No," you counter, "I am very much available for you. Just let me know when." You are saying, "I am ever-available." And that's how God is for us. He is the most accessible help we could ever imagine.

The word for trouble could be rendered as a "tight place." God is ever-present to help us in the tight places we get into in life, when we are between a rock and a hard place. If someone is ever-present, it means they are easy to be found. We don't have to go looking for them. In fact, we can't. We're stuck in a tight place!

The reason God is always with us, even in our tight places, is because of what He told Moses in Exodus 33:14: "My presence will go with you." So when we are stuck and can't move, God is there because He is always with us.

Loving and Keeping

If you love Me, keep My commandments.

John 14:15

When Eddie Taubensee of the Cleveland Indians was sidelined by an injury, he saw a divine plan behind it. "I'm not in the spotlight anymore, which is okay," he said. "I can handle that. In one sense, I'm free to do anything I want. But I'm going to make myself a slave to everybody—to my teammates, to whoever I come in contact with—to win as many as possible for Christ."

When Jesus said, "If you love Me, keep My commandments," He meant for us to make every occasion in life, good or bad, an opportunity for obedience. As we celebrate God's Christmas gift to us, why not ask yourself, "What gift of obedience can I give to Him today?"

Perhaps you need to bring your temper under Christ's control. Perhaps you need to change your vocabulary. Maybe God is nudging you to forgive an offense or overlook an insult. Do you need to express your love more freely to your wife? Are you presenting yourself modestly in your wardrobe (1 Timothy 2:9)?

As this year slips away, it's a good time to leave behind some old habits. Confess your sins to God and determine to give Him not idle words but obedient deeds as the new year dawns.

Fellowship Forever

Behold, the tabernacle of God is with men, and He will dwell with them, and they shall be His people. God Himself will be with them and be their God.

Revelation 21:3

There will be no sanctuary or tabernacle or temple in heaven—and no churches. Revelation 21:22 says that "the Lord God Almighty and the Lamb are its temple." Because God will be dwelling in the midst of His people, just as He started off doing in the garden of Eden, there will be no need for a sanctuary for Him to dwell in.

We incorrectly call our churches "sanctuaries" today because they are where we draw together once a week to worship God and hear His Word proclaimed. But God does not dwell in buildings in this age; He dwells in His people. At present, we cannot "see" His presence as we will be able to in heaven. Instead of dwelling "in" us in heaven, He will dwell "among" us, in our very presence.

The same Jesus who healed the sick, raised the dead, fed the multitudes, died on Calvary, was raised from the dead, and ascended into heaven will be walking among us in heaven. We will have unbroken, personal fellowship with Him forever.

Passion

I press on, that I may lay hold of that for which Christ Jesus has also laid hold of me.

Philippians 3:12

Josh Davis, winner of three gold medals during the 1996 Olympics, is a Christian who credits Christ with his success. One of the keys to his intensity, he told an interviewer, is Colossians 3:23: "And whatever you do, do it heartily, as to the Lord and not to men."

This verse has its Old Testament parallel in Ecclesiastes 9:10: "Whatever your hand finds to do, do it with your might."

As we prepare to begin a new year, let's determine to start it with passion, to press on with a desire to lay hold of what God wants us to do—and to do it with all our might.

In 1938, the great writer and preacher A. W. Tozer wrote a New Year's editorial in his magazine, saying in part: "If you ask God to give you a special message for the opening year, one that will be made seasonable and real in every exigency of the unknown future, you will be surprised how faithfully He will fulfill His Word, and how fittingly the Holy Spirit will speak to you of things to come, and anticipate the real needs and exigencies of your life."

Ask God to show you His plan for the New Year, and then live it out to the fullest . . . until He comes.

Sources

Exposing the Myths of Parenthood. Jeremiah, David, with Carole C. Carson. Dallas: Word Publishing, 1988.
Book of Esther, The. Atlanta: Walk thru the Bible, 1994.
Celebrate His Love. Atlanta: Walk thru the Bible, 1999.
Christ's Death and Resurrection. Atlanta: Walk thru the Bible, 1997.
Christians Have Stress Too. San Diego: Turning Point, 2000.
Escape the Coming Night study guide, vol. 4. San Diego: Turning Point, 2000.
Facing the Giants in Your Life. San Diego: Turning Point, 2001.
Fruit of the Spirit. Atlanta: Walk thru the Bible, 1995.
Gifts from God study guide. San Diego: Turning Point, 1999.
Giving to God. San Diego: Turning Point, 2001.
God in You. Sisters, OR: Multnomah, 1998.
God Meant It for Good: The Life of Joseph, vol. 1. San Diego: Turning Point, 1996.
God Meant It for Good: The Life of Joseph, vol. 2. San Diego: Turning Point, 1996.
God's Righteousness and Man's Rebellion. Living by Faith series, vol. 4. San Diego: Turning Point, 2002.
God's Sovereignty and Man's Responsibility. Living by Faith series, vol. 4. San Diego: Turning Point, 2002.
Greatest Stories Ever Told, The. Atlanta: Walk thru the Bible, 2000.
Hearing the Master's Voice. San Diego: Turning Point, 1999.
Heroes of the Faith. San Diego: Turning Point, 2001.
Home and Family. San Diego: Turning Point, 2000.
Home Improvement. San Diego: Turning Point, 2001.
How to Be Happy According to Jesus. Atlanta: Walk thru the Bible, 1996.
In Transit: Moving Confidently through Today's World. Wheaton, IL: Tyndale, 1984.
Investing for Eternity. Atlanta: Walk Thru the Bible, 1999.

Jesus' Final Warning study guide. Atlanta: Walk thru the Bible, 1999.
Knowing the God You Worship. Atlanta: Walk thru the Bible, 1994.
Love in Action. San Diego: Turning Point, 2001.
Man's Ruin and Christ's Redemption. Living by Faith series, vol. 2. San Diego: Turning Point, 2000.
My Heart's Desire: Living Every Moment in the Wonder of Worship. Brentwood, TN: Integrity, 2002.
A Nation in Crisis, vol. 1. Atlanta: Walk thru the Bible, 1996.
Overcoming Loneliness. Nashville: Thomas Nelson, 1991.
Overcoming Loneliness study guide. Atlanta: Walk thru the Bible, 1997.
People God Uses, The. San Diego: Turning Point, 2000.
People Who Met Jesus. San Diego: Turning Point, 2000.
Power of Encouragement, The. Sisters, OR: Multnomah, 1997
Power of Love, The. Atlanta: Walk thru the Bible, 1994.
Powerful Principles from Proverbs. San Diego: Turning Point, 2002.
Prayer—The Great Adventure study guide. San Diego: Turning Point, 2000.
Prophetic Turning Points. San Diego: Turning Point, 2001.
Runaway Prophet—Jonah, The. San Diego: Turning Point, 1998.
Ruth, Romance, and Redemption. San Diego: Turning Point, 1999.
Signs of the Second Coming. Atlanta: Walk thru the Bible, 1996.
Sons of God and the Spirit of God, The. Living by Faith series, vol. 3. San Diego: Turning Point, 2000.
Spiritual Warfare. San Diego: Turning Point, 2002.
Ten Burning Questions from Psalms. San Diego: Turning Point, 1994.
Turning Points magazine and devotional guide, vol. 3, no. 7 (December 2001). vol. 4, no. 2 (March 2002); vol. 4, no. 3 (April 2002); vol. 4, no. 4 (May 2002); vol. 4, no. 5 (June 2002); vol. 4, no. 6 (July 2002); vol. 4, no. 7 (August 2002).
Turning Toward Integrity study guide. Atlanta: Walk thru the Bible, 2000.
Turning Toward Joy. Colorado Springs: Chariot Victor, 1992.
What the Bible Says about Angels study guide. San Diego: Turning Point, 1999.
Worship. Atlanta: Walk thru the Bible, 1995.

NOTES

Notes

Notes

Notes

Notes

Notes

Notes

The Christmas Spirit

Bearing with one another, and forgiving one another.
Colossians 3:13

In their book *None of These Diseases*, S. I. McMillen and David Stern describe the damage we inflict on ourselves when we dislike someone or refuse to forgive him or her. "The moment I begin to hate a man, I become his slave. He controls my thoughts. He controls my feelings. He even controls my dreams. Stress hormones constantly surge through my bloodstream and wear down my body. . . . The one I hate hounds me wherever I go."

As your family gathers this holiday, perhaps there's a member you don't like or haven't forgiven. Perhaps a father-in-law or a stepchild. Maybe a brother or sister who hurt you years ago.

Remember that Christmas is all about God's love and forgiveness. Jesus left the infinite riches of the heavenly palace to sleep in an animal's food trough, choosing to live among unlovely people. He came to forgive and redeem. He can flush all the hatred from your heart if you'll only let Him.

If you're not looking forward to seeing someone in your family this Christmas, offer this prayer: "Lord, I confess that I don't like __________, and I am dreading being with him (or her). Forgive me, and help me to forgive and forbear. May the love of the Christmas Christ be funneled through me this season."

The Sin of Worry

Do not worry about your life, what you will eat; nor about the body, what you will put on. Life is more than food, and the body is more than clothing.

Luke 12:22–23

Let me begin by stating something that you may or may not agree with: worry is sin. Worry is not part of our personality; it is not something to be excused because "everybody does it." From God's perspective, worry is sin. But in order to clarify this (it's important to know when we are sinning and when we are not), let's separate worry from concern.

It is certainly right to be concerned about things that are your responsibility and over which you exercise control. God expects us to be responsible, to be concerned that we follow through on what is ours to do. But worry is concerning yourself about things over which you have no control. Worry is allowing care and concern to escalate beyond the realm of responsibility and into a realm in which you have no authority or control—God's realm. And that kind of concern, which is worry, is sin.

When we worry, we deny the faithfulness of God—and that is why worry is sin.